# *Tied Up in Tehran*

*Tied Up in Tehran* offers a richly interdisciplinary study of ordinary life in Iran since the 1979 revolution and a critical intervention in political theory debates on knowledge and method. Drawing from over ten years of field work in Iran since the 1990s, and originating in the author's surreal experience of being served tangerines during a home invasion in Tehran, Norma Claire Moruzzi examines the experiences of women, young people, artists, and activists: at home, at work, and in the street. These stories – of food and family, film and politics, shopping and crime — reckon with the past, demonstrate resilient democratization in the present, and provide glimpses of a plausible future while offering a refreshing model to ethically engaged modes of study. Moruzzi's lucid and engaging writing explores Iranian daily life as unexpected, contradictory, and full of political promise.

NORMA CLAIRE MORUZZI is Professor of Gender and Women's Studies and Political Science at the University of Illinois, Chicago. She is an associate editor for the journal *Iranian Studies* and a past member and chair of the editorial committee of the journal *Middle East Report*. Her first book, *Speaking through the Mask: Hannah Arendt and the Politics of Social Identity* (Cornell University Press, 2000) won the 2002 Gradiva Book Award.

# Tied Up in Tehran

## Women, Social Change, and the Politics of Daily Life in Postrevolutionary Iran

NORMA CLAIRE MORUZZI
*University of Illinois, Chicago*

CAMBRIDGE
UNIVERSITY PRESS

CAMBRIDGE
UNIVERSITY PRESS

Shaftesbury Road, Cambridge CB2 8EA, United Kingdom

One Liberty Plaza, 20th Floor, New York, NY 10006, USA

477 Williamstown Road, Port Melbourne, VIC 3207, Australia

314–321, 3rd Floor, Plot 3, Splendor Forum, Jasola District Centre, New Delhi – 110025, India

103 Penang Road, #05-06/07, Visioncrest Commercial, Singapore 238467

Cambridge University Press is part of Cambridge University Press & Assessment, a department of the University of Cambridge.

We share the University's mission to contribute to society through the pursuit of education, learning and research at the highest international levels of excellence.

www.cambridge.org
Information on this title: www.cambridge.org/9781009540247

DOI: 10.1017/9781009540285



When citing this work, please include a reference to the DOI 10.1017/9781009540285

First published 2025

*A catalogue record for this publication is available from the British Library*

*Library of Congress Cataloging-in-Publication Data*
Names: Moruzzi, Norma Claire author
Title: Tied up in Tehran : women, social change and the politics of daily life in post-revolutionary Iran / Norma Claire Moruzzi.
Description: New York : Cambridge University Press, 2025. | Includes bibliographical references and index. | Summary: "'Post-revolutionary Iranian life is unexpected, contradictory, and full of political promise. Norma Claire Moruzzi examines the experiences of women, young people, artists, and activists at home, at work, or in the street. Stories of food and family, film and politics, shopping and crime demonstrate resilient democratization in everyday practice'"– Provided by publisher.
Identifiers: LCCN 2025004832 | ISBN 9781009540247 hardback
Subjects: LCSH: Tehran (Iran)–Social conditions–21st century | Iran–Social conditions–1997- | Middle class–Iran–Tehran | Women–Iran–Tehran–Social conditions | Social change–Iran–Tehran
Classification: LCC HN670.2.T44 .M67 2025 | DDC 306.0955/25–dc23/eng/20250403
LC record available at https://lccn.loc.gov/2025004832

ISBN 978-1-009-54024-7 Hardback
ISBN 978-1-009-54026-1 Paperback

# *Contents*

# *Acknowledgments*

**Some parts of this title have been reproduced with kind permission:**

Part of chapter 1 was originally published in "Women in Iran: Notes on Film and From the Field," in *Feminist Studies* 27, Spring 2001.

Part of chapter 2 was originally published in "Tied Up in Tehran: A Metaphor," in *MERIP, Middle East Report and Information Project* 250, Spring 2009.

Part of chapter 4 was originally published in Norma Claire Moruzzi and Fatemeh Sadeghi, "Out of the Frying Pan, Into the Fire: Young Iranian Women Today," in *MERIP, Middle East Report and Information Project* 241, Winter 2006.

A version of chapter 7 was originally published in "Through the Looking Glass: Reflexive Cinema and Society in Post-Revolution Iran," copyright 2015 from *Iranian Cinema in a Global Context: Policy, Politics, and Form* edited by Peter Decherney and Blake Atwood. Reproduced by permission of Taylor and Francis Group, LLC, a division of Informa plc.

Part of chapter 7 was originally published in "Women's Space/Cinema Space" Representations of Public and Private in Iranian Films," in *MERIP, Middle East Report and Information Project* 212, Fall 1999.

The epigraphs from chapter 11 are from Guy Debord, trans. James Brook, *Panegyric*, copyright 1991, reproduced by permission of Verso; and Carlo Levi, trans. Frances Frenaye, *Christ Stopped at Eboli: The Story of a Year*, copyright 1947, 1963, reproduced by permission of Farrar, Straus and Giroux, Inc.

# *Tables*

# Preface

## How to Read This Book

This book is written for a broad reading audience. It is intended to be relevant for scholars of Iran and the Middle East, and for those concerned with social and political theory, yet also to be interesting and accessible for curious readers who are nonspecialists. This combination presents a challenge: How to keep the nonspecialist engaged while providing the depth of empirical and theoretical engagement expected by the scholar? With this in mind, I pursued a writing strategy: the chapters open with more personal narrative observations of everyday Iranian life experiences before elaborating on their complexity and significance, and the engagement with the extended apparatus of related scholarship is mostly confined to the notes. The notes matter; they are often where the full extent of the analysis is explored, and where the theoretical implications drawn out. But that academic engagement is intentionally kept mostly out of the flow of the text.

I also offer a reading strategy: feel free to skip through the chapters as you find appropriate. The chapter order is intentional; they interrelate and build an argument. But they are not strictly linear. In particular, while nonspecialist readers are encouraged to start at the beginning with the Introduction, readers more familiar with the modern history of Iran, its society and politics, might find that a review of that background information is superfluous and delaying. The Introduction does contain an extended discussion of the process of interpreting a film. The specific film interpretation matters, but the discussion also functions as a consideration of methodological issues, of interpretation, perspective, and positionality. How do we recognize what we don't know? And how do we learn from that experience? This account of interpretation as a shared experience sets the tone for the development of the rest of the book.

Sometimes that experience is funny, sometimes it is tragic, and sometimes it takes a while. Each chapter is discrete, concerned with a different aspect of everyday life: rituals of hospitality, changes in family structure, the practices of cultural intimacies, the challenges to gender roles and identities in a modern, increasingly consumer-identified society. They intersect through a loose organization that is horizontal and vertical: the relational logics of metonymy (narrative flow) and metaphor (analytical focus).

An underlying preoccupation throughout the book is power-how it shifts and informs the most ordinary aspects of our daily lives. Power in everyday life is rarely only about domination, especially when the state is not the primary agent of its manifestation. This book intentionally sidesteps direct focus on the Iranian state. The threat of state repression can be itself an effective tool, and that threat is much more immediate to local actors than to those farther removed. In order to write about the contradictions of contemporary Iran and the daily complexities Iranians negotiate, I had to find another way of discussing them that did not involve a head-on confrontation with state power or institutions, especially for my local interlocutors. I chose to focus on the Iranian life experiences to which I had the most direct access: the experiences of the educated, secular-identified segment of the Tehran middle class. The category of "middle class" in this context refers to social markers (such as education, profession, models of nuclear family organization, generational trajectory) that are not always matched by economic security. This is not a book about working-class, provincial, or faith experience. The Tehran community in which I found myself was all too like the communities in which I participate in the US and elsewhere. But it was also very different. The exploration of those differences and similarities – the tone, texture, and significance of life lived every day in a particular context – provided the project of this book.

*Tied Up in Tehran* uses the prism of everyday life to explore the contradictions of a vibrant postrevolutionary society caught between the unfulfilled and tarnished past promise of revolutionary liberation and the flickering future beacon of consumer fulfillment. In doing so, the book provides an alternative contribution not only to mainstream assumptions about Iran but also to contemporary theoretical debates about how power is experienced, displayed, and transformed. *Tied Up in Tehran* combines a study of postrevolutionary Iranian society, an intervention into current conceptions of how to use political and social theory to understand the significance of daily life, and a reframing of how examinations of daily life can provide insights into larger questions of cultural, social, and political transformation. Against the backdrop of political deadlock and economic insecurity, detailed analyses of everyday experience reveal a democratizing social culture that is being shaped by utopian ideals of collective freedoms as much as authoritarian state pressures and increasing economic inequalities. Caught in the present between past and future, Iranians are working out unexpected new combinations of familiar cultural identities and practices, while negotiating between idealistic promises of change and stubborn private and public institutional structures.

This book has been a long time coming, and many people helped me along the way. I want to thank them and provide proper acknowledgments. I am grateful to the University of Illinois at Chicago, the Woodrow Wilson Center Middle East Section, and the Eurasia Foundation for grants and fellowships that enabled my research. The publication by *Middle East Report* of "Tied up in Tehran: A Metaphor" gave me the courage to pursue the narrative writing style first adopted in that essay. But how do I thank all the individuals? For one thing, I am sure to leave someone out. More importantly, I do not know how properly to thank all the people in Iran whose generosity, patience, insight, and guidance made this project possible. The issue is not only their number. It is also the presently unanswerable question of whether or not I can name them while feeling assured that this association will not cause them problems. Under current political conditions, I do not know this. I could name a comparably long list of friends, comrades, colleagues, students, and others outside of Iran who have been similarly invaluable. But that does not seem fair to those in Iran and would inescapably create a familiar global hierarchy of credit and anonymity. I do not want to do that.

So I am acknowledging by name only the one individual without whom these stories and this book would have been impossible. To everyone else, I apologize: you know who you are, and I will be ever grateful. To Kaveh Ehsani, who is already stuck with me, publicly and privately, past, present, and future, I dedicate this book. Thank you.

# 1 *Introduction: The Personal Is Political – How I Came to Write This Book*

This book is based on more than ten years of fieldwork conducted in Iran from the 1990s until 2007. During that period, I conducted in-depth interviews, engaged in participant observation, and researched multiple aspects of Iranian history, social life, and culture. Over time, I was able to establish working relationships and personal friendships with Iranians inside and outside the country that have extended beyond the period of the fieldwork and despite geographic distances. The analyses in this book are based on painstaking hours of careful research, questioning and requestioning what I thought I knew and what I didn't know. Iran was not an obvious research choice for me, until it became one. This introduction tries to explain how it became my central focus, a focus refracted through varied and often oblique perspectives on underlying questions of power, freedom, and agency in everyday life. It also tries to demonstrate the interpretive methodology of my research in Iran by providing a detailed description of an interpretive experience: an Iranian film I saw in Chicago, but only understood as an effective representation of postrevolutionary Iranian life after I could talk to people about it in Iran. This example – of an initial understanding, the recognition of misunderstanding, and a more inclusive comprehension that depends on acknowledging metaphor as a political strategy as well as a narrative device – provides a model of the method of reflexive interpretation that is at work throughout the book.

## Beginnings (The Personal Is Always Political)

I met Kaveh in graduate school (Johns Hopkins). I was studying political theory (focusing on Hannah Arendt); he was a human geographer (working on Iran); we met in a Hegel reading group (we really did). He was one of the group organizers, attended the first session, and then left Baltimore for the summer. I was the last person he saw driving out of the neighborhood: standing on a corner by the farmers' market, talking to a friend, market bag over my shoulder. I was the first person he saw at the end of the summer, driving back into the neighborhood: standing on a (different) corner, waiting to cross the street. Kaveh suspects I was lurking in wait all summer. I deny this. Our paths often crossed (literally) on a small campus with an interdisciplinary intellectual and social identity (students got to know each other), in a small city with great cheap housing stock (students could afford to live within walking distance of the campus), and not a lot of expensive distractions (this was still John Waters' Baltimore). We shared an interest in social theory. We shared an interest in film. That's how it started.

In March 1992, I went to Iran for the first time. By then we were married, and he wanted me to see the place he was from. I wanted to see it too. Kaveh was from Iran; his parents were still in Iran; his fieldwork had been in Iran. I had known him long enough; I had talked to enough people – Iranian friends, relatives, and colleagues – that I had a sense of what to expect for a visit. We had saved some money, and I was getting ready to begin in the fall as a tenure track assistant professor at the University of Illinois at Chicago, so we had some financial stability in front of us. But I knew no Persian, and next to nothing about the country. This would be simply a family visit; there were no expectations other than those of domestic negotiation and accommodation that exist for any new family entrant.

Our first few trips were mostly like that. I was the privileged guest who didn't know the local rules, but wasn't expected to; that was the advantage of not being Iranian-American, and being almost totally ignorant of how things should be done.[1] I got cultural credit just for trying to fit in, and even for my mistakes: kissing everyone around the

[1] I was even more unprepared than Elizabeth Fernea when she accompanied her graduate student husband Bob to his field site in southern Iraq in 1956. Fernea may have been naïve about gender roles in both Chicago and El Nahra, but at least she knew some Arabic. She traveled to Iraq as an academic wife with no initial expectations of taking her local role seriously except as helpmeet, in terms of making their dilapidated cottage more homelike and helping her husband gain access by proxy to the segregated social world of the village women, both prospective contributions helpfully pointed out to her by her husband at the start of their stay. See Elizabeth Fernea, *Guests of the Sheik: An Ethnography of an Iraqi Village* (New York: Anchor Books, 1969), the culturally attentive, self-reflexive ethnographic memoir that became the basis of Fernea's own impressive academic professional career.

room at an extended family reunion; bowing formally, hand on heart, to the teachers in a village school; traveling in the war-torn province of Khuzestan in the far south of the country. Iranians kiss on each cheek, but only if you are already closely connected, not on first introduction; the hand-on-heart bow is for men, not women; there were hardly any tourists from Tehran, let alone Americans, in Khuzestan in the early 1990s. But the relatives thought I was open and warm-hearted; all the schoolchildren poured out of the school to view the clueless stranger suddenly in their midst; ordinary people were extraordinarily generous and welcoming. I enjoyed my family visits, but I wasn't taking them seriously as scholarly work.

I was a political theorist, so I thought a lot about power, understood not only as hierarchical domination but also as more comprehensive systems of possible empowerment, positioning, and control. I knew I didn't know anything about Iran, or even more generally about the Middle East, beyond what a reasonably intelligent person could read in the newspaper (not much). I went over the proofs for *Speaking through the Mask*, my book on Hannah Arendt, in Kaveh's parents' house. I'd been working on the political intersections of social identities, especially gender and religion, not only in Arendt but also in more contemporary issues involving Muslim women, including the first big national headscarf scandal in France.[2] For that essay, I read a lot of newspapers. I appreciated the nuance of the everyday, and I liked to pay attention to social detail, but I worked on ideas and on texts. Texts don't move around in the multidimensional way that people do.

## Politics (History, the State, and Society)

In 1978–1979, Iran experienced a revolution. A revolution is not a coup: not an exchange of elites at the top of the state, but a bottom-up overturning of the established political and social order. Revolutions are not common. They change everything, because no matter what happens, they establish a precedent that change can happen, that the

[2] The first research project I engaged in independent of my dissertation research was an analysis of one of the early significant controversies over European minority/immigrant identity, agency, and representation: the 1989 French *l'affaire du foulard*. See "A Problem with Headscarves: Contemporary Complexities of Political and Social Identity," *Political Theory*, 22/4 (November 1994), 653–672, additional response 678–679.

status quo of power and hierarchy is vulnerable to human action. The 1979 Iranian Revolution overthrew a strong state, a key and strategic US ally with a well-organized military, ruled as an absolutist monarchy with a modernist veneer. But it was not the first revolution in Iran; for Iranians, the first modern revolution is the Constitutional Revolution of 1905–1906.[3]

The Constitutional Revolution (*Enghelab-e Mashruteh*) established a Constitution (*Mashruteh*) and a Parliament (*Majles*) and the principle of popular sovereignty in Iran in 1906, a period when most European governments were monarchies, the Great Game of empire was at its height, and democracy was still a global dirty word. Iran was never formally colonized, in part because it was a neutral, independent buffer state between the competing expansionary dreams of Russian and British imperial power. But by the twentieth century, the ruling Qajar dynasty was already in its decrepit end days, a dynastic story in itself of ruthlessness become decadence become decline. In the summer of 1906, 12,000 men took refuge on the grounds of the British Embassy compound in leafy north Tehran, tolerated by the British and advocating for constitutional limits to Qajar monarchical rule. Then the Anglo-Russian Convention of 1907 (agreed upon by the two imperial rivals in order to counter the shared expansionist threat of German alliance with the Ottomans) recognized two "spheres of influence" in Iran, each to be the legitimate arena for intervention, by Russia in the north and by the British in the south. The British turned against the Constitutionalists, but having lost faith in the Qajars, eventually helped ease the impressive Reza Pahlavi into power and a new dynasty.

Reza Shah was from the north, the last and only Iranian commanding officer of the Persian Cossack Brigade. Tall, illiterate, and extremely capable, in a photograph taken before the dynastic change he towers impressively behind the short, round, sleepy-looking figure of the last Qajar ruler, Ahmad Shah. I saw this photograph in an

[3] The following, very abbreviated version of modern Iranian history is included only to provide orientation for readers who are unfamiliar with Iran's national history and politics. It is for that reason very much a "potted history": a grinding together of significant bits into an easily and quickly consumed substitute for a more distinguished historical offering. Readers are encouraged to avail themselves of the excellent available scholarship on nineteenth- and twentieth-century Iranian state and society, much of which will be referred to in the various footnotes throughout this book.

exhibit of monarchical relics in the basement of the Niavaran Palace in Tehran in the early 1990s, on what was probably my first trip to Iran. At that time, I didn't know anything much about Iranian history or politics, let alone enough to recognize individual personalities. But I knew enough to pick out the tall man with the piercing eyes in the background of the snapshot and to ask, "Who is *that*?" And then to ask who was the rotund figure in front (Ahmad Shah Qajar). And then I thought I knew everything I needed to know about early twentieth-century Iranian political history (not quite).

During the twentieth century, the Pahlavi monarchy followed an abbreviated version of the Qajar dynastic trajectory. Reza Shah ruthlessly centralized the political and military structure of the state and built infrastructure (railways, tunnels, urban boulevards) that still endure as the pride of visible Iranian modernity. The story is that he supervised the planting of the trees along the main north/south Tehran thoroughfares, *chenar* (local variation of English plane trees or American sycamores) that can grow for hundreds of years and now tower benevolently over the street unless they have been killed off by more recent combinations of drought, construction, and pollution. But in 1941 Iran's strategic location, its oil, and Reza Shah's preference for affiliation with the Germans rather than Iran's traditional, rival Great Power foes led to the Anglo Soviet Invasion, and Reza Shah was forced to abdicate in favor of his son, Mohammad Reza Pahlavi.

During the postwar period, Iran experienced another efflorescence of popular sovereignty, this time under the nationalist prime minister Mohammad Mossadegh. Mossadegh nationalized the Iranian oil industry, which had been developed as an exclusive British concession by the Anglo-Persian Oil Company (later renamed the Anglo-Iranian Oil Company).[4] But national sovereignty outside the metropole was suspect, and in 1953 Great Britain and the US coordinated a coup in Iran that deposed the elected government, placed Mossadegh under house arrest for the rest of his life, and solidified monarchical control by the more pliable Mohammad Reza Shah.[5] The reformulated Pahlavi

[4] See Kaveh Ehsani, *The Social History of Labor in the Iranian Oil Industry: The Built Environment and the Making of the Industrial Working Class (1908–1941)*, PhD diss., University of Leiden, the Netherlands, 2014.

[5] In 2013, the sixtieth anniversary of the 1953 Iranian coup, the CIA for the first time publicly admitted its role; the British would neither confirm nor deny their role, although it had been obliquely referred to previously.

regime became a favored foreign ally of the US and was held up as a model of enlightened absolutism and shiny top-down modernization. But its internal politics were elitist, exclusionary, and corrupt, and the role of benevolent despot was an ambiguous one by the 1970s. Despite the international glamour of the 1971 celebration of 2,500 years of glorious Persian Empire, ordinary people in Iran were becoming more and more dissatisfied. The luxurious tent city built by the Shah at Persepolis (*Takhte-Jamshid*), the ceremonial capital of the ancient Achaemenid Empire (550–330 BC), welcomed Iranian and foreign dignitaries and celebrities and was flatteringly covered by the international press. But it was itself an anachronism, even in its location. Persepolis is outside the more recent, but still venerable city of Shiraz, itself the site of the mausoleums of two of the most beloved Persian poets, Saadi (thirteenth century) and Hafez (fourteenth century), and the capital of the enlightened ruler Karim Khan Zand (circa 1705–1779), who named himself Representative of the People (*Vakil-e Ra'aayaa*) rather than Shah, already in the eighteenth century.

The Iranian Revolution of 1978–1979 was a national phenomenon, and not specifically Islamic until it became so with the foundation of the Islamic Republic of Iran in 1979. History always is claimed by the victors, even if it does not belong to them, and revolution is always a two-part process, initially of liberation (from the old) and then of foundation (of the new). The Iranian Revolution was an effective mass movement of national liberation from an autocratic and dictatorial monarchy. It was also the problematic foundation of a republican form of government with a formalized Islamic ideology and leadership only loosely institutionalized. And then in 1980 Iraq under Saddam Hussein, receiving military support from the US, invaded Iran. The revolutionary dreams of political utopia, already under pressure from the realities of ideological and popular divisions (crisscrossing among the right and the left, the religious and secular, the urban and the rural, the center and the provinces, not to mention between genders, generations, sects, ethnicities, and regions), were blown apart by the immediacy of violence coming from the outside as well as within.

The Iran–Iraq War ended in 1988, and the country had to rebuild, although since Iran remained under widespread international sanctions that was a slow process. By the later 1990s, most people's ordinary daily life had normalized enough to open some room for political experimentation. When I first went to Iran in 1992, we boiled the milk because Kaveh's mother didn't trust the pasteurization process. A few years later, we didn't have to anymore: we knew the milk was pasteurized. People could manage to look up and look around and reconsider what they had been through and where they were going as a collective. In 1997, Mohammad Khatami was elected President of Iran in an unexpected and massive victory. The election ushered in what came to be known as the Reform period and signified a widely shared popular desire for change, and for the easing of the political, cultural, and social pressures that had accompanied the experiences of the 1978–1979 Iranian Revolution and the eight years of the Iran–Iraq War.

The postrevolutionary Iranian government is a complicated structure of elected and nonelected branches that have often fought out their intense rivalry by attempting to contradict each other's control and/or initiatives. The elected branches of government are the Parliament, the Presidency, and the Assembly of Experts; the nonelected branches include the Judiciary, the Supreme Leader, the Guardian Council, and the Expediency Council. Throughout much of the postrevolutionary period, the elected branches provided more support for increased democratic participation in public life and increased social freedom in private life, while the nonelected branches endorsed a vision of governance based on theological authority. Within the unstable balance of competing powers within the Islamic Republic of Iran, popular pressure from below has often manifested itself in the street, the independent newspapers, and the Parliament. More authoritarian resistance to political and social change has come from the nonelected governing institutions of the Judiciary, the Guardian and Expediency Councils, the state-run television, and formal and informal elements of the security apparatus. Balancing within this framework, sometimes tilting it from side to side or regaining a balance, are the offices of the President (elected, although candidates must be approved by the nonelected Guardian Council, as are all candidates for Parliament), the Supreme Leader (selected by the Assembly of Experts), and the Assembly of Experts itself (elected, although all candidates for the Assembly must be approved by the Guardian Council before election, and approved after election by the Supreme Leader).

This complicated and interlocking structure is intended to provide a system of checks and balances, overseen by a uniquely respected Leader above the partisan fray. Ayatollah Khomeini, the face of the

Islamic Revolution and the first Supreme Leader until his death in 1989, theorized the rule of *velayat-e-faqih* (rule/guardianship of the Islamic jurist) as the governance basis of the new Islamic Republic and the supreme arbiter of legal and moral questions through the interpretation of religious ethics, precedent, and law. Khomeini himself emphasized that the legitimacy of the Faqih (the Supreme Leader) rested on the will of the people and was not incompatible with democracy, although his role was to interpret, guide, and correct popular will. In practice, the theory of *velayat-e-faqih* and the governing structure of the postrevolutionary Islamic Republic have provided for ongoing factional struggle since its inception. During periods when the factional rivalries were less evident, it has usually been because of intensifying state repression. But as soon as the unsteady balance of the system is regained, the competitive struggle between contradictory visions of a postrevolutionary political system reasserts itself.

Over time, *velayat-e-faqih* has been used to justify more explicitly antidemocratic positions, including the argument that those with state-sanctioned Islamic authority have the priority of power and decision-making over those whose legitimacy comes from the people and the republican form of government. This increasing tension between the Islamic and republican interpretations of power within the hybrid Islamic Republic has occurred concurrently with the increasing realization by the electorate and the nonelected stakeholders that the majority of voters want a much more limited version of religious political authority. Despite and because of the creation of a theologically defined state, Iranian society has become more secular, as ordinary people, no matter what their personal level of faith and religiosity, have become more skeptical of the close intertwining of religious and political authority.

In a national situation that combined limited political freedom with a state that legitimated itself through a narrative of revolutionary popular (Islamic) sovereignty, Khatami's 1997 election as President provided widespread recognition of shared dissatisfactions and the beginnings of a wider conversation of who and what a postrevolutionary Islamic Republic would represent. During the Reform period under the two terms of Khatami's Presidency, from 1997 to 2005, the hidden struggles over the present and future relations of power in the Islamic Republic became much more visible as they permeated all levels of Iranian society. While the governing factions contested each other's institutional control through competing practices of power (democratic or authoritarian) and authority (electoral or theological), most people experienced political transformations through the minor but significant struggles of the everyday: who makes the decisions in a family (the revalorization and slow disintegration of classic patriarchy); exactly how a woman adjusts her headscarf (the contestations over control of bodies and public space); what opportunities are available during free time (the contradictions of state censorship and social desire in a country recovering from revolution and war). The wider political implications of personal social decisions were often intentionally implicit rather than explicit: representations can sometimes be most eloquent when most imprecise.[6] Small gestures could speak for big ideas, coded in a locally recognizable vernacular that enabled both recognition and deniability. Daily life suddenly became full of promise.

President Khatami sponsored the beginning of an independent press, and "a dialogue of civilizations" that had implications inside and outside the country.[7] New newspapers sprang up and were read cover to cover, handed around from reader to reader, only to be shut down by the Judiciary, which remained controlled by more conservative elements of the regime. Days later, a new newspaper would usually open with a different name but the same staff and editorial policy. Ideas mattered; there were red lines of public discussion, but there was excitement in the air as people recognized in each other similar, previously hidden desires for collective change. The questions of how that change should happen, who should control it, and what it should entail were debated in the pages of the papers, in private conversations, and increasingly in public places – in taxis, in grocery lines, and in the street. I realized I was seeing a society democratize itself, incrementally but every day. This was speech as action, the mutual self-recognition of

6 For a discussion of how small individual decisions can add up to collective "non-movements" for change, especially under conditions of very limited political participation, see Asef Bayat, *Life as Politics: How Ordinary People Change the Middle East* (Stanford, CA: Stanford University Press, 2013).

7 Khatami's "Dialogue of Civilizations" phrasing was intended as a rebuff to the "Clash of Civilizations" rhetoric of Samuel Huntington, as well as the aggressive self-presentation the Iranian state was perceived to be taking to its perceived enemies both at home and abroad. See Samuel Huntington, "The Clash of Civilizations?" *Foreign Affairs*, 72(3) (Summer 1993), 22–49; Michael Rubin, "Iran's 'Dialogue of Civilizations' – A First-Hand Account," *Middle East Quarterly*, 7(1) (March 2000), 31–38.

the citizens' subjectivity through their engagement with each other and their collective creation of a space of participatory appearance. I was seeing the transformative power of politics happening right in front of me. I realized I needed to pay attention.

## Action (Film as Text and Politics)

Arendtian politics is premised on action, and action is mostly speech. As I recognized that my theoretical interests were occurring in real time around me, I also realized how much I needed to learn, both about Iran (history, religion, and economics) and about how to work on the instability of speech and action in process (fieldwork), rather than waiting until it is written down (texts). As an intermediate step, I began to write about films.

When we moved to Chicago in 1992, the same year that I first visited Iran, we discovered that the Film Center of the School of the Art Institute held an annual month-long Festival of Films from Iran. The New Wave of Iranian cinema was just emerging, and every weekend through the month of October, two new films were screened, often accompanied by visiting filmmakers and actors as special guests.[8] We'd already been going to the films, and we had the chance to meet the filmmakers because Kaveh had volunteered to do the question-and-answer translations. (During this period, relatively few Iran-based intellectuals and artists spoke English well; it was more likely that they could speak French.) Out of the luck of geography, I was ideally positioned to observe the flourishing of the Iranian cinematic New Wave and to watch a lot of Iranian movies, some now well known, some generally forgotten.

The innovative auteur-influenced filmmaking that exploded in Iran during the 1990s and through the 2000s was a primary vehicle for

[8] The Festival began in 1989 and continues. The initial Director of Programming, Barbara Scharres, and the then Associate Director of Programming, Alissa Simon, attended the Fajr International Film Festival in Tehran and were able to organize the screening of new productions that otherwise had limited or no international distribution. I could not have written on Iranian cinema or begun to get to know Iranian culture, without the benefit of those intense Octobers of multiple screenings and accompanying weekend visits by Iranian directors, cinematographers, and actors. The Film Center is now the Gene Siskel Film Center of the School of the Art Institute of Chicago; the annual Festival of Films from Iran no longer occurs in October but continues.

social critique and cultural experimentation. The films had to abide by strict representational controls and avoid any overt political references. They were supposed to provide models of proper Islamic behavior as educational postrevolutionary entertainment. But in a society in which the exact degree of coverage provided by a woman's headscarf was a daily issue of public morality vs. private freedom, apparently anodyne representations of daily social life conveyed powerful, recognizable political messages. Working within a peculiarly limited vocabulary of cinematic representation (supposedly private scenes had to conform to norms of public behavior), Iranian screenwriters and directors had to innovate with the conventions.[9] Because their national audience could recognize the unreality of the representation (no ordinary woman gets into bed wearing full outdoor *hejab*, including an overcoat, as was often the case in films during the early 1990s), clever filmmakers began experimenting more explicitly with the artifice of representations in order to avoid scenes appearing clunkily artificial. The nuances of social life became highly significant in their representation. And on film, if you don't catch it the first time, you can try to see the scene again.

Watching films, thinking about them, and writing about them became my bridge to doing actual fieldwork in Iran. Because the conventions of Iranian cinematic representation during that period were so deeply enmeshed within the nuances of social representation, the films provided insights into opaque relations of social power. But sometimes it was necessary to interrogate actual social relations in order to appreciate what was going on in the films. I couldn't just watch people, on film or on the street or in the household. I had to talk with them.

Talking with people helps you learn. It can also help make very clear how much you don't know.[10]

[9] The censorship codes prohibited representations of violence or (sexual) immorality. In practice, this meant non-related adult men and women actors were not allowed to touch each other, even when playing close family members; women actors had to observe full *hejab* – completely covering the hair and the contours of the body as they would in public or when interacting with unrelated men – even when they were playing intimate indoor family scenes or supposed to be inside and alone at home.

[10] I am indebted to Shiera el-Malik for identifying the theoretical method in the following account describing the process of misunderstanding and then reconsidering a film. El-Malik points out that the key analytical recognition is the crucial role of subjectivity for the researcher and the research subject: for the

## Looking into a Representation (Inquiry and Reflexivity)

During the 1999 Festival of Films from Iran, which was also its tenth anniversary season, the Chicago Film Center screened two separate films with surprisingly parallel stories: Tahmineh Milani's *Two Women* (1999) and Fereidun Jayrani's *Red* (1999). Both films portrayed women being controlled by possessive, abusive husbands; in both, the heroine has to argue for a divorce to release her from her oppressive marriage before a mullah who represents an unsympathetic legal system; and in both, the heroine is only released from the misery of her marital bondage by the eventual violent death of her husband.[11] But the films were also very different. The heroine of *Two Women* was a perfect overachiever who was reduced to absolute passivity by her husband's jealous control, finding release only after her stalker murdered her husband. By contrast, the heroine of *Red* was a strong-minded nurse and devoted mother who insisted on her independence all through the movie; when her crazed and violent husband eventually tried to gain ultimate control by killing her, she killed him in self-defense. (And that film was identified as "based on a true story.") Stylistically, the films were equally opposite. *Red* was in the familiar style of a Hollywood domestic abuse drama: conventionally realistic, smoothly professional, and especially toward the end, effectively suspenseful and scary. But *Two Women* had the heightened characters and theatrical stagings of a melodrama: the virtuous heroine romanticized in her passivity; the villainous psychopath who threatens the heroine by glowering at her and brandishing a tiny knife; a key scene in which the heroine pleads for a divorce before an Islamic religious judge by delivering an emotional, futile polemic on the general issue of a woman's right to be treated like a human being.[12]

researcher to recognize "the subject as both *contextually embedded* and *historically contingent*, and simultaneously *remain cognizant of her own subjectivity*." See Shiera S. el-Malik, "Subjectivity," in *Critical Imaginations in International Relations*, eds. Aoileann Ní Mhurchú and Reiko Shindo (Routledge, 2016), 212–227.

11 The parallels between the films were only emphasized by the fact that the same actor played in both of them: the charismatic Mohammad Reza Foroutan played the psychopathic stalker in *Two Women*, and a psychopathic husband in *Red*.

12 In *Red*, as in the documentary *Divorce Iranian Style* (Kim Longinotto and Ziba Mir-Hosseini, 1998) the women plead effectively for divorce by enunciating the specific failings of their errant husbands, rather than making passionate but vague claims for human rights.

I found *Two Women's* style too broad to be convincing, and I was suspicious when I found the Chicago audience tended either to love *Two Women* and hate *Red* or love *Red* and hate *Two Women*. (I was leaning toward the latter.) It seemed to me that what most divided the two films (and the audience response to them) was the role of agency. In *Red*, the heroine maintains her agency throughout; even as a victim, she maintains her claim to her autonomy. In *Two Women*, the heroine becomes so passive under the jealous browbeating of her husband that during the climactic scene in which the psychopathic stalker, newly released from prison, tracks her down in an empty street, she falls to her knees screaming, "Kill me, kill me!" The stalker then declares his love and instead kills the husband, who shows up at an inopportune moment. Finally released from her marital predicament by the timely, violent intervention of her crazed suitor, the end of the film has the heroine of *Two Women* telling her best friend that she is ready to put her life back together, even ready to learn to drive; it doesn't seem to matter that early in the film she was offering to give her friend driving lessons or that a key middle scene involved her driving a car.

Both movies had been huge popular successes in Iran, but it was Milani's *Two Women* that was being hailed abroad as a feminist achievement, while *Red* received almost no critical attention or distribution. For audiences in the US, *Two Women* seemed happily to confirm the worst stereotypes about Iranian/Islamic/Middle Eastern men, and the absolute misogyny of Iranian society, state, and culture.[13] But *Two Women* didn't match up at all with what I'd seen of the assertive tenacity of postrevolutionary Iranian women. So I was shocked when I discovered that women in Iran were finding a feminist message in Milani too.

I saw the films in October, and by March I was in Iran. I knew *Two Women* had been a huge box office success, but I was surprised when so many of the women I knew told me how much they liked the film. They were active professional women (teachers, urban planners, publishers, and social workers), some married, some single, and some divorced, all of whom wouldn't seem to have had the trouble with

[13] See the film critic Richard Peña, writing in *Film Comment* about *Two Women*: "... unsparing in its portrait of the brutality suffered by women who question traditional roles ... Milani's most impressive film to date." Program notes for *The Tenth Annual Festival of Films from Iran at The Film Center at the School of the Art Institute of Chicago* (October 1999), 5.

agency that I had associated with the heroine of the film. It didn't make sense to me that these independent and determined women would have been drawn in by the heavy-handed sensationalism and passivity of *Two Women*. Yet they described an emotional connection to the film that puzzled me, all the more so because I was sure it was quite different from the projection of utter feminine victimization I had encountered in Chicago among both the US and Iranian exile audience.

My interpretive impasse was only resolved through the course of a long evening conversation among several friends, women and men, who had been in and out of the country for different durations over the past twenty-odd years. We all had slightly different reactions to the film, but as we started comparing those reactions, we also began to realize that we were reacting to the representation of different experiences. My impression, and one shared by several other Iranians in the room, had been that *Two Women* had provided an almost Orientalist version of an Iranian woman's feminine oppression and that the very excesses of this representation (the heroine's polemics and the uniform hostility of all the men around her) had been part of the film's refusal to engage with the specific (rather than the rhetorical) historical and material conditions of Iranian women's lives.[14] But not everyone agreed. As we talked, it became clear that the Iranian women who had been in the country through the Revolution and the Iran–Iraq War had a very different interpretation: they had seen a different film. For them, *Two Women* was not an ahistorical melodrama of generalized masculine oppression but an accurate emotional representation of their own experience under the specific historical, cultural, and political conditions of the early years of the Islamic Republic.

The difference in our interpretations of the film depended on a few very small but key details that I hadn't even noticed. The film's title refers to the heroine and her best friend, and the different life trajectories that lead to their encounter fifteen years later, one a successful architect in partnership with her loving and supportive husband and the other an oppressed housewife and mother still persecuted by the crazed stalker/suitor from her past. Although this time frame meant

[14] This criticism – of an Orientalist representation perpetuated under the guise of feminism – had been addressed to Tahmineh Milani, the writer/director, when she appeared in Chicago for the film's screening. Her response that the film was a universal story and that even women in Italy had loved it had not been reassuring.

that the women would have been university students during the Revolution, the film had seemed to avoid political references: these were just "two women," certainly not two revolutionaries. But that evening, one of the women who had been in Iran during that period, and who had been the same age as the characters would have been in the film, pointed out the particular references that would have signaled political context for an audience attuned to them. These were the codes of representation (essential for communicating social critique within a context of political censorship) that I hadn't known how to read and that I realized I had to learn if I wanted to understand the multidimensionality of postrevolutionary Iranian experience, and its essential intermingling of political and social nuance.

The most important of these signals is a brief remark early in the film. In a conversation about homework and tutoring (and the one in which the heroine offers to teach her friend to drive), the two friends also mention, seemingly in passing, rumors that the universities will be closing. It's a brief discussion, seemingly unimportant, but it locates the friends as students immediately before the period of the Cultural Revolution (1980–1983), the three-year period shortly after the Revolution itself when the universities were closed, and students and faculty were politically evaluated to determine their appropriate Islamic credentials for readmission to the reconstituted university community. The universities were closed to everybody, men and women, but for young women who did not yet have their degrees this was especially problematic. Like the young women in the film, they often had families who had been willing enough to let them go off on their own to study, but who now, with the universities closed and the country in upheaval, wanted their girls to come back home. And what was the alternative? The residence halls were closed, the Iran–Iraq War and the US-led embargo devastated the economy, and the popular ideology of the Revolution reemphasized a traditional domestic role for women. Even young women who had been raised in a seemingly entirely Westernized and modernized middle-class social environment (coeducational schools, mixed parties, the liberationist texts and music of the 1970s) found themselves newly pressured by families having second thoughts about the cultural trends they had encouraged in their children, especially now that the whole nation seemed to be in a backlash against them. A lot of young women got married. What else could they do? But that isn't all that happened.

My friend described the change in gender attitudes after the Revolution, how it seemed that all the men around you, in the middle of national turmoil and their own personal dislocation, found some stability in the cultural reinscription of a gendered hierarchy. And how women, themselves confused, equally caught up in the Revolution's dynamic of renewal and rejection, found themselves going along with this. Maybe it was true, after all, that Iranian national identity had become so deeply contradictory because it had abandoned its (Islamic) roots. And maybe it was further true that a return to those roots, even for the less religious, could be accomplished by a return to those family values that secured women's energies (sexual, intellectual, and practical) firmly in the home. So they got married and had their children. And eventually, as time passed and they got a little older, as the early days of Revolutionary confusion and idealism gave way to ordinary life under a new regime, they felt themselves to be trapped. Individually, each young woman had her personal situation. But collectively, they felt betrayed by a national shift that had cut them off from the future they had expected, and stranded them in a landscape of changed gender relations that proscribed the conditions of their individual fulfillment. It wasn't just that times were tough, politically and economically. It was the feeling that they had personally paid the price for a national experiment in gender relations, and the experiment hadn't worked.

For these women, this was the story that *Two Women* told. The polemics, the passivity: the heroine's problem wasn't merely with the men around her; it was that the men around her represented her problem with a whole society. The heroine was trapped, not simply by her marital situation but by her national situation, as experienced during that period. She was passive because there really wasn't that much she could do individually about changing the national context, and she was released from her situation by actions outside herself, even if she was a part of them. Twenty years later, often with university student daughters of their own, these women weren't trapped any longer. (Many women and men identified the 1997 election of President Khatami as the defining moment when they knew that things had really changed.) And it was precisely because they had changed, as had the society, that the film functioned as such a powerful cathartic experience.

The young women who had been through the emotional experience portrayed in the film were precisely the independent Iranian women whom I had been unable to connect with the film's narrative representation. But they made the connection. They recognized their younger selves in the young heroine, and they also recognized the portrayal of a national political experience in personal terms. In particular, they recognized the ending of the film: the heroine's sudden frantic need to get going and catch up and to learn (and relearn) the skills that allow for independence in the contemporary global world. (This was the significance of the references to knowing how to drive.) This is what one friend said about the film's meaning for her:

> This woman in the film, her story continues. And it's my story, it's the story of every woman who wants her identity, her self-respect. She wants to change herself, because now the society is changing. Because she truly needs to learn. You must remember the last thing Niki Karimi [the well-known actor playing the heroine] says at the end of the film, "I have no time, I have to hurry." She has to catch up. In everything. Learn computers. Learn her life.[15]

As an allegory of the national experiences of a specific generation of Iranian middle-class urban women, *Two Women* functions brilliantly. But on first viewing, and even on fairly careful consideration, I had completely missed this aspect.[16] I was still applying an interpretive model in which private life can be assumed to function independently of public events. But for the women who had lived through this period, the political was personal. The present openings of political and cultural reform were not only about regaining a separation of the public and the private (about getting the government out of decisions about who could watch satellite television and who would wear a head scarf) but also about recognizing the intersections of personal and political life.

At the same time, my conversations in Iran with Iranian women made me realize that my interpretive ignorance was not at all unique but was in fact recognized by my friends as part of the problem

15 Personal conversation with the author.

16 One would think I would have been more alert to the use of allegory and metaphor (strategies of representational allusion and substitution) in postrevolutionary Iranian films. After all, I was well aware of how directors had adapted the genre of children's films (films with children as protagonists, supposedly for children but eagerly viewed by audience members of all ages) to avoid state censorship while exploring larger social questions, especially regarding heterosexual intimacy and the very strict prohibition of any kind of on-screen physical contact between unrelated adults of opposite genders. For a fuller discussion of filmic representation, see Chapter 7, "Through the Looking Glass."

represented by the film itself. The heroine in *Two Women* gets cut off; her friends don't know what has been happening to her. Part of her urgency at the end of the film is to catch up with them, with a life lived with others involved in the world. She needs to know about what has been going on, and she needs the people outside her immediate experience to know what has been going on with her. Here is another comment on the film's function as a representation of that experience:

> The Revolution happened when our generation was 18, the age of our socialization. We lived every step of the Revolution within its processes. We were starting and crossing the way with it, growing with it and becoming mature with it. Each steps of its trial and error was paid with our lives. And this was not limited to our public and social life, such as status and career; we also paid in the personal and private realms of our lives. Who would say that the return-to-your-roots experience was not more of a personal rather than a social challenge? When you are facing the challenge of respecting traditional ways of life once you have been raised with modern attitudes. We paid the price of it, as women, also at the national level, by embodying the symbol of a radical change in cultural and social attitudes. Now, after a long fight for every basic principle, the society – the same as each individual – is able to find its/her/his life choice. I am, as an Iranian women, a part of that "national woman" who is now able to separate from this cycle of passivity and victimization. We want to compensate this gap in our development. My endeavor is to overcome by all means this lack. For this goal, I need more than ever to establish a dialogue, to know the "other" – inside and outside Iran – and also to be known by the other.[17]

After these discussions, I understood several things more clearly than I had before. I better understood the film *Two Women*, or at least many Iranian women's response to it. I better understood something very important about the intersection between the personal and the political in Iranian women's lives. And I better understood that the most important thing was the effort at understanding itself; the actual engagement in a dialog about our own and each other's lives.

For everyone in Iran, the decades years since the Revolution have been a profoundly political construct. Everything has been politicized, sometimes especially when politics seem to be most overtly absent. Throughout these years, the tense push-and-pull between reformers and hard-liners over every aspect of public and private reform has

[17] Personal conversation with the author.

meant that almost every social critique has formal political implications, and attendant risks. Under these conditions, the public presentation of a seemingly strictly personal story may function as a very different narrative to an informed audience. The women I spoke with couldn't at that time make a critical public analysis of the effects of the Revolution and national ideology on their own available life choices. But they could recognize such an analysis when they found it, even when apparently styled as a marital melodrama.

I still don't really like the film *Two Women*, and I still think that Rakhshan Bani-Etemad's *The May Lady* (1998) is a better feminist analysis of the postrevolutionary cultural pressures shaping Iranian women's lives. But it was only by going to Iran and talking to women in Iran that I was able to comprehend that the film could also be functioning as an allegorical aesthetic project, and not simply as the Orientalist melodrama I feared. Without my friends' conversation, I was unable to appreciate the different levels on which the film might be working, and the different levels of experience that had shaped their lives.

Every woman's life is personal, but it can also be a prism of the national experience. In Iran, this may be particularly true and, in a time of national transformation, particularly hard to grasp. Everything is more complicated than an outsider would first expect, and the codes seem impossible to comprehend. It's easy to make mistakes; it's easy to misread the signs. But it's also not too difficult to have a conversation, to ask questions, and to listen to what people have to say for themselves. It's not that Iranian women don't speak up. The problem is the gap in knowledge; the gap in life experience which the heroine of *Two Women* is in such a hurry to overcome, the gap in shared understanding about which my friends spoke. A gap that can begin to narrow in the course of a conversation, or through the viewing of a film, or the reading of a book.

## Analysis through Narrative (Metaphor and Metonymy)

This project grew out of my attempts to make sense of what I saw, what was happening around me when I was in Iran, and what mattered to the people around me. Politics and the public sphere mattered: the elections, the newspapers, and the competitive jockeying of political figures. But the sphere of Iranian formal politics was extremely volatile and extremely fraught. Making a mistake within or about that sphere could lead to imprisonment or worse.[18] And one thing I had learned from watching films but also from reading social and political theory is that the realm of personal, private life can also be a window into the structural ramifications of political and social power. The question for me was how to write about it.

For a long time, I struggled to find an academically conventional, scholarly approach to writing about the profound political and social changes I was observing in Iran. I wanted to get across the sense of unexpected dynamism I had myself discovered in postrevolutionary Iranian people and society, while conveying the knowledge I had gained to make sense of the changes I was seeing. Working within the norms of contemporary academic writing, this meant that, intentionally or not, I was trying to be as staid as possible. But it turned out that what most people, especially Iranians, really wanted to hear was the funny story that forms the basis of Chapter 2 and the title of this book: being tied up in Tehran. I told the story almost as often as I was asked. And as I told it more often, I thought about it more, and I realized it taught me quite a bit about Tehran and Iran, but something even more specific about writing. The story was funny, but it also provided a rich basis for interpretation and analysis.

The tied-up anecdote itself was a metaphor, and a point of beginning for the rest of the book I wanted to write. Each chapter of this book begins with a similarly positioned narrative telling; a story of immediate, day-to-day practice that sticks the specificity of personal experience to a fabric of social analysis.[19] The stories began as accounts of

[18] Real dangers included the "chain murders" of dissident intellectuals in Iran, 1988–1998; imprisonment of local activists as well as visiting researchers and scholars, often as pawns within internal power struggles within the regime, 1997–present. For a fuller discussion of crime and insecurity, see Chapter 9, "Being a Public Woman."

[19] I am indebted to Sadeq Rahimi's brilliant online essays on Lacanian metaphor and metonymy, part of his series on "Political Subjectivity in Psychoanalytic and Anthropological Work Today," on the website *Somatosphere*. See Sadeq Rahimi, "The Unconscious: Metaphor and Metonymy," posted April 29, 2009; Sadeq Rahimi, "The (Lacanian) Unconscious: Structure and Negative Ontology," posted May 3, 2009; Sadeq Rahimi, "Subjectivity at the Intersection of Metaphoric and Metonymic Functions," posted December 16, 2012; Sadeq Rahimi, "Subjectivity after the Subject," posted April 27, 2017.

experiences and observations I wanted to share, and that I recognized sooner or later as metaphors representing larger, more significant, and complex issues I needed to explore. Metaphor functions as a rhetorical logic of poetic representation and substitution: a word or an image or an anecdote that provides a concise expression of a longer explanation. In (Lacanian) psychoanalytic terms, metaphor is linked to repression (vertical stasis) and the symptom: the surface indication of the underlying state of being.[20] Metaphor provides focus; it is the grip.

The chapters themselves, and the discussions within the chapters, are organized to accommodate their narrative and analytical momentum. Although they intersect in their subject matters and analyses, they are also independent entities that can be read independently and not necessarily in a strictly linear, although nonetheless systemically connected, process. This is the rhetorical logic of metonymy: a lateral linking of one thing to another, a horizontal movement of contingency, relation, and association.[21] In (Lacanian) psychoanalytic terms, metonymy is linked to displacement.[22] Metonymy enables change and movement toward the discovery of a utopian horizon. Metonymy is freedom.

In combination, metonymy and metaphor construct the narrative. Metonymy is the relational logic between disparate ideas, the analytic momentum of the narrative. Metaphor is the precise selection of word and image that stitches the thoughts together while allowing for the lateral tension and flow. This is indeed a linguistic and analytical metaphor of sewing: the stitch that connects (the vertical hold) and the cloth that flows (the horizontal movement). The stories in this book, often funny but sometimes not, are intended to provide the vertical hold within the horizontal movement of the social analysis. The stories should catch your attention; the analysis should keep and develop it.

## The (Larger) Logic of (Everyday) Practice

This book is an analysis of contemporary everyday practices in order to illuminate fundamental issues of social and political power in

20 See Jacques Lacan, "The Insistence of the Letter in the Unconscious," *Yale French Studies*, No. 36/37, Structuralism (1966), 112–147.

21 Rahimi, "The Unconscious" and "Subjectivity at the Intersection."

22 Lacan, "Insistence of the Letter."

contemporary Iran. Every chapter is focused on a different practice or associated set of practices that preoccupied me, and every chapter therefore relies on a different subset of the literature of scholarly research that helped me solve a particular puzzle of social and political meaning. Within each chapter, I make use of what seemed the most relevant scholarship; sometimes this makes for an eclectic choice. But a few social and political theorists provide the analytical backbone for this book: Hannah Arendt, Pierre Bourdieu, Michel de Certeau, Michel Foucault, and hovering in the background, but asserting that an absence is not a lack when it can be a multiplicity, Luce Irigaray. Sometimes these theorists and their theories make their way explicitly into the text. More often, they are implicit within the analysis. All have helped me to think about power in unconventional ways and to pay attention to the nuances of power in the most ordinary and everyday interactions and practices.

In order to sidestep the problems of writing about formal politics in the Islamic Republic of Iran, I have chosen to write about the social politics of a postrevolutionary society. But the line between society and state is always blurred. As I have written elsewhere, the exact beginning and end of a revolution is hard to pinpoint.[23] To speak in Arendtian terms, revolution is a process of liberation and foundation. Bringing down a regime is not the same as transforming a state, and the society in which the state is embedded. Do ordinary people think of themselves as subjects or citizens? Do they look to a figurehead as either a savior or villain? Or do they recognize power as located in each other and themselves, with all the difficulties and challenges that constantly entail?

Voting matters, as do political parties and government pronouncements. But especially under conditions of state repression, political transformation may be more evident in the informal sectors of the economy, society, and the state. How have ordinary people changed the way they do things, the way they treat each other and themselves? What do they expect of themselves, and how have social relations of

[23] See my book review of Afary and Anderson's collection of Foucault's essays on the Iranian Revolution: review of Janet Afary and Kevin B. Anderson, *Foucault and the Iranian Revolution: Gender and the Seductions of Islamism* (Chicago: University of Chicago Press, 2005), *International Journal of Middle East Studies* 38 (2006), 492–494.

power and intimacy changed between the generations, the genders, between friends and in families, in private and public spaces, and in our own bodies? These are ongoing questions in any society, and especially in one as dynamic as Iran has been since 1979. This book is my effort to address those questions and to share my interest and preoccupations with those who choose to read it.

# 2 *Tied Up in Tehran: A Metaphor*

I want to begin with a story. Like the best of stories, it is true.

In mid-March, 2003, I am sitting in the living room of my Persian teacher's house, in an established older neighborhood on the north side of Tehran. We have been chitchatting for a few hours, catching up. I haven't been in Iran for about a year, and this trip is a short visit, so now is our chance to exchange news. I have been hearing the latest about the house, which is a very big, very old, Qajar era summer mansion set in a large, overgrown garden off a small street leading from a good-sized main road. When the house was built, in the nineteenth century, it would have been the hot-weather summer retreat for a wealthy family from central Tehran, a fairly simple two-story structure with open balconies running around four sides of the building, in a big walled garden, surrounded by other gardens, orchards, fields, and forests. By now, a good one hundred years later, the ground-floor balconies have been glassed in, the *chenar* (plane trees) in the garden are some of the biggest I've ever seen, and the pastoral surroundings have been replaced by a combination of building sites, high-rise apartments, abandoned upper-middle-class properties, and the manicured villas of the newly rich. (I have recognized the house we can see if we climb the stone wall in the glossy photos of an architectural exhibition.) For the past few years, the question has been, what will be the future of this house, or more specifically, this property?

My teacher shares the house with a woman whose family owns the property, which is really a compound with at least two other, smaller, more modern, normal houses on it. Other members of the family live there. The whole property is jointly owned, a shared inheritance that is simultaneously a white elephant and a gold mine. The garden is too big to manage easily, everything needs renovation, and there's no money. But the land itself is a speculator's dream and is worth literally millions (dollars, US). But any developer willing to pay that price will knock down all the buildings, including the Qajar mansion, cut down all the trees, including the huge chenars, and happily forward the process of turning all of north Tehran's former green space and gardens into cheap construction, low-design, residential high-rises. The siblings have wanted to go for the money: sell and be done with it. My teacher's friend, a classical pianist with a strong corollary appreciation of her own cultural heritage, has been urging her family to accept an offer from the municipality and the national heritage foundation. They would landmark and purchase the property and eventually convert the old house into some kind of cultural center; they are offering at least a million dollars, although they can't match a speculator. Amazingly enough, the family has just agreed to accept the municipality's offer. On this unexpectedly bright note, I am just wondering if it is time for me to get up and go, when the door bursts open, and the evening takes a turn.

Literally, the door burst open, propelled by three young men standing in the frame, wearing kerchiefs tied over their noses and mouths, and carrying fruit knives. They look like comic bandits, and it is quite several minutes before I understand that this really is a home invasion, and not a joke related to *Chehar-Shambeh Souri*. That's a holiday close to the Persian New Year, mostly celebrated by children and young people, which involves getting rid of the last year's old bad spirits by jumping over a bonfire and reciting a rhyme, preferably in the street at night in the dark. It doesn't involve dressing up, but for some reason it has always reminded me of Halloween, which is probably why I thought our young visitors might be playing a prank. In any case, *Chehar-Shambeh Souri* was only a day or two away, and I sat there smiling welcomingly until I figured out that something else was happening.

It wasn't really my fault that I was confused. I don't think my friends really knew what was going on either. Our visitors' entrance was so sudden and unexpected, their appearance so bizarre, and their behavior so theatrical, that there were a few minutes when it was really unclear what the genre of our drama was. They would only say "*Saket, saket*" ("Silence, silence") in low threatening voices; they moved with an attempt at controlled menace, but they were basically three skinny kids with scarves and fruit knives. I still think that if we had been quicker to realize what was going on and had simply thrown the coffee table at them while jumping around and screaming, they might very well have run away. But would they have? And they were armed, even if only with fruit knives. In any case, by the time we realized they were serious, it was clear what our parts were to be. This was a robbery, we needed to cooperate, and they were going to tie us up.

Actually, that came a little later. Initially, there was a certain amount of negotiation, which involved the apparent leader of the operation asking where the gold was, and my teacher, annoyed, telling them to look on the roofs of all the mosques (she is not overly fond of the Islamic Republic). They were arguing the point when one of the others noticed my wedding ring, which is gold with a carved carnelian stone. Not roughly, he tried to take it from me, but the shock of being touched made real to me that this was not a joke, and I freaked out. Also, it's my wedding ring, which as they say has a certain sentimental attachment, and it made no sense to me that he should have it. So I folded my hands tightly in my lap, looked at the ceiling, took a deep breath, and introduced myself. "*Man arous farangi hastam*," I said. "I am the foreign bride."

It is hard to convey the precise hit of meaning this statement carries in Iran. For one thing, it is an anachronism; "*farangi*" is more precisely the word for European foreigner, based on the Crusader-era term for the European Christian armies, the Franks. It is exactly what a woman like me, an educated, cosmopolitan, multiethnic professional, would not usually term herself. It is a two-generation joke in the family, originating with the Austrian wife of one of my husband Kaveh's uncles (father's brother, the particular affiliations matter), who lived in Iran for more than thirty years, before, during, and after the Revolution. The first few years they lived in the extended family home of her father-in-law, Kaveh's grandfather, where Kaveh's father, my father-in-law, mischievously assigned Elisabeth the "foreign bride" label, an identity that easily fell to me in the next generation. The term is an anachronism precisely because those families that might find themselves in receipt of an *arous farangi*, a European or Western daughter-in-law, are typically precisely the kind of secular, middle-class families that would go out of their way not to replicate the old-fashioned terminology of fixed social roles. But that is also why the term is a useful self-identification for me: it locates me exactly where I am, both inside and outside of Iranian traditional social culture, and it makes specific demands on that traditional culture's obligations toward me. If I am the *arous farangi*, I am simultaneously both a guest and a member of the local community; having chosen to marry in, I am reciprocally owed the validation of that choice. Self-identifying as the *arous farangi* means laying claim to an informal kinship with the national community, and therefore to the social obligations of that kinship; a mutual recognition that structured relations of social hierarchy imply reciprocal obligation. In the ongoing context of Iranian social negotiations, announcing myself as the *arous farangi* is both deeply serious and very funny, and it is occasionally my most canny card to play, especially with those, whether thieves or petty government officials, who would demand an automatic obedience.

Given that my Persian is not really good enough to engage in the politesse of negotiation, I had been careful not to open my mouth until this moment. But now my accent and my announcement confirmed my status as a foreign guest. Not to mention my grammatical mistakes. "*Een baraye arous*," I added, pointing to my ring. "This for bride," a sentence neatly lacking any trace of a verb. But it worked. When in doubt, always count on the intractable obligations of Persian hospitality. The one thief immediately backed off from my ring, and the third one who had been going through my bag and had already removed all the money now replaced everything (including all the cash) and gently set it down by my side. My property was inviolable, although unfortunately this did not apply to my Iranian hosts, and I still got tied up. From experience, I can tell you that a silk scarf knots more tightly than a cotton one; the scarf around my wrists eventually had to be cut off, and my hands stayed red for days because of the lack of circulation, but my teacher was able to shrug off her coarser cotton scarf when the time came. But that wasn't for hours. From about eight pm until eleven, we all entertained each other. Two of the thieves insisted my teacher come with them while they searched the house. Her friend, the actual owner, and I remained in the living room with the one who seemed the youngest of the three, keeping an eye on each other. My teacher had whispered that she thought she had seen a gun. Did she imagine it? But a gun, like being a foreigner, changes everything, so we were taking things seriously. Tied hand and foot, we sat in the living room and ate tangerines.

How is it possible to eat tangerines while tied up, hands behind the back? You have to be fed, of course. Or to be more exact, my teacher's friend, whose hands were tied in her lap because she was older and should be treated with respect, started to talk to our guardian and then to smoke, and he leaped to light her cigarette. She was leading him out about his plans in life, and why he wasn't in school. Then, so I shouldn't feel left out, she gave me a piece of tangerine. Except tangerines have pits, so when the thief noticed I needed to spit them out, he jumped to offer a saucer. Pttt, pttt, pttt. At some point, he even got up, took a few steps, swooned and fell down, and then gloated at us for our concern, having proven to us what a good actor he was. In the meantime, my teacher was having to witness the stripping of anything valuable from her own household, forced to accompany the thief who seemed to have the gun as he searched from room to room. The phone kept ringing. I was sure it was Kaveh, worried about what had happened to me. We tried to explain to the thief in the room with us that they should leave soon, that my husband would be concerned that there was no answer when there should be, and might come looking or even call the police. In fact, I was quite worried about this. Kaveh might come looking for me, hop the garden wall when there was no answer at the gate, and walk in unannounced. Then what? Kaveh is a senior black belt in two separate Japanese martial arts, and ordinarily he could lay out all three of our skinny thieves very easily. But that afternoon he had badly sprained his ankle (a side effect of other old athletic injuries), and then there was the question of the gun. So what if he limped in, surprised the robbers, and then they shot him? The edge of my concern was real enough, and it got our thief a little worried too. The young thief made a suggestion: I should call my husband, tell him that my teacher's friend, the respected older woman, had gotten sick, and we had had to take her to the hospital. No need to worry! Except I knew this would raise more questions at home than it answered: if someone was sick, why was I tagging along to the hospital and causing an extra burden to my poor friends instead of heading home where I belonged? We were now at such an absurd stage of experience that I had to convince him that I shouldn't use the phone; it was clear he didn't speak English, but the complications of effectively explaining our situation over the phone while actually sitting under our minder's nose, without further risking anyone's participation, were more than I could handle. We were neither truly scared enough to attempt risky subterfuge nor quite relaxed enough simply to call home and give excuses for being late. So we waited.

In the end, the thieves loaded up everything they could find – jewelry, electronics, a camera, a guitar, and small appliances – stowed it all in a car and drove off, leaving the three of us tied up there in the living room. After about two minutes of silence, we agreed they must be gone. My teacher pulled her hands from behind her back and started untying the rest of us. I was the only one who had to be cut free. She called the police. They claimed they couldn't find the address, although the local police station is only blocks away. I called home. I tried to be very calm, but my conversation gave a good indication of why an earlier phone call might have been a bad idea. It turns out English is a bit linguistically ambiguous on some points.

> "Kaveh? I'm here at my teacher's. We were held up, but we're fine."
> "Good. What have you been doing?"
> "We were tied up, but they've left, we're ok."
> "Did you have a good time?"
> "No, thieves broke in, they tied us up and robbed us! But they've left and we're alright!"
> "What?!? You were tied up and robbed? Are you all right?"

Apparently he had called but hadn't worried. He knew I had been at my teacher's and assumed we had gone out to one of the open-air traditional late-night cafés that are not too far from her neighborhood. He further assumed I had simply been too distracted or preoccupied to call, an assumption based on intimate experience. But as soon as he realized what had actually happened, he came right over.

So did the police, after they figured out where the house was. It turned out our visitors had been part of an organized robbery of the entire compound; there had been two cars, and simultaneous robberies in the other houses. The police wandered around, not quite sure what to do until one of them suggested it was possible that the gang might still be hiding in the garden. Then the sergeant started yelling excitedly because the Tehran police force had just been issued brand new Mercedes sedans, and they had left the car with all the doors wide open, keys in the ignition, unattended in the garden. The officer suggested my husband take our statements; Kaveh suggested that was his job but offered to take mine, so I could give my evidence in English. About an hour later, we went home. All I lost was my leather jacket, which was Iranian and had been hanging with the other coats in the hallway, and so wasn't adequately associated with the *arous farangi* to be exempt from predation on one's fellow countrymen. In a house containing at least two pianos, lots of old Russian furniture, fine carpets, and other antique bric-a-brac, the thieves took exactly what the same kind of generalist would have taken in the US: mobile items easily saleable, nothing too distinctive or too hard to fence. I don't know if they were ever caught. But I think I may have seen them a week or so later; they might have been working construction on the high-rise apartment building going up on a neighboring lot. In any case, I know they were disappointed. They must have thought they were raiding a paradise of fabulous wealth, the old mansion in the middle of that big garden, in a neighborhood where the families of some of the wealthiest members of the present regime are reputed to live. Instead, they found the run-down remnants of aristocratic glories from former days, the meager wealth of the current resident artistic intellectuals, and three moderately genteel ladies drinking tea and eating bread and cheese. And tangerines.

End of story.

Now, let's begin again.

## Analysis

So, what are the layers of social meaning trapped in this little anecdote about one evening in Tehran?

To start with, there is the specific geography of the local urban political economy. Iran is that particular economic construct, a rentier oil state. That means that the government can count on a stable oil stream from a tightly managed export market. It's a truism that oil-based economies are notoriously corrupt, and oil income easily makes its way into the pockets or the pet projects of regime insiders. Oil money tends to stunt the development of other aspects of the national economy, not to mention when the nation has experienced an eight-year war with its neighbor and an international economic embargo. But oil wealth can also be used to fund other social development projects, and although the Pahlavi shahs are credited with initiating Iran's national modernization, the nationwide distribution of literacy, electricity, and road networks wasn't effectively accomplished until after the Revolution. In other words, Iran is now a modern country with a literate population, an integrated system of passable roads, and electricity in even the smallest villages.[1] This national integration has

[1] Detail regarding Iran's postrevolutionary social development is presented in Chapter 4, "Food as a Social Relation."

also led to increasing urbanization, while further accentuating the dominance of Tehran as the national administrative, economic, and cultural center.

Tehran is where the big questions get posed and the decisions get made, even if the main actors come from elsewhere. In the past decades, it has sprawled east, west, and especially north into the foothills of the Alborz Mountains.[2] The old mixed central neighborhoods are now déclassé, the solidly bourgeois neighborhoods of the north side now equally choked by smog and traffic. If they can, people move out of their old neighborhoods and head farther north. If they were already in north Tehran, aging parents either convert what had been a large single-family home into apartments that can accommodate grown children's households, or sell the property to a developer in exchange for a deal that usually involves cash and ownership of two or three out of six or eight apartments in the new building. The problem is that because both houses and apartments have to be bought outright, cash in hand, the only way to get into the property market is already to own property. And because of the opacity and stagnation of the rest of the economy, the property market is the only economic sector that simultaneously offers the chance of both profit and security. If you own land, you have a future; if you only have a salary, you are trapped in the present.

For the established professional middle class, land is usually the only tangible material asset they can provide for their children. So families are either cash poor and land rich, usually meaning that they are still living in a house they already owned well before the Revolution, or they have sold some or all of the family home in order to fund an appropriately middle-class existence for the next generation. My teacher's friend's house was exceptional because it was so big and so old that, despite the ramshackle state of the property, it transcended its existence as mere real estate and had value as a cultural commodity, which is why the municipality was willing to buy it. But the family story is all too familiar, and the usual outcome is reflected in the adjoining individual lots of the immediate neighborhood. If the family have all relocated outside the country, the property is mostly

[2] For a discussion of Iran's geographic sprawl and its political implications, see Kaveh Ehsani, "Municipal Matters: The Urbanization of Consciousness and Political Change in Tehran," *Middle East Report*, No. 212, Pushing the Limits: Iran's Islamic Revolution at Twenty (Autumn 1999), 22–27.

abandoned, like the house across the street, awaiting the resolution of competing inheritance claims so it can be sold for unsupervised development. If the family is still based in Tehran, they might renovate an upper floor into an apartment for married children; if the house is big enough, still has a garden, and is located in a northern but easily accessible neighborhood, they can rent it for well above local market rate to foreigners whose income is in hard currency. If the house and garden are exceptionally large, the family can rent them out for weddings and other private functions, like the older building in the lot next door. But even a normal-sized house in a reasonably sized garden in an old neighborhood of north Tehran can most profitably be sold for development as a twenty- or thirty-story high-rise (zoning limits the height of most new construction to four to five storys in the old mid-north neighborhoods). This is what had happened to the lot around the corner, where the building skeleton already overlooked my teacher's friend's family's property. Their house was unusual: neither open in any way to the public, like the wedding-rental or the architectural showpiece across the back wall, nor abandoned, like the empty house across the street. To a working-class construction worker unfamiliar with the postrevolutionary economic trajectory of the old middle class, an inhabited villa that kept its privacy would be assumed to be an easy source of riches.

Why not take some, then? Reliable crime statistics are hard to get, but there is certainly an increased sense of crime and insecurity. It's hard to separate perception from reality. After repeated crackdowns on the independent press effectively closed them down as forums for public debate on political reform, the remaining newspapers reestablished the prerevolutionary practice of printing a regular crime sheet, including as many gory details as possible. Everyone knows everything about all the latest murders, robberies, or assaults and is convinced that Iranian society is a cesspool of moral degeneracy and random violence.[3] If you live in an American city, this can't but seem like a joke. My own story is a case in point. Within days, it had made the rounds of social circles in northern Tehran, so that during a casual chat with a shopkeeper in a store I had never set foot in, I was actually told about the three women who were tied up in

3 Discussion of perceptions of (women's) insecurity and street crime is presented in Chapter 9, "Being a Public Woman."

Niavaran, and I had to explain that one of them was me. The story is by now widely enough known that it's become part of my informal résumé, a kind of street cred. When you meet someone in Iran, you first go through a general accounting of shared references: who's your family, where you live, where you went to school, and who your friends are. The same as anywhere, but more personal than it might be in the US, since in Iran personal networks are more kept track of, are more densely interconnected, and are more necessary to the management of daily life. So it often came up fairly quickly that I was one of the women – the foreigner – who was tied up in the neighborhood of Niavaran.

What this tells me is precisely that my story became well known because it was unusual. People tell the story not because they know the details about the tangerines, but because it's shocking, and it's shocking because random personal violence, although much feared, is still relatively rare. People talk about it because, although violence looms large as a social threat, the actual experience is unusual. It's not common enough to be an accepted fact of life. I used to try to explain to friends in Tehran that the robbery hadn't really been terribly scary, but that only led them to conclude I was some kind of fearless American superhero. I was left making vague relativist arguments; it wasn't nearly as terrifying as the same sort of thing would have been in the US, where the assailants almost certainly would openly have been armed with guns rather than fruit knives. There is random violence in Iran, and it is probably increasing. But there is also a deeply embedded local culture of negotiation that relies on certain predictable social and material continuities. Being tied up in Tehran means that life still goes on. You eat; you talk about the past, the present, and the future; you respect certain codes of behavior and authority while breaking others; you don't quite know if you are involved with something deeply serious or you are playing roles in a game; you're kind of scared, but you have a fairly sure sense that everything will be all right in the end, if you can only get through the crisis of the moment.

This is the status of political life in Iran, writ large. Being tied up in Tehran is indeed the perfect political metaphor: fairly serious, a bit surreal, inconclusive. Was my experience a thriller, a melodrama, or a farce? Has the ongoing emancipatory project of the Revolution ground to a halt, or is it percolating at a domestic level even if the evident public signs are threatening?

## Theory and Method

Why did I start this book with this anecdote? What does it mean? I first went to Iran in 1992. From 1999, I visited regularly, collecting interviews and information for a project on contemporary women's lives after the Revolution. Of all my observations, this story was the one that most lent itself to the telling: it had happened to me, it perfectly captured the surrealism of the Iranian experience, and it was self-enclosed enough to be accessible to the minimal attention most people are willing to give to an academic going on about their research. Perfect dinner party conversation, but I kept having a nagging feeling it was something more than that. Eventually, I realized this story was too good to ignore just because it was interesting (and funny).[4] It was the perfect metaphor for my understanding of Iran, a metaphor that worked on an immediate level but also needed to be unpacked. Being tied up in Tehran was an unusual but ordinary experience, in that it seemed to be easily separable from the serious analysis of public activism and political change I thought I was supposed to be studying. But I had already been thinking about the significance of ordinary social practices in terms of enabling or prohibiting political positions and alliances. In fact, I was in Tehran that March in order to present a paper on Pierre Bourdieu's conception of social capitals at a workshop

[4] It also was what prompted me to investigate further the background and significance of minor details. For instance, why would we continue to eat tangerines and engage in social chitchat during a home invasion? Arab culture traditionally encourages no lingering over a meal, as the Prophet didn't encourage unnecessary chitchat or socializing over food. See Ianthe Maclagan, "Food and Gender in a Yemeni Community," in Sami Zubaida and Richard Tapper, eds., *A Taste of Thyme: Culinary Cultures of the Middle East* (New York: Tauris Parke Paperbacks, 2010), 159–172. But Persian meal etiquette has always been much more leisurely, and Iranians include food, at least snacks, at every gathering, from university symposium lectures to religious *rozeh* (ritual mourning gatherings commemorating the martyrdom of Shi'a Imams). Medieval Persian handbooks of practical ethics explicitly recommended that dinners should include conversation with a meal, according to "the rule of Islam" (*shart-i Islam*). See the references for the eleventh-century *Qabusnāma* by Keikavūs ibn Wushmgīr (a member of the ruling Ziyarid dynasty), and the twelfth-century *The Alchemy of Happiness* (*Kīmīyā-ya sa'ādat*) by Abu Hamid Muhammad Ghazālī (a theologian) in Pamela Karimi, *Domesticity and Consumer Culture in Iran: Interior Revolutions of the Modern Era* (New York: Routledge, 2013), 123 and notes #14 and #15 on 210.

on participation, public space, and the political sphere.[5] My paper focused on the different fields of signification of religious and secular symbolic capital within the Iranian context. I don't think my presentation was very clear, but I knew I had a theoretical thread to something. The thread of the theoretical significance of symbolic social practices kept getting twisted up with the thread of the story of being tied up in Tehran. Eventually, I realized I had the narrative cord of a book; the presentation of the most ordinary of daily experiences, re-examined in terms of their extraordinary significance as markers of fundamental change in an evolving social revolution.

In 1978 and 1979, Iran went through a convulsive social and political revolution. Outside Iran, and to some extent inside as well, there is a general assumption that the revolution failed, either because of the repression associated with the postrevolutionary Islamic state or because the new Islamic Republic could not achieve a promised utopia of justice and egalitarianism. But revolution is a long process, not simply a quick-fix change of regime. Even a revolution that succeeds at national liberation but fails to found an adequately representative, stable state (to make use of Hannah Arendt's two-stage theory of revolution[6]) achieves something of lasting relevance to the ongoing process of national political development. As Michel Foucault wrote, referring to the Iranian Revolution,

> The collective will is [supposed to be] a political myth with which jurists and philosophers try to analyze or to justify institutions, etc. It's a theoretical tool: nobody has ever seen the "collective will" and, personally, I thought that the collective will was like God, like the soul, something we would never encounter. I don't know whether you agree with me, but we met in Tehran and throughout Iran, the collective will of a people. Well, you have to salute it; it doesn't happen every day.[7]

If this collective will is driven from the public space of the streets and the public sphere of formal politics through some combination of externally sponsored military violence, state-sponsored political

[5] Pierre Bourdieu, *Distinction: A Social Critique of the Judgement of Taste*, trans. Richard Nice (Cambridge, MA: Harvard University Press, 1984).

[6] Hannah Arendt, *On Revolution* (New York: Penguin Books, 2006).

[7] Michel Foucault in "Iran: The Spirit of a World without Spirit" (conversation with Claire Brière and Pierre Blanchet) in *Foucault and the Iranian Revolution: Gender and the Seductions of Islamism*, Janet Afary and Kevin B. Anderson, eds. (Chicago: University of Chicago Press, 2005), 253.

repression, social divisions, and individual exhaustion, it may still go underground. And underground, it may still have the ability to shake things up.

My argument in this book is that the fundamental changes in Iranian national political identity that have occurred since the 1979 Iranian Revolution can actually best be observed through deconstructing the ordinary practices of quotidian social life. This is especially true for issues involving gender, but it is also true for more conventionally formal political evaluations as well. There are several reasons for this. The most obvious of these is probably the very volatility of the formal political sector, and its sensitivity to the leveraging of influence, including commentary from outside Iran. In other words, while activists on the ground can get in trouble with the government for what they say and what they do, or even for what others outside the country write about them, writing about Iranian political culture is a problem, especially from the security of outside, from where it is much harder to keep track of the constantly shifting political red lines. But there is also always another problem with a preoccupation with formal electoral politics and juridical statutes, and that is the relative size of the always-existing gap between public facts and social realities. In other words, a Constitution or an election is one thing, but its face value doesn't mean much if ordinary people don't have access to the law or if state power is predominantly extra-electoral. When the political system is in flux, the question of the vibrancy of civil society may be best addressed informally, by focusing slightly away from the struggles at the center of the political sphere.

## Narrative and Analysis: Metaphor and Metonymy

Two strategies are at work in this book. One is a narrative of funny stories, and some not-so-funny ones: an evening robbery, mothers and daughters, etiquette, jokes, dress codes, crime, shopping, and art. They are about the habitual enforcement of social logics in the private sphere, and their representation in the public. Those stories are then reexamined for their more significant (and serious) social meaning as instances of daily life and habitually normalized behavior, whether religiously or socially formalized. They reveal disparate themes of agency and insecurity; family and gender dynamics; issues of sexuality;

and frameworks of social and spatial organization, transgression, and representation. But this book is intended to be not only an analysis. It is also intended to be a calculated intervention into assumptions about the conceptual and material structures of Iranian social life broadly defined, including both private and public aspects. The method of the intervention relies on disparate but linked analyses of a variety of social practices. These add up to the presentation of a larger social fabric, punctuated by detailed examinations of experience: the unexpected complexities and significations of the politics of daily life in postrevolutionary Iran.

Iran is a modern, cohesive society with deep social and political fractures. Contemporary Iranian identity is itself hybrid and contradictory, and nowhere more so than in Tehran. Iranians, and especially Iranian women, are willing to assert themselves, but they are also bound by conventions of practice and power that seriously limit their capacities. Yet these limiting conventions are not necessarily what they seem to be, or the ones that are expected. The formal restrictions of life in the Islamic Republic are severe, but they may be less essential than the ambiguous logics of practice that govern the social sphere. Elaborate, naturalized codes of personal behavior and social etiquette provide an unexamined social basis for the reproductions of inequality, especially of gender; they also provide the evidence of substantive change. These logics of practice are less embedded in any particular religious or secular identity than in an inclusive field of cultural experience that emerges from more than a century of volatile national history. These underlying logics and trajectories may be more productively examined through the apparently tangential patterns of ordinary daily experience than the central arguments of ideology. In Iran, the truth is in the details. And the details are the only place to begin.

The *arous farangi* is always both an insider and an outsider, with a foot in both camps and a doubled gaze that can provide for either crossed vision or a fuller perspective. The access I have had to the daily workings of people's lives has only been given because I have been accepted as a member of a local community; knowledge of individuals' intimate lives is premised on intimacy, whether acknowledged or not. I couldn't have written this book without the welcome and patience of those around me. Because of that welcome, I struggled to fit in with local practice and to fit in by respecting, and therefore trying to make sense of, the whys and the hows of what was being done. I learned to be sometimes almost a local, while simultaneously being clearly recognized as an outsider. It is from this perspective that I have written this book and am attempting to share that doubled insight, balancing surface and depth, with my readers.

# 3 *How Our Mothers Drive Us Crazy: Hospitality, Ritual, and the Burden of the Social*

## How to Serve Tea: The Role of Social Ritual

*Nowruz* (Persian New Year) is a pre-Islamic holiday celebrating the first day of Spring, the Vernal Equinox, March 20, the big Iranian national celebration, with its own very specific set of traditions. Every household, and often restaurants and other public spaces, sets up a special table arrangement, called a *Haftsin* (Seven S), named as such because it is composed of seven things beginning with S, as well as several other non-S items. There are always sprouting herbs (*sabzi*), usually vinegar (*serkeh*), coins (*sekeh*), certain dried spices and fruits (*sumac, senjed*), garlic (*seer*), apple (*seeb*), a mirror, a book of Hafez's poems or the Koran, depending on the religious leanings of the household, and a glass bowl with a goldfish.[1] We have all these things, as well as mosquito netting over the goldfish bowl in order to keep the cat out of it.

It is not only a beloved national holiday but also a cherished cultural symbol. The formal beginning of Spring, Nowruz is meant to be a holiday to celebrate the rebirth of nature and to appreciate the beauties of the gardens and orchards that are the treasures of traditional Iranian architecture and daydreams. The most famous poets have written about Nowruz: its fresh breezes and intimations of new life and loves.

> *You are not human if you don't fall in love in Springtime's ray*
> *In the breeze of Nowruz only dead leaves don't sway* (Sa'di)
>
> *The breeze of Nowruz wafts from the alley of the one I adore*
> *If you wish to kindle a light in your heart here are sparks*
> *galore* (Hafez)[2]

[1] In the movie *The White Balloon* (Jafar Panahi, 1995), one of the first postrevolutionary Iranian films to receive wide distribution (and popularity) in the US, the plot rests on the small girl protagonist's stubborn attempt to buy her New Year's goldfish.

[2] My thanks to Ahmad Sadri for bringing these poems to my attention. The English translations are his.

They call us to go out of the house and out of the city, to picnics and pleasures and the enticements of fresh beginnings. This is the poets' *Nowruz*, the romantic *Nowruz* of high Persian culture and the artists – mostly men – who have celebrated it. The poets are themselves a part of the national cultural fabric, and their poems are shared across generations and classes. Because of its pre-Islamic origins, *Nowruz* lends itself as an adaptable symbol to secular, mystical, and nationalist versions of Iranian identity.[3] But in my experience, *Nowruz* is actually a much more practical affair.

The calendar moment of the transition to the New Year is calculated exactly, so that everyone celebrates it at the same moment, which is announced on the radio. Rather like Western New Year, only because this moment is geared to the position of the planet rather than a clock in a public square, it changes every year. Some years, this can mean getting up and dressed and acting excited at 4 am, because at the exact moment of *Nowruz* everyone should be sitting around the *Haftsin* to wish each other Happy New Year and then exchange presents. Elders also give children some money in new bills, special for the New Year. Later there is a big lunch, at which everyone around the country eats fish and rice cooked with green herbs; the same sort of seasonal demand for a particular food item as are turkeys for US Thanksgiving. If the beginning of Nowruz comes too early, everyone gets up and gets dressed and goes through the holiday motions and then goes back to bed to try to get some more sleep. Resting up is necessary, both for the coming day and the coming fortnight, because although the New Year itself is a family day, the two weeks following are for visits. Unless you choose to use the holiday to flee the house and get away on vacation, the real work of the holiday is the ritual of visiting.

## Ritual Practice: *Eid Deedani*

*Eid Deedani* literally means Holiday Seeing, but actually means holiday visiting, particularly the formal process of paying and receiving calls for the New Year. Although the holiday is calculated precisely to a

[3] The leftist-Islamist political theorist and sociologist Ali Shariati wrote a short piece that demonstrates how Nowruz can represent nature, nation, religion, and history in a single multifaceted symbol. See Ali Shariati, "Nowruz," trans. Mehdi Abedi, *Iranian Studies* xix (3–4) (Summer–Autumn 1986).

moment of seasonal transition, Nowruz now also means a two-week vacation during which all the important business of the country is put on hold. Even most newspapers cease publication, so that whatever the news, whether of a death in the community or a national political controversy, there is almost no coverage (other than the state radio and television). But this enforced isolation from outside events only emphasizes the priority of local obligations. On the day of New Year itself, one pays calls to the elders of one's family. In our case, these are my husband's grandmother, his mother's aunt (on her father's side), his father's eldest brother, and, out of courtesy, his sister's mother-in-law. But this is only the beginning. Over the next few days, we pay further calls, and calls are paid to us, in part because Kaveh's father is himself an elder within an extended social circle and is also ill. Some days, we have continuous guests from late morning, through lunch, all afternoon, and into midevening. By 9:00 pm, everyone groans at the ring of the doorbell, not because of the identity of the actual individual behind the door but at the idea of anyone else coming in. Yet every guest is individually welcomed and enjoyed, whether they are close friends, or the family of the sister of an uncle's wife.

Iranian hospitality is both formal and spontaneous. Even in a relatively informal household like ours, there are certain things you have to do for each guest. For one thing, whenever anyone new comes into the room, everyone gets up, and the newcomer shakes hands, or gives kisses, all around the room. As soon as they are seated, they should be offered tea. This does not mean you ask them, "Do you want tea?" This means you physically offer them tea. This is the process:

Go to the kitchen, fill small glasses with fresh tea and boiling water from the samovar, put the glasses on saucers (or, for special occasions like the New Year, the tea is offered in small glasses in silver holders), put the saucers on a tray, along with a bowl with sugar cubes, and then offer each new guest tea and sugar from the tray. You should also be checking if other guests want fresh tea, or if they are finished, in which case you should whisk away the dirty glasses. Then you should offer sweets, again individually, bringing the serving dish to each person so they can help themselves comfortably. And you should have already remembered to set a small plate in front of them; this should really have happened between serving the tea and offering the sweets. Nuts, dried fruit, and dried seeds get offered along with the sweets, or a little later. After a while, you should get up and make up a fruit plate for each guest: one of each, according to the season, at this time of year usually an orange, a tangerine, and a cucumber (Iranian cucumbers are small, sweet, crunchy, and are eaten like fruit), or maybe an apple. The fruit plate, along with a fruit knife and fork, is set alongside the sweet plate, which you might need to clear now, if it is full of pistachio and pumpkin seed shells. Usually about now the doorbell rings, and if anyone has left, you should quickly clear their plates, so that new guests don't have to sit down to dirty dishes. Be sure to welcome in the new guests and to usher out any who might be leaving. Also, be sure to keep an eye on the tea in the kitchen, which is probably close to running out. Keeping the tea supply going in this situation requires careful timing, as Persian tea is brewed over boiling water for about twenty minutes by the samovar method (like the Russians), not simply steeped in the pot for five (like the British). Mistiming the tea supply can lead to a horrifying hospitality gap between finishing the pot presently on the samovar and having ready the freshly brewed tea for the new set of guests. But by now this also means that the counter in the kitchen is piled with tea glasses and small plates and cutlery, and if someone doesn't sneak off to wash dishes, we might actually run out of tea glasses, which would be a calamity and a total humiliation for the whole family.

## Ritual Matters: Social Relations, Social Reproduction

Everyone is wearing their best clothes, nibbles a lot, and has a fine time, although everyone complains about visiting. Despite the complaints, there is a point to all this; paying calls is not simply the apparently formalized, overly modulated waste of time it would seem to be in the US. This is because social networks matter in Iran, not just for socializing but also as the practical structure of social, and even economic, life. Iran is a less economically individualized, less rationalized, and routinized society than the US. This does not mean people are less developed as individuals. Quite the contrary; it seems there are more characters here, more people with eccentricities and highly defined personalities. But precisely because of this, people are less interchangeable and less standardized, and therefore it is much more important to know the right specific individual for the right job, in a literal sense. Everything is less regularized here, so whether it is for a mechanic, a doctor, or a husband, you want to get recommendations from people you trust. This is where the social network matters. As in most places, women are the caretakers of the social network, and it's mostly women who offer tea and clear the glasses (but Kaveh does this too). But because this work of the keeping of the social does matter so much, this women's work matters too and is not just the attenuated refinement of domesticity that highly polished etiquette seems to be in places like the US. It's practical, in ways that are quite obvious, even while you grumble about it.

Who is responsible for this work of producing and reproducing the social? Mothers. One year, after hostessing a full Nowruz day of *Eid Deedani*, Kaveh's mother's back gave out and she couldn't stand up straight for three days. But during that very full day, she barely sat down, and she didn't cede her obligation, or her role, as mistress of the hospitality ritual. This work, the women's work of creating and maintaining an intangible network of social relations – supervising their boundaries while facilitating their connections – is made through practice: both the "practice" of accumulated experience and the "practice" of material techniques. To practice the proper hospitality of *Eid Deedani* is to wield authority within the formal logics of Persian culture and the informal workings of Iranian family life. This is the authority of and over the domain of the social. It is the authority Iranian mothers practice ruthlessly over those other, lesser practitioners who are expected both to acknowledge and inherit the dominating power of the social: their daughters.

Within this generational calculus, my generation – women in their midlife who often have growing and near-grown children of their own – still function as daughters. The real mothers, the women who fully comprehend the possibilities of the magisterial deployment of control over practices within the fixed realm of the social, are the women of an earlier generation. Prerevolutionary in their formative experiences, modern in their expectations of life's benefits, they nonetheless adhere to fairly rigid assumptions about set gender roles and hierarchies. For women of this mature generation, many of whom are well educated and have worked at professional careers outside the home, the distinction between the private realm of the family and the public realm of politics and public life is also a gender distinction, mediated by the intermediary sphere of the social. Private, domestic space is an area under the practical control of women and is the arena of women's primary identity. Men may be welcome into the home (under certain conditions), but its practices, rituals, and boundaries are considered the domain of women.[4] Although men may patrol the outer boundaries of the private household and limit (their) women's passage through its doors, by the very logic of gender segregation, within the sphere of the home, women are expected to maintain appropriate social order.[5] Even women who may themselves have moved freely in and out of private and public spaces from an early age, who have negotiated the social transitions between changing state regimes and are fluent in the workings of public life, nonetheless may regard the outer world as primarily the realm of men. Their stake in it has not been the same as their husbands' and is not the same as their daughters'. Outside of the domestic sphere, the mothers' efforts, whether economic, intellectual, or political, are considered supplemental. Whether because of formal institutional barriers or internalized social pressures, their identity is located in managing the women's work of household reproduction in its myriad social and material forms. Precisely to the extent that women feel excluded from full participation as engaged subjects in the public world, they will claim

[4] A pre-Islamic seasonal holiday, Nowruz is considered a nonreligious (rather than secular) holiday and is practiced by most religious communities in Iran and among Persianate-origin communities regionally (Afghanistan, India, Iraq, and Bahrain) and in diaspora. But its rituals are often overlooked precisely because they are not religious. In the extensive scholarship about women's control of shared social rituals performed within the home, both in Iran and in other Muslim cultures, most of the works address women's religious rituals, or social rituals that are premised on a religious basis. For a discussion of piety circles and related social exchanges among Iranian women in the early 1990s, see Azam Torab, *Performing Islam: Gender and Ritual in Iran* (Boston, MA: Brill, 2007); for a discussion of Iranian women's food-centered hospitality at home-based religious gatherings, see Faegheh Shirazi, "The Sofreh: Comfort and Community among Women in Iran," *Iranian Studies*, 38(2) (June 2005), 293–309.

[5] The social logic of women's expected responsibility for the domestic sphere and space exists even under the most classical forms of patriarchy: patriarchal social order depends on familial hierarchies of gender and age. A senior woman (with a direct family connection to a senior man) functions as the enforcer of masculinized social order within the realm of women's space and sphere. The gendered division of labor and authority is not limited to communities that practice formal gender segregation; it continues through the conventions of labor and authority within the modern family and home. For an overview of the transformations and continuities in the social order and the spaces of Iranian homes from the late nineteenth through early twenty-first centuries, see Pamela Karimi, *Domesticity and Consumer Culture in Iran: Interior Revolutions of the Modern Era* (New York: Routledge, 2013).

their strength within the compensatory, while socially necessary, life of the family.

They claim their stake here by insisting on the priority of social ritual, and their own obligation and entitlement to enforcing the practical nuances of its maintenance. Men's contributions (whether economic or patrilineal) may be fundamental to the reproduction of the household economy, but as social actors they tend to be peripheral to its workings. The targets of these mothers' management are their daughters: by the ongoing logic of the sex segregation through which the mothers' lives have been both restricted (in the public sphere) and entitled (in the private domain), the daughters are the handmaidens and guarantors of mothers' social power. The legitimacy of the mothers' domestic dominance depends on the daughters' generational accommodation and is justified by reference to the necessary continuity of not only social but also cultural reproduction.

## Generational Change

But the daughters have become restless, and they chafe at the mothers' expectations. The daughters' lives are different from the mothers', and the easy continuity of generations has been broken. This has as much to do with legal and political changes as with the modernization of the material conditions of family life: urbanization, and related changes in the arrangements of domestic space, domestic labor, and domestic identity. Two generations ago, the normal family home was a house. A house (rather than an apartment) did not necessarily imply more space, as young families often lived with parents and in-laws, and even a house with a large or extended family might only contain a very few rooms. Urban tenements were usually single-storied courtyard structures in which a number of families inhabited individual rooms around the central, shared open court. Traditional villas were built on the same model but inhabited by a single, possibly extended, family and their servants. Middle-class families could expect to maintain a live-in servant, and working-class urban families could still count on the domestic labor of multiple women: daughters, unmarried sisters, divorced and widowed aunts, grandmothers, etc. Prerevolutionary urban residential housing was either located in traditional mixed-use (and mixed-class) neighborhoods or in the newer, more elite residential neighborhoods that may have been at a distance from the workplace but nonetheless involved only a quick commute for wealthy individuals whose private automobiles were still a privileged luxury.

For contemporary families, the situation has changed. Decades of urban real estate speculation beginning after the end of the Iran–Iraq War have meant that in much of the city, older one- and two-storied houses have been replaced by mid-rise or high-rise apartment buildings, while the square-meter price of housing has skyrocketed. Only the very poor or the very rich in Tehran now live in houses. Cars are more affordable and more common, which means the city traffic is notorious, and it can take hours to cross town from one neighborhood to another. The combination of changed living space and changed labor relations means that families can no longer rely on the kind of in-house supplemental (paid or unpaid) domestic labor their parents took for granted. Middle-class mothers of the earlier generation, whether they worked outside the home or not, often had a woman or a couple living in, as well as other paid helpers who came regularly during the day or for special occasions, whether for a dinner party or spring cleaning. Their daughters with families now live in apartments that are often farther from both the workplace and family networks, and their travel time, whether to work, shop, or visit, is longer and more unpleasant (more polluted, more congested, and more stressful).[6] Female relatives are not immediately available to help with household chores, and although domestic workers are not uncommon for middle-class households, a weekly cleaning lady does not supply the integrated domestic support of a live-in servant. In these respects, the daughters' lives are modern: they live in nuclear families in single-family domestic spaces, typically at a distance from work, friends, and family. To the extent that they are themselves integrated as workers in the formal economy, their lives are even more modern, in that they face the typical burdens of women's double day: the responsibility to balance

[6] This repositioning of urban residential geographies, particularly for young families, and the social pressure it brings to bear on young women, particularly young mothers, is not limited to Tehran or Iran. For an intriguing study of how one urban generation of young lower-middle-class urban Egyptian women responded to their situation, see Arlene Elowe MacLeod, *Accommodating Protest: Working Women, the New Veiling, and Change in Cairo* (New York: Columbia University Press, 1991).

professional and domestic responsibilities through their own initiative and labor.[7]

The daughters' lives are familiar and frenetic: they have to meet deadlines, pick up children, cook dinner, keep track of details, and keep their heads. When the two-week Nowruz vacation looms, they speak wistfully of the dream of being "alone," which means only with their husband and children. But unless they manage literally to leave town, as many now do, there will be other obligations. Nowruz is two weeks of "family" time, which means extended family, friends, and the families of friends. Nowruz means two weeks of *Eid Deedani*.

Men don't complain about Nowruz in the same way. Everyone rolls their eyes at the prospect of the endless visits, but men don't seem to dread it. Perhaps they don't feel the same burden or feel freer to escape it. But almost every woman of the middle generation I know in Iran has at some point made the same haphazard, defensive, desperate comment: they love their "family," they love Nowruz, and it's a beautiful tradition, but they wish they could just avoid it.

Why can't they? After all, it's just tradition: a series of visits, a ritual of hospitality, an exchange of pleasantries and tasty treats. But because it's tradition, it's a locked yoke on the necks of young women, a yoke they bear but do not even recognize as such. In the most modern and self-consciously enlightened families, among the most anti-religious of individuals, the burden of secular tradition weighs down unremarked and inexorable: the fixed law of the social.

## Hannah Arendt and the Threat of the Social

Hannah Arendt's antipathy for the social is well known, well remarked, and still regarded as either stubbornly anti-modern or objectionably

[7] Although the prerevolutionary middle class was tiny, middle-class women have participated in professional work for several generations. But previous generations of middle-class working women could rely on an array of domestic workers at home. Contemporary Iranian working women now find themselves, like their cohort elsewhere, with fewer support resources for their domestic responsibilities, while also possibly taking their responsibilities as workers as more fully part of their identities. Chapter 4, "Food as a Social Relation" provides a much fuller discussion of the enduring relevance of the domestic half of Iranian women's double day or second shift, and of their very low participation in the paid labor force.

anti-feminist.[8] Scholars have pored over her writings on the social, particularly in *The Human Condition* and *On Revolution*, and tried to rationalize the visceral quality of her objections.[9] What exactly did Arendt mean by the term, which she distinguishes from both the private and the public? She claims it is modern, rather than classical or traditional, and initially associates it with the rise of capitalism and the nation-state.[10] In her writings, "the social" is linked either to the rise of instrumental economic thinking and a preoccupation with economic rather than political goods (*The Human Condition*) or with the bursting in and overwhelming of the free space of public appearance by the miserable, belabored bodies of the (female) abject urban poor (*On Revolution*). In *The Human Condition*, "the social" seems to stand in for capitalism (which she doesn't actually mention by name until page 163) and to represent the modern degradation of political practice into mere administration. In *On Revolution*, it carries more emotional weight and stands for an embodied demand that cannot be withstood, most characteristically presented by mothers whose claim cannot be humanly refused.

Yet her use of the term remains confusing, not only because of the discrepancies in her use of it but also because of her own other, more admiring writings on social figures, particularly the eighteenth- to nineteenth-century salon society hostess, Rahel Varnhagen.[11] Arendt is sympathetic to Varnhagen's struggles with social convention, but her Rahel only becomes admirable when Arendt reads a political inflection into Varnhagen's own narrative of her social identity as a Jew. In Arendt's early text on Varnhagen, social existence is an existential

[8] Arendt was of a generation of professional women who often prided themselves for being considered along with the men, and who rejected feminism as a personal political position. But Arendt's particular hostility to the social is distinct and has provided a stumbling block for her feminist readers. For a direct attack on Arendt's apparently unreasonable opposition to the social as a realm that blurs distinctions of gendered roles and authority, see Hannah Fenichel Pitkin, *The Attack of the Blob: Hannah Arendt's Concept of the Social* (Chicago: University of Chicago Press, 1998).

[9] Hannah Arendt, *The Human Condition* (Chicago: University of Chicago Press, 1958); Hannah Arendt, *On Revolution* (New York: Penguin Books, 1965).

[10] Arendt, *The Human Condition*, 68–73.

[11] See Hannah Arendt, *Men in Dark Times* (New York: Harcourt Brace Jovanovich, 1968); Hannah Arendt, *Rahel Varnhagen: The Life of a Jewish Woman* (New York: Harcourt Brace Jovanovich, 1974).

mire that must be transcended by the individual; in Arendt's later texts on political life, the social is a threat to freedom itself. Why?

For many contemporary readers, Arendt's use of the term "the social" is at best idiosyncratic. The sense she gives to it, of an inescapable reality – other than the state – that cannot be resisted despite its obvious drawbacks, has no clear resonance. Within the paradigm of modern Western societies, social identity and identity politics contain an element of choice: a possibility for self-creation that presumes autonomy, individuality, and control. But "the social" can only gain its full weight of domination when there is no apparent individual alternative: when the immediate compulsion is neither a law nor an argument, but the implacable authority of intimate collective obligation. "The social" is "our tradition," and its model is the family.

Arendt implicitly recognizes the crucial role of the family in opposition to the freedom of the individual, but she herself confuses the issue by equating the family with the household, and the household (the *oikos*) with housekeeping as an economic function. In *The Human Condition*, she opposes the public, political sphere of the *polis* to the private, household sphere of the family. The household is the site of "the maintenance of life" in terms of reproductive labor, and the implication is that the bodies necessitated to that labor – particularly the gendered bodies of women and the class- or caste-defined bodies of slaves – are trapped within the household by the obligation to what they do.[12] They are also kept there by the "despotic one-man rule" of their governing patriarch (or boss).[13] As a political alternative to the *oikos*, the polis is the site in which free individuals create themselves and their shared reality in a context of mutual equality. The public world, with all its jostlings and agonistic interactions, is the refuge of the freedom-seeking individual from the fixed hierarchies and absolute identities of life in the family. (That the free individual is presumably and traditionally male is, within this neatly ordered division of the public and private, simply a given.)

Certainly, this is a bleak view of the family, and seemingly unnecessarily so. Arendt's opposition between the private family and public political life would seem to reverse the modern liberal equation, in which the family is the (male) individual's private refuge from the state

[12] Arendt, *The Human Condition*, 28.
[13] Arendt, *The Human Condition*, 29, note 15.

and the market. But the modern equation rests on a modern understanding of the nuclear family: based on romanticized versions of heterosexual partnership marriage, the cult of the child, and the sanctity of the home. Arendt's equation is more in keeping with earlier notions of the family as a functional social unit in which individual emotional ties are secondary to collective interest: a sexually inflected economic contract that guaranteed the reproduction of the lineage's material and social capital.[14] Arendt's premodern Athenian family is concerned less with personal romantic or sexual self-fulfillment than with the proper functioning of established social roles and the appropriate satisfaction of material duties. These family relations are necessarily intimate and they may also be affectionate, but the bonds of traditional family are the bonds of kinship, work, and context: blood, labor, and community rather than individual choice.[15]

These bonds can be the hardest to escape, the hardest to reject or avoid. Even and perhaps especially those who claim to break with the family often simply replicate its bonds and roles in displaced forms elsewhere. Family relations are tied with emotion as well as obligation and internalized in the body of the subject more deeply than any legal injunction or rational argument. Strengthened by the normativity of conventional family relationships, they bind the individual more tightly than formalized rules. These are the bonds of identity in community, the warm commonality of belonging that can also sacrifice the individual self to the generic standards of local suitability.

This is the model of family as threat to individual freedom that Arendt identifies with the social. Its authoritative face is not necessarily the despotic patriarch mentioned in *The Human Condition*, but even more effectively, the mothers marching on Versailles in *On Revolution*.[16] The mothers are a threat to free political choice because

[14] This model of the family as an economic kinship unit that works toward its collective interest and maintenance even at the expense of its individual members is evident in Bourdieu's work on French provincial peasant families. See "Pierre Bourdieu on Marriage Strategies," trans. Elborg Forster, in *Population and Development Review* 28(3) (September 2002), 549–558.

[15] Arendt's version of the classical Athenian family is also very different from Foucault's, in which the organization of private life within the family is nonetheless also deeply implicated in the functioning of political life beyond it. See Michel Foucault, *The Use of Pleasure, Volume 2 of The History of Sexuality*, trans. Robert Hurley (New York: Random House, 1985).

[16] Arendt, *On Revolution*, 99.

they cannot be denied, not because they back their demands with physical force but because they manifest the strength of emotional and moral authority, institutionalized not in their individual relations but in their social roles.

Arendt's brilliant insight is her recognition, even if inadequately developed, that emancipation from ingrained social constraints is more daunting than the overcoming of formal political obstacles. In *The Human Condition*, she herself almost immediately conflates family obligations with bodily necessities, yet in *On Revolution* she returns to the problem of insistent familial authority – in its maternal role – breaking in on the apparent fantasy of free political deliberation. Her antipathy to "the social" is not only a rejection of instrumental, economic, and technocratic thinking, which it is. It is also an attempt to identify and limit the insidious power of "the social" when its model is the (traditional) family, not necessarily in any of its many particular kinship forms but as a system of encompassing and institutionalized obligations of mutual loyalty so profound they can seem inarguable.

## "It's Our Tradition": The (Secular) Social as Absolute

I only understood Hannah Arendt's emphasis on the social through living in Iran, and I only understood why so many Iranian daughters had a problem with Nowruz through teaching Arendt in Iran. The idealized concept of the modern Western family has become fragmented, isolated, and burdened by its nuclear specificity, and this is as true for the daughters' marital families in Iran as it is for families in the West.[17] The couple may be at the center of the daughters' family experience, but the example of the modern (nuclear) family (based on partnership marriage) is fairly new in Iran, and the model of the traditional family (as kinship household) still holds sway.[18] Even if

[17] For a left feminist analysis of how the family, as a remnant locus of social reproduction and care, has been eroded by capitalism's demands as well as feminism's critiques, see Nancy Fraser, "Contradictions of Capital and Care," *The New Left Review*, 100 (July/August 2016), 99–117. And Fraser wasn't even considering social media or climate change.

[18] For a discussion of when partnership heterosexual marriage (the basis of the modern nuclear family) became a norm in Iran, see Afsaneh Najmabadi, *Women with Mustaches and Men without Beards: Gender and Sexual Anxieties of Iranian Modernity* (Berkeley: University of California Press, 2005). A more detailed discussion of postrevolutionary changes in women's experience of

the daughters' mothers' marriages were self-chosen love matches rather than family arrangements, their marital experiences took place in a context of more extensive family relations. The sense of filial respect toward the older generation, and the sense that the family is a kin-based network of membership, rather than a singular partnership, is still present, even if markedly less so in the daughters' relations with their own children.

Arendt's identification of the social as threat doesn't seem to make sense in the modern world, except as possibly a reflection of an archaic sensibility. But even the modern Western world has never been completely modern, despite its confidence in the self-evidence of its own modernity. Modernity is always in contradiction with itself, and with both past and future. In Iran, the contemporary social world intimately and obviously commingles with the traditional one, especially in the family. This is a blessing and a curse, a source of both continuity and friction. We all love our mothers, and along with the rise of the modern confessional, a taboo remains about airing our own resentments too seriously. Good daughters are good girls, in a different capacity from the characterization of good sons. As the daughters also struggle to be each her own woman, the tension between generations becomes more pronounced.

For the mothers, *Eid Deedani* is a pleasing ritual, a happy confirmation of their own role in the centrality of home and hearth. It may occasionally be exhausting, but it is also reassuring. For the daughters, *Eid Deedani* is an additional burden in already overstretched lives. Its rituals are for them more nostalgic than legitimizing, a return to culturally embedded practices and relations that exist concurrently with newer, radically different assumptions about the proper commitments of the wife, the mother, and the working woman in the modern nuclear family. Caught in between, the modern daughter must find her own sense of self.

The power of the Nowruz traditions is precisely that they are secular and nonjuridical. They are not rules to be broken, or rulings to be interpreted. Faced with the whining evasions of a resentful daughter attempting to avoid another seemingly pointless social call, it is the absolute power of the social the mother calls on when she answers

marriage, education, and motherhood is included in Chapter 4, "Food as a Social Relation."

simply, "It is our tradition." In that phrase, the mother invokes an enormous structure of loyalties to history, place, and nation, refracted through a particular personal relationship, and onto an apparently minor social commitment. Who is any daughter, any individual, to reject such a small request, when the rejection would be of something so much larger?

## Whose Ritual, Whose Burden: Religious, Secular, Social

Everyone celebrates Nowruz, although it is a secular holiday. But it is hard to tell if the Nowruz *Eid Deedani* has always been as central to the social reproduction of family life as it is now. Although the Islamic Republic has emphatically reemphasized the centrality of public and private Islam, through much of the twentieth century the Iranian state prioritized the social aspects of pre-Islamic Iranian national identity and practices. Did *Eid Deedani* become more important in families in which the traditional rituals of social practice, usually linked to religion, had been abandoned? Could it have been as intensive and exceptional a period of holiday visiting in the period before most families had access to motorized transportation, when extended families tended to live in closer proximity to each other but did not expect to see those who lived at a distance? Is the dynamic of maternal authority over ritualized material practices an adaptation of similar patterns, based on religious rather than secular justifications?

The women I knew who complained so resignedly about *Eid Deedani* were all from secular middle-class families. They and their parents were educated, professional, Westernized products of the pre-revolutionary secular Iranian state, and they and their parents would be shocked to be called "traditional." Within this particular class of Iranians, "traditional" means religious, bound by the conventions of Shi'a piety and the rituals of its practice. And that is exactly what they are sure they have emancipated themselves from.

Daughters from more religious families did complain about the tyranny of their mothers, although it was not over Nowruz. They complained about their mothers' attempts to enforce the material rituals of religious purity. Purity practices are neither completely public nor private; like Arendt's version of the social, they are an intermediate set of embodied relations – with oneself and with others – that maintain and reenforce membership in a community. Even in clerical families, in which the father was a public and official expert on Islamic law, the mothers insisted on maintaining authority over the actual practices within the home. Because so much of religious ritual purity deals with bodily functions (related to food, hygiene, sex, etc.), their enactment is often located in the domestic space, and the supervision of these pure and impure bodies is therefore within the domestic sphere. Male clerics may be the interpreters of texts and the writers of laws; women are the ones who make sure children learn to wash themselves properly and that the decorum of proper cleanliness, ritual or otherwise, is maintained.

Daughters of religious families might laugh at their mothers' over-insistence on observing the absolute letter of religious law, especially when even the fathers were willing to be more lax. In the domestic sphere, the mothers claimed their authority over the boundaries of the proper and the right, and the practices necessary to maintain correct and appropriate relations. A clerical father might object that extreme observation of ritual purity practices "isn't Islam." But his wife could respond by asserting her own greater expertise and material knowledge of how things actually had to be done. Dismissing the husband's formal credentials, the mother laid claim to being a "better Muslim" through her insistence on the obligations of practice.[19] The practices, and contested authority over them, were justified within a religious context with extended significance. In Iran after the revolution, the public sphere was Islamicized, and (male) religious authority became explicitly public authority. Yet while women might be blocked from equal authority as engaged actors in the formal religious sphere, religious mothers could stake their authority in the attendant, intermediate social sphere of required domestic practices to maintain and reproduce the proper religious body.

Like the daughters in secular families, the daughters in religious families often rebelled. With more access to formal education (both secular and religious), and more possibilities for public participation in the institutional world of Iranian religious politics, the daughters no longer felt they needed to abide by the mothers' authority or to take its limits as their own. They had other options, and they took them. Religious daughters, often following in their father's footsteps by

[19] (Conversations related to the author.) Daughters in religious families thus could find themselves skeptical of both maternal and paternal claims to religious authority.

educating themselves in religious law and its interpretations, have been able to find leverage in challenging their mother's (or father's) insistence on rigidly orthodox practices and behavior. The rituals of religious purity are based on religious law and textual exegesis; they are righteously subject to interpretation and argument.

## Who Are We? What We Do

A generational break has occurred in both the secular and religious families. More options for women in the public world have meant women have less need to build their authority primarily through their role in the family. The older mothers, a transitionally modern generation formed in the mid-century context of traditional hierarchies between men and women in both the public and the private worlds, have attempted to hold on to their authority through passing on a cultural paradigm of specific practices to their daughters. The daughters, modern whether they liked it or not and whether religious or secular, often find their mothers' insistence on proper practice, especially the rituals of proper behavior, whether social or religious, to be impractical and irrelevant.

Yet for all these modern daughters, the power of the social seemed harder to resist when it was manifested through mothers' insistence on secular rituals like *Eid Deedani*, rather than when it was tested through mothers' insistence on religious laws. Often with more education, and in a more formally institutionalized national religious environment, daughters could challenge their mothers over religious issues by arguing, interpreting, or rejecting religious texts and rules. Texts exist to be interpreted as much as to be applied, and rules can be modified or broken. But the social convention of secular tradition is informal; it exists neither as a text, nor a set of formal rules, nor an abstract institution. It is both general and particular, located in a set of relations that are supported by a vast continuity of constitutive realities: a habitus of embodied expectation, practice, and identity.[20]

[20] Pierre Bourdieu developed the concept of the habitus in relation to complex versions of class. But in Iran, religious community identity – whether an individual and a family identify as religious or secular – is a fundamental component of cultural capital, and therefore of class identity, as Bourdieu understands it. See Pierre Bourdieu, *Distinction: A Social Critique of the Judgement of Taste*, trans. Richard Nice (Cambridge, MA: Harvard University Press, 1984).

At an extreme, the daughter of a religious family could reject rigidly orthodox religious practice and identify as secular. In doing so, she might free herself from the authority of her mother's religiously based social demands and claim the independence of her own subjectivity. But as a secular woman, she still confronts the social in its other traditional aspects, in community life embedded in the murky realm of family expectations, personal obligations, group loyalties, and thwarted desires. Writing in 1908, the American Progressive Era reformer, domestic feminist, and early home economist Ellen Swallow Richards noted, "Tradition has held longer sway over home life than over even religious life."[21] In twenty-first-century Iran, a young woman, no matter what her religious or secular identification, will still face the implacable social that is "our culture," even if only through the beloved rituals of *Eid Deedani*.

[21] Ellen Swallow Richards, "Ten Years of the Lake Placid Conference on Home Economics; Its History and Aims," *Lake Placid Conference on Home Economics, Proceedings of the Tenth Annual Conference* (American Home Economics Association, 1908), p. 19.

# 4 *Food as a Social Relation:* Sabzi *and the Question of Household Skilled Labor*

## Household Labor: *Sabzi*

(March 4, 2007)

Every time I come to Iran, I look for the thing that has changed, the symbol of what has been happening to society while I have been gone. There's always something, usually something small. The small things are the best symbols of the big changes. Since my second trip, in the mid-1990s, I have tried to note the small, symbolic change. For years, it was dress: the manteaus got ever shorter and tighter, the colors got brighter, and there would be more hair extending in front and in back of the scarf. Lots of makeup. Scarf styles changed: from tied-under-the-chin babushka style to longer rectangles thrown over the shoulders. In 2005, young women's fashionable manteaus were hot pink, turquoise, or lime green, and some especially out-there girls had matching sets: scarf, bag, shoes. I haven't seen those this time, but they were summer colors, and it's still snowing. This year, this season, young women's scarves are multicolored wool in an open weave. But this trip, the symbolic change isn't about women's self-presentation; it's about vegetables.

When Iranians speak of "vegetables," what they usually mean are *sabzi* (literally, greens), a selection of fresh herbs eaten raw as an accompaniment to, or a substantial part of, the meal. *Sabzi* are like a salad, except without dressing, and eaten with the fingers even in the most cosmopolitan company. Depending on the season, the selection can include parsley, basil, mint, cilantro, radishes and small radish leaves, dill, tarragon, scallions, and a number of herbs I didn't used to know the names for, including a mild, flat, rasp of green-onion (garlic chives) and a spicy, arugula-type leaf (costmary).[1] The herbs

[1] The most complete combination of Iranian food studies scholarship with practical (and historical) cooking information available in English is Margaret Shaida's *The Legendary Cuisine of Persia* (New York: Interlink Books, 2002).

are served all mixed up in a pile and can be eaten on the side of the main dish, as a sort of refresher, or with bread and cheese, as a substantial snack. Everybody loves *sabzi*, and they are one of the delights of Persian cuisine. The problem is their preparation.

How complicated can serving raw food be? For one thing, they're organic: real, back-to-basics organic, which means fertilized with manure. So they have to be chemically disinfected, and in summer especially you have to be very careful about this. (This is the big irony of original organic; that lack of chemical input during the growing means a certain amount of required chemical treatment before consumption.) There's a special fruit and vegetable disinfectant you can buy; add a few drops to a basin of water, soak the vegetables for the prescribed time (ten minutes, twice), and you should be able to avoid dysentery. But the other problem with *sabzi*, even before washing them, has always been cleaning them. *Sabzi* are sold in big piles at fruit and vegetable sellers, and you basically buy an armful that gets wrapped up in newspaper, and you take it home, where you begin the painstaking process of separating the leaves and tender stems from the roots, branches, dead shoots, and general muck that is also included in the bundle. When you finally have a stack of what looks much more like what you would buy in an American grocery store or even at a farmers' market, you can wash and disinfect it. Then you can eat it. And since herbs are easy and quick to munch, they go quickly, so this is a regular process. And a huge pain.

A few years ago, some stores started selling prepared bags of sorted, chopped, and presumably disinfected *sabzi*, but these were really for cooking, not the fresh herbs for table eating. However, this year is different. We went food shopping in the neighborhood, and a whole row of fruit and vegetable sellers had their *sabzi* sorted and lined up in neat, prepared rows of tied, trimmed bunches. No roots, no mud, no dead leaves. You went down the line and picked the selection you wanted: a few of these, a few of those, one or two others, a big bunch of something else. You still have to wash them, but the really time-consuming task has been done. Of course, you pay some for this privilege, but not too much; ours is a middle-class north Tehran neighborhood, but not known as rich or fashionable. The thing is, the work has been taken care of: the kind of grudging household labor that most of us who cook in the West usually don't have to do. This is the kind of labor that makes household management a full-time job and gets in the way of women, especially, really being able to do anything else.

So finding cleaned, prepared *sabzi* available at the ordinary local fruit and vegetable market (even if they still have to be washed at home) is a big deal. A small practical thing, but a big symbolic change, because of what it means about the changing value of household labor (which here is usually but not always women's labor), and women's work. Once a substantial number of women are working outside the home, but in positions other than as paid domestic labor in the homes of others, the time/labor equation of the household economy has to rebalance. This often implies a shift in diet, not always for the better but also an increase in "labor saving devices." In the US, this phrase is practically a joke: How much more household labor do we need to save before we completely deskill ourselves domestically?[2] But in Iran, labor-saving devices really help. If Marx's ideal society would allow a man "to hunt in the morning, fish in the afternoon, rear cattle in the evening, criticize after dinner, just as I have in mind,"[3] then prepared *sabzi* allow some modern, domestic, more feminized version of this: the ability to prepare a balanced meal and write an article too. Like the commodity itself or labor in the market economy, labor in the household can become a fetishization of its own process. To quote again from Marx: "This fixation of social activity, this consolidation of what

[2] It's been well established that "labor saving devices" actually don't save time; technical innovations making housework less labor intensive have usually simply increased the expected standard of domestic work (clothes washed more frequently than on a regular "washing day"; carpets cleaned more frequently than during seasonal "spring cleaning"). See Ruth Schwartz Cowan, *More Work for Mother: The Ironies of Household Technology from the Open Heart to the Microwave* (New York: Basic Books, 1983). But emotional arguments about whether mainstream Americans' lack of domestic skills is to be lamented or celebrated have become part of the American "mommy wars": the vituperative accusations hurled back and forth in the popular press between women who are identifying with a domestic role – "stay at home moms" – and women who identify with a non-domestic profession – "career women." Training manuals for updated but traditional domestic skills often explicitly claim a rehabilitated familial legacy: the knowledge of one's grandmothers, generously shared with an orphaned public. See Cheryl Mendelson, *Home Comforts: The Art and Science of Keeping House* (New York: Scribner, 2005).

[3] Thanks to Omid Maljoo for bringing these quotations to my attention. Both quotations, Karl Marx and Frederick Engels, *The German Ideology*, Part I, "Feuerbach: Opposition of the Materialist and Idealist Outlook," section on "Private Property and Communism" (New York: International Publishers, 1988), 53.

we ourselves produce into an objective power above us, growing out of control, thwarting our expectations, bringing to naught our calculations, is one of the chief factors in historical development up till now."

Within the system of Iranian household production, prepared *sabzi* might mark the beginnings of a domestic revolution.

## Reproductive vs. Productive Labor: The Question of Work

In the Anglo-American domestic tradition, food preparation is considered unskilled labor, its monetary and time expenditure to be minimized as much as possible.[4] This attitude has so saturated conventional feminist analyses of household labor that it is taken for granted that domestic work is unskilled reproductive labor; something from which women need to be emancipated if their contribution is to be integrated into an economy of value.[5] Modern political economy has had difficulty assigning an economic value to household reproductive labor because its products are considered essentially transient, continually consumed in the maintenance of our ongoing daily existence that is reproductive labor's ultimate accomplishment.[6] The household itself is assumed to be the last sphere of non-monetarized social relations, either precapitalist in form (unpaid family agricultural labor as part of a peasant

[4] This dismissal of the work done as drudgery that (to add insult to injury) is expected to be performed as a loving (or at least dutiful) service rather than for monetary compensation is characteristic of the Anglo-American "wages for housework" debates of the 1970s. See Pat Mainardi, "The Politics of Housework" (originally published in 1970), in Estelle Freedman, ed., *The Essential Feminist Reader* (New York: Modern Library, 2007), 288–294; Silvia Federici, *Wages against Housework* (Bristol: Falling Wall Press, 1975).

[5] The classification "unskilled housewives" is used without question in the otherwise excellent and insightful paper by M. Ghazi Tabatabaei, N. Mehri, and M. Messkoub, "What Is Unpaid Female Labour Worth? Evidence from the Time Use Studies of Iran in 2008 and 2009," Working Paper #562, International Institute of Social Studies, The Hague, The Netherlands, August 13, 2013.

[6] Gary Becker's Nobel Prize-winning work provides an economic rationalization of how the family functions as an institution for the site of investment in human capital. His analyses apply a conventional economic logic to the family; he does not particularly consider how a different social logic prevalent within the household might itself affect other formal economic structures (except insofar as a precapitalist or noncapitalist logic is assumed to be detrimental to proper forms of human social development).

economy) or apologist for capitalism in function (the "angel of the house" as the compensatory fantasy of refuge from the stresses of market competition).[7] Household reproductive labor is ordinarily considered unskilled work because by the time the mid twentieth-century postwar Western feminists and political economists were considering the relationship of unpaid domestic labor to the local economy, most of their own societies had achieved a high level of household capacity in terms of material infrastructure (electricity, piped water, and cooking fuel), and resources (the new consumer "white goods" to make use of the available utilities). Labor-saving devices such as refrigerators, washing machines, and vacuum cleaners accomplished the same process for domestic work and domestic workers they had in other working sectors: an improvement in efficiency and a deskilling of labor, with a concomitant devaluation of the work being performed.[8] Within this conceptual framework, reproductive labor is absolutely essential but also absolutely frustrating for anyone whose gaze rises above the temporal horizon of the everyday. It is locked in its own immediacy: absolutely feminine. Reproductive labor is women's work.[9]

We should be attentive to that turn of phrase, from work to labor, or back again. The common understanding of work as labor is that which

7 These arguments often skip over the paid domestic work that employed enormous numbers of workers, both women and men, and was legally recognized as formal contractual employment ("work") in the eighteenth and nineteenth centuries. In early modern England, any household that could scrape together discretionary funds employed at least a "girl" to help with the most laborious forms of household work. See Carolyn Steedman, *Labours Lost: Domestic Service and the Making of Modern England* (Cambridge: Cambridge University Press, 2009).

8 In evaluating the market value of women's labor, Ghazi Tabatabaei, Mehri, and Messkoub estimate "unskilled housewives" (i.e., housewives) to be the equivalent of "unskilled female cleaning workers." See "What Is Unpaid Female Labour Worth? Evidence from the Time Use Studies of Iran in 2008 and 2009," p. 4.

9 There is a specific literature of the social history of housework in the US that takes seriously the social relations of women's domestic labor as actual work. Along with Schwartz Cowan's *More Work for Mother*, some classic best examples include Sarah Fenstermaker Berk, ed., *Women and Household Labor* (Beverly Hills: Sage Publications, 1980); Susan Strasser, *Never Done: A History of American Housework* (New York: Henry Holt & Co., 2000); Glenna Matthews, *"Just a Housewife": The Rise and Fall of Domesticity in America* (New York: Oxford University Press, 1989); Jeanne Boydston, *Home and Work: Housework, Wages, and the Ideology of Labor in the Early Republic* (New York: Oxford University Press, 1994).

is done because it must be done, and perhaps for pay, but without glory (the high regard of others), satisfaction (the achievement of something lasting), or skill (the performance of a complex practice learned over time and with its own set of techniques, standards, and cumulative accomplishments).[10] Often, the two terms are considered interchangeable, cohabiting sullenly across the border from the sunny realm of leisure and fun. But this binary opposition of work and leisure betrays its own assumption: that these activities are being performed in the context of a modern capitalist society. Work, under conditions of alienated labor, is not particularly done for pleasure, but in order to gain the resources for pleasure when work is done; leisure is the worker's time of pleasure outside of work.[11]

The modern terminology for domestic labor as work is itself troublesome: housework is mostly a more respectful term for housecleaning; homework is paid productive work from elsewhere transported into the domestic space, but with no intrinsic relation to the domestic sphere. Homemaking is a term to rescue a vocation for housework from its modern futility; once the home is no longer a realm of production, it inevitably comes to be regarded as a backward remnant, rehabilitated only by a sentiment for embattled values, rather than the value of economic reasoning. Hence the emergence of the classification of "care work" (and care worker) for the remnant of domestic work that we are not socially content to classify as completely frivolous and/or unskilled, even if that is its typical level of economic remuneration: physical and emotional labor for vulnerable persons (children, the ill or disabled, the elderly) that traditionally occurred in the household.[12]

[10] Hannah Arendt takes this common understanding as the basis for the conceptual development of the categories of labor, work, and action in *The Human Condition* (Chicago: University of Chicago Press, 1958).

[11] This is Karl Marx's argument that "life" for the laborer begins – "at the table, at the tavern seat, in bed" – only when the activity of commodified labor ceases. But Marx is only concerned with alienated productive (men's) labor; his analysis is unconcerned with the labor (or work) of social reproduction, except as the basis for the determination of wages. See Karl Marx, *Wage-Labor and Capital*, trans. Harriet E. Lothrop (New York: New York Labor News Company, 1902), p. 25.

[12] Earlier generations of feminist social theorists and home economists evaluated domestic labor differently. Charlotte Perkins Gilman wanted to liberate most women from "house service" by professionalizing domestic work according to the new scientific standards of nutrition, hygiene, and public health. Childcare would be similarly professionalized according to new insights from early

The only term available to remind us of the productive possibility of domestic work may be the very old-fashioned one of housekeeper: a manageress of the resources of the household economy, its persons, and materials. But the term housekeeper is a referent back to the *oikos*: the household (not the home) as the building block of larger systems of productive social and economic relations. The *oikos* may be private – domestic – but it is a place of work, and work is not only the production of things: work builds our social world.[13]

Work, when it is not yet fully assimilated into the market (let alone the capitalist) economy, retains the possibility for some degree of creative endeavor, personal satisfaction, and autonomy over the conditions of the labor process (time, space, and materials). This is a conception of work as craft; a conception that has only been tenuously maintained within a capitalist system of valuations. Ironically, it may be in the household that the values of craft work have most tenaciously held. In particular, to the extent that household cooking is work, it is often not experienced or valued in the same way as the waged work of alienated labor. Household cooking, when it is valued, is experienced more as craft. Not all contexts value food, in its preparation and consumption, as craft work. At its most basic, food is a universal bodily necessity. Even under conditions of relatively less scarcity, food can still be regarded simply as that which is consumed, and cooking as a process easily commodified. But for some cultures, the relationship between cooking and craft is part of cultural identity itself: cooking as cuisine. And cuisine is not necessarily what you get in restaurants; for many cultures, cuisine is what you eat at home.

## Home Cooking: Identity and Practice

It is a modern truism that all cultures valorize a nostalgic cult of "home cooking," which memorializes a closed circle of intimate belonging,

childhood education, leaving the home a domestic space for emotional intimacy rather than labor. See Charlotte Perkins Gilman, *Women and Economics* (New York: Harper & Row, 1966), originally published in 1898.

[13] This conceptualization of work – as the sovereign production of that which endures, whether a material product or a cultural meaning – is borrowing and adapting from several sources, including both Marx and Arendt. But even for Arendt, a social world is not quite the same as the social.

whether familial or national.[14] The exceptions to the rule – like the Dutch insistence that "we don't care about food" – only proves the fundamental significance of food as the practice of a historicized shared identity – "we don't care about food because we're Calvinists." Whatever the general outside opinion is of mama's or the nation's food, home cooking is the essence of intimacy: you have to know it in order to recognize it; to belong in order to know. This common but intimate knowledge of local food practices is so tied to basic everyday life that it can be assumed to be universal: the recipes and techniques may differ, but the attitudes must be shared. This is clearly not the case if home cooking – unpaid household reproductive labor – still functions locally not as a nostalgic endeavor or an economic waste but as an expansive set of cultural and material practices.

A taste for home cooking, in and of itself, doesn't indicate much about how the daily labor involved with household food preparation – cooking – is valued. The strict monetarization of labor is not necessarily helpful here; the fact that domestic labor has traditionally been unpaid and underpaid is a complex part of the gendered history of capitalism, not a definitive indicator that domestic labor is unskilled. To understand the comparative cultural value of household food production – the labor of home cooking – we need to try to track the attitudes that inform practices, rather than the comparative wage

[14] The "food memoir" is by now an established literary subgenre. One of the most original as well as complex narrative voices is still M. F. K. Fisher, whose writings are – almost uniquely – never nostalgic (remembrance and mourning are not necessarily nostalgia) and do not valorize a family past of home cooking. Quite the contrary: Fisher makes clear that the food she grew up with was as bland and boring as could be and that the discovery of delicious food was for her always a route beyond the internalized limits of the natal home and culture. For discussion of how Middle East food memoirs do deploy specific nostalgias for familial and national belonging, see Nefissa Naguib, "Doing the Right Thing: Fathers, Husbands and Food in Contemporary Egypt," Paper presented at the 2013 Annual Meeting of the Middle East Studies Association, New Orleans; Naguib, "The Fragile Tale of Egyptian Jewish Cuisine: Food Memoirs of Claudia Roden and Colette Rosant," *Food and Foodways*, 14(1) (2006), 35–53; Carol Bardenstein, "Transmissions Interrupted: Reconfiguring Food, Memory, and Gender in the Cookbook-Memoirs of Middle Eastern Exiles," *Signs: Journal of Women in Culture and Society*, 28(1) (Autumn 2002), 353–387. Bardenstein's work is itself striking for how she places into question the cultural authenticity of the authors she discusses (Sephardic Jewish, Muslim, Christian) while herself claiming an unbroken lineage of maternal Ashkenazi Jewish food tradition.

tables of domestic workers who may be replacing the traditional army of reserve labor: women at home.

## Different Cooking Cultures: The French and the English

Food studies scholarship can be helpful here. It may not be surprising that food studies as a field (rather than the study of food within the disciplinary parameters of public health or anthropology) seems to have initially burgeoned in France and Italy rather than within the Anglo-American scholarly community.[15] The encompassing and integrated studies of social and economic history developed by the Annales School provided a background of intellectual endeavor that could then be modified into more precise areas of focus, including food and cooking,[16] while the sociology of everyday life practices initiated in different ways by Michel Foucault, Michel de Certeau, and Pierre Bourdieu provided fresh insights into the significance of the ordinary.[17] These varied efforts helped to make clear that cultural and culinary

[15] Reay Tannahill, the groundbreaking British author of the early classic *Food in History* (London: Penguin Group, 1973), revised edition 1988, was not a professional scholar and took up the serious historical study of food despite the initial desires of her employer and publisher. See "Reay Tannahill: Accidental Pioneer of Food History and Bestselling Romantic Novelist," *The Independent*, Tuesday, November 27, 2007, www.independent.co.uk/news/obituaries/reay-tannahill-accidental-pioneer-of-food-history-and-bestselling-romantic-novelist-760621.html

[16] The Annales methodology and perspective are recognizable throughout the comprehensive volume edited by Jean Louis Flandrin and Massimo Montanari, *Food: A Culinary History* (New York: Columbia University Press, 1999), first published in 1996 in French (Librairie Arthème Fayard) and Italian (Gius. Laterza & Figli). See also Montanari's *The Culture of Food* (Oxford: Blackwell, 1994), first published in Italian by Laterza, 1993.

[17] The resistance within the Anglo-American academic community to taking seriously the French preoccupation with food in the household is reflected in the publication delay of the second volume of de Certeau's *The Practice of Everyday Life*. First published in France in two volumes in 1980, the English translation of the first volume was published quickly as *The Practice of Everyday Life*, trans. Steven Rendall (Berkeley: University of California Press, 1984). But "the American publisher had judged [volume two] too closely linked to something specifically French to interest the American public," and an English language version did not appear until 1998. See Michel de Certeau, Luce Giard, and Pierre Mayol, *The Practice of Everyday Life, Volume 2: Living and Cooking*, trans. Timothy J. Tomasik (Minneapolis, MN: University of Minnesota Press, 1998), xlii.

"taste" is deeply embedded in material experience and naturalized almost beyond recognition as a social construct.

But tastes are not the same, as any comparison of English and French food cultures makes clear.[18] In *All Manners of Food: Eating and Taste in England and France from the Middle Ages to the Present*, Stephen Mennell provides a thorough historical analysis of what has happened to make the twentieth-century French and English eat the way they do.[19] Mennell's work is worth a digression, here, because it is one of the few directly comparative studies of related but divergent food cultures, and because it is important for making the case that Iranian food culture – and its household preparation – functions much more like the French rather than the English or Anglo-American model.

Mennell makes the case that English "cookery" among the upper and middle classes was "decapitated" in the nineteenth century by the elite fashion for French cuisine (and the condescension toward "plain" English cooking), and the lack of engagement within the kitchen by both upper- and middle-class women (who disdained the traditional knowledge and the daily work of the "plain English cooking" with which they would have been familiar).[20] Cautioning that cookbooks

[18] A comparative analysis of anything as naturalized as taste is always helpful. In his 1961 article "Towards a Psychosociology of Contemporary Food Consumption," Roland Barthes began his analysis of French food significations with a discussion of the American preference for sweet and sugary foods. See Roland Barthes, "Vers une psycho-sociologie de l'alimentation moderne," *Annales: Économies, sociétés, civilisations*, 16(5) (September–October 1961), 977–986; republished in English in Carole Counihan and Penny Van Esterik, eds., *Food and Culture: A Reader, Second Edition* (New York: Routledge, 2008), 28–35.

[19] See Stephen Mennell, *All Manners of Food: Eating and Taste in England and France from the Middle Ages to the Present* (Chicago: University of Illinois Press, 1996). Mennell focuses on food preparation, but the commodified ingredients modern French and British cooks had to work with also differed. From about 1820 until the late nineteenth century, the French state was much more willing to enforce regulation of food purity that had been lost after guild control was broken; the British faith in laissez-faire made a negative difference in the general quality of ingredients. See John Burnett, *Plenty and Want: A Social History of Food in England from 1815 to the Present Day*, 3rd ed. (London: Routledge, 1989), especially chapter 10, "The Quality of Food," 228.

[20] As devalued as English cooking skills became, it seems they were still considered superior to those practiced by the North Americans. English novelist Frances Trollope, traveling in the US in the early nineteenth century, frequently bemoans the low level of domestic comforts provided even within American middle- and upper-class households. In particular, she despairs of finding good "help"

and novels cannot be taken as transparent representations of English practices, Mennell nonetheless finds some telling examples, including Jane Austen's description of Mr. Collins' *faux pas* at the Bennet's family table when he asks, trying to be complimentary, which of the daughters has cooked the food, and Mrs. Bennet has to remind him "with some asperity" that none of her daughters needs to set foot in the kitchen.[21] A good cook might be valued, but cooking as a skill was not.[22]

This lack of English appreciation for cooking as a skill is well reflected in Mennell's evaluation of recipes and food columns from comparable early twentieth-century women's magazines: the British *Woman's Life* (1895–1934) and the French *La Femme chez elle* (1899–1938).[23] Both magazines aimed at similar national middle- and lower-middle-class readerships, maintained similarly long publication runs during the same period, and published similar contents: cooking columns and recipes; household tips and family advice; practical handcraft projects (sewing and knitting). *Woman's Life* included short romantic fiction, while *La Femme chez elle* recommended current published popular literature and some music and cultural events. Otherwise, the main difference between the two publications was in their approach to cooking and food.

Consistently, the French publication gave more emphasis to the food columns (sometimes as a leading article) and discussed the cooking

(women servants) in the US. According to Trollope, young (white) American women would prefer even to work in the mills than as household domestics: they object to being called servants and won't contract for a year, as they intend either to marry or to leave for better options. In addition, although the quality of the food available (except for fruit) is generally good, the Americans don't have the knowledge to prepare sauces and "made dishes" (*entrées*). See Frances Trollope, *Domestic Manners of the Americans* (London: Routledge, 1927), originally published in 1832.

21 Mennell, *All Manners of Food*, 212.

22 This nineteenth-century attitude easily carried over into the twentieth century: kitchen work was inconceivable for a middle-class English woman, no matter how dissatisfied she might have been with her cook and her cook's cooking. See E. M. Delafield, *Diary of a Provincial Lady* (Chicago: Academy Chicago, 1982), originally published in England in 1931. Delafield presents a sort of interwar, married version of *Bridget Jones' Diaries* (the entries were first published in serial form in the weekly *Time and Tide*) in which one of the running themes is the heroine's inability to manage to get better cooking provided for herself and her household.

23 Mennell, *All Manners of Food*, chapter 9, "The Enlightenment of the Domestic Cook?" 230–265.

project at hand with energetic enthusiasm. Cooking was consistently connected to the sensual pleasures of food, its handling as well as consumption, and the practice of cooking was treated as a craft rather than a burden. "In France, the housewife seems to be assumed not only to enjoy cooking and eating, but to have inherited knowledge of certain basic skills."[24] These skills were maintained: the same recipe for *galettes* (filled pastry tarts) appears in 1899 and again in 1937, except in the later version the proportions are halved.[25] By contrast, the English cooking columns tend to emphasize efficiency of outlay – money, time, and effort – rather than pleasure.[26] There are regular references to "the servant problem," making it unclear who exactly is expected (or desired) to do the cooking. In 1933, the same decade in which the French magazine was republishing the galette recipe, *Woman's Own* (the in-house successor to *Woman's Life*) recommended, "Use Up Those 'Left-Overs' and You'll Find 'The Way to a Man's Heart' by Keeping Down Expenses."[27]

In the postwar period, Mennell includes some newer magazines and finds they maintain much of the national cultural distinctions even as the slow increase of postwar leisure and consumer goods, including packaged and prepared foods, provides some more homogenization both within each national culture and across national lines. Nonetheless, differences are still evident. The end of British food rationing (which continued until 1954) injected a celebratory tone into the English magazine's food columns, but it is noticeable that the end of scarcity (of meat, sugar, butter, etc.) was interpreted as an opportunity either to spend less time in the kitchen or to engage in "hostess cooking." For the postwar British household cook (increasingly the woman of the household herself, rather than a paid employee), the return of desirable foodstuffs meant either the ability to prepare an

24 Mennell, *All Manners of Food*, 240.
25 Mennell, *All Manners of Food*, 211.
26 In contrast, in the final long interview chapter, "'When It Comes Down to It, Cooking Worries Me'" in *The Practice of Everyday Life, Volume 2: Living and Cooking*, the interview subject, an editor and proofreader, repeatedly insists she is not an accomplished cook and that she doesn't cook particularly varied or interesting food because of time and budget constraints. Nonetheless, in the course of the interview, she describes grinding her own meat for stuffings, using leftovers and beating egg whites by hand to make a soufflé, making cassoulet, etc. These skills, which would mark her as an accomplished cook under other cultural circumstances, are apparently taken for granted in the French context.
27 Mennell, *All Manners of Food*, 244.

acceptable, economical family meal without the struggle to make up for the lack of favored ingredients or the ability to cook new and fancy foods (usually foreign and especially French recipes) for occasions of competitive social display. But by the 1970s, even English food writers were treating cooking as closer to a pleasurable hobby rather than a necessary chore, and associating meals with enjoyment as well as nutrition and economy.[28]

Mennell is careful to note that household cooking has always been an intermediate responsibility between work and leisure, involving both obligation and time-discipline (like work) along with possibilities for creativity and enjoyment (like leisure).[29] In both postwar France and England, capitalist consumer society and its values were thriving, even if France has often been regarded as arbitrarily resistant (devoted to its own cultural exceptionalism) by its more wholeheartedly economically liberal neighbors.[30] But within the conventions of Anglo-American cultural and scholarly analyses of household labor, French maintenance of household cooking as skilled craft work could be regarded either as a holdover idiosyncrasy of French culture or a brilliant strategy for sustaining a higher standard of public health through well-managed reproductive labor. In other parts of the world, recognizing the household as a site of craft work has tended

[28] Mennell, *All Manners of Food*, 250–265. Mennell also includes a thorough debunking of Roland Barthes' famous essay on "Ornamental Cookery," in which Barthes decried the travesty of postwar French women's corruption of French culinary taste by a turn to visual extravagance (elaborate garnishes, pink food, etc.), as evident in the pages of the woman's magazine *Elle*. Although "Ornamental Cooking" was published in *Mythologies* (Paris: Éditions du Seuil, 1957), the fifty-three essays for the collection were written between 1954 and 1956. Mennell points out that Barthes' examples of pretentiously status-conscious cooking seem to come from a few unusual weeks in early 1955. Before and after January 1955, the magazine's recipes and illustrations are consistent with the traditional emphasis on flavor and craft; even in those exceptional weeks, *Elle* included plenty of usual food articles and recipes.

[29] Mennell, *All Manners of Food*, 265.

[30] From 1971 until 1984, Michel Foucault gave a series of regular lecture "seminars" at the Collège de France that eventually developed into his sustained investigation into the triumph of capitalist society across Europe (and Great Britain); France was quite clearly a participant in this historical development. See the published lectures, particularly beginning with the volume Michel Foucault, ed. Michel Senellart, *Security, Territory, Population: Lectures at the College de France, 1977–1978* (New York: Picador, 2007), published first in France in 2004.

immediately to be equated with a regrettable lack of economic and social development.

## Women's Work and Working Women

The trimmed and sorted *sabzi* I observed in Tehran in Spring 2007 seemed to indicate that the labor-intensive aspect of Iranian domestic work was becoming less. The Iranian household might still be a site of craft work, but apparently Iranian women were benefiting from similar conveniences in terms of food preparation and production that most middle-class Western women have been able to take for granted since the postwar period.[31] Are Iranian women participating at higher numbers in formal employment?[32] The answers are inconclusive. Iranian women's "economic activity rate" (the classification the Iranian Statistical Center uses in its National Labor Force Surveys to include any individual, whether employed formally, employed informally, or unemployed, who participates in economic activity, i.e., productive labor) has hovered around 12 percent for more than a decade.[33] During the same period, the official economic participation rate for the country as a whole rose from 36 percent to 40. 9 percent in 2022–2023, with slightly higher rates consistently reported in rural

[31] Janet Afary discusses the valued household role of wives in what she terms "premodern" formal (arranged, legal) marriages (as compared to the companionate marriage model associated with "modernity"), and the prestige that could accrue to those who displayed skill in managing domestic networks of food and social relations, as well as "keeping her house meticulously clean." See Janet Afary, *Sexual Politics in Modern Iran* (New York: Cambridge University Press, 2009), 8.

[32] The most comprehensive overview of why the issue of women's labor force participation rate has been so perplexing for scholars of Iran is Roksana Bahramitash and Hadi Salehi-Esfahani, *Veiled Employment: Islamism and the Political Economy of Women's Employment in Iran* (Syracuse, NY: Syracuse University Press, 2011).

[33] The rate between 2012 and 2023 has ranged between 11 percent and 14 percent, with seasonal variations. (The survey is published quarterly.) In the Iranian year 1401 (March 21, 2022 to March 20, 2023), the rate for women was 13.6 percent; in the previous year, it was 13.3 percent. See *A Selection of Labor Force Survey Results – The Year 1401 (21 March 2022–20 March 2023)*, Statistical Center of Iran, www.amar.org.ir. Similar phrasing is used in the previous surveys, which are also available on the site for comparison. See also Iranian Labor Force Survey results for Summer 1391/2012, Spring 1392/2013, Summer 1392/2013 and Autumn 1392/2013; *A Selection of Labor Force Survey Results Autumn 2013 (September 23–December 21, 2013)*, all Statistical Center of Iran.

areas (more than 75 percent of the Iranian population is urban).[34] So even if the Iranian population generally is facing challenges in finding work, women's economic participation rates are about one-third of the national rate (and this is without comparing rates of unemployment).[35]

Low women's participation rates in economic activity are conventionally presumed to be an indication of either cultural or economic problems: women aren't employed because of entrenched patriarchal resistance ("Islamic values") or inappropriate economic development ("the oil curse").[36] Higher levels of women's employment are generally presumed to indicate better integration of women into public life and higher levels of social and economic empowerment. A fairly low women's employment rate is not really very unusual for the Middle East region or for mid-level economies, other than those that have intensively developed an industrial export sector in textiles or electronics. But in India, a women's labor force participation rate of around 22 percent caused public handwringing in 2013.[37] By comparison, the French labor force participation rate for women (as a percentage of the

[34] In 2022–2023, the rural economic participation rate was 42.7 percent and the urban was 40.3 percent. The Iranian population became majority urban around the time of the revolution in 1979; since then, the urban population percentage has been consistently climbing, with 75 percent recorded in 2019. See entries from Iranian National Labor Force Surveys and Iranian National Population and Household Census; Statistical Center of Iran.

[35] In 2022–2023, women's economic participation rate was 13.6 percent compared to the national rate of 40.9 percent. See *A Selection of Labor Force Survey Results – The Year 1401 (21 March 2022–20 March 2023).*

[36] See Valentine Moghadam, "Hidden from History? Women Workers in Modern Iran," *Iranian Studies*, 33(3/4) (Summer–Autumn, 2000), 377–401; Michael L. Ross, *The Oil Curse: How Petroleum Wealth Shapes the Development of Nations* (Princeton, NJ: Princeton University Press, 2012), especially chapter 4, "Petroleum Perpetuates Patriarchy," 111–144.

[37] Indian National Sample Survey Organization female labor force participation rate, quoted in Rupa Subramanya, "Why Female Labour Force Participation in India Is Low," *Business Standard*, October 8, 2013. *The Times of India* journalist Rukmini Shrinivasan frequently addresses the issue of low reported Indian female labor force participation; her work often points out problems in the statistical evaluations or difficulties capturing Indian women's self-employment or work in the informal economy. See Shrinivasan in *The Times of India*, "Working Women Numbers Don't Add Up" (May 19, 2013); "No Country for Working Women: A Story in 5 Graphs" (March 10, 2013). In 2022, Indian women's labor force participation rate was 24 percent, compared to a national rate of 73.6 percent. See https://genderdata.worldbank.org/countries/india.

female population aged 15–64) has been close to 50 percent since 2000.[38] The low levels of Iranian women's workforce participation are often taken as indicators of their disadvantage after the Revolution; if Iranian women's economic participation rates only returned to their prerevolutionary levels in 2006, isn't that an indication of how much they lost – socially, politically, and economically – after the Revolution?

A closer examination of the changing Iranian economic and labor data yields a somewhat different picture. First of all, there is the question of basic definitions: Who is a worker, and what is work? This is not as obvious as it may first seem.[39] The International Labor Organization (ILO) for years reported much higher Iranian female labor force participation rates: from 20.6 percent in 1986 to 38.6 percent in 2005. The ILO utilized somewhat different criteria to identify workforce and economic involvement. Significantly, the ILO (as well as most other international data sets) uses fifteen as the age threshold for beginning workforce participation, while Iran until very recently was using changing but much lower age limits.[40] The Iranian Labor Force Surveys for the years following the revolution thus included large numbers of enrolled primary and secondary students who were counted as not economically active.[41] Before the revolution,

38 In 2022, the women's labor force participation rate in France was 52.5 percent. See https://genderdata.worldbank.org/countries/france.

39 The problem of classifying who is a worker is ideological as well as statistical. Joan Wallach Scott makes a perceptive analysis of the political implications involved in the mid nineteenth-century attempt to reclassify many Parisian proletarian homeworkers (including washerwomen) as "heads of 'enterprises'" (i.e., entrepreneurs) if they took in work from multiple employers. During a period of intense political and labor unrest, "The effect of this categorization was to reduce significantly the number of people who had come to think of themselves as workers in the Parisian population." See "A Statistical Representation of Work: *La statistique de l'industrie à Paris*, 1847–1848," in Joan Wallach Scott, *Gender and the Politics of History* (New York: Columbia University Press, 1999), revised edition, 123.

40 The 2022–2023 Iranian *Labor Force Survey Results* published by the Statistical Center of Iran includes data for the population aged fifteen and over.

41 The problem of determining the accurate interpretation of Iranian statistical indicators is not confined to the question of labor force participation; a similar problem arises with statistics about HIV infections, which are often pointed to as unreasonably high for the region. International public health experts point out that this is at least partially because Iran actually has reasonably functioning HIV surveillance and treatment policies, in comparison with many of its neighbors. See Mohammad Karamouzian, Maryam Nasirian, Abbas Sedaghat,

the much lower school enrollment of girls would have meant their higher participation rate in economic activities, particularly carpet weaving. Thus the postrevolutionary lower economic participation rate of girl children (who were still counted as adults in the national labor surveys) actually indicated a postrevolutionary improvement of women's status indicators: presumably women's empowerment is better supported if the primary occupation of under-fifteen girls is school work rather than integration into economic activity.[42] The ILO also tries to take more of an account of the informal economy and includes as labor force participants "persons engaged in the production of goods or services for their own final use." It is generally assumed that the ILO numbers thus include large numbers of unpaid (family) agricultural laborers, which the Iranian national statistics miss. But the continuing migration of the rural population to urban areas (according to the national census, Iran achieved an urban majority between 1976 and 1986), plus the integration of rural society (through provision of public education, healthcare, and utilities), means that even if many rural women may still be engaged in family-run agricultural enterprises, most women are not.[43]

But the ILO's inclusion of "persons engaged in the production of goods or services for their own final use" returns us to the question of what counts as work. In general, it is considered preferable for all concerned if "work" is done within the structures of the formal

and Ali-Akbar Haghdoost, "HIV in Iran," *The Lancet*, 383 (March 22, 2014), 1040; Maryam Nasirian, Mohammad Karamouzian, and Ali-Akbar Haghdoost, "Why Is the Number of HIV/AIDS-Related Publications Low in the MENA Region?" *Sexually Transmitted Infections*, 89 (2013), iii10.

42 The very low labor-force entrance age initially used by Iranian national data collection meant that (especially rural) schoolchildren were counted as nonworking (unemployed) labor. The almost universal postrevolutionary enrollment of Iranian children into school, both boys and girls, is part of what has caused a massive contraction in the Iranian carpet industry; carpet weaving is now mostly done by Afghan refugees (women and children) who have few other options. See Zahra Karimi, "The Effects of International Trade on Gender Inequality in Iran: The Case of Women Carpet Weaver," in Bahramitash and Salehi-Esfahani, *Veiled Employment: Islamism and the Political Economy of Women's Employment in Iran*, 166–190.

43 See Jennifer C. Olmsted, "Gender and Globalization: The Iranian Experience," 25–52, and Roksana Bahramitash and Hadi Salehi-Esfahani, "From Postrevolution to the Reform: Gender Politics and Employment," 83–122, both in Bahramitash and Salehi-Esfahani, *Veiled Employment: Islamism and the Political Economy of Women's Employment in Iran.*

economy: having or looking for a regularized paid job enables the state to collect taxes and workers to claim institutionalized economic rights and benefits. The alternatives to the formal economy are presumed to be less developed and less desirable: non-remunerated family agricultural labor or craft production that is sold onto the market by another family member who retains control of the payment, or participation in the informal economy, meaning cash and barter exchanges for undeclared goods and services, whether legal or illegal. Iranian postrevolutionary social transformations, including urbanization and higher levels of education, mean that unpaid family-based agricultural labor is no longer a viable option for large-scale women's economic participation. This leaves the possibility of participation in the informal economy. Most labor analysts, including the ILO, regard the informal economy as a less attractive option for workers: clandestine work in sweatshops; irregular work as day labor; exploited domestic labor in someone else's home.[44] Nonetheless, the presumption is that the normal progress of economic and social development runs from a peasant economy incorporating kinship as a basis of social organization (unpaid family agricultural labor), to opportunities for modern individuation through access to paid employment, preferably in the formal sector.

Missing from this common equation is a serious analysis of household labor, which is conventionally assumed to be unskilled and unproductive. Postrevolutionary Iranian women's lack of participation in the categories of work that can easily be captured in national labor statistics has been interpreted prima facie as evidence that women in the Islamic Republic are confined to the home and lacking opportunities for public participation and individual empowerment. This is a mistake.

[44] Although global studies of the informal economy are increasingly acknowledging its diversity, it is still primarily associated with increased risks of household poverty and worker vulnerability. "Our analysis ... shows how large poverty and occupational risks, combined with lack of access to social protection and risk management instruments, render many informal economy workers – especially women, and their families – particularly vulnerable." OECD/ILO, *Tackling Vulnerability in the Informal* Economy, Development Centre Studies, OECD Publishing, Paris, 3, 2019, https://doi.org/10.1787/939b7bcd-en.

See also Florence Bonnet, Joann Vanek, and Martha Chen, *Women and Men in the Informal Economy: A Statistical Brief* (Manchester: Women in Informal Employment: Globalizing and Organizing (WIEGO), 2019), sponsored by the ILO.

## Iranian Women: Status Indicators

In evaluating women's position in the contemporary Islamic Republic, it is at least as important to look at the social, as opposed to the juridical, aspects of citizenship; defining Iranian women's political realities by attention only to their legal rights may be as misleading as describing their productive contributions only with reference to their apparent economic participation.[45] Iranian women are visible and active in public, and the postrevolutionary Iranian state, whatever its ideology and despite the juridical barriers to women's equality, has invested heavily in women's health and education. In the decades since the 1979 Revolution, Iranian society has become resolutely more urban, literate, and youthful, despite the public face of elderly tradition it still presents through its clerical political elite.[46] Underneath the formal surface of political governance, Iranian society has been evolving forward on its own terms.

The postrevolutionary trends in social development indicators make clear that while Iranian women are legally disadvantaged (in terms of rights of inheritance, divorce, and custody; juridical authority; etc.) they are generally much better able to claim the rights they do have than they were before the Revolution. In terms of the two key statistical indicators of women's social position  education and fertility – Iranian women have experienced dramatic postrevolutionary improvement. In 1976, although the majority of Iranians were illiterate, there was a very large (more than 20 percent) gender gap between male and

[45] Even when Iran's elected political body (the *Majles* or Parliament) has passed progressive legal and juridical gender reforms, they are often blocked by the unelected religious bodies of the Guardian and Expediency Councils. See the discussion of the multiple legislative initiatives of the Sixth Parliament, many of which were stymied by the Councils (although some were enacted) in Elaheh Koolaee, "Iranian Women from Private Sphere to Public Sphere, with Focus on Parliament," *Iran & the Caucasus*, 13(2) (2009), 401–414.

[46] As the geographer Bernard Hourcade eloquently put it, the Revolution was made by the "Sons of the Shah," and for the most part, these elder statesmen ("white beards," *reesh sefid*) still dominate formal politics. But postrevolutionary society has been predominantly made up of the "Sons and Daughters of Khomeini" and their children. These younger generations have had a radically different experience of social development in terms not only of state ideology but also of demographic change. See Bernard Hourcade, "Iran: From Social to Political Change?" *Woodrow Wilson International Center for Scholars* (25) (June 2006), 1–3.

Table 4.1 *Iranian literacy rates, age 15+*

| | Total | Men | Women |
|---|---|---|---|
| 1976 | 37 | 48 | 24 |
| 1986 | 52 | 63 | 41 |
| 1991 | 66 | 74 | 56 |
| 1996 | 73 | 80 | 66 |
| 2002 | 77 | 84 | 70 |
| 2006 | 82 | 87 | 77 |
| 2011 | 84 | 89 | 78 |
| 2016 | 86 | 90 | 81 |
| 2022 | 89 | 93 | 85 |

*Source*: UNESCO Institute for Statistics

female literacy rates (see Table 4.1). In the years following the revolution, massive efforts to enroll both boys and girls in primary education were probably helped by the postrevolutionary state's policy of single-sex schools, which encouraged more socially conservative families to overcome their hesitations and enroll their daughters.[47] By 2008, the 15–24 age group had achieved 98 percent literacy, with essentially no gender gap (a gender parity index of .99) (see Table 4.2). Similar positive trends in status indicators are evident in the population growth rate, which rose dramatically immediately before and during the revolution and fell just as dramatically within a decade: both trends appeared before major changes in state population planning policy.[48]

47 Like the 1961 Cuban Literacy Campaign, the Iranian postrevolutionary efforts to expand literacy to an underserved population have been both remarkably successful and surprisingly overlooked in the global literature.

48 There are ongoing arguments regarding to what extent the postrevolutionary state's population policies directly influenced the birth rate. The fertility rate was declining before the revolution, but began to rise sharply in the years of the revolution (1976–1978), before any changes in the state's population policies (the postrevolutionary state dismantled previous population control programs and supported pronatalist policies); similarly, the sharp decline in the fertility and population growth rate began between 1984 and 1986, well before the state's re-implementation of energetic family planning programs. See Hassan Hakimian, "From Demographic Transition to Fertility Boom and Bust: Iran in the 1980s and 1990s," *Development and Change*, 37(3) (2006), 571–597. For an overview of the Iranian fertility transition and its links to postrevolutionary public policies and social practices (especially changes in marriage and contraception use), see Mohammad Jalal Abbasi-Shavazi, Peter McDonald, and

Table 4.2 *Iranian literacy rates, age 15–24*

| | Total | Men | Women |
|---|---|---|---|
| 1976 | 56 | 71 | 42 |
| 1986 | 75 | 85 | 66 |
| 1991 | 87 | 92 | 81 |
| 1996 | 93 | 96 | 91 |
| 2006 | 97 | 97 | 96 |
| 2012 | 98 | 98 | 98 |
| 2016 | 98 | 98 | 98 |
| 2022 | 99 | 99 | 99 |

*Source*: UNESCO Institute for Statistics

Facing a sharp increase in population (from 34 million in 1976 to almost 50 million in 1986 to 79 million in 2016), the pronatalist postrevolutionary state began to support effective family planning programs, including available birth control and required family planning classes before a couple is permitted to obtain a marriage license.[49] But the population growth rate had been dropping since its high point in 1986 (when it peaked at 3.9 percent) and had fallen significantly by 1991 (to 2.5 percent), one of the sharpest declines recorded globally.[50] Between 1996 (1.5 percent) and 2016 (1.2 percent), the Iranian

Meimanat Hosseini-Chavoshi, *The Fertility Transition in Iran: Revolution and Reproduction* (New York: Springer, 2009).

49 "Family planning" in Iran is taken to mean the ability to plan children, including both birth spacing (contraception) and support for conception (available IVF and related procedures, although not surrogacy).

50 Rising female literacy and enrollment in education, at least as much as population programming, have influenced individual and familial decisions to limit the number of births. The correlation between women's literacy and the population growth rate seems actually to be closer than the correlation between the population rate and state policy on fertility and family planning: between 1986 and 1991, the majority of the Iranian female population became literate, and the population growth rate peaked and then began its sharp decline. See Azadeh Kian-Thiébaut and Marie Ladier-Fouladi, *Survey of the Social, Cultural, and Economic Situation of Families*, a survey of 6,960 households and 30,715 individuals conducted in all the provinces of Iran, sponsored by the Statistical Center of Iran (Tehran) and Monde Iranien (Paris), 2002. Selected data from the survey are available on the web at www.ivry.cnrs.fr. For an overview of the survey results, see Azadeh Kian-Thiébaut, "From Motherhood to Equal Rights Advocates: The Weakening of the Patriarchal Order," *Iranian Studies*, 38(1) (March 2005), 45–66.

Table 4.3 *Iranian population growth rate*

| 1956 | 1966 | 1976 | 1986 | 1991 | 1996 | 2006 | 2011 | 2016 |
|---|---|---|---|---|---|---|---|---|
| 3.1 | 3.1 | 2.7 | 3.9 | 2.5 | 1.5 | 1.6 | 1.3 | 1.2 |

This very low population growth rate, combined with a youthful but aging population, has pushed a shift back towards pronatalist approaches in the state's population and family planning policies. This mirrors similar state concerns in other modern and modernizing societies that are facing declining future numbers of working-age adults combined with longer life expectancies (and higher expectations) for the present adult generations.
*Source*: Statistical Center of Iran

population growth rate has stabilized at what for the state is now a worryingly low level, despite continuing improvements in child mortality and life expectancy (see Table 4.3). The age of first marriage for women also rose significantly after the revolution, despite the legal age of marriage initially being lowered to nine (and later raised to thirteen) for girls, and fifteen for boys.[51] This discrepancy, between the post-revolutionary legal age for girls to marry at nine and the social reality that after the revolution the age of first marriage for girls has consistently risen from its prerevolutionary low, is indicative of the need to attend not only to the institutional and legal indicators of Iranian women's experience but also to their social and material realities (see Table 4.4).

The 2011 National Population and Housing Census (Statistical Center of Iran) was full of information that helped illuminate the material conditions of ordinary Iranians' everyday lives. In a country

[51] The Shah's Family Protection Law, introduced in 1967, raising the legal age of marriage to eighteen; after the Revolution, it was lowered and set at different ages for boys and girls. In 2002, Article 1041 of the Iranian Civil Code was amended to raise the legal age of marriage to thirteen (solar) years for girls and fifteen (solar) years for boys; marriage for younger children can only be approved with guardian and court permission. A comparison can be made with Japan, where in June 2023 the legal age of sexual consent was raised to sixteen from thirteen (an age limit introduced in 1907). Since April 2022, Japan's legal age of marriage is eighteen for both men and women; previously the legal age of marriage was sixteen for women and eighteen for men. Note that in Iran, there is no separate legal age for sexual consent outside of legal marriage. See Michelle Ye Hee Lee, "Japan (Finally) Changes a Century-Old Law: The Age of Consent Is Now 16," *The Washington Post*, June 16, 2023.

Table 4.4 *Mean age at first marriage*

| Mean age at first marriage | Total men | Total women | Urban men | Urban women | Rural men | Rural women |
|---|---|---|---|---|---|---|
| 1345/1966 | 25.0 | 18.4 | 25.6 | 19.0 | 24.4 | 17.9 |
| 1355/1976 | 24.1 | 19.7 | 25.1 | 20.2 | 22.7 | 19.1 |
| 1365/1986 | 23.6 | 19.8 | 24.2 | 20.0 | 22.6 | 19.6 |
| 1370/1991 | 24.6 | 20.9 | 24.9 | 21.0 | 23.5 | 20.8 |
| 1375/1996 | 25.6 | 22.4 | 26.2 | 22.5 | 24.5 | 22.3 |
| 1385/2006 | 26.2 | 23.2 | 26.5 | 23.3 | 25.5 | 23.4 |
| 1390/2011 | 26.7 | 23.4 | 27.1 | 23.6 | 25.8 | 23 |
| 1395/2016 | 27.4 | 23.0 | 27.8 | 23.4 | 26.5 | 22 |

*Source*: Statistical Center of Iran

of 75 million,[52] 71.4 percent of the population were urban, and ten million Iranians or 18.3 percent of the population were graduates or students of higher (postsecondary) education; the percentages of men (18.2 percent) and women (18.4 percent) postsecondary students and graduates were almost identical (in the following years, women became the majority of postsecondary students). The median age for both sexes was twenty-seven; the life expectancy for men was 72.1 years and for women 74.6. In 2011, the mean age at first marriage for men was 26.7 and for women 23.4, with little difference between urban and rural women's age of first marriage.[53] The average national household size was 3.55 persons (3.48 in rural areas and 3.73 in urban), with quite a bit of regional variation; 12.1 percent of households were female headed (it was 7.3 percent in 1976).

The data that most clearly demonstrate widespread experience of the material conditions for modern living are the changing household characteristics. In 1390/2011, 22.8 percent of households had a motorcycle, 42.1 percent of households had an automobile, and 33.4 percent

[52] The 2011 census population of 75 million total population included 73.4 million Iranian citizens, 1.45 million Afghan citizens, and assorted others.

[53] The closing of the age difference between rural and urban women parallels a narrowing of the age gap between women and men. Thus, most first marriages across the country now more closely match the model of partner marriage: marriage between peer age-mates in their mid-twenties rather than the former common hierarchy of a much older man and a much younger woman.

Table 4.5 *2011 National Population and Housing Census;*[a] *and Summary Results of the Urban and Rural Household Income and Expenditure Survey – The Year 1400 (March 20, 2021–March 20, 2022)*[b]

| |
|---|
| 2011: 78 percent of households use natural (piped) gas for cooking, heating, and hot water |
| 2021–2022: 95.2 percent of urban and 78.1 percent of rural households use natural gas (piped networks) |
| 2011: 20 percent of households use liquefied natural gas (tanks) for cooking |
| 2021–2022: .3 percent of urban and 1.5 percent of rural households use liquified natural gas |
| 2011: 96.5 percent of households have access to piped water |
| 2011: 91.3 percent of households use a public water distribution system |
| 2011: 99.5 percent of households have access to electricity |
| 2011: 95.2 percent of households have a bathroom (was 87.1 percent in 2006) |

[a,b] *Source*: Statistical Center of Iran.

of households had a computer.[54] In 1400/2021, only 18.7 percent of households had a motorcycle, but 35.9 percent of rural households and 53.9 percent of urban households had a private car.[55] But what becomes clear very quickly is that most households have access to modern domestic material infrastructure, meaning most women's lives are not defined by subsistence reproductive labor (Table 4.5).

If the majority of households in 2011 were using a form of natural gas for cooking, women's domestic labor was not spent in gathering fuel. Similarly, if almost 97 percent of households had access to piped water (and 95 percent have bathrooms), most women were not carrying water or emptying slop jars. Iranian women's domestic labor is not excruciatingly labor intensive. Given the massive level of basic education and developmental integration among the Iranian population, for both men and women (cooking with natural gas and piped water

[54] *Selected Findings of the 2011 National Population and Housing Census*, Statistical Center of Iran. www.amar.org.ir.

[55] *Summary Results of the Urban and Rural Household Income and Expenditure Survey – The Year 1400 (20 March 2021–20 March 2022)*, Statistical Center of Iran – the year 1400. The *Summary* presents the data in a comparative table collating "Percentage of Households Using Major Household Appliances in Urban and Rural Areas in the Years 1399 and 1400." The phrasing implies that households may possibly own or rent the specified appliance, but have personal direct access to it. (The information does not include hire cars and taxis.)

means being integrated into a well-developed infrastructure system of supply), the further question arises: if Iranian women are apparently still not participating at high levels in the paid labor force, what are they doing?[56]

Some of these women are students, whether girls enrolled in primary and secondary school or women in postsecondary education. Some of them are indeed working or looking for work at regularized paid jobs that show up in formal employment statistics. Increasingly, women's household-based activity is entrepreneurial, in that it is consciously directed at income production, even if these business efforts are intentionally kept informal.[57] According to a woman professional with her own registered company, "Many of my other [women] colleagues, we have the same cultural background, but they prefer to have their business in their house. Antique business, dance school business, teaching business, many other businesses you can have in your house without any certification, without any permission, and being at your ease, without any constraint, without any pressure, having coffee, not struggling."[58] The reference to being able to drink coffee when you want to is not an idle comment: during the fasting month of Ramadan, security patrols have been known to check businesses to ensure that the teakettle isn't hot. A warm kettle could indicate that tea (or coffee) has been brewed and therefore that individuals working in the business aren't observing the religious fast and might be subject to disciplinary measures. Similar issues of social regulation over proper observance of *hejab* within a formal workplace mean that for many women, a home-based informal business can indeed offer a greater degree of personal freedom from regulatory social scrutiny.

But many Iranian women are primarily involved in skilled craft work within the household that is not usually even considered to be part of the informal economy: the production and reproduction of the

[56] Narjes Mehdizadeh argues that the low level of employment of well-educated (postsecondary) women in professional positions is the lack of available childcare and other support for better work/life balance. See Narjes Mehdizadeh, "Gender and Reconciliation of Work and Family in Iran," *International Labour Review*, 150(3–4) (2011), 405–417.

[57] Roksana Bahramitash, *Gender and Entrepreneurship in Iran: Microenterprise and the Informal Sector* (New York: Palgrave Macmillan, 2013).

[58] Personal interview, woman publisher. She was willing to deal with the regulatory controls (both behavioral and bureaucratic) of formalizing her business, "because I wanted to be in the public sphere."

material and social networks of cultural identity that sustain daily life under specific political conditions.

## The Social Economy of Food: The Production and Reproduction of the Iranian Habitus

To what extent can household work, whether "the production of goods or services for their own final use" or for exchange in the local market economy, be considered productive work (even if informal) rather than unskilled reproductive labor? The majority of Iranian households are sites neither of subsistence domestic labor (collecting fuel and carrying water) nor of superfluous femininity (the sentimentalized cult of "home-making" that tries to relegitimize a gendered domestic role under conditions of hyper-commodification). Reproductive work, including "doing cooking,"[59] in contemporary Iran may still be labor intensive, but it is not regarded as drudgery. The definition of "drudge" is someone who does menial work, almost exclusively associated with domestic labor within the household: an unskilled, undervalued kitchen maid. But Iranian kitchen work is both skilled and valued, and food is integral to the maintenance of the social networks that sustain all the other forms of productive accomplishment, economic and otherwise.

Iranian households are the social and spatial context for the valued and valuable skilled work that creates and recreates the material and social realities of daily life under the particular conditions of contemporary Iranian modernity. Like many other aspects of postrevolutionary experience, the Iranian household is an unusual hybrid, shaped by unique political as well as social and material circumstances. Iranian women who are participants in the common daily practices of "the production of goods or services for their own [household's] final use" maintain a social economy that may be as valued and as necessary in the postrevolutionary state as any form of paid employment. Thus food as a social relation; domestic labor as skilled work; a social economy that is valued because it produces and reproduces the material basis of cultural identity; the recognizable habitus of Iranian life.

[59] "Doing cooking" is translator Tomasik's admittedly "rather awkward" translation of "*faire-la-cuisine*," Luce Giard's own term to play off of Michel de Certeau's term "*arts de faire*," itself translated as "the practice of everyday life." See *The Practice of Everyday Life, Volume 2: Living and Cooking*, 275.

## Iranian Home Cooking: Identity/Culture/Skill

Part of that habitus is a legacy of home cooking that participates in a very long cultural heritage of cuisine.[60] Modern Iranian home cooking is an amalgamation of two nearly opposite dietary regimes and techniques, reflecting two very different but coexisting strands of a diverse national history: a sophisticated urban and imperial court culture and a large pastoral tribal population with extensive herds.[61] Classical and Medieval Persian court culture produced a cuisine of painstakingly cooked combinations of varied and refined ingredients, especially a taste for sweet and sour combinations of meat simmered with fruits and spices. Pastoralist animal husbandry produced techniques for quick cooking meat (grilled kabobs), preserving cultured dairy products (*kashk*, a drained, dried, and reconstituted yogurt with a pronounced umami flavor), and a taste for fresh foraged herbs and greens (*sabzi*). Over time, and particularly with the Safavid dynasty, these two cultural and culinary traditions became one, without denigration for the pastoral tribal inheritance of grilled meat and green leaves (since this was the background of the new ruling dynasty), and without disdain for the niceties of urban imperial court culture (the Safavids legitimized their rule by

60 Shaida's *The Legendary Cuisine of Persia* provides an overview of the geographical and historical range of influence Persian culinary practices and tastes have had globally: from Herodotus' grudging admiration of the sophistication and bounty of their table to the "Persianization" of Arab and Mongol/Mughal conquerors' food preferences and their dissemination of those preferences along the geographic routes (both westward and eastward) of their further conquests. Shaida also has written a witty and quite comprehensive overview of the treatment of food – from the sublime to the satirical – within Persian poetry: see Margaret Shaida, "The Poetry of Persian Food," in Harlan Walker, ed., *Food in the Arts: Proceedings of the Oxford Symposium on Food and Cookery* (Devon: Prospect Books, 1998), 182–189.

61 European culinary traditions are similarly made up of two broadly distinct food culture legacies, each with its own accompanying aesthetics of the dietary regime: a Mediterranean Graeco-Roman agricultural regime based on grain (bread), grapes (wine, raisins, and vinegar), and olives (cured olives and olive oil), with some (sheep) cheese and fish as the primary animal protein, and accompanied by an aesthetics of bodily moderation; and a northern Germanic/Celtic forestry regime based on meat (game that was hunted or free pastured in woodlands), fish, and foraged fruits, accompanied by an aesthetics of bodily satiety and appetite. See Massimo Montanari, trans. Carl Ipsen, *The Culture of Food* (Cambridge, MA: Blackwell, 1994), 1–37.

sponsoring the arts and making Isfahan into a showplace of architectural grandeur and intimacy).[62]

Of course, as in any culinary culture, changes in preparation and consumption happened over time. The Safavids solidified the union of the two main Persian culinary traditions by introducing a preponderance of the complex rice dishes that have become the hallmark of Iranian cuisine. But the unique four-step process that characterizes Persian rice cooking (washing, soaking, parboiling, steaming/baking to obtain individually distinct grains and a disk of crispy browned *tadiq* or bottom crust) seems to have been developed by the Qajars.[63] The most evident culinary transformation was probably the later near-total switch away from coffee, which was first associated with medicinal purposes and then became a convivial drink associated with guests and conversation, whether in private receptions or in shared social settings like the *hammam* (bathhouse) or the *qahveh khaneh* (coffee house). From the beginning of the seventeenth century, coffee was a common luxury beverage in Safavid Iran, but by the late nineteenth century under the Qajars, tea had become the dominant national beverage and had all but replaced coffee drinking, even among elites. Unlike coffee, tea also seems to have been domesticated in its Iranian consumption; tea is a ubiquitous food staple, brewed and consumed at home, work, and in the street, without the associations of public occasion that historical Iranian coffee consumption seems to have had. Through the nineteenth century, well-to-do travelers would still carry dried coffee in tablet form, which they would nibble like chocolate (presumably for its stimulant effect during long and tiring caravan trips), but coffee almost completely disappeared as a known drink. The ghost of its presence remained. A traditional Iranian tea house is still called a *qahveh khaneh* even though coffee is never served; a modern *qahveh khaneh* serves tea, possibly with some snacks, occasionally with live recitations or music for entertainment, and almost

[62] The scholarship on the Safavids and their capital city of Isfahan is enormous. For a particularly insightful account of their unique contribution to a political culture that combined political authority with popular access and spatial intimacy, epitomized in the new architecture of Isfahan, see Sussan Babaie, *Isfahan and Its Palaces: Statecraft, Shi'ism and the Architecture of Conviviality in Early Modern Iran* (Edinburgh: Edinburgh University Press, 2008).

[63] See Shireen Mahdavi, "Women, Shi'ism and Cuisine in Iran," in Sarah Ansari and Vanessa Martin, eds., *Women, Religion, and Culture in Iran* (Richmond, Surrey: Curzon Press, 2002), 10–26.

always with available *qalyun* or tobacco water pipes. Coffee is now served in cafés.[64]

But other culinary and cultural continuities have been retained. The combined Iranian traditions of pastoralist and urbanized court culture are epitomized in the dish of *kashk-e-badamjun*: eggplant that is blackened over an open flame, peeled, cooked and mashed, then sautéed with fried onions, spices, and liquid *kashk*, and preferably served with fresh garlic and dried mint that have been fried in oil until crispy. Blending ingredients associated with settled agricultural production (eggplant), with trade route spices (turmeric) and a heritage product of pastoral herding (*kashk*, even if it is now ordinarily processed in modern dairy plants) in a complex, multistep preparation, *kashk-e badamjun* is a homely but delicious staple of Iranian cooking, served both as a meatless entrée for family and a proper first course or side dish for guests. Many of the other most common and most beloved examples of Iranian home cooking demonstrate a similar national heritage of cultural hybridity. *Ghormeh sabzi* is an herb stew cooked long and slowly with some dried beans and a little meat; the sophistication of what probably began as a pot of foraged greens now comes through the appropriate mix of the various herbs, which must include but not be overly dominated by the strong-smelling fenugreek (which is otherwise not often used in Persian cooking).

These dishes have little or no meat, but until recently, that lack would not have been a reason to consider them less satisfying. The common Iranian diet has changed drastically within the past two generations. Like much of the rest of the world, Iran has rising rates of the diseases (obesity, type-2 diabetes, hypertension) associated with changes in lifestyle and diet, and the problem of junk food consumption, especially by children, is a recognized public health problem.[65] But changes in

[64] For a fascinating and very complete account of Iranian coffee and tea habits, see Rudi Matthee, *The Pursuit of Pleasure: Drugs and Stimulants in Iranian History, 1500–1900* (Princeton, NJ: Princeton University Press, 2005).

[65] The sudden prevalence of these diseases – indications of large-scale changes in the production, distribution, and consumption of foodstuffs – does not mean that the older issue of food insecurity has disappeared. This new combined challenge has encouraged a sense of necessary collaboration among members of the multiple professions struggling to develop policy responses, including media and advertising professionals; nutritionists, public health, and medical experts; and educational and development specialists. Some of the most innovative local initiatives are the result of these joint efforts (author's discussions with

meat consumption, so that eating meat every day is now expected as a norm, while its absence from the daily diet is a deprivation, have been less remarked. Informal investigations among older Iranians indicate that through the middle of the twentieth century, even a well-to-do family would not necessarily expect to eat meat every day. Meatless dishes that might include eggs or dairy, or soups and dishes cooked with only a very small amount of meat or bones for flavoring, were not a sign of the absence of meat. A dish, a meal, or a diet was judged not by the presence of meat but by the proper balancing of hot and cold.

Hot and cold refers not to temperature, but to the classification of foods according to the dietary regime of Hippocratic and Galenic medicine: the balance of the body's four humors (blood, yellow bile, phlegm, and black bile), each associated with a particular temperament. Humorism, and the resulting close attention to diet as a means of influencing the body's fluid humors, has been supplanted by the orthodoxies and pharmacological interventions of modern medicine, although most Iranians still do pay attention to the balance of cold and hot foods they are consuming.[66] Everyone knows which foods are "hot" and which ones "cold," although there are some regional variations and there isn't necessarily a single authoritative answer to disagreements.[67] But in general, the classifications are not only conceptually known but present on the plate. Eggplant is hot, while kashq is cold: *kashk-e badamjun* is a balanced mix. Fenugreek is hot, as are most of the other ingredients in *ghormeh sabzi*, making it a very hot and potent meal. But it is always served with rice, which is cold (except in the rice-growing region of Rasht, where rice is considered to be hot).

The most famous Iranian culinary dish, and the one that may best represent the far-flung permutations of both culture and cuisine, is

conference participants, Shahid Beheshti University of Medical Sciences and Health Services, Tehran, May 2007).

66 Even people who otherwise don't pay much attention to "hot" and "cold" foods will inevitably be reminded of the need for appropriate choices under specific conditions. For instance, a professional woman with two daughters stated that she is often advised that if she wants a son, she should take better care to modify her diet according to the appropriate hot and cold choices (personal interview).

67 For a discussion of the system of food classifications, including its possible regional variations and a list of classified foods, see Christian Bromberger, "Eating Habits and Cultural Boundaries in Northern Iran," in Sami Zubaida and Richard Tapper, eds., *A Taste of Thyme: Culinary Cultures of the Middle East* (New York: Tauris Parke Paperbacks, 2010), 185–201.

probably *fesenjun*. *Fesenjun* can be served with roasted duck or chicken or small meatballs; the meat is variable, but the sauce is not. *Fesenjun*, like Mexican *mole*, is the sauce: a long slow simmering of ground walnuts, fried onions, and a thick pomegranate reduction. Pomegranates are very cold, but walnuts are hot, as are duck, turkey, wildfowl, and sometimes chicken (depending if it is a cock or a hen, and on regional variation); *fesenjun* is hot, but the rice with which it is always served gives the dish its balance. The preparation must be careful and attentive: the walnuts need to be ground fine so as to blend into the sauce; the sugar in the pomegranate reduction means the sauce has to be stirred often, so as not to caramelize and burn. The chosen meat is usually cooked separately and added at the end, at serving. *Fesenjun*, which is always a festive dish but also a common one, maintains the legacy of older Persian techniques of cooking sweet and sour fruits with meats, and of using pulverized nuts for thickening, while maintaining the essential healthy balance of hot and cold combinations. It is one of the glories of Iranian cooking, but not limited to present-day Iran. In her 1965 ethnography of life in a tribal Shi'a village in southern Iraq, Elizabeth Fernea describes the favored youngest wife of the sheikh preparing a special, cherished dish: *fesenjun*, which the local women also call "Persian chicken."[68] And the mole comparison is not accidental. Mole is considered the Mexican national dish because it is a mix of American "New World" ingredients (chiles, turkey, and the later addition of chocolate to some recipes) and "Old World" Spanish, Moorish, and Arab flavors, techniques, and

[68] Elizabeth Fernea, *Guests of the Sheik: An Ethnography of an Iraqi Village* (Anchor Books, 1969), 270–271. The southern area of Iraq is historically mostly Shi'a and has had close economic (trading) and religious (pilgrimage) relations with Iran. Many of the local foods that the village women cook are recognizably Persian, including the rice preparations: both rice cooked with other ingredients mixed in (*polo*) and rice cooked to emerge from the pot with a crisp browned crust (*tadig*) (Fernea, *Guests of the Sheik*, 34). The village women insist on teaching Fernea the proper way to prepare and cook rice, a process of multiple steps that is specific to Persian cuisine: the rice is rinsed and soaked (to remove excess starch) and then parboiled and drained; the pot is dried, and oil or fat heated in the bottom; the rice is then returned to the pot (some of it being mixed with the hot oil to coat the grains) and steamed until done (Fernea, *Guests of the Sheik*, 78–79). The result should be individual grains that are fully cooked but do not stick together, preferably with a golden disk of *tadig* (a delicacy in itself) in the bottom of the pot.

spices.[69] This acknowledgment of well-traveled culinary influences leads back to the eighth-century Muslim "Arab" conquest of Spain from North Africa. But the influences on Muslim court culture, whether in Al-Andalus or Moghul India, trace back to the Persianization of the Abbasid dynasty in terms of imperial administration, urban architecture, and courtly protocol. Mole, a New World hybrid and itself a glory of Mexican cuisine, is the distant genealogical cousin, separated and linked by both history and geography, of Persian *fesenjun*.

Why does the fragile thread of culinary kinship matter? Because to lay a cultural claim to cuisine, rather than merely to cooking, is to make claims for a distinctive set of techniques, ingredients, and flavors that are not only defined by the regional specificities of *terroir*. When an Iranian home cook makes *fesenjun*, she is probably completely unaware of the cultural *mestizaje* that connects her to the culinary practices of her Mexican colleague, although she may know that *fesenjun* is cooked in Iraq. What she is aware of is the cultural continuity that making *fesenjun* provides for her, and for anyone participating in the resulting pleasures of its consumption. *Fesenjun* is an ongoing cultural achievement – history and identity on a plate – maintained through familiar cultural practices. It is cooking as craft, but not cooking as science; Iranian home cooks rarely use written recipes. These are culinary skills that have been learned and passed on through practice – observing and doing – not through a catalog of procedures: the "doing cooking" in Giard's discussion of undocumented domestic knowledge, no matter how complex and skilled the work.[70]

## Food as a Social Relation: We Are What We Eat (Together)

The product of such labor-intensive skilled work is usually meant to be shared beyond the immediate members of the household: with

[69] Rachel Laudan, "The Mexican Kitchen's Islamic Connection," *Saudi Aramco World*, 55(3) (May/June 2004), 32–39; Louis Werner, "Mexico's Colors of Three Cultures," *Saudi Aramco World*, 61(1) (January/February 2010), 34–43. For a discussion of the more recent Middle Eastern (early twentieth-century Ottoman "Lebanese" immigrants from the instability of greater Syria) origins of one of the apparently typical dishes of Mexico City – *tacos al pastor* – see Katy Watson, "Shawarma: Taco al pastor's Culinary Ancestor," *BBC Magazine*, September 2, 2015, www.bbc.com/news/magazine-33993719.

[70] Luce Giard, "Part II: Doing Cooking," in *The Practice of Everyday Life, Volume 2: Living and Cooking*, 149–247.

extended family, neighbors, and friends. Even if they are not invited to share the meal at home, a pot may be filled and sent over; eventually, it will be returned, filled with another household's home cooking. Food – the social reality of its preparation and consumption, of both cooking and eating – is the basic currency of the Iranian social economy. It is a circulation of capital and credit that is less easily debased than coinage and more accessible than economic wealth. Even strangers are invited to share in the material exchange of a cultural identity reproduced through food and sociability. A *nazr* is a vow to fulfill a beneficent act, often to provide food for strangers, and *nazri* (food cooked and distributed as part of a religious vow) is considered by everyone to be especially delicious. It is not exactly alms; eating *nazri* is not an embarrassment or an indication of straitened circumstances; it is a blessing alike on the one who gives and on the one who receives. Thus it is a mutual benefit, a sociability of reciprocity that does not require immediate social or material equivalence. Sharing food both sustains and creates a network of community.

Once, in downtown Tehran in a famous old *piroshky* shop, three young street children came in, two very small boys and a slightly older girl, begging for money.[71] I offered to buy them a snack; Kaveh suggested I get them the piroshkies with the meat filling. Overhearing us, the little girl calmly stepped forward and informed me that they would like potato and cabbage (I prefer these fillings as well). When they received their piroshkies, they didn't run off; the girl shepherded the boys to the counter, had them pull up stools, and they all sat down quietly and properly and, without rush, enjoyed their meal. They were

[71] The piroshky shop itself is a remnant of an earlier overland arrival of 100,000 Polish refugees, including a large contingent of orphan children, during WWII. Piroshkies and *paczki* (pronounced by Iranians as "*ponchik*," a sweet-filled doughnut with a rich dough) were adopted as specialty snacks into the food culture of the cities where there was a substantial presence of Polish refugees in the 1940s. They still tend to be sold out of shops located in the now somewhat run-down neighborhoods that were fashionable midcentury and postwar entertainment destinations, although the Polish association with the snacks and the shops has long since been lost. See Parisa Damandan, *The Children of Isfahan: Polish Refugees in Iran, Portrait Photographs of Abolqasem Jala, 1942–1945* (Tehran: Nazarpub, 2010). For discussions of the Russian influence on Iranian consumption habits, and specifically how tea (brewed in a samovar) replaced coffee to become the dominant national beverage in nineteenth-century Iran, see Rudi Matthee, "From Coffee to Tea: Shifting Patterns of Consumption in Qajar Iran," *Journal of World History*, 7(2) (Fall 1996), 199–230.

very young street children, as marginal an identity as it is possible to have in contemporary Iran. But as soon as they had the opportunity, they knew how to claim a propriety of cultural participation. In that afternoon pause, the simple fact of joining the counter to sit down and eat their cabbage and potato – not meat – piroshkies provided a momentary claim to an inclusive civic identity that was otherwise, for those three, probably all too elusive.

That was a fleeting moment, and I have wondered often what has happened to that young girl. I don't know, although I fear the probability. I do believe that whatever options might have become available to her, she knew how to speak up to assert some agency, and how to sit down to take a place at the table. That is not much; maybe it has been enough.

For most Iranians, shared food is not an exceptional opportunity for civic participation, but it is the essential practice that maintains the ongoing network of necessary social relations. This network is not just about socializing, although that is culturally valued and religiously approved.[72] In the Islamic Republic of Iran, social networks are how you get things done. Given the strictures the state puts on ordinary daily behaviors (no too-relaxed mingling of unrelated adult men and women; no non-wearing of *hejab* by women if unrelated men are present; no non-wearing of *hejab* if unrelated men are not present but might be able to see you; no consumption of alcohol unless a member of an approved religious minority, etc.), finding someone to do even ordinary household repairs means finding someone who will be at least tolerant of the private habits of the household. For this kind of relation – an

[72] Although some versions of Islam hold that food should be best consumed in silence and one should get up from the "table" as soon as one is finished (so as to make room for others and not inflict one's company unnecessarily on one's fellow diners), the Persian tradition is different. From at least the eleventh century, Persian books of advice combined ethics, etiquette, and theology to recommend approved personal and social behavior, noting that according to the "'rule of Islam' … while eating with others, one must take time from consuming food to converse with one's fellow diners." This is a reference to the *Qabusnāma*, compiled around 1082 by a member of the Ziyarid dynasty, Keikavūs ibn Wushmgīr, as quoted in Pamela Karimi, *Domesticity and Consumer Culture in Iran: Interior Revolutions of the Modern Era* (New York: Routledge, 2013), 123. This scholarly observation is echoed in the conversation of an excellent Iranian cook, married to an Arab Jordanian man, who recalls her disquiet at how quickly his relatives would eat and leave the table. They obviously enjoyed the food, but she could never get over that they never lingered!

intimacy with strangers that is different from the more impersonal service transactions paid for in other state contexts; it isn't enough to rely on anonymous user reviews or commercial advertisements. No one is going to publicize that they are comfortable working in an "immoral" household (where the women might not wear *hejab* around visitors) or that the behavior in their own household is open to (legal) reproach ("wanted: someone to repair the roof gutter, but not to report the presence of the illegal satellite dish"). Getting things done – whether finding a cleaner to help with the housework, a plumber to repair the pipes, or a home-visit nurse to help care for a dying family member – means relying on a circle of trusted friends and family, a social network that is maintained at least in part through the regular preparation, consumption, and exchange of food, preferably home cooking.

This is really the product of Iranian women's skilled domestic work: the reproduction of the social world. The work and the world are integrally allied and equally valued, although also both taken for granted to some extent: the normative nature of the ordinary allows us to overlook its presence even as we are shocked to note its unexpected absence. Given the choice between the possibility of a fairly low-skilled but highly supervised job outside the home (whether clerical, retail, or industrial), and the skilled and relatively autonomous work of the household, it seems that many Iranian women are choosing not to participate in formal economic activity, at least in terms of pursuing waged labor.[73] This may change, as economic pressures and increasing levels of education encourage more women to consider employment. In this process, an ideology of women's domestic role, whether that ideology is apparently traditionally Islamic or the modern convention of the separate spheres, is probably of much less importance than the possible availability of prepared fresh *sabzi*.

[73] Iranian employed women and housewives don't experience statistically significant differences in life satisfaction, at least according to a study in one provincial area. See Fatihe Kerman Saravi et al., "Comparing Health-Related Quality of Life of Employed Women and Housewives: A Cross Sectional Study from Southeast Iran," *BMC Women's Health*, 12(41) (2012).

# 5 Elegy or The Rule of the Fathers: The Break with the Past

## Household Labor: Waiting for Death

(Wednesday, March 14, 2007)

We're all waiting for death. From the moment we're born, we run toward it. Life itself is the process of continuing to an end; every step of the living continuity a step closer to its mortal finish. And toward the end of life, the goal becomes . . . confused. Is life's goal its end, or a final resistance? When we cling to life, do we deny its most fundamental reality, our mortality, or do we honor the miracle of our daily breath? And when our bodies slow toward the finish, are we holding back, or are we learning the pace that will take us to our end?

These are not uncommon thoughts. Prompted by illness, loss, and tragedy, they are the questions of being, and of its end. But in the US, ordinary death is hidden, unless you take a professional interest. And the decline of the body at the end is especially intangible. We visit our relatives, our friends, in the hospital, or in their places of care, but we are less often responsible for the care ourselves. For the American middle classes, nursing is more often a profession than a noun related to the ill, and we forget, unless we are the patients ourselves, how demanding is the body of its care. Losing a loved one is an emotional loss, but it is less often the close physical experience of meeting death's growing presence every day. We are spared that, our lives easier and our losses cleaner, at least for those left behind.

In the US, my father died alone, in the hospital. It was a good hospital, and he had good care, but we were not the ones caring for him, and we were not with him when he died. It's not like that here. In Iran, in our house, death is present, and it waits. We are living with it every day, getting used to it as a part of daily life. Resisting death, clinging to life, we have made of death a constant presence, a companion who is unwelcome, except that now its absence would bring a finality we also dread. We wait.

And we do laundry. Lots of laundry. Make and remake the bed. Prepare some meals. Listen for a call. Serve tea. Prepare a meal, prepare a tray, do the dishes. Put them away. Care for the body, reach for the mind. Wait. Do it over again. The rhythm of the body outside of its learned routine, which is no rhythm at all, a rhythm of its own demanding and its own need. This is the rhythm of life, life near its end, death in the midst of ordinary living. The rhythm of our days.

Sometimes I knit. Women's work, the traditional work of idle hands in a spare moment, the work of waiting. But it is important to be making something, to create. Is that what they were doing, those women waiting with their knitting by the tumbrels? Not only to mark the dramatic fall but also to make something ordinary, make something new, in the midst of closure and the extraordinary? Those women who knew how to live with death … were they also claiming a daily task of continuity? My role is not so public; our experience not so extreme. I sit in a comfortable chair in the living room, and sometimes I find it is good to have something to do with my hands that is a quiet accomplishing.

When I was a child, my grandmother was the knitter. As she failed, my mother took it up and outfitted us all with sweaters. I learned from her, but even though she can't manage it anymore, my knitting is only intermittent. This sweater has lasted for years, a joke in the family, a possibility that never ends. But I'm getting close to finishing. What then?

Kaveh's father died midmorning Sunday, March 18, 2007. March 18 is my birthday.

An hour later, the heating pipes burst. We hadn't known anything was wrong with them. But it was as though the soul of the house had died. Kaveh's father built that house: added to it, reconstructed it, tended and cared for it, over forty years. In the last decade of his life, as he got sicker and weaker, the house was his home and his retreat. His room overlooked the garden, and for as long as he could, and longer, he worked in it every day; when he couldn't, he supervised those who did. He read the papers in bed, a prospect that during the height of the reform period could take hours, accompanied by the cat. Part bedroom, part sitting room, part study; we collected there, visiting, paying respect, passing time. But when he died, the house expired. Everything went cold. We didn't really notice at first. The oldest uncle came, the neighbors across the street offered soup, we put on black, and the plumber had to be called.[1] When death does arrive, it keeps you busy. Since in Iran the burial is the next day, the arrangements are hectic, no matter how well planned. The pipes got fixed; the heat came back on. We loved that house. But it wasn't the same.

When they opened up the wall to get at the heating pipes, the foundation was all rubble. The house was solid, the walls nearly a foot thick, brick and mortar and finished plaster that we thought would stand through anything. We thought it was built on a rock foundation, but it was built on gravel. Tehran is built over major seismic fault lines, and the fact that there hasn't been an earthquake in living memory makes it all the more likely that when the next one comes, it will be bad. This had been discussed in the family, with the satisfaction of knowing that the house was sound, and we could depend on what had been accomplished. But then Agha Ehsani died, and the pipes burst, and we found out that life, space, and place are all ephemeral.

## House and Home: A Space of Relations

(April 23, 2000)

Our problem as a family is that we are, like the gentry in nineteenth-century English novels, cash poor and land rich. We are not even really that land rich, but we own some orchard land outside the city (*Ab-eh Sard*, an orchard district meaning "cold water," but that's another story, and involves a pickup truck), and we have a house. Actually, in Tehran, we are house rich; we are one of the few middle-class families I come across who are still living in a house rather than an apartment, and who haven't contracted part of the house out as a separate rental apartment. It's a good-sized house, with lots of

1 "In the kitchen, *one battles against time*, the time of this life that is always heading toward death. The nourishing art has something to do with the art of loving, thus also with the art of dying. In the past, in the village, a burial was the chance for an extended family reunion around a solid meal, serious and joyful, after the internment. People thus began the work of mourning by sharing earthly foods. In the past, death was a part of life; it seems to me that it was less alarming that way."

Luce Giard, chapter 10, "The Nourishing Arts," Michel de Certeau, Luce Giard, and Pierre Mayol, *The Practice of Everyday Life, Volume 2: Living and Cooking* (Minneapolis, MN: University of Minnesota Press, 1998), 169. In our house, in Tehran, we offered what was expected: dates, made appropriate to mourning with a sprinkle of rosewater and coconut.

comfortable, airy rooms, and it's an old-fashioned house, in that all the internal doors are multi-paneled with colored glass, the kitchen has room for a table, and there are enough nooks and crannies in the layout for both privacy and sociability to happen at the same time. And we have a garden. This is really the reason why we worked hard to convince Kaveh's parents not to sell when they were considering moving to an apartment several years ago. The house and the garden require constant work, and apartment living seemed so convenient. But what the house and the garden give us is space. Slowly becoming the ultimate luxury, space in an urban setting is the privilege of the rich and the reduced. Space gives us room to move, the chance not to be on top of each other and constantly in each other's way. And space gives us history.

Tehran used to be a low-rise city of family homes no more than two stories tall. It's a twentieth-century city built into the foothills of the Alborz mountains; the historical capitals of earlier dynasties are the architectural destinations of Isfahan (the Safavid capital from the sixteenth to the eighteenth century) and Shiraz (the Zand capital during the eighteenth century). The ancient city of Rey had been built on the flat plain just south of the mountains, but it lost its importance after being sacked by the Mongols, and all that remains is the contemporary south Tehran neighborhood of *Shahr-e-Rey* (City of Rey), a tough working-class enclave that used to be the location of the city's main cemetery and brick kilns. The sixteenth-century Safavid ruler Shah Tahmasp was the first to fortify the town, and the walls were reconstructed by the Zand ruler Karim Khan. But at the very end of the eighteenth century, Mohammad Khan Qajar defeated the last Zand ruler and established a new dynasty and a new dynastic capital. The Qajars chose Tehran because it was in the geographic center of the country and had fertile flatlands, and because despite the fortifications, it had little historical significance, and no one else had chosen to make it their own. By the early nineteenth century, they had settled into their new capital city; they spent the next hundred years losing territory, spending money, and fathering children.[2] Nineteenth-century Tehran

[2] They did expand the city, tearing down the old wall – with its 114 towers, one for every *sura* (chapter) in the Quran, designed by Shah Tahmasp – and building a new octagonal wall enclosing land previously outside the city limits, most of which was owned by the minister responsible for the new wall. See references in Mina Marefat, *Building to Power: Architecture in Tehran 1921–1941*,

seems to have been a dusty backwater, a ramshackle bazaar, and a new palace and court built in the elaborately decorative Qajar style, and a progression of independent small villages that backed up above the city into the northern piedmont. Travelers complained about the dirt, and the locals' reputation as brigands. By the time of the 1906 Constitutional Revolution, the Qajar dynasty and the state were both economically and politically bankrupt.

But by the twentieth century, Tehran had been consolidated as the capital city, no matter who was in power. Under the Pahlavis, father and son, under Mossadegh and during the coup that overthrew him, and under the Islamic Republic, Tehran has kept its place as the center of the state. Isfahan may be "half the world" according to the poets; Mashhad is still the most important Iranian shrine city and the gateway to Central Asia, and I love Shiraz, but Tehran is the recognized national capital. For better or worse, Tehran is the central urban space of the twentieth-century history of Iran.[3]

When Gholamhossein Karbaschi became mayor of Tehran, he built parks, restricted traffic in the city center, and set up trash bins around the city that were marked with the slogan "My City, My Home."[4] He financed these initiatives to improve the urban experience by selling air rights to build multifamily apartment towers, and suddenly city land prices became sources of speculative windfall, and apartment living became fashionable for the middle class. Apartments, whether

unpublished dissertation, Massachusetts Institute of Technology, June 1988, vol. 1, pp. 31–38.

3 Most scholars agree that Reza Shah Pahlavi's most lasting legacy was the vast amount of built infrastructure he sponsored, mostly in Tehran but also in multiple other provincial cities. Although his efforts at dress reform (forcibly discouraging *hejab*) didn't last, and he was deposed by the Allies (suspicious of his anti-British and pro-German sympathies) during WWII, his projects of state-sponsored urban renewal (including a public architecture of municipal buildings, and expansive arterial roadways that pushed through traditional neighborhood fabrics and out into suburban destinations) have shaped Iranian urban experience throughout the twentieth century, and into the twenty-first. On Tehran, see Marefat, *Building to Power*, and C. Adle and B. Hourcade, *Téhéran, capitale bicentenaire* (Tehran: Institut français de recherche en Iran, 1992); for discussion of other regional architectural urban histories, see Ali Modarres, *Modernizing Yazd: Selective Historical Memory and the Fate of Vernacular Architecture* (Costa Mesa, CA: Mazda Publishers, 2006).

4 Karbaschi was Tehran mayor from 1989 to 1998. See Kaveh Ehsani, "Municipal Matters: The Urbanization of Consciousness and Political Change in Tehran," *Middle East Report*, (212) (Fall 1999), 22–27.

skyscrapers or five-story housing blocks, included conveniences like elevators and dishwashers. This was especially appealing to families, like Kaveh's, in which much of the younger generation was now abroad, leaving aging parents and maybe a lone sibling to take care of increasingly decrepit real estate. War shortages, and the bombing of the city during the Iran–Iraq War, had taken their toll, and many middle-class families sold up and moved further north into shiny new apartments in which the appliances all worked and there wasn't any urgent structural repair.

On the other hand, being land rich and cash poor means that everything in our household is quite dilapidated. For a long time, I thought everything in Iran was a bit the worse for wear, until I finally realized that this was a personal and not national phenomenon. Other people have newer cars and modern kitchens with dishwashers, while everything in our household (except the pickup truck) seems to be more than twenty years old, and sometimes much older. This is partly because, having been here through the Revolution and the War, Kaveh's parents have developed what in the US is referred to as the Depression-era mentality, which means that they won't throw anything out, and buy in bulk (everything from kitchen sponges to toilet paper), to avoid shortages. So we have everything we need or want, but some of it is so old, tattered, or scratched that eventually a replacement has to be supplied. That doesn't mean we throw the old ones out! Everything is in duplicate, the old and the new coexisting and intermingled: not quite trusting that a single modern version can replace the tried and true; not quite willing to make do with whatever was good enough before. This Fall, new sheets were provided (you can't say bought, because getting new sheets in fact involves buying material and having them sewn), and everyone is delighted with the colorful cotton matched sets. But the old sheets are still piled in the linen closet. New serving trays were purchased, since the old ones are scratched beyond respectability, but we use the old ones in the kitchen. Kaveh took down a 1960s era pop painting of a waif with big eyes and hung a calendar in its place in the kitchen; we hid the picture behind the vacuum cleaner in the back kitchen, but after a few days it was on the wall again (at least in the back kitchen this time). The back kitchen itself is an extension of the original kitchen, part mudroom, part pantry, and part prep space, built when the house and the national economy were experiencing their own now-distant periods of energetic expansion. For some reason, both Kati and Kaveh have focused on a contraption that sits on a table in the main kitchen; I don't know what it was originally, but it looks like the base of a blender, functions like radio if you press a button or bump it, and has a single clear flame-shaped lightbulb screwed into a bare socket on the top. This is used as a nightlight, so actually is practical, but I think Kaveh and Kati have decided it represents all the tinkering and frugality of their parents' combined talents. The nightlight rests on a portable dishwasher that is never used and may or may not work. The whole house needs to be painted, and in the kitchen none of the cabinets or drawers close unless you slam them.

It's true that the economy in Iran is terrible, and many people have to struggle either to make ends meet or to make them meet in the ways they want them to. But our combination of spatial luxury and shabbiness is particularly ours. We are not spiffy! If the family moved and the house were sold, everything would be smooth and shiny, inside and outside the new apartment. But we wouldn't have the garden, we wouldn't have the terrace, and we couldn't all spread out the way we have been accustomed to in this house. Most likely, Kaveh and I wouldn't even be here or would be here under very different circumstances. We have noticed that among families in which the parents have moved from houses to apartments, the children from abroad only come for short visits and do not stay. The children feel trapped and complain less about family dynamics than the noise, pollution, and stress of the city. But we have our oasis, our garden, our terrace, and our small pool, and enough room in the house to be both private and sociable. So it's dilapidated. But it's ours and we love it.

(March 2012)

The house has been sold.

The morning that Agha Ehsani died, the neighbor from the house across the street knocked on the door to give us a big pot of *ash-e-reshteh*, the thick homemade noodle soup that has to be cooked and stirred for hours, and that I had seen the women of their family making outside on their *aivan* (the terrace). Like *shol-e-zard* (the golden rice pudding made with saffron) and *gheymeh-pollo* (rice cooked with dried yellow peas, cinnamon, and lamb), *ash* is one of the traditional foods cooked, given away, and eaten as a *nazri*, a beneficence. People say *nazri* food always tastes better, and although the recipes can be prepared in family-sized portions, when made for *nazri* they are usually cooked outside, whether in the courtyard, on the terrace, or in the street, in enormous metal pots above portable kerosene stoves. Individuals or families may cook a *nazri* to fulfill a vow or as thanks to a vow fulfilled; our neighbors' gift to us on the morning of a death was part of a deeply established mutual decorum of neighborly exchange and reserve, the generosity not to mind each other's business only still possible in stable, older neighborhoods.

It was a sensible decision to sell the house. We were not alone in selling. The established middle classes, the residents in neighborhoods like ours, have been especially squeezed by the postrevolutionary economy. Land speculation is the only sure way to make money or guarantee the economic security of yourself or your children; family relations have been transformed by the commodification of residential space, and the accompanying pressure to exploit the space you have. The ground space and air rights for what was a modest single-family home in a middle-class neighborhood can be leveraged into a small fortune and/or several apartments for the now dispersed members of that former household. One by one, the individual family residences around us were sold, knocked down, and replaced by the new five- to seven-story apartment buildings. The shared, mixed social fabric of the neighborhood gave way to anonymous strangers, their perspectives unknown, their buildings looming across the street and above the garden walls, implying no longer a neighborliness but a dissolution of both privacy and mutual respect. In the Islamic Republic, privacy is everything; with reasonable discretion, behind your own walls you can do what you want. But if your neighbors can look into your garden, then it is "public" space and women can be reported for not wearing a headscarf, let alone wearing shorts or using the pool. This is the problem with higher-rise apartment buildings going up in a lower-rise neighborhood: privacy and the freedoms it preserved are now exposed, and without long-standing community memories to share and build neighborly respect, everyone is made insecure. The municipality built an extension to the subway line, rerouting traffic through our small residential street and turning the peace and quiet of the back alleys into a constant jam of traffic. In the spring, in the weeks around Nowruz, camels would appear in our street: short processions of one, two, or three animals walked northward through the city and up our street, saddle-bagged with the best organic fertilizer (dried camel dung) to be spread in walled family gardens. But now the courtyard gardens have been replaced by apartment buildings flush to the street, the street is full of cars and noise, and the familiar neighbors are gone. Not knowing each other, everyone is afraid of being watched by the others. It made sense to sell the house, to move away, and move along, like everyone else.

It's a tragedy.

## Spaces of Relation 2: Pamenar

Kaveh didn't grow up in a normal house. He grew up in Pamenar. Pamenar is the name of an old downtown neighborhood, but in the family, it is the name of a house. Pamenar the neighborhood is near the bazaar, a rundown remnant of an older Tehran. Given the relentless northern expansion of the city and the continual movement of the urban elites toward the north, Pamenar's location means the neighborhood is now a gritty mix of small workshops, businesses, and working-class families. It is definitely déclassé. But until the postwar expansion of the city, central urban neighborhoods were desirable and mixed spaces. Just as multiple generations of a family could be expected to share the space of a single domestic household, a variety of class and social identities could be expected to share the space of a single urban neighborhood. Pamenar means "at the foot of the minaret" of the local mosque, and while the main street leading to the mosque is lined with shops and workshops, the side alleys were a mix of larger and smaller family homes. Because there was no easy transportation around the city, workers and employers lived close to each other, by necessity. The spatial segregation by class is a new urban phenomenon, and part of the reason the middle-class residential neighborhood around our family house – Kaveh's father's house – was so comfortably cohesive. It is precisely the heterogeneous class and social mingling of the old neighborhoods that now makes them resolutely unfashionable for anyone with the means to get away.

Pamenar the family house is almost a myth, a lost spatial paradise that crumbled away with the passage of generations and the wreckage of time. We went to visit once. It was built of *kahgel*, the traditional local mud and straw adobe, so without constant upkeep, the outer walls had gone to ruin. The courtyards were desert, the big walnut tree was dead, and I never saw the kitchens, the baths, or the back courtyard.[5] But I saw the *orsi*, the formal family salon that had always been referred to by the term for its wide colored-glass sash windows, and walked down the few stairs from the courtyard into the summer basement sitting room, now decrepit, with the painted wall tiles still showing stories from the *Shah-Nahmeh*, the Persian national epic *Book of Kings*. The basement room had held a small pool with a fountain, a cool tiled refuge from the heat and intense sun of summer. Directly above it, the inside of the *orsi* was bordered with an elaborately sculpted geometric plaster cornice all around the ceiling, and the wall onto the central garden courtyard was set with enormous floor-to-ceiling wood-framed sash windows of small-paned colored glass. The windows pushed up and down, opening the whole room to the garden. When Kaveh was a child, the lower walls of the room were set with inlaid and painted stone tablets, big enough to be a backrest for someone sitting against the wall. Formal seating for Iranians still tends to mean a large circle of guests spaced around the room, whether on chairs or carpets on the floor. The stones would have been as inviting as armchairs, marking a favored spot to sit. I saw stone wall tablets like that in the *Arg*, the courtyard castle-fortress of the Zand dynasty in Shiraz: pale translucent stone, but without the painted birds, flowers, and branches of the Pamenar work. The Pamenar stones were taken out when the family left the house, divided up, and put into storage. When I saw it, the *orsi* was still beautiful, elaborate and simple at the same time, a haunted ruin.[6] We took a small curved pane of painted stained glass from an upstairs doorway, and we left. Kaveh was angry.

5 The kitchen and other resolutely private spaces would have been as spatially separate as possible from the main living spaces, not only for modesty's sake but also because of the problem of the smells and dirt associated with cooking and washing. For discussion of changes in these residential spaces and practices, see H. E. Chebhabi, "The Westernization of Iranian Culinary Culture," *Iranian Studies* 26(1) (March 2003), 43–61, as well as Pamela Karimi, *Domesticity and Consumer Culture in Iran: Interior Revolutions of the Modern Era* (New York: Routledge, 2013).

6 A newspaper story on the history of the house, with a photo from the central courtyard facing the large stained-glass windows of the salon, appeared in *Ettela-at*, Mordad 27, 1352 (August 18, 1973). See Mohammad Ali Najafi, "*Yek Emarat-e Tarikhi-i Digar dar Khatar-e Virani*" ("Another Historic Building in Danger of Ruin: Urban Renewal Assessments as Blight on Beautiful Historic Buildings"), *Ettela-at*, Mordad 27, 1352 (August 18, 1973). Photographs of Iranian houses comparable to the family Pamenar house can be seen in Jassem Ghazban-pour, *Iranian House* (Tehran: Urban revitalization Office, Ministry of Housing and Urban Development, Winter 1375/2006).

A few years later, the roof caved in, and then even that space of memory was gone.

Pamenar was the house Kaveh's father grew up in. It was built by a Qajar princeling who was at one time the foreign minister, and who would have run the bureaucratic details of his administrative duties from the official residence that was also his home. We know this because the house is identified as such on an early map of the then-walled city of Tehran.[7] After the Qajar minister, the house was sold to Kaveh's great-grandfather, a well-to-do urban notable from an extended merchant family spread across the nodes of the Persian trade routes: Tehran (Iran), Baku (Russian Azerbaijan), Kashmir (India), and Karbala (Iraq). Pamenar was a family house built for an expansive model of domesticity that included both extended kin and the long-time live-in household workers who helped care for the family and the living spaces they shared: a house built with multiple spaces for the plural roles of many people. A long corridor from the street entrance allowed for a transition from the dirt, noise, and public bustle of the street toward the graduated private sanctums of the family. The corridor opened into a first small guest courtyard, fronting a mirror-work reception room for male guests not admitted to the more internal domestic spaces; a small hallway led into the big internal family courtyard, squared off by the variously private or shared spaces of the extended family. Along one side just above ground level was the big family salon, the *orsi* with its wide colored windows and elaborate plasterwork; the tiled summer basement sitting room was directly below, down some steps from the garden courtyard. Kaveh's family's apartment, bedrooms and a sitting room, ran along the middle wall; the grandparents' rooms were along the courtyard wall facing the *orsi*, with the unmarried uncles' rooms above. The kitchen, baths, and work-yard were in a third space further back, another degree of distance along the shared-out distributions of collective family life.

Pamenar was a house built for a patriarchal family: a family ordered around relations of kinship and loyalty centered on the rule and the

[7] Known as the "Abdol Ghaffar Map of 1891," the map was drafted by Soleyman Khan Sartip under the supervision of Abdol Ghaffar Najm-ol-Molk, professor of mathematics and geometry at the Dar-ol-Fonum Polytechnic College. See Marefat, *Building to Power*, vol. 1, pp. 14–16, and Fig. 1/9 in vol. 2 (plates).

lineage of the father.[8] Patriarchy in its nineteenth-century Qajar spatial and historical context was not necessarily the arbitrary monopoly of power, but it was the dominant social model of political and familial organization. It was also a fairly loose structure of control, with competing sites of agency and surprisingly diverse possibilities for identity and relation: the Pamenar house was not a panopticon; the Qajar state had only a slack grip on security, territory, or population. Pamenar was a Qajar house, although it became the home of a non-aristocratic merchant family: classic members of a nascent bourgeoisie. Pamenar remained a patriarchal house, a bourgeois house, while Iran underwent an early twentieth-century Constitutional Revolution, and then the transition to a new dynasty under Reza Shah Pahlavi. Despite the challenges, the patriarchal state seemed to remain intact, and with it the patriarchal family. Reza Shah settled the tribes, built a railroad, and tried to unify the country under his lone authority. With the help of the Allied Powers, he was deposed and replaced by his son, a man of lesser stature both physically and politically. In 1953, again with outside help, a coup deposed the popularly elected government of Mohammad Mossadegh, and the patriarchal state – the model of the state in which the father rules (for) all and everyone knows their place – again seemed to remain intact, although perhaps cracked around the edges.

According to Aristotle, "The state is by nature prior to the family and to the individual, since the whole is of necessity prior to the part."[9] The origin of human social organization may be in the relations of primary reproduction, but a hegemonic social and political order requires more formal legitimation. Over the course of the twentieth century, the form of the patriarchal family and household did not last so well as the apparently stable structure of the patriarchal state. New relations of affiliation, new possibilities for individual achievement and loss, began to be more common. The couple began to replace lineage as the core relation of the family: a horizontal bond rather than a

8 The expansive house and the extended family construct each other. To the extent that space is understood to be composed of social relations (and thus of social and political powers), social relations themselves are always spatialized, that is, social relations occur within a specific space (and a specific time). Thus, both space and time shape social relations (and social powers), while social relations shape space (and the experience of time). See Doreen Massey, "Thinking Radical Democracy Spatially," *Environment and Planning D: Society and Space*, 13 (1995), 283–288.

9 Aristotle, *Aristotle, "Politics": A New Translation*, trans. C. D. C. Reeve (Indianapolis, IN: Hackett, 2017), Book I, chapter 2, paragraph 1253a, lines 19–20.

vertical one.[10] The question of citizenship – who is a citizen and what are his or her rights – became more and more contested. Extended family kinship exerts its own bonds of authority, but there can be strength, and discretion, in numbers. Within the model of the essentialized nuclear family, patriarchy no longer represents the potentially benevolent guardianship of collective, extended family; it just gets reduced to someone's petty dictatorship.

Over the past decades, classical patriarchy as a logic of social control, whether at the level of the family or the state, has been subjected to a relentless and quite justified political critique, in Iran and elsewhere. "Patriarchy" has come to represent a kind of shorthand for the arbitrary and exclusive deployment of social and political power, and even further, an archaic form of premodern social organization. But "patriarchy," like any other social logic, involves a more complex set of social experiences than its contemporary caricature (whether offered as critique or justification) would imply. To the extent that the representation of the patriarchal family unit emphasizes the hierarchical deployment of authority through masculine descent and affiliation, it is recognizably overbearing and all too often repressive. But family is always essentially a collectivity: it must involve more than a singular individual. Only in its mythologized origins or lonely finality can a family be reduced to one person who is all that remains of a collective experience, or a singular ancestor who is considered to be a family's founding progenitor. A family is fundamentally a set of relationships, whether defined by the bonds of lineage (shared origins over time), domesticity (shared household space), or affection (shared appeals to taste and experience). Not all of these aspects need be present to define a collective as a family, but at least one of them usually must be. And to the extent that the possibilities available for any one aspect of the relations of family – definitions of kinship; spaces of household organization; diversities of taste – change, the experience of the collectivity of family will also change.

[10] See Afsaneh Najmabadi, *Women with Mustaches and Men without Beards: Gender and Sexual Anxieties of Iranian Modernity* (Berkeley: University of California Press, 2005) for a discussion for the uneasy rise of partnership marriage, and Camron Amin, *The Making of the Modern Iranian Woman: Gender, State Policy, and Popular Culture, 1865–1946* (Gainesville: University Press of Florida, 2002) for a history of the symbolic modernization of women subjects under Reza Shah.

## Families and Their Spaces: Fathers and Sons

By the 1960s, Kaveh's was the only family with children in the Pamenar house, his father the only married son choosing to raise the next generation in the space of the extended family. By that time, successful middle-class families were moving north, following the fashion being set by the second Pahlavi Shah, now well ensconced as a modernizing absolutist, productively married to his third (but consecutive) wife, a decade and more after the 1953 coup. The Shah's ideological justification for benefiting from the quashing of Mossadegh's democratic government was that he was dragging Iran into modernity, and those of his subjects most enlightened or aspiring should hang onto his mantle on the magic carpet ride. In Tehran, the ride headed north, up to the new residential neighborhoods built among the former villages in the mountain piedmont. The low-rise, streamlined apartment buildings and single-family villas built in midtown in the 1930s under Reza Shah were becoming unfashionable; downtown courtyard houses, no matter how originally opulent, were becoming tenements. Pamenar was becoming a space of the past.[11]

Agha Ehsani was a middle son, not the expected inheritor of family authority, lineage, or home. But more than his siblings (four brothers, two sisters, and another who had died in childhood), he was the guardian of historical memory. An intellectual, a free thinker, a collector, an expert on the crafts of traditional handwork, a champion of the poetry duel of verse challenge and exchange (the last word of the recited couplet required to be the first word for the opponent's response, all the verses being the memorized poems of the national literary heritage; good players could keep the challenge going for hours and even days), and an intimate of the most radical writers of his day, he was a classic polymath and ardent secularist. But he was not necessarily a modernist.

[11] For multifaceted discussions of how changes in political, economic, and family organization are reflected in changing urban spatialities, see Morteza Mirgholami, "From Traditional *Mahallehs* to Modern Neighborhoods: The Case of Narmak, Tehran," *Comparative Studies of South Asia, Africa and the Middle East* 32(1) (2012), 214–237; Hamed Khosravi, Amir Djalali, and Francesco Marullo, eds., *Tehran: Life within Walls: A City, Its Territory, and the Forms of Dwelling* (Berlin: Hatje Cantz Verlag Gmbh, 2017), and in particular the chapter "Dwelling: Contested Spaces: Toward New Frontiers for the City," Hamed Khosravi, 105–143.

In the second half of the twentieth century, choosing to raise his family in Pamenar was an unfashionable, almost a quixotic choice. It was not nostalgia, certainly not tradition: it was shaped by a dedication to keep alive the spatial experiences that make a cultural inheritance. Realizing that space provides us with the possibility of the experiences that make our identity, he chose to raise his own children within the multifaceted possibilities of classic Iranian architecture. Pamenar represented a built lineage rather than one that was born, a way of being in the world that was less about the hierarchy of a fragmenting patriarchal authority than the tangible multiplicity of a lived identity rooted in material culture. For Kaveh's father, raising children in Pamenar meant continuity with a cultural patrimony that was already being lost. There is a tape of Kaveh and his paternal grandfather reciting the memorized verses of the *Shahnameh* together during afternoon naptime in the *orsi*, the old man and the little boy reenacting the practice of poetry as a familiar oral tradition. Then the grandfather died. And Pamenar had to be sold.

The other uncles had married and moved away, and Pamenar wasn't a house for a nuclear family. It was a house that literally needed to be inhabited by many people: the building required the chronic, careful attention of the handful of domestic workers who had also lived in the house and tended to its needs and were themselves tended in turn when they became infirm. The mid twentieth-century professional middle classes weren't interested in or capable of maintaining the network of personal responsibilities and mutual obligations that accompanied classically patriarchal structures, whether a house or a family. Plus, inheritance laws meant the value of the property had to be split among the inheritors; if one child inherited, the others had to be bought out. This is the classic problem of non-primogeniture inheritance: all children benefit, but the domain of the family is fragmented and must be reconstituted at each generation. There were efforts to have the house dedicated as a historical monument, bought by the municipality as a museum.[12] But the 1960s weren't much of an era for historical preservation, in Iran or elsewhere, and most of the family wanted to sell. Pamenar the house became a workshop, a warehouse, a ruin, a lost space of historical memory. Pamenar the neighborhood became more

12 Najafi's *Ettela'at* newspaper story (Mordad 27, 1352/August 18, 1973) bemoaned the failure to preserve such an exceptional building.

uniformly working class, less central, and more rundown, a space of what had been left behind by the shiny goals of urban modernization's theory, practice, and identity.

Like other members of the modern middle class, Kaveh's father moved his family north, buying a modest house made of modern building materials – fired brick and reinforced cement – in the new residential neighborhood of Golhak, a mile or so north of the *hoseiniyeh* where Ali Shariati was giving his lectures on a newly engaged Islam to an overflowing, attentive audience. Kaveh's family did not attend the lectures. They were the wrong age (the parents too old and the children too young, compared to the youthful student audience), and the wrong cultural class (resolutely secular in their identification, uninterested in possible reforms to the ideology of Islamic identities), to be inspired by such goings-on.[13] The children grew, the house was expanded and renovated, and the garden tended with care. The persimmon tree grew to provide enormous crops of fruit; the white magnolia grew to provide exceptionally fragrant flowers. Ivy covered the garden walls; all the doors inside the house held panes of colored glass. The new house became a home, became a bit dilapidated, and became a space of possibility itself out of keeping with the relentless development of the city north, the move to smaller residential spaces and more spatial social exclusivity. The house became a touchstone remnant of the past, a space of possibility and being.

Then Agha Ehsani died. The pipes broke. The house was sold.

Like Pamenar, the house has become a space of memory.

## Rule of the Fathers: The Break with the Past

What does it mean to break with the past? So often, when Iranians were telling me about their family histories, they would proudly emphasize an abrupt break with tradition that was also inevitably a break with family, and especially a break with the father. Breaking with a traditional family structure meant breaking with the patriarch, and that usually meant leaving home. This break with the past was considered a sign of a new beginning, and a choice of freedom and

[13] For a more developed discussion of Shariati's influence, see Chapter 8, "Women, Life, Freedom: One Movement Out of Two Legacies".

modernity over outmoded forms of authority and tradition. It was expected to be applauded. It was often the fact of the break that was celebrated; the succeeding story was not always especially successful.

What is the compelling force of this historical model? Why the expectation that the past, in its social relations and material culture, must be – or can be – erased for the present to be made anew? Inevitably, the past then hangs on to haunt the present in another form; the return of the repressed indeed.[14] The Safavids, Zands, and Qajars all chose different capital cities, preferring to build a new geographical power center rather than appropriate the symbols of the previous regime. When the Qajar dynasty gained power in Iran, they set up their capital in Tehran. Almost one hundred years later, the new prince-ruler of Isfahan could find no better way of demonstrating his questionable loyalty to his elder brother, the Qajar shah ruling in Tehran, than by having the internal walls of the Safavid palace systematically defaced. Instead of painting over the frescoes or replastering the walls, workmen hacked at them with chisels to the height of a man's reach.[15] The destruction is still visible: the point being not so much to make room for the new, as to reject and humiliate the old; the claims of the present secured only by the obliteration of the past. A century later, the official vandalism presents itself as a puzzle: Why destroy your own patrimony? Is the rule of the father so all-encompassing, his role so overwhelming, that not even his death, and the destruction of his built material world, can free the living to make their own choices and rue their own mistakes?

Or is this the inevitable inheritance of patriarchy, a model of dealing with the past that can only change when the social relations of inheritance – inheritance of social identities and social spaces, not simply

[14] For a brilliant, extended consideration of how the repressed past haunts us in plain sight, see Avery Gordon, *Ghostly Matters: Haunting and the Sociological Imagination* (Minneapolis, MN: University of Minnesota Press, 2008).

[15] This was a doubled familial rivalry: internal within the unsteady rule of the Qajar princes, and external between the Qajar dynasty and the taunting historical memory and material evidence of the Safavids' dynastic glory; the younger Qajar brother appointed in Isfahan having to appease the elder ruling in Tehran that he would not try to mount a separate challenge to power, from the Safavid's previous center of power. For an internal account of familial structure and rivalries within the Qajar court, see Soltan Ahmad Mirza Azod al-Dowleh, ed. and trans. Manoutchehr M. Eskandari-Qajar, *Life at the Court of the Early Qajar Shahs* (Washington, DC: Mage Publishers, 2014), translated from the Persian original *Tarikh-e Azodi of Soltan Ahmad Mirza Azod al-Dowleh*.

loot – have themselves been changed? Agha Ehsani treasured the built world of the past because he was not bound by it: the patriarchal model already broken; the patriarchal household already dispersed. Kaveh's parents chose each other; his mother was college educated and worked as a teacher all her life, both before and after her marriage and the birth of her children. Theirs were the social relations of a new freedom, with all the pains and loss that it implies. If they chose to live their early married life in the extended household of the patrilocal home, they were free to do so because almost nobody else around them did: it was unconventional, almost eccentric, and bohemian rather than traditional. In making such a choice in defiance of the familial, generational, and contemporary social trend, Kaveh's parents discovered the utter modernity of recuperating the charm of the half-forgotten past from its vintage remnants; in choosing the space of the past, they bequeathed to their children the foundation of the new.

Around the same time that Kaveh's family was deciding to leave Pamenar, Hannah Arendt considered the disintegrating modern relation between authority, religion, and tradition in her essay "What is Authority?" Arendt was certainly no modernist, but she was no traditionalist either. Thinking about the role of the past in the contemporary world, she had this to say:

> With the loss of tradition we have lost the thread which safely guided us through the vast realms of the past, but this thread was also the chain fettering each successive generation to a predetermined aspect of the past. It could be that only now will the past open up to us with unexpected freshness and tell us things that no one has yet had ears to hear. But it cannot be denied that without a securely anchored tradition – and the loss of this security occurred several hundred years ago – the whole dimension of the past has also been endangered. We are in danger of forgetting, and such an oblivion – quite apart from the contents themselves that could be lost – would mean that, humanly speaking, we would deprive ourselves of one dimension, the dimension of depth in human existence. For memory and depth are the same, or rather, depth cannot be reached by man except through remembrance.[16]

[16] Hannah Arendt, "What Is Authority?" in *Between Past and Future: Eight Exercises in Political Thought* (New York: Penguin Books, 1977), 91–141. A partial early version of the essay was first published in 1958 and the full version in the collection in 1961. Many of the same concerns and textual resources are incorporated within Arendt's discussion of the circular nature of revolution as both return and beginning, in *On Revolution* (New York: Penguin Books, 1965), first published in 1963.

To make the new is to found creation in the old. To lose the past is to find that the present is resting on a very shallow foundation.

We didn't want that break. The house was our tradition, a built space of lived memory, our link with the past, with the previous generations, and the foundation of our freedom too. Now it is sold. We are like everyone else, become flotsam and jetsam swept into the contemporary flow: commodities, persons, tides of history, political currents. Out of our depth. Unmoored, we have lost our bearings. Sink or swim.

# 6 *Democratic Intimacies: Jokes, Sex, and* Ta'arof

## Jokes

This is one of my favorite Iranian jokes.

*Three men are sitting around, discussing their home lives. The subject gets around to their wives, and the men start comparing stories of their expertise in the bedroom. The first man, from Isfahan, begins by describing how he has been able to keep the magic in his marriage:*

On Thursday evenings, after a week of work, I come home knowing I have a day off ahead of me. I make sure to stop off and buy my wife a little present; something special that will tickle her fancy. And I get some sweets. I come home, and I find my wife waiting for me. She takes my coat and brings me tea, we nibble the sweets, and slowly we make our way to the bedroom. I bring out the present, and as she begins to unwrap it, I slowly begin to unwrap her. As she unwraps her present, she becomes more and more excited; as I unwrap her, I become more and more excited. Soon we are both overcome by our excitement, and we fall on the bed. I prove to her that I am still the same man I was when we first married, and ... I drive her crazy!

*The other two men are suitably impressed. But they each have stories of their own, and the second man, the one from Shiraz, gives his own account:*

That's very nice, but I don't have to bribe my wife with presents. When I come home on Thursday evening, I just make sure I bring home an armful of flowers, whatever is in season and has the sweetest perfume. I go into the bedroom, and I scatter petals on the bed; I leave flowers on the pillows and put them around the room. Then I call my wife. When she enters the room, the heady perfume of flowers is overwhelming, and their colors and textures charm the eye. My wife swoons with pleasure, and I catch her and carry her to the bed. Murmuring a poem in her ear, I cover her with flowers and caresses, and ... I drive her crazy!

*Rivals in their seductive accomplishments, the first two men eye each other. The third man, who is a Turk, looks at them both. Then he tells his own story:*

You two are just wasting your time with all this folderol. I don't need any of this to impress my wife. When I come home on Thursday, I just go straight to my wife, grab her and bring her into the bedroom. I toss her on the bed, throw off my coat, and jump straight on her; sometimes I don't even take off my shoes! We do our business, no fuss, and then I get up and wipe myself off on the curtains. And ... I drive her crazy![1]

If you are not an Iranian, reading this, and especially if you are an American, this joke is crude, shocking, and absolutely problematic in all its aspects. It makes use of ethnic and regional stereotypes. It refers humorously to what all too closely resembles a form of marital rape. It relies on a heteronormative conception of masculine sexual dominance. It crosses all sorts of red lines of cultural propriety. And I find it hysterically funny.

What does it mean to cross this line? I kept wondering about including that joke in this book. What will readers think? It depends on which readers. The American will presumably be horrified. The Iranians will probably crack up. We are different audiences of readership on either side of a cultural threshold, invisible but fundamental.

I've had to ask myself: Why do I find this joke funny? Isn't this another example of (hetero)sexual humor among men, presuming a privileged male gaze on the situation, at the expense of any other gender perspective, whether within the narrative of the joke, of the narrator, or of the audience? Yet I understand the perspective of the Iranian joke as otherwise: if anything, it is the perspective of the wife exasperated by her clueless husband (a perspective that may well be shared by the Isfahani and Shirazi wives, whatever their husbands' smug assertions). The main point of the joke is the humiliation of the man who seems to have no idea how to behave with a woman, or even

[1] "Thursday night" is a common contemporary Iranian social code for established couples to have sex. It seems to refer more to the schedule of the workweek (Thursday night being the start to the one-day weekend, meaning no need to get up early the following day), than to any possible religious connotations (despite the common but unsubstantiated rumor that intercourse on a Thursday night is more blessed than otherwise). "Thursday night" has become a sort of Iranian equivalent to "date night," except staying home rather than going out, and with a clear sexual meaning.

inside the home (the curtains!). It also slyly sends up the caricature of orthodox romantic behavior that the other men's gestures represent. It is indeed based on caricatures of regional identity: the merchant/artisanal culture of Isfahan (with its associated miserliness and petty craftiness); the flowers, poetry, and "softness" associated with Shiraz (the city whose accent is supposed to be the "sweetest"); the inevitable comic role of the Turk (referring to a Turkish or Azeri speaker from the northwest Iranian province of Azerbaijan). "Turks" are a ubiquitous butt of the joke for Persian speakers, but there is a covert *ressentiment* here as well; the Turkish-speaking tribal dynasties of the Safavids and Qajars conquered and ruled all of Iran for most of the last five hundred years, from the beginning of the sixteenth into the early twentieth century. So the sophisticated Farsi-speaking urbanite's joke at the expense of the supposedly rural ("Turks" in jokes are never characterized as urbanites coming from the city of Tabriz) "Turkish" clueless bumpkin is also a late-arriving lowly commoner's vengeance against the courtly warrior's identity associated with the modern history of Iranian monarchy.

Iranian political humor tends to neglect the Safavids, who are still respected, and skip over the Pahlavis, who were not Turks; the high-point of low humor in Iranian satirical writing was aimed in the early twentieth century at public figures during the late period of the Qajar monarchy and the Constitutional Revolution.[2] But Reza Shah Pahlavi was born in Mazandaran, a north-central province on the Caspian Sea, and the dynasty is past but not gone, still too present to be easily

[2] There is a wonderfully rich if relatively small scholarship on Iranian political satire during the late nineteenth and early twentieth centuries, especially the period of the Constitutional Revolution and the early Pahlavi dynasty, and often but not only highlighting the scatological sexual invective of the reformist poet Iraj Mirza and the lexicographer and political satirist Ali Akbar Dehkhoda. See Hasan Javadi, *Satire in Persian Literature* (Rutherford: Fairleigh Dickinson University Press, 1988); Paul Sprachman, *Suppressed Persian: An Anthology of Forbidden Literature* (Costa Mesa, CA: Mazda Publishers, 1995); Ali Gheissari, "Despots of the World Unite! Satire in the Iranian Constitutional Press: The Majalleh-ye Estebdad, 1907–1908," *Comparative Studies of South Asia, Africa and the Middle East*, 25(2) (2005), 360–376; Homa Katouzian, "Private Parts and Public Discourses in Modern Iran," *Comparative Studies of South Asia, Africa and the Middle East*, 28(2) (2008), 283–290; and the extensive discussion in Janet Afary, *The Iranian Constitutional Revolution, 1906–1911: Grassroots Democracy, Social Democracy, and the Origins of Feminism* (New York: Columbia University Press, 1996).

humanized or trivialized. This isn't true of more recent political figures. As soon as a public figure, especially a powerful one, falls from grace in the public eye, a whole new panoply of jokes start to circulate about him; given the dynamics of Iranian public life, the subject is almost always a "him" rather than a "her," and he is often a cleric. If he redeems himself – distancing himself from an aura of corruption and reclaiming his integrity, both political and economic – the jokes mostly stop.[3]

I didn't always find Iranian humor funny, and it doesn't help that the humor often incorporates regional accents or characterizations that require a fairly sophisticated knowledge of both language and cultural nuance. Often enough, I have sat in a room with Iranians who quickly moved to establish and reestablish their social ties by circulating all the newest jokes. Even if I could follow most of the lead-up, I usually missed the point; humor is almost never literal. I didn't feel excluded by these exchanges, just ruefully aware of my own inadequate inclusion in a circle of mutual exchange. It took me quite a while to learn enough about Iranian contemporary culture, to be immersed in it long enough and deeply enough, to share the joke.

The ability to "get" the joke is always a sensitive line of cultural integration in any foreign cultural milieu, whether or not that involves national and linguistic boundaries. But perhaps the preconceptions about Iran provide for additional barriers. The journalist and writer Elaine Sciolino, who famously traveled on the same plane with Ayatollah Khomeini back to Iran from Paris in 1979, describes being offended in 1997 by the sexual jokes told by an Iranian cleric during an after-dinner gathering at a European conference. Sitting in the evening in a hotel garden, with Iranian musicians playing and after serious "theoretical and esoteric" conversation including at least one other European participant (the eminent and regionally experienced scholar Olivier Roy), the ayatollah announces he would like to tell a joke, and tells one about a Rashti finding another man under the marital bed (jokes about men from the city of Rasht, in the Caspian province just west of Mazandaran, almost always involve their being cuckolded, plus a squeaky accent). Sciolino is appalled. The ayatollah's assistant tells

[3] For an analysis of the political landscape of postrevolutionary cartoon satire in the Islamic republic, see Nikahang Kowsar, "Being Funny Is Not that Funny: Contemporary Editorial Cartooning in Iran," *Social Research*, 79(1) (Spring 2012), 117–144.

another sexual joke, and Sciolino tries to move the conversation back to serious topics, questioning the reason for state-mandated *hejab*. The ayatollah explains that since it is not forbidden for unrelated men and women to interact, or for a man to look at a woman, *hejab* helps keep inappropriate sexual thoughts at bay. His statements endorsing the mingling of unrelated men and women are themselves noteworthy. But to illustrate the relative propriety of such behaviors, he pretends to leer at Sciolino (thus demonstrating when such behavior is inappropriate), then returns to a normal gaze (while explaining the significance of the concept of the gaze), and then demonstrates the leer again. Sciolino decides she's had enough and leaves. Later she hears that another American, a "serious academic," had also joined the conversation and also been appalled. The cleric had recited poetry, including a rueful, explicitly bawdy poem about an old man sexually obsessed with a young girl; by the time the girl had grown old enough to be womanly, the old man had withered into impotence. The serious American academic wants to know why all the cleric's comments reflect an obsession with sex. "Because I do not have any of it," the ayatollah replies.[4]

Sciolino investigates the meaning of this incident of clerical impropriety, and her Iranian sources explain that Iranian clerics have a well-known reputation for humor, especially for dirty jokes, since so much of their formal training involves religious rules for the most intimate behaviors: excretions and bodily interactions of all kinds.[5] She understands that the cleric was sharing a "private" perspective with "outsiders"; for her, this glimpse of shared social intimacy is nonetheless difficult to comprehend within an assumed context of "serious," let alone "esoteric" theological authority and social modernity.[6]

I have always understood this anecdote as revealing a regrettable failure of mutual acknowledgment. Even after the cultural explanations, Sciolino doesn't seem to realize that by telling jokes and reciting bawdy poetry (Sciolino compares the poems to *The Canterbury Tales*),

[4] One wonders if by this stage, the after-dinner evening conversation had continued on into the early morning. See Elaine Sciolino, *Persian Mirrors: The Elusive Face of Iran* (New York: The Free Press, 2000), 204–206.

[5] In order to be recognized as a senior cleric, every ayatollah must write and publish a treatise on religiously accepted rules of behavior, including appropriate ablutions of all kinds. See, for instance, Ayatollah Sayyed Ruhollah Mousavi Khomeini, trans. J. Borujerdi, *A Clarification of Questions: An Unabridged Translation of Resaleh Towzih al-Masael* (Boulder, CO: Westview Press, 1984).

[6] Sciolino, *Persian Mirrors*, 206.

the Iranians may have been using humor as an invitation to an informal social sphere of inclusively shared camaraderie, rather than as a breaching of the appropriate (gender-specific) barriers surrounding a forbidden realm of the abject. Ironically, in this case it is the professional American woman who insists on the segregation of properly gendered social roles in a public gathering. Pity the poor Iranian cleric, who thought that they were all getting comfortable enough to start telling jokes and really get to know each other.

## Transgressions: Modernity and Its Repressions

Like the experience of home cooking, shared humor is a mark of intimacy.[7] It is also a boundary, and the boundary lines are not always where we expect them to be.[8] Even within the same national context, one side's humor is another side's utter seriousness, or absolute taboo. Some Iranians still tell stories of the funniest show broadcast on state television soon after the revolution: Ayatollah Gilani's program explaining the religiously proper response to unexpected human dilemmas. The program was completely in earnest, but many of the viewers seemed to have watched it for its comic potential (there were also rumors that Gilani was consistently drunk or high while presenting). Certain lessons from the program have become legend:

[7] Sciolino displays a similar lack of comprehension around the subject of food: trying to make friendly small talk (in the context of a public appearance and photo op), President Khatami asks Sciolino if her Persian language skills have improved and if she has learned to cook Persian food. Sciolino is offended, convinced Khatami has condescended to her as a woman. Later, it is explained to her that language and food are the most essential parts of Iranian cultural identity; she has misunderstood a friendly gesture of cultural inclusion for a rebuff. Sciolino, *Persian Mirrors*, 83–84.

[8] Outsiders may assume that sexual transgressions of orthodox expectations would provoke the most severe (or humorous) responses. But an earlier example demonstrates that blurring the boundaries between ecstatic religious mysticism and the homely pleasures of the table may be at least as unexpected, and therefore shocking and funny. Shah Ni'matullah, the fifteenth-century Sufi spiritual leader and religious poet, is revered for his mystical writing. His follower and fellow Sufi Bushaq At'imah parodied Ni'matullah's (and others') mystically yearning religious poems by rewriting them as hymns to delectable foods: sweet puddings (*shol-e zard*), boiled sheep's head (*kal-e pacheh*), and yogurt-meatball stew. See Nasrollah Pourjavady and Peter Lamborn Wilson, *Kings of Love: The Poetry and History of the Ni'matullahi Sufi Order* (Tehran: Imperial Iranian Academy of Philosophy, 1978), 80–86.

*Question: is it ever permissible for a Muslim man to father a child with his aunt?*
*Answer: if you are a Muslim man sleeping naked on the second floor, while your aunt is sleeping on the first floor, and if while you are asleep you have an erection, and if while you are asleep naked with the erection there is an earthquake, and if the earthquake causes the floor to collapse, dropping you in your bed naked with your erection down onto the floor below, and if you – still asleep and naked with your erection – are dropped out of your bed and onto your aunt in such a way that your penis enters her and she conceives and bears a child, then this is permissible.*

*Question: is it ever permissible to kill another person?*
*Answer: if you are sleeping face down on the bed, and if someone else sneaks up behind you with the intention to kill you with a poison pill, and if they intend to administer the poison pill by inserting a hollow reed into your anus and blowing the pill into your anal cavity, and if the person inserts the hollow reed with the pill into your anus and then puts it to their lips to blow the pill into you, but at that moment you fart, thus blowing the pill back up the reed and into the would-be killer, and if they then die, then killing them has been permissible.*[9]

This is the outer edge of humor: a common disbelief that the abjectly absurd has traded places with, and indeed has become, deadly serious. It was funny for so many of the immediately postrevolutionary viewing audience precisely because it was so foreign to their own social expectations, of themselves and of the jokester. Especially for the secularized members of the Iranian middle class who had become culturally accustomed to the Pahlavi monarchy's model of Westernization, having a cleric appear on television openly talking about the forbidden – whether sex or farting – was so unthinkable – the world turned upside down – that it became the signification of all the taboos that the Revolution had broken: the ultimate joke.

Freud claims that "tendentious" jokes "are able to release pleasure even from sources that have undergone repression." The tendentious joke is an insult modified into another form, so that the suppressed

[9] These are paraphrases of versions of the programs I have been told; I have never viewed the program myself. For another written account of Gilani's advice regarding fathering a child with your aunt, see Karim Sadjadpour, "The Ayatollah under the Bed(sheets)," *Foreign Policy*, 193 (May / June 2012), 74–80.

aggression finds its way through a permissible alternate route.[10] The joke is a discharge of the psychical energy otherwise bound up – cathected – with a focused object of inhibited desire, whether positive or negative.[11] Ayatollah Gilani, pontificating on state-television, regularly aired the most repressed topics of modern bourgeois propriety and did so from the position of the newly empowered theological class and state that the Pahlavi-era bourgeoisie regarded as backward and inherently puritanical.[12] Like Sciolino, they could not reconcile the open discussion of bodily transgressions with their own sense of a modern hierarchy of appropriate decorum, in which the Westernized perspective is assumed to be far more serious and liberated than any structurally traditional voice. But while Sciolino could leave the party when she disapproved of the conversation, the secular middle-class Iranians who were in Iran after the foundation of the new state couldn't so easily withdraw from a foreign cultural milieu. Instead, Ayatollah Gilani's television program became a subject of fascination, a momentary release in which a cleric's breaking of modern sexual taboos enabled the expression of the political tension that was otherwise personified by – and cathected onto – the new regime.

There are endless arguments as to the meaning of "modernity." There is modernity as a euphemism for the present, the here-and-now, and there is the long philosophical modernity of the historical period

[10] Sigmund Freud, trans. and ed. James Strachey, *Jokes and Their Relation to the Unconscious* (New York: W. W. Norton, 1960), 134–136. It must be pointed out that Freud's writing about jokes is almost entirely humorless and reduces the play of humor to a sadly desiccated analysis that is, in his own terms, entirely without "wit" (which he takes pains to separate from "intelligence, imagination, memory, etc."). See Freud, *Jokes and Their Relation to the Unconscious*, 140.

[11] Freud, *Jokes and Their Relation to the Unconscious*, 148–149.

[12] I am using "bourgeois" here as a cultural identification rather than a category of political economy. The proprieties of the modern bourgeoisie have been appropriated by the middle classes, even while the formal bourgeoisie (those who control the means of production) have often now achieved the behavioral standards of ostentatious self-presentation that were previously associated with aristocratic privilege. But the prevalence of norms of middle-class reticence over bodily functions, enabled by the provision of material infrastructure, is fairly recent. To realize how rudimentary were the sanitary provisions for much of urban England even through the mid twentieth century, see, "A Study Made in 1939–1942 with Certain Recommendations by the Hygiene Committee of the Women's Group on Public Welfare (in association with the National Council of Social Services)," *Our Towns: A Close-Up* (London: Oxford University Press, 1945).

beginning perhaps in the sixteenth century, and leading up to but only possibly including the immediacy of the contemporary. There is modernity as a stylistic or conceptual reference to a speeded-up, clean-lined breaking with the inherited techniques of the past, whether artisanal or intellectual. And there is modernity as identity and ideology: a "we" who are modern, and others who are not: being modern has been a smoothly given identity for some communities since the term became a positive attribute; for others, it has been an endlessly delayed goal and possibility.[13] From about the nineteenth century, being modern has been presumed to be equivalent to being "Western," at least when Western is assumed as a stylistic, rather than a geographic, identity; there are long-standing communities within the Western metropole that are still considered shamefully "backward" in their inadequate modernity (the Roma are probably the exemplars of this problematic of identity), while there are fractions of communities dispersed around the globe that are recognizably "Western(ized)" and therefore modern.

What is a modern identity? Philosophical categories aside, the social conventions of modern identity are based on a particular stylistics of learned bodily practices, more bourgeois than aristocratic: a discretion of bodily management and corporeal necessity, whether alone or with others. This discretion extends to the spoken: ribald exuberance has no easy place here, the pleasures of such open joking relegated to beloved but archaic literary classics, children's delight in questionable puns, and the quarantine of the stand-up routine and the comedy club. Reserve has to be learned and maintained. Gilani's television

[13] Modernity also solidifies the cultural opposition between "Western" European identity and Eastern "Oriental" identity in a different form from the sectarian oppositions of the earlier Crusades. When Jean Chardin (1643–1713) was traveling in Iran in the middle and late seventeenth century, the modern divide between an "us" and a "them" was not as geographically fixed. Chardin found the culture of courtly absolutism in Safavid Isfahan to be fundamentally comparable to the Paris cultural milieu of Louis XIV, despite all the details of customary difference he chronicles so minutely (including forms of seating, dress, cooking, present-giving, etc.). Even alcohol was not an obstacle. Wine was common in the Safavid court, and Chardin was impressed by the cultivation of his Muslim hosts. He was more shocked by the uncouth behavior associated with visiting Russians, who were still tainted by a notorious story of a previous second ambassador who, at a banquet given by the Shah, got so drunk that he threw up into his hat, which he then obliviously set upon his head, disgracing himself while amusing the entire company. See Sir Jean Chardin, *Travels in Persia, 1673–1677* (New York: Dover Publications, 1988), 88–89.

statements were not intended to be funny, but they broke through the modern conventions of private bodily propriety while utilizing the utterly modern and public medium of television, and they dislocated expectations. Breaking taboos of sexual discussion is one of the conventions of modernity; speaking seriously about farting is not (unless within a modern medical discourse, when exception may be made). Gilani's scandalous expositions were met with disbelief and then dismissed as a joke; the alternative would have been to acknowledge that the conventional proprieties of modern identity were themselves being challenged with a competitive set of stylistics and practices, even if no one really took Gilani's particularly idiosyncratic public version very seriously.

## Toilets

Like all major revolutions, the Iranian Revolution posited a new ethics of the individual body, as well as the body politic. After the Revolution, the governing bodies of the Islamic Republic zealously set about changing the toilets: public "facilities" were changed from the "foreign" seated style ("*toilet farangi*") to the squatting style of "Islamic" toilets. This was a question of moral as well as physical hygiene; what is "clean" and what is "dirty" are not arbitrary distinctions but classifications integrated within a cultural structure of judgments and practices. But it was not a sanitation issue: it was automatically assumed that all styles were flush toilets with available running water. At stake was the proprietary management of the modern body (the body that uses and expects to use flush toilets), and with it the claim over the right to modern identity.[14]

[14] The prevalence of modern "Western" (seated) flush toilets has its own tortuous history. See Lawrence Wright, *Clean & Decent: The Fascinating History of the Bathroom and the Water-Closet* (London: Penguin Books, 1960); Maureen Ogle, *All the Modern Conveniences: American Household Plumbing, 1840–1890* (Baltimore: Johns Hopkins University Press, 1996). Although not usually addressed in property-rights scholarship, the intimate relation between a privileged modern identity and access to designated toilet facilities is codified in legal inheritance and rights of access. See the discussion of how favored working-class individuals could be granted (as a willed bequest) legal right of access to "the necessary" (usually an outhouse), in Carolyn Steedman, *Labours Lost: Domestic Service and the Making of Modern England* (Cambridge: Cambridge University Press, 2009), 99–104.

Cleanliness as an aspect of propriety is always culturally defined, but contemporary modernity has become a contest of alternative claims, with their accompanying logics of bodily practice and implicit regimes of power.[15] The great cultural divide in toilet habits, as opposed to the public health issue of access to sanitary facilities, may be between water and paper, washing and wiping.[16] Those who wash themselves use water and their hand; a cleaner result that includes direct contact. Those who wipe themselves use paper and thus can avoid getting their hand dirty, but perhaps do not achieve a "squeaky clean" result.[17] Each technique requires training; ordinarily this is done at such an early age that there is no question of a child who is not yet toilet trained claiming an autonomous identity. Proper training involves the ability to manage the intimate physical realities of personal hygiene (itself a phrase that is often a euphemism for menstruation) so well that they do not need to be spoken of: the discrete silence over bodily functions of modern bourgeois identity.[18] A friend's mother used to spend the

15 The distinction between toilet habits (washing vs. wiping) is in Iran tied to distinctions between religious or secular cultural identification, and the distinctions of practice that thereby define, separate, and distinguish so many aspects of daily life, from the most private behavior in the bathroom to public political affiliations. In daily life, these differences of habituated practice, and the cultural assumptions that are embodied in them, create a self-separation between groups that is often considered to be, and therefore essentially is, almost unbridgeable. The separation is not really about faith or politics. It is more a matter of competing networks of ideas, conventions, and relationships, laid over with moral justification; a lack of hegemony over what are the dominant national forms of social, cultural, and symbolic capital, and therefore an ongoing competition over legitimate social power.

16 The extent to which civilizational identity is bound up with proper hygiene (however that is understood) is exemplified by a hapless early nineteenth-century Mughal official who asked, in reference to the economic and political domination of the East India Company, "What honor is left to us when we have to take orders from a handful of traders who have not yet learned to wash their bottoms?" See William Dalrymple, "Lessons for Capitalism from the East India Company," *The Financial Times*, August 29, 2019.

17 One of the religious demands for ablutions after passing one's bowels is that the area must be washed until it "squeaks like glass" (Iran, private conversation). For a discussion of the initiation of sanitary regulations (public health and hygiene regulations, particularly as part of efforts to limit cholera epidemics) in Iran, see Amir Arsalan Afkhami, "Defending the Guarded Domain: Epidemics and the Emergence of an International Sanitary Policy in Iran," *Comparative Studies of South Asia, Africa and the Middle East*, 19(1) (1999), 122–136.

18 This silence over the organization of practices is so complete, even within the genre of the intimate memoir, that the exception can be startlingly original and

duration of her menstrual period in the family *hōz* (the shallow pool that contains enough water to make it Islamically clean and therefore purifying) in order to minimize her own experience of religious pollution. My own initial practical efforts to manage clothes, hands, and the spraying water from the flexible water hose that is now built in next to an Islamic toilet, were not well done. A cultural shift in the proprieties of cleanliness involves a dislocation of the physical maintenance of modern identity; if you don't know how to clean yourself properly (without splashing about or otherwise making a mess), then how can you make political claims or otherwise contest those in a position of guardianship or authority?

## From Freud to Foucault: "We 'Other Victorians'"

Both humor and hygiene are so profoundly intimate and culturally specific that it is often easier to ignore or reject the immediate challenge they present to anyone who goes into the field, wherever it may be. Not so sex, which is one of the most reliably excavated forbidden realms of modern preoccupation. Michel Foucault's writing on *The History of Sexuality* should have taught us that while sex in and of itself may be endlessly banal (at least as a subject of scholarship), sexuality as a set of embodied social practices can provide a sharply defined analytical lens

almost revolutionary in its implications. Sandor Márai begins his early twentieth-century memoir of growing up properly bourgeois in late nineteenth-century Austria-Hungary, by querying the social contradictions produced when physically mingling bodies are expected to observe a carefully ordered hierarchical spatial segregation. Within the family apartment, the intimate realities of respectable bourgeois moral and physical hygiene must be established, but the servants are not allowed to use the bathroom: the "modern" character of the building is most explicit in its provision of toilets in the service stairwell for the domestic servants (who hesitate to use them; their bodily requirements remaining mysterious). Within the structure of the apartment building, the wealth and status of each family are manifested spatially according to the location of their apartment, from the high bourgeois families in the front-middle floors to the messy domestic lives of the poor Jewish family living on the ground floor in the back; the neighbors all observe friendly relations, except with the very rich and cultivated Jewish family living in a front apartment, whose wealth and status are considered somewhat unseemly by all. Within the extended family, the neighborhood, and beyond, the contradictions of class, nation, and state are embedded in every intimate encounter. See Sándor Márai, trans. Georges Kassai and Zéno Bianu *Les Confessions d'un bourgeois* (Paris: Albin Michel, 1993), originally published in Hungarian in 1934.

into a constellation of other relations of social power.[19] But one of the less remarked lessons from Foucault's multivolume historical series is that when we are most celebrating our modern freedom from dogma and restriction, we are most bound by our own determined fascinations.

The scopophilia of Western researchers regarding the fact that post-revolutionary Iranians have a sex life can be quite remarkable, even if the sex itself is not, except insofar as it contradicts an assumption that the Islamic Republic is entirely a place of puritanical repression. There is some truly excellent work being published on modern and contemporary Iranian society.[20] There is also much that is eyebrow raising in

19 It may be true that most readers only read volume one, itself published in its English language version as *The History of Sexuality, Volume 1: An Introduction*, and thus never actually encounter the carefully detailed analyses of how changing understandings and practices of sexuality are differently integrated within specific social, political, and cultural contexts. See Michel Foucault, trans. Robert Hurley, *The History of Sexuality, Volume1: An Introduction* (New York: Random House, 1978), subtitled in French as "*la volonté de savoir*" ("the will to knowledge") (Gallimard, 1976). The series was projected to include multiple volumes of focused historical study. The two further volumes published before Foucault's death, and both translated by Robert Hurley, are *The Use of Pleasure* (New York: Random House, 1985, originally published by Gallimard, 1984) and *The Care of the Self* (New York: Random House, 1986, originally published by Gallimard, 1984). A fourth volume dealing with early Christianity was unfinished at the time of Foucault's death and later published as *Confessions of the Flesh*, ed. Eric Gros, trans. Robert Hurley (New York: Pantheon, 2021, originally published by Gallimard, 2018).

20 Among well-known recent studies of Iranian sexual mores, historians have been relatively better able to maintain some critical distance. Afsaneh Najmabadi's provocatively titled *Women with Mustaches and Men without Beards: Gender and Sexual Anxieties of Iranian Modernity* (Berkeley: University of California Press, 2005) focused on the late nineteenth- to early twentieth-century shift from a model of masculine sexual dominance (a model with less emphasis on who was being f***ed, than on who was doing the f***ing) to a heteronormative sexuality that accompanied other forms of social and political modernization, including increasingly egalitarian private and public roles for women. Najmabadi celebrates the homo-social eroticism of early modern Iranian men, but she neglects to inquire into the rigidly structured hierarchy of roles intrinsic to it (a hierarchy very similar to the one Foucault analyzes, between the Greek male lover and his male beloved, in volume two of *The History of Sexuality: The Use of Pleasure*). Najmabadi may not thoroughly investigate the hierarchical power relations that were invested in traditional Persian same-sex masculine sexuality, but her very original work opened up new possibilities for considering the modern genealogy of contemporary Iranian gender relations. Janet Afary's *Sexual Politics in Modern Iran* (New York: Cambridge University Press, 2009) has provided a comprehensive and nuanced evaluation of changing social and sexual gender relations in nineteenth-century and early twentieth-century Iran,

its headlong enthusiasm for the new discovery of the most hidebound cliché.

In the first volume of *The History of Sexuality*, one of Foucault's main arguments was that especially when we are sure we are bravely transgressing the conventions of a repressive sexuality, we are

including a critical analysis of some of the problems of a hierarchically constituted masculine sexuality that Najmabadi overlooked. Afary also provides a briefer discussion (Afary, *Sexual Politics*, 134–140) of some of the satirical publications from the Constitutional period she discussed in more detail in *The Iranian Constitutional Revolution, 1906–1911*. Yet as Afary's discussion approaches the contemporary period, her analysis of mid twentieth-century Iranian state and society becomes more dependent on summarizing well-known published sources, while her presentation of sexual politics under the Islamic Republic tends to privilege Western conventions of social behavior. Afary's association of Western sexual practices or conventions with modern individualism, and Islamic or traditional practices with sexism, repression, and unsanitary risk, leads to some unfortunately familiar moralizations. An example is her treatment of *sigheh* (temporary marriage): she criticizes Islamic support for a practice she characterizes as akin to prostitution, and as promoting venereal disease (VD), while she advocates more open tolerance for Western-style dating as a form of appropriate experimental sexuality. This fairly arbitrary choice between styles of nonpermanent sexual relationships is a contemporary adaptation of the old-fashioned moral scapegoat that only prostitutes are a source of physical infection, and "nice girls" (or boys) can't give you VD. Other scholars analyzing postrevolutionary iterations of the Shi'ia tradition of temporary marriage (*sigheh*, or the Arabic *mut'a*) have been able to employ *sigheh* as a critical lens to productively explore the variety of power dynamics inherent in contemporary Iranian sexuality. Shahla Haeri's *Law of Desire: Temporary Marriage in Shi'i Iran* (Syracuse, NY: Syracuse University Press, 1989) provided a groundbreaking investigation of the practical reasons women might engage in temporary marriage, and the unequal power relations they have to negotiate within such marital relations, while Fatemeh Hosseini's *Whores or Wives: Discourses on Prostitution in Modern Iran, 1969–2006*, unpublished graduate paper (University of Maryland College Park, Middle East Studies Association Graduate Student Paper Award, 2009) further developed the analysis of modern Iranian attitudes toward sexuality and feminine sexual roles. As a scholar and a public intellectual, Fatemeh Sadeghi's "'Temporary Marriage' and the Economy of Pleasure" (available online through Tehran Bureau, www.pbs.org/wgbh/pages/frontline/tehranbureau/2010/03/temporary-marriage-and-the-economy-of-pleasure.html, or Iranian Progressives in Translation, www.iranianvoicesintranslation.blogspot.nl, originally published online in *Alborz*) provided a sharp intervention into ongoing policy debates and the available discourse on sexuality within Iran, while her ethnographic research into youth gender relations, "Negotiating with Modernity: Young Women and Sexuality in Iran," *Comparative Studies of South Asia, Africa and the Middle East*, 28(2) (2008), 250–259, explores the unexpectedly different access to resources for empowerment available to religiously or secularly identified young women as they negotiate modern heterosexualities.

probably reinscribing an underlying pattern of dominant social relations. It is easy to replicate the "Victorian" tendency to load sexuality with the weight of displaced social oppression, and many scholars of contemporary Iranian sexuality align the repressive sexual order entirely with the Islamic state. Thus, any sexual behavior pursued beyond the limits of state ideology can be revealed as essentially political and intrinsically liberationist. But the need to expose the forbidden realities of sex can be another way of reinscribing the power of other fundamental taboos. Foucault's argument is very clear: "In a specific type of discourse on sex, in a specific form of extortion of truth, appearing historically and in specific places ... what were the most immediate, the most local power relations at work?" When he asks this question, he has already explicitly distanced this conception of power relations from the "system of Law-and-Sovereign which has captivated political thought for such a long time." Instead, he emphasizes the pervasive participation in shifting, intersecting social relations of inequality:

> rather than referring all the infinitesimal violences that are exerted on sex, all the anxious gazes that are directed at it, and all the hiding places whose discovery is made into an impossible task, to the unique form of a great Power, we must immerse the expanding production of discourses on sex in the field of multiple and mobile power relations.[21]

Following Foucault, perhaps we should not be looking for the totalizing force of the state or a unitary religion to be shaping contemporary Iranian sexuality, but toward a more dispersed and rampant field of inequalities.[22]

21 Foucault, *History of Sexuality: Introduction*, 98.

22 An historical and continuing example of a fixation on Iranian sexuality as an indication of (im)morality rather than a facet of more complex social life is the authoritative insistence, from the nineteenth century into the twenty-first, that Iranian society was riddled with exceptionally high rates of VD, whether syphilis or HIV. Nineteenth- and early twentieth-century public health accounts assert incredibly high levels of syphilis among all sectors of the population, including rural communities and women and children. Almost no one acknowledged that such high levels of chronic but not necessarily critical infection – apparently a different strain of the syphilis virus – were observed and identified during the same period in Russian villages, where the uncommonly high levels of contagion were attributed primarily to nonsexual contact among family members, including the sharing of food and saliva between mothers and children under conditions of rudimentary sanitation. For a thorough overview of the general

Class is the truly illicit subject latent within many of the recent studies of contemporary Iranian youth culture, gender norms, and sexuality. For a very small percentage of the prerevolutionary population, Iran in the 1970s was indeed the paradise selectively memorialized in family stories and photographs; the combination of technocratically driven social modernization policies and expansionist economic development provided wonderful opportunities for those elites (including members of the relatively small secularly educated middle class) in a position to take advantage of them. These groups did lose tremendously during and after the Revolution, and many of them fled the turmoil and narrowed prospects of their home country; particularly for the most economically privileged sectors of the Pahlavi-era elite, the US provided a familiar social geography. In the recreated oases of Iranian-American diaspora landscapes, it can be easy to project all the repressed knowledge of class privilege back onto a version of Iran that is part lost illusion, part fearful dream.[23] This is

perception, see Willem Floor, "Venereal Disease in Iran (1855–2005): A Public Affair," *Comparative Studies of South Asia, Africa and the Middle East*, 26(2) (2006), 260–278. For an analysis that offers the possibility for a different interpretation of the evidence, see Laura Engelstein, "Morality and the Wooden Spoon: Russian Doctors View Syphilis, Social Class, and Sexual Behavior, 1890–1905," in Catherine Gallagher and Thomas Laqueur, eds., *The Making of the Modern Body: Sexuality and Society in the Nineteenth Century* (Berkeley: University of California Press, 1987), 169–208. Although Engelstein's work is not a discussion of conditions in Iran, the implications would seem to apply to Iran as well. More recently, Iran's relatively high regional rate of HIV infection in the early years of the twenty-first century was often decried by Iranians and outsiders alike. What was less noted was the reality, recognized by global medical researchers examining the comparative epidemiology and policies of countries in the MENA region, that Iran's rate was only relatively high because its public health statistics were relatively reliable, especially compared with most regional countries that were still denying any national HIV or AIDs problem existed. For debunking of these contemporary versions of the panic over venereal infections as an indicator of exceptional sexual and social contamination, see M. Karamouzian, M. Nasirian, A. Sedaghat, and A. A. Haghdoost, "HIV in Iran," *The Lancet*, 383 (March 22, 2014), 1040. The reality of Iran's relatively early and progressive public health responses to HIV and AIDs is also supported by the author's conversations with members of GNR-MENA, an international network of researchers sharing data on HIV transmission and policies in the MENA region, 2004–2008, and incidental observations of public health posters portraying HIV prevention practices in the Tehran Mehrabad Airport, December 2003.

23 There are a number of well-known postrevolutionary diaspora memoirs written by Iranian-American women whose personal experience of living, working, and

the external vision of Iran as a place of universal black chadors, puritanical mullahs, and grim, gray totalitarianism. It has very little to do with the kaleidoscopic realities, some violent and repressive, some exuberant and empowering, of contemporary Iranian state and society.[24] Prepared for a postrevolutionary culture dedicated to mourning and a cult of martyrs, visitors can be overwhelmed by the lively ordinariness of daily life, let alone the counter-top open baskets of individually wrapped condoms displayed in the bazaar.[25] For some, this initial shock prompts a deeper inquiry into the ongoing complexities of contemporary Iran.[26] Others have remained caught up in the thrill of revealing the unthinkable banal: that well-off young people in the Islamic Republic have been going shopping and having sex.[27]

leaving Iran shapes their presentation of an exotic and fraught experience. These include Sattareh Farman Farmanian (with Dora Munker), *Daughter of Persia: A Woman's Journey from her Father's Harem through the Islamic Revolution* (New York: Doubleday, 1992); Tara Bahrampour, *To See and See Again: A Life in Iran and America* (Berkeley: University of California Press, 1999); Roya Hakakian, *Journey from the Land of No: A Girlhood in Revolutionary Iran* (New York: Crown, 2004); Azadeh Moaveni's *Lipstick Jihad: A Memoir of Growing up Iranian in America and American in Iran* (New York: Public Affairs, 2005). A more diversified portrait that more explicitly addresses how exile and the experience of diaspora shape memory and present experience is Zohreh T. Sullivan, *Exiled Memories: Stories of Iranian Diaspora* (Philadelphia, PA: Temple University Press, 2001).

24 A very effective, sophisticated, and accessible riposte to the reduction of Iranian identity to the image of the black chador is presented in artist and journalist Haleh Anvari's online narrated slide lecture and performance, "Power of Cliché" (2006). The piece can be accessed through artist Haleh Anvari's Vimeo website www.vimeo.com/61602790.

25 Observed by the author on the counters of several pharmacy stalls in outer edges of the Tehran bazaar, March 2003.

26 Often written by women who had established professional authority as experts working between Iran and the US until political shifts in Iran shifts forced their withdrawal (often literally), these include Haleh Esfandiari, *My Prison, My Home: One Woman's Story of Captivity in Iran* (New York: Harper Collins, 2009), and Nazila Fathi, *The Lonely War: One Woman's Account of the Struggle for Modern Iran* (New York: Basic Books, 2014). In a class by itself is Azar Nafisi's widely read and quite problematic *Reading Lolita in Tehran: A Memoir in Books* (New York: Random House, 2003), a memoir by a scholar that presents a moving portrayal of a particular period on the cusp of change, as an ahistorical account of postrevolutionary conditions.

27 Shahram Khosravi's *Young and Defiant in Tehran* (Philadelphia: University of Pennsylvania Press, 2007) presents some fascinating material based on serious fieldwork, but the lack of engagement with the unequal class dynamics (and their implications for gender roles and relations) evident in the text leads to a

Pardis Mahdavi's *Passionate Uprisings: Iran's Sexual Revolution* is the exemplary case for this perspective, a resolute exposé of daring and danger that can best be read as (mostly) an unintentional comedy. The problems with the text are evident from the opening anecdote in the "Prologue." Arriving in Tehran in 2000, her "heart beating anxiously," Mahdavi's scarf blows off as she is making her way down the staircase from the plane. She lunges after it, dropping all her luggage on the stairs. The other passengers disapprove: one woman scolds her for pushing; a man cries, "What are you doing, sister?" and looks away. Mahdavi has nightmares about this experience, dreaming that she leaves the house naked and is chased by the morality police.[28] It doesn't seem to occur to her that in 2000 (in the midst of the reform period, and three years after President Khatami was first elected, as Mahdavi observes), her fellow passengers were probably less horrified that she was momentarily and accidentally without her scarf than that she was disrupting everyone's exit from the plane; those push-to-the-plane mobile stairways are quite steep and narrow, let alone if someone has dropped all their luggage in the middle and is trying to push through everyone ahead of them. Since many of the women passengers on international flights to Iran weren't even putting on a headscarf until the crew announced arrival in Iranian airspace, the disapproving man turning his gaze away from bad behavior after a long transatlantic flight may simply have been trying to ignore the overexcited American, let alone look after his own luggage and mind the awkward descent.

Mahdavi's anxious overreaction may be understandable for a young woman raised in the California Iranian diaspora and arriving in Iran for the first time, but she maintains this attitude of slightly hysterical adrenalin-in-the-face-of-danger fortitude throughout her entire time in Iran and her analysis of contemporary Iranian society. This leads to some curiously insistent interpretations. Later in her fieldwork experience, in the chapter titled "Caught!," Mahdavi and a friend are stopped by the *komite* during the summer of 2007 (a period when there was a more intensive crackdown on young people's lack of observation of Islamic dress). Driving in a car and noticing that

sense that an alternative title for the book could be "Paradise Lost: Gone Shopping." See my book review of that title in *Middle East Report* 245 (Winter 2007), 42–43.

28 Pardis Mahdavi, *Passionate Uprisings: Iran's Sexual Revolution* (Stanford, CA: Stanford University Press, 2009), 1–3.

the morality police are making checks, Mahdavi and her friend (who is wearing capri pants) become so frenzied at the prospect of the possible police stop that the friend swerves the car and almost drives into the roadway median; police then do pull them over. While the two young women breathlessly try to strategize with regard to their possible dress code infractions, the police are initially furious at the reckless driving. After a certain amount of negotiation (involving the kind of sincere protests of virtue and acknowledgments of regret that are more or less de rigueur anywhere if anyone has a hope of wriggling out of a police stop), they are let off with a warning.[29] Mahdavi presents this nearly comic set piece as evidence of the almost overwhelming repression against which her youthful informants bravely rebel. Like a bad reading of Foucault, she adamantly celebrates (some, mostly upper class) Iranian youth's escape from an Islamic form of Victorian repressive morality.

Throughout her earnest, exhaustive exploration of the Tehran party scene, Mahdavi is so fixated on the essential sexual repression of the postrevolutionary state that she equates illicit sex – premarital, extramarital, and nonmarital – with Iranian political liberation, achieved through the vanguard of the leisure habits of the upper middle class. But there is almost no analysis of any other aspect of their lives, or of how they do or don't combine their energetic sexual pursuits with the commitments of work, home, or family. Mahdavi's accounts of north Tehran sex parties (especially the one in the empty private swimming pool, which is remarkably similar to another party she describes in an empty private bathhouse) were locally notorious.[30] The working-class equivalent she describes seems to be milder versions: kids hanging out in open land, doing drugs rather than drinking alcohol, and making

29 Mahdavi, *Passionate Uprisings*, 209–212. Although any traffic stop in Iran can be intimidating because of the threat of more invasive questions and punishments for behavior (improper dress, heterosexual mingling, controlled substances, etc.), there is rarely the same level of deadly threat immediately present that minorities in the US face when pulled over by police.

30 There is some skepticism as to whether Mahdavis' accounts are quite reliable; one particular description of a young woman ripping off her clothes in a highly public protest that should be easy to document cannot be verified. See Nahid Siamdoust's book review of *Passionate Uprisings* in *International Journal of Middle East Studies*, 43 (2011), 155–158. Some in the north Tehran youth community even questioned whether Mahdavi's informants had always been sincere (meaning their friends told them they had made up the stories they told her). Author's conversations, Tehran, summer 2007.

out under the trees. It isn't clear how involved the sex is at this less elite party; Mahdavi stays by the bonfire and switches shoes with a poorer girl who "screeches" her appreciation of such upper-class largess.[31]

The supposed sexual revolution Mahdavi observes can also be regarded as a reactionary counterrevolution to the imposed Islamic egalitarianism of the Revolution. The 1979 Revolution and the post-revolutionary Islamic state opened up new opportunities for working-class youth, whether intentionally, through ideologically driven state policies intended to benefit the *mostazafin* (the "downtrodden," the more religious sectors of the working class regarded as the activist backbone of the Islamic Revolution), or unintentionally, through the policies that were intended to Islamicize society (like state-mandated *hejab*) that also made public space more accessible for religious or less Westernized women.[32] As new elites have claimed positions of political, economic, and social privilege, and as some segments of the old elites have been able to regroup their capital and reestablish their own positions of authority, the fractured hierarchies of social and economic dominance have reappeared in Iranian society.

The designer apparel and accessories, "nice" cars, and geographical stratifications valued by Mahdavi's research subjects reveal a class structure of sexual strategies: rich kids are "slumming" when they pick up or pursue a temporary sexual relationship with someone from (poorer) south Tehran; young women make themselves sexually available to young men whose equal or more elevated social position can

[31] See Mahdavi, *Passionate Uprisings*, 91–92 for the pool party, 181–182 for the bathhouse party, and 97–101 for the poor girl who shrieks because rich girls aren't usually as nice to her as Mahdavi. Mahdavi's own sexual behavior is never in doubt; although she spends much of her fieldwork attending petting parties and spending time with women friends while they try to pick up men, she always makes clear that her own sexuality is restrained; not for her the energetic promiscuity she so enthusiastically chronicles. Mahdavi's avowed sexual fastidiousness means her participant observations of the Iranian sexual revolution are never quite fully participant.

[32] Azam Khatam, "The Islamic Republic's Failed Quest for the Spotless City," *Middle East Report* 250 (Spring 2009), 44–49. For an individual example of how the Revolution and the postrevolutionary state enabled one woman to push back against the paternalist pressures of father and brothers in a working-class family, first in order to go into the streets to join the protests and later to become a respected professional, see Sullivan's chapter on historian Mohammad Tavakoli and his discussion of his sister in *Exiled Memories*, 129–130.

provide the classic form of feminine class advancement.[33] Mahdavi uncritically recounts her informants' attitudes, but doesn't explore them further, even when the opportunity presents itself. Attending another party, Mahdavi haplessly walks in on a couple having sex in a darkened bedroom; mortified, she leaves the party, which is raided an hour later. Most of the partygoers are released after spending a night in jail and paying a fine, but the sexually active couple are forced to get married. Worried, Mahdavi contacts the bride, a young woman from a south Tehran neighborhood who works as a manicurist in a north Tehran neighborhood (presumably for richer, north Teheran clients), who explains that "it's fine." The couple are married, but they'll try to have the marriage annulled; even if her "reputation will be ruined," she says she enjoyed the adventure and "it makes a great story."[34] Neither she nor Mahdavi dwell on the implications: that the forced marriage has actually given the young woman unanticipated leverage in what was otherwise a clearly temporary sexual relationship based on a specific scenario Mahdavi has elsewhere described: south Tehran girls available at north Tehran parties to have casual sex with north Tehran boys. Having suddenly managed to achieve the romantic feminine ideal of a marriage of social advancement (i.e., having snagged a richer husband), the bride may be better able to negotiate to her own advantage, even if that involves ending the marriage. At the least, she should be able to demand her *mehr*, the wife's financial settlement that is a requisite inclusion in any marriage contract. Her reputation may have been "ruined" by her having been exposed to having sex before marriage, but the financial settlement may be welcome. The groom will also have shamed himself and his family by being caught with and then married to a woman his class considers only appropriate for casual

[33] Mahdavi, *Passionate Uprisings*, 26–28, 69–70, 140–141, 163–164, and 197–198. For a sophisticated analysis of how class is involved with current Iranian ethnographic accounts, including an eloquent exposition of a working-class feminine experience of cross-class romantic entanglements (a long quote from a young south Tehran working-class woman who describes participating in the 2009 Green movement protests because it is the only chance to mingle with more upper-class youth without being the object of their disdain), see Zuzanna Olszewska, "Classy Kids and Down-at-Heel Intellectuals: Status Aspiration and Blind Spots in the Contemporary Ethnography of Iran," *Iranian Studies*, 46(6) (November 2013), 841–862.

[34] Mahdavi, *Passionate Uprisings*, 197–198.

pleasures; they may be even more eager than she to exit this unexpectedly formalized relationship.

Represented as an example of state repression, this "great story" may be a better insight into something else: how contemporary Iranian youth sexuality plays out the unacknowledged antagonisms of class tension and the narrow possibilities for social mobility. This is indeed revolution as the return of the repressed: the state's Islamic enforcers providing a vestigial counterbalance to the exploitation, gendered and classed, of the sexual freedom Mahdavi so heroically celebrates.[35]

## Stuck in the Door: Performing Equality

Contemporary Iranian sexual relations may all too often be a hierarchical struggle for social power, but going through a doorway can be a performance of mutual acknowledgment and egalitarianism. Of course, this can mean it can take a long time to get through the door. If sexuality, so often valorized as a private realm of individual freedom, is more likely a multiply enforced convention of rigidly structured inequalities, etiquette – that despised tradition of role-appropriate behaviors – can be a means of enacting new forms of equality through a plural dynamic of recognition.

*Ta'arof* is the Persian term for a somewhat ritualized exchange of politeness; many of the usual definitions emphasize compliments and courtesy carried to extremes.[36] *Ta'arof* is fundamental to Iranian social

[35] For an unusually sensitive analysis of how perceptions of class structure urban working-class youth's self-perception and self-presentation, see Manata Hashemi, *Coming of Age in Iran: Poverty and the Struggle for Dignity* (New York: Routledge, 2013).

[36] Many of the earlier (prerevolutionary) examinations of *ta'arof* emphasize hypocrisy and the problematics of cultural insincerity; more recent (postrevolutionary) studies tend to highlight the mutuality of relations. Since *ta'arof* is often identified as a "traditional" cultural practice that continues despite the revolution, there has been little attention to the extent to which postrevolutionary changes in social hierarchies have changed the practice of *ta'arof* itself. See Donald Wilber, "Language and Society: The Case of Iran," *Cross-Cultural Research*, 2(1) (1967), 22–30; William O. Beeman, "What Is (Iranian) National Character? A Sociolinguistic Approach," *Iranian Studies*, 9(1) (Winter, 1976), 22–48; Mary Catherine Bateson, "'This Figure of Tinsel': A Study of Themes of Hypocrisy and Pessimism in Iranian Culture," *Daedalus* 108(3) Hypocrisy, Illusion, and Evasion (Summer, 1979), 125–134; Sofia A. Koutlaki, "Offers and Expressions of Thanks as Face Enhancing Acts: tae'arof in Persian," *Journal of Pragmatics* 34 (2002), 1733–1756. Many of the

life, but most Iranians regard it with a certain disdain: an old-fashioned excess of nicety that doesn't sit well with modern notions of honest straight talk.[37] This contemporary disdain is actually a carryover from class-attitudes from before the Revolution: William Beeman's prerevolutionary study of national character mentions the deep (and characteristic) distrust by an urban "upper-class" Iranian for villagers, who might be courteous but couldn't be trusted to be "truthful." Beeman's friend also points out that "he felt he would be uncomfortable if he had to interact with villagers as an equal, if that were even possible."[38] What is particularly striking in Beeman's account is the level of stratification and antagonism within power relations: between the urban and the rural, between the foreign and the local, between the richer and the poorer, between fathers and sons (there is no mention of the presumed hierarchy between men and women). Beeman's work is both sympathetic and attentive to the nuance of cultural detail, but the hierarchies that structure the social behaviors he examines are taken to be so fixed and unchanging that he introduces his contemporary discussion of "Authority/Submission/Autonomy" with descriptive observations from 1892, 1949, and 1964. Within this Iranian social landscape, *ta'arof* was considered a "ritual courtesy" that was not practiced between "intimates" and barely ameliorated the stark power differences between class status and social positions. Beeman characterizes *ta'arof* as distinct from practices that indicate "genuine respect," or the requests made "absolutely and unequivocally" among intimate equals.[39] It is not quite clear who these equals might be. Within the prerevolutionary Iranian society that Beeman describes,

more recent studies of Iranian/Persian forms of courtesy are linguistic analyses, particularly in reference to Penelope Brown and Stephen Levinson, *Politeness: Some Universals in Language Usage* (Cambridge: Cambridge University Press, 1987).

37 Nazila Fathi, "Taarof" in *Open Democracy*, August 26, 2004. Fathi's essay is a variety of the continuation of journalistic (as opposed to scholarly or general interest) explanations that equate Iranians' cultural obligations for politeness with duplicity and underhandedness; these kinds of accounts often also reduce the foreign policy of the Islamic Republic to exercises in religiously sanctioned dissembling by conflating the Shi'ia permitted practice of *taqiyya* (permission to hide one's faith under conditions of repression) with chronic lying.

38 Beeman, "What Is (Iranian) National Character? A Sociolinguistic Approach," 27.

39 Beeman, "What Is (Iranian) National Character? A Sociolinguistic Approach," 36–37.

tense hierarchies of status cut through the family, the village, and the working group, and the courtesies of *ta'arof* may have been more intimately common than Beeman, or his friendly upper-class informant, knew to admit.[40]

Since the Revolution, both in Iran and in the Iranian diaspora, *ta'arof* seems to have become a more generalized practice: everybody *ta'arofs*, and especially among equals and intimates, *ta'arof* establishes the courteous individual as a self-respecting and respected Iranian. The etymology of *ta'arof* is an Arabic word meaning "mutual recognition," and that is fundamental to the social meaning of its current performance.[41] Contemporary accounts of *ta'arof*, whether online postings or published linguistic studies, all make clear that *ta'arof* has become a fundamental part of establishing Iranian-ness in a postrevolutionary world, whether in Iran or the diaspora.[42] Knowing how to *ta'arof* – how to demonstrate the mutual recognition of Iranian cultural identity and claim status through the overt demonstration of one's generosity and self-effacement – is more essential than language or belief. *Ta'arof* enables the social workings of the political body.[43] It is a mode of being, and its postrevolutionary significance is deeply political: in a postrevolutionary society in which old hierarchies of standing have been undermined or even reversed, *ta'arof* smooths out possible confrontations over status difference, and enables everyone to save face.

40 Zohreh Sullivan mentions "one of the younger Iranians" describing *ta'arof* as part of "a way of caring for others," and a distinctive part of diaspora Iranian culture and identity. Sullivan, *Exiled Memories*, 15–17.

41 Koutlaki, "Offers and Expressions of Thanks as Face Enhancing Acts," 1740.

42 One of the most accurately funny accounts of how to *ta'arof*, as a properly physical as well as linguistic display, is "Presenting our video about 'Tarof'!" (Leyla Shams, July 10, 2013) in the informal online educational series *Learn Persian with Chai and Conversation.*

43 As a social practice of exchange that is linguistic and performative rather than material, *ta'arof* nonetheless structures similar social effects that other studies have associated with the exchange of gifts or relations of debt. On the social significance of gift exchange, see Marcel Mauss, *The Gift: The Form and Reason for Exchange in Archaic Societies*, trans. W. D. Halls (New York: Routledge, 2002); on debt as a fundamental social relation, see David Graeber, *Debt: The First 5,000 Years* (Brooklyn: Melville House, 2011); for a study that combines aspects of gift and debt exchange, see Azam Torab, "Conditional Gifts for the Saints: 'Gift' and 'Commodity' as Gender Metaphors in Shi'a Ritual Practices in Iran," in *Women, Religion, and the Gift*, M. Joy, ed. (Sophia Studies in Cross-Cultural Philosophies of Traditions and Cultures), vol. 17 (New York: Springer, 2017), 139–157.

Since the Revolution, the fixed hierarchies of status and power have been eroded, and no one takes dominance for granted: Iranians may not all be equal, but no single position is hegemonic. Within an institutional context, there may be clear hierarchies of authority. But in social settings – and Iranian daily life is always socialized – *ta'arof* provides for the problem of equality. If we are all equal, who goes through the doorway first? If you and I *ta'arof*, then I will insist that you should go first, that I defer to your status and excellence compared to my humble self. You will similarly insist. And if I succeed, and you precede me through the doorway, then you may get to pass through first, but I have proven my superior ability to impose the subtle art of deference within the mutual game of Iranian cultural recognition and reciprocity. There is usually a similar ritualized exchange over paying for a meal, a snack, or a drink; Iranian men of equal status will physically engage each other (and resort to devious strategies like cornering the waitstaff) in order to gain the privilege of hosting the group. Like the North Pacific Native American custom of potlatch, the one who gives (a)way is the one who is then owed respect through a cycle of mutual exchange.[44] Everybody wins. But don't necessarily try this with non-Iranians; they will usually walk right past you through the door or happily let you pick up the check.[45]

44 Like potlatch, *ta'arof* works as a cohesive social system when it is based on mutual exchange over time; it can be exploited if one side only doesn't respect its mutuality. In contemporary Iran, the most evident failure of the *ta'arof* system is in the relations between nomadic Qashqa'i communities and touristic groups of expectant middle-class Persians who drive into tribal areas specifically in order to enjoy the abundant (free) benefits of tribal hospitality: food (freshly cooked meals to be served to guests and fresh ingredients like meat, yogurt, and herbs that can be carried away), exotic sleeping arrangements (in traditional tribal tents), and the liberty to indulge in bad behavior (guests often bring along alcohol, opium, or other prohibited substances that they consume in front of their hosts, expecting that they will neither be shared nor be censored). As with North American potlatch, ethnic outsiders who presume on the ritualized hospitality of the tribal group can justify their material exploitation of their hosts' remarkable generosity by denigrating it as a cultural relic, a folkloric practice they are entitled to experience by virtue of their civilizational/ethnic superiority. See Lois Beck and Julia Huang, "Manipulating Private Lives and Public Spaces in Qashqa'i Society in Iran," *Comparative Studies in South Asia, Africa and the Middle East*, 26(2) (2006), 303–325.

45 Some comparative language studies have focused on implications for the enormous cultural differences between Persian-language deployment of ritual courtesies and English-language briskness. See Zohreh Eslami-Rasekh, "Face-Keeping Strategies in Reaction to Complaints: English and Persian," *Journal of*

*Ta'arof* is so essential to the ritualized performance of postrevolutionary Iranian social life that it is practiced even between intimates who would seem to have clearly differential status positions. Even though everybody *ta'arofs*, there are still certain expectations of deference, especially to age, and to some extent to gender. If *ta'arof* as a performance of mutual recognition is too insistently demanded by those who nonetheless consistently expect to be accorded deference – and would in fact be offended if their offer to defer was accepted by the proposed "equal" – it can lead to the same kind of accusations of insincerity that were voiced by Beeman's prerevolutionary urban friend about the performed deference of the rural peasants. The impatience and annoyance that are often expressed by younger (especially diaspora) Iranians about the "hypocrisy" of *ta'arof* are often related to these situations, which are usually associated with the negotiation of social relations within the hierarchy of the (extended) family.

In Iran (as opposed to the diaspora), it may be no surprise that *ta'arof* is usefully employed to smooth over the inherent inequalities and tensions of an institution that fits awkwardly but necessarily within the postrevolutionary Iranian social context. A few generations ago, relations within the extended family might be intimate, but they would also be ordered according to clear hierarchies that privileged gender and age; the system of mutually evident obligation and responsibility that has been classed as the "patriarchal bargain."[46] *Ta'arof* would have been inappropriate if everyone already recognized who should proceed first through the door. But now that clarity of proper role and response has become blurred. In our family roles, are we intimates (who do not need to *ta'arof*) or equals (who do)? How should we perform the rituals of mutual recognition that can bind together dissonant autonomies? The practice of *ta'arof* within the family is a compromise between emotional immediacy and the distance that enables respect; a bridge over the possible distance between relations of affection and those of kinship. But the performance can become tiresome, like a joke repeated

*Asian Pacific Communication*, 14(1) (2004), 181–197; Biook Behnam and Niloufar Amizadeh, "A Comparative Study of the Compliments and Compliment Responses between English and Persian TV Interviews," *3L: Language, Linguistics, Literature (The Southeast Asian Journal of English Language Studies)*, 17(1) (2011), 65–78.

[46] See Deniz Kandiyoti, "Bargaining with Patriarchy," *Gender and Society*, 2(3) (September 1988), 274–290.

too often. The hypocrisy of *ta'arof* in the family – the *ta'arof* experience that young people (especially second-generation diaspora immigrants) so often object to – is the knowledge that the outcome is already fixed: we all know who proceeds first through the door. The offer might be made, but woe to the hasty or unsuspecting youthful relative who strides ahead; they will be guilty of a huge breech of etiquette. Iranians know this and therefore sometimes regard *ta'arof* within the family as a trap in plain sight, and therefore all the more annoying since it is so unlikely that anyone will fall into it.[47]

As a foreign woman first visiting Iran, I was initially not expected to negotiate the performance of deference, and the *arous farangi* could graciously accept proffered hospitality or walk through the door without creating much social disturbance. But there were definite expectations I had to learn, fast. Iranian hospitality to a foreign guest may be almost absolute, but it is socially dangerous to presume precedence over age. Early during my first visit to Iran, while paying a family call for the forty-day mourning ceremony of a distant relative, I started up the stairs in front of Kaveh's grandmother, thinking I would open the door for her. Kaveh's sister grabbed the back of my manteau and sharply yanked; I almost tumbled backward down the stairs. But Kati had actually saved me from myself: any incidental physical accident would have been preferable to the ignominy of such rudeness to the matriarch of the extended family. I hadn't even known to *ta'arof*; I simply hadn't yet recognized that I needed to learn a new vocabulary of practices as well as one of words. Some cultural trainings collide, and it can be hard to be courteous when the behavior seems inherently impolite according to a different set of cultural practices. I have always had difficulty announcing myself by saying "Salam" first when I enter a room of Iranians, especially if they are older and more dignified; blurting out a greeting before I have been acknowledged feels wrong, even though I know it is the locally proper thing to do. And I still have

[47] *Ta'arof* tends to be particularly resented by younger diaspora Iranians. But this may have more to do with the very limited communities in which they experience the practice, among immigrant gatherings of extended family and family friends. Among non-Iranian friends or Americanized Iranian peers, second-generation young people would not necessarily *ta'arof*. Therefore they rarely experience the practice of *ta'arof* among equals, but always the version in which the young person's experience is of required formal assertions of mutual deference that are in fact all predicated on the strictest forms of social hierarchy-those enforced by the family.

trouble letting older people get into the back seat of the car first, when that means making them have to scoot themselves across the seat, rather than getting in first and scooting over myself, so they can comfortably sit down by the open door.

In the family, *ta'arof* can seem to be a caricature of social relations that are performed as among equals but experienced and judged according to more fixed hierarchies. But in the wider political realm, *ta'arof* bridges the further distances of reciprocal recognition that present themselves to political equals, and provides a mutual engagement for the structures of friendship.[48] The Revolution abolished the semifeudal rankings of the Pahlavi Shah's modernism, and the Islamic Republic established Iranians as uneasy citizens. The political promise of equality may be always endlessly delayed; political equality being the continual struggle implicit in modern conceptions of citizenship. But in social terms, the Revolution provided radical possibilities for the disruption of traditional power relations: between the rural and the urban; between the provinces and the center; between the youth and the aged. The intimate social relations between women and men have been some of the most contested, and class and labor relations remain charged. But now we find ourselves all equal. Face to face, we hover and balk in the doorway, offer each other hospitality, both sincere and ritualized, and engage in a performance of mutual acknowledgment and respect. When I *ta'arof*, is my deference in respect to you, or is it an acknowledgment of my own self-respect? And when you *ta'arof* in return, are you sincere in respect to me? Is our practice one of mutual acknowledgment, or are you simply condescending?[49]

Maybe sincerity is overrated. According to Hannah Arendt, hypocrisy might be death to politics (since the hypocrite lies to himself as well

[48] This contemporary Iranian practice of friendship as a means of consolidating relations among social equals harkens back to much earlier but equivalent political practice of "friendship" among royal equals. See Mana Kia, "Indian Friends, Iranian Selves, Persianate Modern," *Comparative Studies of South Asia, Africa and the Middle East*, 36(3) (2016), 398–417.

[49] "Condescension" was considered the favor of acknowledgment graciously bestowed by one of superior status on an obvious inferior; it only achieved its negative connotation with the rise of a democratic social culture in which such fixed hierarchies of status were no longer uncontested. See the discussion of the term in Don Herzog, *Poisoning the Minds of the Lower Orders* (Princeton, NJ: Princeton University Press, 1998), especially the chapter on "The Politics of the Emotions," 202–243.

as the world), but the search for an essential inner authenticity is a path to authoritarian terror. We cannot ultimately know the truth of another; in the end, in a democracy, we must trust each other on our word and our deeds, and rely on the rich complexity of a shared world of appearance that has accumulated over time. Arendt prized Machiavelli because she understood him to recognize this version of a truth of presence and being as that which we perform and practice in common. "'Appear as you may wish to be', by which he meant: 'Never mind how you are, this is of no relevance in the world and in politics, where only appearances, not "true" being, count; if you can manage to appear to others as you would wish to be, that is all that can possibly be required by the judges of this world'."[50] The social world of our embodied representation, and performative appearance, is the stage on which we enact ourselves as citizens. Do I really mean it, if I insist you precede me through the door? Is my respect for you sincere, or is it *ta'arof*? And if I perform the ritual courtesies of *ta'arof* well enough, is there any difference? Perhaps there is, in my heart. But if our shared world of social practices is the expansive modern bridge between our apparent public persona and the depths of our own inner mysteries, then my proper performance of *ta'arof* should be all the truth of appearance you should need.

## Back to Jokes

I hear that young people in Iran don't *ta'arof* as much anymore; I don't know if it's true. But times change. Context effects how the body is used to make a statement, and context is changing all the time. During the period of political ferment around the Constitutional Revolution, one of the most common forms of published political satire was through extended scatological and sexual insults directed at public figures, often in rhyme, published openly in the press.[51] The blatant (contemporary) impropriety of these scurrilous diatribes, often written

[50] Hannah Arendt, *On Revolution* (New York: Penguin Books, 1965), 101.

[51] Chahryar Adle and Bernard Hourcade's *Téhéran capitale bicentenaire* (Teheran: Institut français de recherche en Iran, 1992) mentions the appearance of newspapers that were "nationalist, partisan and sensationalist, often bitter in tone" after the Constitutional Revolution of 1906, compared to previous newspapers that were "government sponsored, dull, and limited in scope" (p. 131).

by now highly respected champions of political liberty and national development, can come as a shock. They seem to be completely disrespectful. But what is public respect under conditions of absolutism? Whether because of the inadequacy of its authoritarian achievement, or the presence of its republican promise, published political satire in the Islamic Republic is not lewd in the style of the Constitutional Revolution. Postrevolutionary political satire appears in Iranian publications mostly in the form of graphic art and cartoons.[52] Verbal satire is circulated primarily through jokes.

Jokes go in and out of circulation: changes in political conditions shape humor as well as bodies. For years after the Revolution, the first thing many Iranians would do when they got together socially would be to exchange the latest of an endless supply of jokes (now the new equivalents are circulated online). Some of these were simply funny stories: jokes about losing a watermelon; jokes depending on a clever pun or mispronunciations; jokes about a husband finding a lover under the bed. But political jokes are of a different quality from the often ribald style of apolitical humor. They could be ruthless, but not through sexual humor. Contemporary Iranian political jokes only function within a general terrain of shared stakes. This means that those who set themselves emphatically beyond the law are not the subject of humor: jokes about former president Ahmadinejad only really began to circulate after he was out of power. It also means that the scurrilously personal political attacks of the Constitutional Revolution period, or Ayatollah Gilani's wild postrevolutionary expositions, are no longer respectable in contemporary Iran.

When postrevolutionary political humor has deployed sexuality, it has almost always done so in order to accommodate a conflict of

[52] Two of the best known and best loved are Kambiz Derambakhsh (1942–1921) and Ardeshir Mohassess (1938–2008). Derambakhsh lived and worked in Iran and published his work in Iranian and international newspapers; his witty line drawings were not overtly political but functioned as deeper internal commentaries on the gentle absurdities of life. See his 2016 interview with writer, translator, and editor Poupeh Missaghi, "Kambiz Derambakhsh, *Literary Series*" in New York-based online journal *Asymptote*. Mohassess' work was always elliptical but more political; he moved to New York in 1976 after receiving unwanted attention and warnings from the Shah's security services and remained there after the Revolution. But his work has been celebrated by a younger generation of Iranian artists; see *Ardeshir Mohassess: Art and Satire in Iran*, eds. Shirin Neshat and Nojoomi Nikzad (New York: Asia Society, 2008); reviewed by Katja Föllmer, *Iranian Studies*, 44(2) (March 1, 2011), 302–306.

agency (action) and desire (intention): the problem of democratic responsibility. This sexuality-as-politics tends to be rueful and self-reflexive, like the cleric's jokes and his comment to Sciolino's friend that his delight in sexual stories was directly related to the absence of his practice. Or like this story:

A boy's mother died, and his father decided to remarry. Considering what kind of stepmother he would like, the boy hoped she would be young, kind, and pretty, and indeed, his father found such a wife. But the boy was already almost a youth, and so when he looked at the lovely young woman living in his house, he began to have other thoughts about her. What if, after his mother, his father also died? Only he would be left alone, the man of the house, to care for the grieving widow. And his mind filled with fantasies of the possibility...

Time passed, and the father did die. The youth realized that his dreams were coming to fruition, and he looked at his stepmother with burning eyes. But the young widow had other ideas. She quickly married a new husband, the local butcher, big, hearty, and strong. The widow's needs were met on a regular basis, the evidence of which the orphan could follow from the other side of the wall. But the butcher was a man of appetite, and his tastes were varied. On nights when he was not busy with his bride, he took his pleasure from the youthful flesh of his hapless stepson. Lying face down under the heaving bulk of the panting butcher, the young man would think to himself, "Oh, what I thought would happen, and what it was I actually got!"

If there is some bitterness there, it is subsumed within a skeptical self-criticism that comes from hard-won political experience and maturity. This is a joke that acknowledges deeply political realities of power and expectation: sometimes just when you think you will do the f***ing, you are the one who gets f***ed. The insight is framed sexually, but the humor is directed at the self's own culpability. The point of the joke is not a denigration of same-sex experience or identity; the point is the rueful realization that phantasies of omnipotence and domination are the flip side of domination, and all too likely to end up with the would-be dominator being dominated. We might wish to be the lords of our domain, but we are all too unsteadily equal to regain absolutism, too self-reflexive not to recognize ourselves in abject musings. Despite the jokes and the fleeting fantasies, Iranian society has matured beyond the phantasy of an all-encompassing political savior or a scapegoat: we are all in the political game. But we can *ta'arof*! Please, be my guest: after you.

# 7 *Through the Looking Glass: Reflexive Cinema and Society in Postrevolutionary Iran*

PANAHI: Don't look at the camera, Mina.
MINA: I'm not acting anymore!
PANAHI: Cut.
(Mina rips the sling and bandage off her arm, pulls off her *maghneh*, Panahi enters the frame.)
PANAHI: Mina...
MINA: I want to get off!
PANAHI: What's the matter?
MINA: I'm not acting anymore!
(Mina finishes removing her school uniform)
PANAHI: Has somebody bothered you?
MINA: Open the door! Let me off!
DRIVER: What shall I do?
PANAHI: Stop the bus.
MINA: Open up!
PANAHI: Tell me what's wrong.
(Pause)
PANAHI: Won't you say?
MINA: No, I won't.
PANAHI: Let her get off.
(Mina exits the bus, walks over to a storefront, sits down, begins to take off her shoes.)

—*The Mirror* (Jafar Panahi, 1997)

This scene takes less than a minute, just about a third of the way into a ninety-five-minute feature film. Until that moment, Jafar Panahi's *The Mirror* has followed the trajectory of a standard Iranian children's film: a low-key story of an individual child's simple quest in ordinary surroundings. But between minute 38.53 and minute 39.52, the cinematic fourth wall breaks, and the film itself tracks off in a different direction in pursuit of Mina, its errant child protagonist. For the rest of the film, the filmmakers follow after their reluctant actress, who is no longer acting. Or is she? The original film sets out to tell a story of a little girl who has to make her way home on her own because her mother has failed to collect her from school. When Mina suddenly erupts in her temper tantrum, rips off her uniform, and refuses to continue acting, the film becomes the chronicle of her autonomous trip home. So it is the same film, except now Panahi himself and the film crew are also in the scene, and the main character is no longer following directions. Or is she? To what extent is the rest of the film simply a cleverly reflexive version of the first third? It is impossible to know. And that is the point.

When Mina looks straight into the camera and then begins to speak on-screen to the director rather than the audience, the film breaks with the most fundamental convention of cinematic realism: the invisible fourth wall that allows the audience to enjoy the illusion that the cinematic representation isn't artifice but is actually "real." We know that a movie is a highly artificial work of craft. But we are used to a cinematic style that allows us to lose ourselves in the fiction that appears before us; we are invisible and absent from the reality before us and therefore enabled to be fully present, without obligation, within its narrative frame. Rare is the film, in any national cinematic tradition, that dares to break with this realist convention; a nod and a wink from the actor to the audience is a clever aside, not a disruption of the form.[1] Bertolt Brecht may have advocated a politicized dramaturgy of "defamiliarization" to make the playgoer self-conscious of the theatrical

[1] In-joke references or asides may break the fourth wall, but they don't challenge its convention. One of the only commercial feature films that really seems to try to do this (with mixed results) is *Adaptation* (directed by Spike Jonze and written by Charlie Kaufman, 2002), the film about adapting Susan Orlean's nonfiction book *The Orchid Thief*. The entire film is explicitly about the difficulties of making a feature film of an "unfilmable" text. But the conclusion, in which the rambling story of the earnest screenwriter making a serious film is highjacked – in the plot and on-screen – by the alternative, popular shoot-em-up ending suggested by the supposed screenwriter's more commercially successful brother and alter ego, has often been mistaken as an unfortunate capitulation to popular expectations, rather than as an enactment of the protagonist's dilemma; the feature film's abrupt change of genre mirroring the screenwriter having given up the unfilmable project in favor of the compromised, but more popular, action ending. *American Fiction* (written and directed by Cord Jefferson, 2023) does something very similar, including the self-hijacking with an action ending. But the "unfilmable" text in the more recent film is the bleak impossibility of commercially representing US Black experience without reductive racialized exploitation; for better or worse, viewers and critics got the joke.

experience. Clement Greenberg celebrated the auto-critique of modernist painting and its narrowed autonomy from generalized inclusivities.[2] But self-conscious is not the same as self-reflexive, whether in the audience or the representation.[3]

After the 1979 Revolution, Iranian filmmakers faced practical and political barriers to developing films that would be acceptable to censors and audiences alike. In response to the combination of state support for the production of a new national cinematic form, and state constraints on the cinematic portrayal of daily life (including heterosexual intimacy and women's private dress), filmmakers developed a style of self-reflexive cinema that acknowledged the limits of representational naturalism and incorporated issues of audience response and directorial control directly into the cinematic project. In particular, Iranian reflexive filmmakers broke down the almost universal reliance on the cinematic "fourth wall" of modern realism: the representational and philosophical construct (articulated in the eighteenth century by Diderot) that the audience is viewing a self-contained "real" world rather than an artificial composition. Breaking through the fourth wall disrupted the representational autonomy of cinema and placed into question a number of other apparent distinctions: between the genres of documentary and feature films; between the viewer's role as passive observer or active participant; between the authority of the director and the quiescence of the actors.

## Cinema as Mirror for Society

In a contested postrevolutionary context, Iranian reflexive cinema became a parallel project of aesthetic representation and experimentation that reflected simultaneous struggles over social and cultural life, and political representation in more formal institutional spheres.[4]

2 Clement Greenberg, "Modernist Painting," *Art and Literature*, (4) (Spring 1965), 193–201.

3 My use of the term "reflexive cinema" is an effort to examine how a genre of Iranian postrevolutionary cinema came to embody the dynamic form of "discourse" (as opposed to "story") the film theorist Christian Metz discusses in "Story/Discourse: A Note on Two Kinds of Voyeurisms," *The Imaginary Signifier: Psychoanalysis and the Cinema* (Bloomington: Indiana University Press, 1975).

4 In his book on Iranian cinema, social anthropologist Michael Fischer identifies its role as a "vehicle of ethnography . . . a descriptive medium, of cultural patterns, of patterned social dynamics." See Michael M. J. Fischer, *Mute Dreams, Blind*

By often inserting themselves in the narrative and representational frame, Iranian directors making use of reflexive strategies focused their audience's attention on the arbitrary logic of cinematic narrative and authority, and on the contradictory parallels between on-screen and off-screen social relations. Reflexive films (including films about filmmaking, films that converge the autonomy of the realities on-screen and off, and films that force the audience to recognize their own complicity in the representational project) became themselves political positions in the ongoing national power struggle over democracy, representation, and citizenship. For nearly two decades during the 1980s and 1990s, Iranian cinema was the refractive lens through which postrevolutionary Iranian society could most clearly view itself, inside and outside Iran. Despite heavy-handed government censorship and immense filmmaking challenges, films provided the most exciting, dynamic, and creative forum to mirror the liveliness, contradictions, and originality of postrevolutionary Iranian experience. Iranians, inside and outside Iran, went to the movies to see themselves, realistically represented through a language of recognizable artifice a viewer sometimes had to know already, in order to understand.[5]

## Necessity Is the Mother of Invention

After the Revolution, Iranian cinema became a problematic and hugely symbolic national entity. Before the Revolution, films and film going were associated with the Westernized cultural atmosphere encouraged by the second Pahlavi shah. The default position of the religious establishment regarding cinema was condemnatory, and the burning of Cinema Rex in Abadan in 1978, causing the death of at least 400 people, was a key event in building popular momentum and

*Owls, and Dispersed Knowledges: Persian Poets in the Transnational Circuitry* (Durham, NC: Duke University Press, 2004), 231.

5 Polish filmmaker Agnieszka Holland mentions Soviet filmmakers developing a similar style of sophisticated coded metaphor: "censorship created 'intelligent directors who were using all the language of metaphors and symbols and stylistic figures that the audience could perfectly read'. Now, she says, directors have less intense life experiences and their audiences want simple story lines: 'Everything has to be straight and, on top of that, you have to put that it's [based on] a true story'." See Raphael Minder, "Lunch with Agnieszka Holland: 'It's Possible to Commit the Worst Crimes and Never Pay'," *Financial Times US*, October 14, 2023.

revolutionary participation.[6] But after the Revolution, even Khomeini (who had condemned cinema as decadent and a cause of moral and cultural corruption in his prerevolutionary writings) stated that

> We are not opposed to cinema, to radio, or to television ... The cinema is a modern invention that ought to be used for the sake of educating the people, but as you know, it was used instead to corrupt our youth. It is the misuse of cinema that we are opposed to, a misuse caused by the treacherous policies of our rulers.[7]

Thus emerged the postrevolutionary problem of how to develop a properly educative and Islamic national cinema for the citizens of the new Islamic Republic.

If the appropriate use of a new Iranian cinema – postrevolutionary, properly Islamic – was for the education of the people, there were two obvious genre possibilities: a nationalist cinema to educate and mobilize the population toward its own role of dedication, sacrifice, and achievement within the new Islamist state, and a children's cinema to educate the next generation of modern, postrevolutionary citizens. Initially, revolution, war, and the perfidy of the previous regime were

[6] The Cinema Rex tragedy has become an acknowledged national symbol of a contested revolution. At the time, the arson was assumed to be the work of the Shah's secret police (the SAVAK), because the theater was showing a politically critical film that had had difficulty passing the censors. It has since been definitively established that the fire was set by Islamist radicals seeking to provoke popular antagonism against the Pahlavi government.

[7] Quoted in Hamid Naficy, "Islamizing Film Culture in Iran: A Post-Khatami Update," in Richard Tapper, ed., *The New Iranian Cinema: Politics, Representation and Identity* (New York: I. B. Tauris, 2004), p. 29. Some say that Khomeini's change of heart regarding cinema was prompted at least in part by seeing Dariush Mehrjui's prerevolutionary film *The Cow* (1969), a work that is considered to have established a new national standard for both aesthetic sophistication and engaged social realism. Several earlier feature films, including Ebrahim Golestan's brilliant, convention-defying, and under-referenced *Brick and Mirror* (1965), are at least as innovative, and more so in terms of grappling with representations of urban experiences of gender and sexuality. But *The Cow* combined dramatic visual style with a story of one man's alienation in a village setting; an inverted rural idyll that could appeal to multiple versions of the national psyche. Khomeini was not alone in revising his attitude toward the possibilities of cultural production in the immediately postrevolutionary period. In *Iranian Cinema: A Political History* (New York: I. B. Tauris & Co., 2006), Hamid Reza-Sadr quotes a number of other contemporary political figures (as well as Mohsen Makhmalbaf) making similar statements about the need to develop a new Iranian Islamic cinema; see chapter 7, "The 1980s," 169–172.

the overwhelmingly obvious themes for an Iranian nationalist cinema, which would eventually consolidate itself around the genre of war films, mobilizing the mixed emotional legacy of the Iran–Iraq War through a cinema of "Sacred Defense."[8] But within the time frame of its immediate aftermath, any revolution tends to be too freshly potent and fragmentary an experience to function as a generically unifying symbol. Most of the Iranian feature films made shortly after the revolution are critically dismissed, and even decades later, films dealing with the experiences of the years of and immediately after the revolution have been controversial.[9] The overwhelming turmoil of those years, the enforced Islamization of society, and the Iran–Iraq War made it almost impossible for Iranian filmmakers to find a stable reference point from which to establish an acceptable and effective perspective for representing their society. Filling the gap were foreign films, including a large number of films from the Soviet Union and others with impeccable third-world revolutionary credentials that had been banned under the previous regime: Costa-Gavras' *Z* and *State of*

[8] There is almost a separate literature on the Iranian national defense cinema; a number of serious studies of modern and postrevolutionary Iranian cinema and filmmaking don't even mention it and skip completely over the contributions of some of its most impressive genre directors (Ebrahim Hatamikia, for instance), while some film scholars focus almost exclusively on the war films. There are some welcome exceptions to this tendency. Agnès Devictor has written sensitively and extensively on Iranian film and the cinema of sacred defense, although mostly in French; an example of her work available in English is "How Can Faith Be Filmed on the Battlefront and Experienced by TV Spectators?," in Pedram Khosronejad, ed., *Iranian Sacred Defense Cinema: Religion, Martyrdom and National Identity* (Canon Pyon: Sean Kingston Publishing, 2012), 161–173. Two other scholars who have written thoughtfully about the war films are Roxanne Varzi and Hamid Reza-Sadr. See Varzi, "A Ghost in the Machine: The Cinema of the Iranian Sacred Defense," in Tapper, *The New Iranian Cinema*, 154–166; Reza-Sadr, "Contemporary Iranian Cinema and Its Major Themes," in Rose Issa and Sheila Whitaker, eds., *Life and Art: The New Iranian Cinema* (London: National Film Theatre, The British Film Institute, 1999), 26–43; and Reza-Sadr, *Iranian Cinema*, especially "Blood and Battle: War Comes to Iran," 192–199.

[9] Tahmineh Milani's films are cases in point: *Two Women* (1999) and *The Hidden Half* (2001) were both controversial and risked being banned upon their release not so much because of their depiction of women's issues, as for their depiction of women's issues within the context of the social upheavals and political divisions of the revolution.

*Siege*, Guzman's *Battle of Chile*, Akkad's *Mohammad, Messenger of God*, and Pontecorvo's *Battle of Algiers*.[10]

*Battle of Algiers* (1966) was particularly popular; in 1981, it was being shown simultaneously in twelve theaters in Tehran and ten in the provinces.[11] The postrevolutionary popularity of this particular film – with its newsreel-like recreation of actual events from an earlier anti-colonial revolution, and some of the original revolutionary actors playing themselves – may be significant in regard to later developments in Iranian cinema. *Battle of Algiers* is usually considered to be unique: a combination of an emphatically political sensibility with a formally innovative challenge to standard conventions of cinematic narrative and representation. It looks "real," like a documentary, and nonactors recreate their own original actions: neorealism taken to the edge.[12] But it relies on a developed script, careful staging of scenes, professional actors in key roles, and the nonactors certainly can act. It is neither a straightforward documentary nor a conventional original feature film. Straddling the apparent distinction between reality and fiction, *Battle of Algiers* places into question the truth of representation in cinema and politics; a decade after the Iranian Revolution, Iranian cinema will begin to offer something very similar.

## Censorship and Creativity: "Children's" Films

In the mid-1980s, a whole genre of Iranian films developed that focused on child protagonists. Not exactly children's films, they were low-key neorealist feature films intended for both children and adults, in which children were the main characters, struggling with familiar issues of practical responsibility and social obligation within

[10] Most of these films fit the category of the "militant image" of cinema associated with the nationalist liberation struggles of the later twentieth century. Despite their impact on Iranian filmmakers, and the support of the Islamic Republic's government, Iran has not produced a similar cinema of the militant image. Instead, the ongoing contestation over national identity and politics has produced the reflexive cinema I discuss in this chapter. See Kodwo Eshun and Ros Gray, "The Militant Image: A Ciné-Geography," *Third Text*, 25(1) (2011), 1–12.

[11] Naficy, "Islamizing Film Culture in Iran," 31.

[12] For an insightful study of how the spaces of the film provided a further layer of recognition and realism to viewers who were familiar with the spatial and historical geography of the city, see Alan O'Leary, *The Battle of Algiers* (Milan: Mimesis International, 2019).

recognizably contemporary surroundings.[13] During that period, the restrictions surrounding the representation of women were particularly tight: the requirement to wear full *hejab* (headscarf and overcoat or *chador*)[14] at all times, including during indoor domestic scenes; no physical contact between adults of the opposite sex unless the actors themselves were close relations; disapproval of close-ups or lingering camera shots on adult women.[15] This censorship made any conventionally realistic representation of private life seemingly impossible: a scene of family life in which the women were all always dressed as though they were living among strangers (i.e., wearing the *hejab* that they would outside the home or in the presence of unrelated male guests) seemed too artificial to be "real."[16]

During a period in which Iranian cinema had not yet found reliable techniques to represent realistic social interactions within the confines of postrevolutionary censorship, children became the alter egos for audience members of all ages.[17] Given this situation, children became

[13] See Reza-Sadr, "Contemporary Iranian Cinema and Its Major Themes," 36–37, and in *Iranian Cinema*, 223–234.

[14] The term *hejab* has come to be accepted to mean a scarf or proper head-covering over a woman's hair, but it is intended to include all aspects of "modest decorum," including both dress and behavior. A *chador* is a typically Iranian form of traditional modest dress: a large drape of material that rests on the top of the head and falls down the back like a cloak; it is held closed under the chin (the edge of a *chador* can be pulled across to cover all or part of the face, but after the revolution even the most orthodox Iranian women usually leave their faces uncovered).

[15] Negar Mottahedeh points out that these restrictions work to produce a cinema that carries through the 1970s feminist critique of cinematic voyeurism as continually recreating the objectifying male gaze. See Negar Mottahedeh, "Iranian Cinema in the Twentieth Century: A Sensory History," *Iranian Studies*, 42(4) (2009), 529–548.

[16] This marked unreality is especially evident in some of the early efforts to portray serious women's concerns within Islamically approved private spaces. In Tahmineh Milani's *Legend of a Sigh* (1991), the audience is distracted from the problems of the heroine when she pops out of bed fully clothed. A few years later, filmmakers will finesse this apparent contradiction by making the practical decision to set scenes with women in public spaces where *hejab* would be normally expected, thus also confounding the Islamic Republic's official ideology that women belong in the private sphere.

[17] This was also the period when there were suddenly a lot more small children in Iran. The Iranian population growth rate had been slowly dropping before the Revolution and was 2.7 percent in 1977/1978. It spiked at 3.9 percent (one of the highest in the world) in 1986/1987, before falling back to 2.5 percent in 1991/1992, and 1.5 percent in 1996/1997 (Statistical Center of Iran). This is one of the most effective family planning reversals recorded in modern population

the stand-ins for representations of intimacy, or any personal emotion that would seem to transgress the standards of appropriately dignified postrevolutionary behavior. Children could embrace adults; as importantly, adults could embrace children, and children could provide the sympathetic focal point around which the rigors of contemporary society could be demonstrated. A child's vulnerability and confusion in the face of overwhelming events (whether recognizably tragic or humorously banal) was immediately engaging rather than contemptible; a child's stoicism or perseverance could be quietly heroic rather than merely expected.

Many of the children's films, and their filmmakers, were associated with the Center for Intellectual Development of Children and Adolescents, usually known simply as the *Kanun*.[18] The significance of this one organization in the development of an innovative and internationally recognized postrevolutionary Iranian cinema cannot be overemphasized.[19] A prerevolutionary institute that supported the making of both documentary and feature films for children, the Kanun's early films had been children's films in the usual sense: they were not expected to be crossover films appealing to adults. But the explicit Islamization of cinema, and most other aspects of Iranian public life and institutions, pushed many filmmakers, who might under other circumstances have produced more conventional mainstream feature films, to turn to children's films as a possible genre through which to produce properly "educational" films that were not overtly religiously didactic. After the Revolution, the Kanun provided an

policy. See Norma Claire Moruzzi and Fatemeh Sadeghi, "Out of the Frying Pan, into the Fire: Young Iranian Women Today," *Middle East Report* 241 (Winter 2006), 22–28, as well as discussion and notes in Chapter 4, "Food as a Social Relation."

18 The *Kanun-e Parvaresh-e Fakri Kodakan* is sometimes translated as the Center for the Intellectual Development of Children and Adolescents (CIDCA), sometimes as the Center for the Intellectual Development of Children and Young Adults (CIDCYA), and sometimes as the Institute for the Intellectual Development of Children and Young Adults (IIDCYA). Given the multiplicity of possible versions, it is commonly known as the Kanun, the first word of its Persian name, meaning Center.

19 Godfrey Cheshire identifies the combination of revolutionary isolation and the institutional support of the Kanun as the two crucial elements that preserved a "modernist-cinematic '60s/'70s" aesthetic in Iran during a period when the rest of the global film industry was "swept up in an increasingly globalised and video-dominated media climate." Godfrey Cheshire, *Projection* (London: Faber & Faber, 1998), quoted in Reza-Sadr, *Iranian Cinema*, 237.

apparently uncontroversial platform of support for the careers of a cohort of filmmakers whose more secular perspectives put them in a delicate political position, including both established prerevolutionary directors like Bahram Beyzaie (born 1938) and newer figures like Abbas Kiarostami (1940–2016), Jafar Panahi (born 1960), and Majid Majidi (born 1959).[20] And it continued to support children's films even when the genre had become a recognizable general audience category, and the films themselves were representing some of the more painful aspects of social inequality, discrimination, and exclusion.

The seeming ubiquity of the genre of Iranian children's films, both in Iran and internationally, lasted for about a decade, from Amir Naderi's *The Runner* (1985) to Majidi's *Children of Heaven* (1997). The films tend to share certain stylistic elements: a cinema of neorealism, with a loose plot structure following a series of small-scale ordinary life events linked by the trajectory of a child's simple goal, with children as the central characters who are all played by found or unknown child performers, interacting with a variety of social actors in public or semipublic spaces (streets, alleys, parks, shops, buses, etc.). Some of the most noteworthy examples of the genre include Bahram Beyzaie's *Bashu, the Little Stranger* (1986), Ebrahim Forouzesh's *The Key* (1987),[21] Abbas Kiarostami's *Where Is the Friend's House* (1987), Kiarostami's documentary *Homework* (1988), Jafar Panahi's *The White Balloon* (1995), and Majid Majidi's *Children of Heaven* (1997). With the exception of *Homework*, which, as a documentary, is more unexpected and unsettling in its portrayal of public surfaces and overlooked realities,[22] these films tended to be modest, lyrical

[20] A very different institution that nonetheless provided comparable early support for a dedicated cohort of politicized Islamist filmmakers was Ayat Film (see Naficy, "Islamizing Film Culture in Iran," 35–36).

[21] Kiarostami was also the writer for *The Key*.

[22] *Homework* is often taken to be a covert critique of the postrevolutionary imposition of militarized Islamic discipline within Iran's schools. But it is more noteworthy for what else it reveals: the playground insubordination of the children who don't pay much attention to the efforts to keep them in order; the terrified youngster who cries uncontrollably when he finds himself alone in the room with only adult men and the door closed, but who calms down if another child is allowed to join him. Gently questioned about his fears, he describes having to do "homework" in his room every evening, alone with his father, with the door closed, and no one else in the family allowed to enter. Remarkably, these scenes, central to the film, have generally been accepted as revealing a child's terror about schoolwork, rather than about the hidden abuses of family life.

stories of a child – mostly but not always a little boy – on a quietly familiar but imperative quest. *Where Is the Friend's House* is an especially popular and beloved film, a simple story of a little boy who realizes he has accidentally taken his friend's homework assignment and tries to find his friend's house in order to return it to him. The film, in which the big-eyed young hero has to find his way through the neighboring village as the shadows of evening close in, achieves a child's version of an Iranian rural gothic fable, mysteriously brooding and comforting at the same time.[23] These films helped establish international recognition for the elements of the "new" Iranian postrevolutionary cinema, whether in films for children or adults: slower paced, avoiding obvious violence or sexuality, character and event driven rather than relying on a complicated plot or theatricalized spectacle.

## The Pivot Point: *Bashu*

But the Kanun was also connected to the film that arguably set the stage for all the subsequent Iranian innovations in genre, narrative, and cinematography: Bahram Beyzaie's *Bashu, the Little Stranger*. *Bashu* is

[23] The title of the film is a reference to the poem *Address* by Sohrab Sepehri; even in this apparently simple children's film, Kiarostami was reaching for the kind of intertextuality that he would develop within a cinematic framework.

> *Address*
> (translation by Leili Adibfar)
>
> "Where is the friend's house?" At dawn, the rider asked.
> The sky grew still.
> The passerby offered the branch of light held between his lips
> to the darkness of the sands
> and pointed with his finger to a poplar tree and said:
> "Before the tree,
> there is a garden path that is greener than God's dream
> and in it, love is as blue as the feathers of truthfulness.
> You go on to the end of that path, which reaches behind adolescence,
> thus, you turn toward the flower of loneliness,
> two steps to the flower,
> you remain at the eternal fountain of earthly myths
> and a lucid fear will seize you.
> In the fluid intimacy of the space, you will hear a rustling:
> You see a child
> climbing a tall pine tree to take a birdling from the nest of light
> and you ask him
> where the friend's house is."

an extraordinary cinematic achievement masquerading as a deceptively simple rural story about a war orphan finding a second family. Fleeing the Iraqi bombardment of the arid Gulf coast city that kills his Arabic-speaking Iranian family in the chaotic opening scenes, a young boy stows away in the back of a truck and is transported from the far south to the far north of Iran, and into another landscape (lushly green), another language (Persian), and another world. There, war and revolution are present through absence: the father of the family where Bashu ends up is mysteriously away; the ghosts of Bashu's own lost family hover mysteriously near. For postrevolutionary Iranian cinema, *Bashu* is the linchpin film, the pivot that connects all the elements of the subsequent innovation and genre development.[24] It is at once a film about the war,[25] a film with a child protagonist, and film with a strong, central female character whose role addresses gender questions in both society and the family. (The close-up first shot of the veiled Soosan Taslimi rising from the field breaks a postrevolutionary gender taboo by re-centering the camera on the striking eyes of a handsome woman.)[26] The plot foregrounds Iran's ethnic, linguistic, and regional differences, and their national spatial distribution.[27] And it is formally innovative; while *Bashu* is mostly filmed in a realistic style, there are notable exceptions: the recurring fleeting image of the black-veiled woman (presumed to be Bashu's dead mother's spirit) in the

24 Shahla Mirbakhtyar argues that Amir Naderi's *The Runner* (1985) is the film that establishes a genre of Iranian feature films that utilize child protagonists to poetically explore issues of poverty, struggle, and redemption. I am arguing that *Bashu* is distinct in that it incorporates a broader range of social issues (including gender and regional/ethnic differences) along with significant formal experimentation in its representation. See Shahla Mirbakhtyar, *Iranian Cinema and the Islamic Revolution* (Jefferson, NC: McFarland & Co., 2006), 115–129.

25 In his 1999 essay (rather than his 2006 book), Reza-Sadr includes *Bashu* within his discussion of films dealing with wartime experiences, rather than within his discussion of children's films. He also includes Mohsen Makhmalbaf's *Marriage of the Blessed* (1989) and Masoud Kimia's *Snake's Fang* (1990) among these depictions of the war's effect on social experience, but not, for instance, Kianoush Ayari's *The Abadanis* (1993).

26 See Reza-Sadr, *Iranian Cinema*, 189–190; Naficy in Issa and Whitaker, *Life and Art*, 58-60.

27 It does so while acknowledging the unifying elements of national experience, including the state (through public education and national Persian-language schoolbooks) and the war (which effects everyone, from one end of the country to the other). See Negar Mottahedeh, *Displaced Allegories: Post-Revolutionary Iranian Cinema* (Durham, NC: Duke University Press, 2008), 15–88.

background of his scenes with Taslimi's character Na'i, his substitute mother figure; the rhythmic, almost choreographed movements of the children's planting game or Na'i's fevered trance; the panoramic vision of death and the war circling around Bashu toward the end of the film, as he makes his peace with his new home and family. These phantasmagoric elements make explicitly clear that *Bashu* is not only a child's (or children's) story but also a more complicated adult consideration of death, disorientation, and redemption. Coming unexpectedly in the midst of an otherwise realistic pastoral representation, these scenes catch the viewer off guard, breaking us out of our spectator's reverie and reminding us that the film is an intentional made construction, not simply a seamless, organic fantasy of the real.

*Bashu* subtly breaks with the conventions of film representation in ways that both hearken back to Dariush Mehrjui's *The Cow* (1969), the film that began Iran's "New Wave," and prefigure the reflexive cinema that will emerge a few years later in association with the new generation of Kiarostami, Makhmalbaf, and Panahi.[28] Given how much is going on in the film, it is not surprising that it is mentioned in almost every analysis of Iranian cinema, and its various aspects selected and discussed depending on the focus of the particular discussion. But I want to emphasize something that is not so often acknowledged: *Bashu* as a breaking point. This is the film that connects and also makes distinct two of the most significant trends in postrevolutionary Iranian filmmaking, trends that sometimes but rarely overlap: the trend of children's films as mainstream adult cinema, and the trend toward a reflexive cinema in which filmmaking as an issue of both political and aesthetic representation becomes explicitly part of the representational narrative.

## Censorship and Creativity: Reflexive Cinema

The self-consciously innovative cinema that I am terming reflexive cinema has sometimes been called auteur cinema, acknowledging both

[28] A striking but seemingly underappreciated reference in *Bashu* to *The Cow* is the presence in both films of mysterious figures silently viewing the action from the background. But their symbolic role is reversed: in *Bashu*, the guardian shades are of the child's dead family, eerily but benevolently watching his progress; in *The Cow*, they are enigmatically threatening, the distant silhouettes of "outsiders" observing the unfolding village tragedy.

its identification with a handful of particular directors (especially Kiarostami and Makhmalbaf) and referencing the now established innovations and cachet of the original French New Wave. But the technique of cinematic reflexivity was not only confined to a few well-known Iranian auteur directors. And while Truffaut, Godard, et al. broke with cinematic convention, especially eschewing the theatricality of stage sets and designs for a new convention of naturalism in setting, sound, and plot, they did not necessarily challenge the basic premise of the film as autonomous entity: the convention that a feature film is an original work of art that is separate from the happenstance of the real, no matter how realistic its impression.

Kiarostami has to be given credit for making this genre a category unto itself. His 1990 *Close-Up* owes a recognizable debt to Pontecorvo's *Battle of Algiers*, offering a cinematic recreation of a "real" event, filming in the same location and with many of the original participants acting themselves.[29] Like *Battle*, *Close-Up* seems almost to be a documentary, its realism a bit grainier and rougher than expected from an original scripted feature. The key difference is scale: Kiarostami chooses to recreate an event that is not about revolution but about postrevolutionary society. *Close-Up* observes the unraveling of popular belief in charismatic leadership, reflected through cinema and its realities. A sincere fan takes on the role of Mohsen Makhmalbaf, the well-known Islamist filmmaker. The family who initially accept his impersonation later become disillusioned and accuse him of being a fake. They had believed that their ordinary lives had been transformed and that they were becoming (film) actors themselves. And of course, it turns out that they are.

This filmic recreation of cinematic enthusiasm, with its reflexive view of filmmaking as a creation of truths that extend beyond the frame, would be an odd footnote to the annals of moviemaking, were it not

[29] In both *Battle* and *Close-Up*, most of the on-screen participants are nonactors playing a version of themselves, including the main protagonists of the events depicted. In *Battle*, Saadi Yacef, a revolutionary leader of the FLN (Algerian Liberation Front), played a version of himself in the film, and the only professional actor was Jean Martin, who played the colonial enforcer, the French Colonel Mathieu. In *Close-Up*, Hossain Sabzian plays himself as the impersonator to the same family he originally convinced, while the professional with a late cameo role is Mohsen Makhmalbaf, the impersonated director.

for the time and place in which it is made.[30] The national project of a postrevolutionary Iranian cinema focused attention on the question of who, exactly, are the Iranians that the nation would recognize in their representation. Muslims? Martyrs? Child protagonists? What about women? What about ordinary people who went to the movies and saw themselves on-screen in the films of their favorite filmmakers? What about a nation of individuals who had broken with the past and created something new, and now wondered who that meant they could be, and how they should represent themselves, to themselves and to each other?

During a period when most political options and other forms of media (newspapers, journals, theater, and television) were still firmly limited, Iranian cinema provided a medium in which to be explicitly experimental with the realities and the questions of the postrevolutionary experience. Whose story gets told? Who gets to tell it? Who controls the telling? And most compellingly: Is it true? These are not only cinematic questions but larger sociological and political issues as well. The dynamics of class and education, and of urban and rural status and knowledge, are all involved in the problem of representation, in both Iranian postrevolutionary film and postrevolutionary society. But the familiar contradictions of postrevolutionary daily realities with national revolutionary goals – whether for social justice or Islamic piety – became the basis for a reflexive cinema that set out to capture the tragedy and absurdity of Iranian daily life through a self-consciously self-referential representation.

That *Close-Up* is the film that establishes this new Iranian genre is appropriate, as it succeeds in intertwining two categories of filmmakers whose work after the revolution had until this point been fairly distinct: more secular figures, identified with Kiarostami; and more politicized or religious figures, identified with Makhmalbaf. It is Makhmalbaf's fame that prompts the incident that sets the stage for *Close-Up*; it is Kiarostami who decides to follow up with the other director's fans. This transcendence of the categories of secular and religious is as significant as it is unusual; film becomes one of the few spaces of representation in which the social reality of the merging of

[30] Hamid Naficy touches on some of these issues in his very perceptive essay about the film, "Close-Up (1989), Abbas Kiarostami," in Jeffrey Geiger and R. L. Rutsky, eds., *Film Analysis: A Norton Reader* (New York: W. W. Norton, 2005).

varieties of popular expectations and agendas can be acknowledged. Over the next decade, most of the noteworthy Iranian films, including a number that don't make much of an international impression, will include elements of this self-reflexive filmmaking, establishing a community of recognition through exchanged images, references, and shared acknowledgments.[31]

Well-established figures like Kiarostami and Makhmalbaf were not the only practitioners of a cinematic style that directly incorporated self-conscious references to the artifice of filmmaking, pushing at the borders of the realist convention and audience expectation. To some extent, the necessities of postrevolutionary film production led to its innovations. In particular, the restrictions on adult interactions between opposite genders strongly pushed a different sensibility in both filmmaking and film viewing. Children's films provided one possible form of recognizable local experience, and a means through which to begin its representation. But the genre entailed its own limits, and both audiences and directors still wanted to see films about adult issues with adult actors playing in them. The neorealism that was adopted by the children's film genre couldn't quite take hold in the same way for adult stories, because private or intimate scenes between adults couldn't be realistically filmed. Filmmakers had to adapt themselves to the rules mandating the public appearance of women in *hejab*, but at the same time, everyone – the filmmakers, the film audience, and the film censors – knew that the conventions of behavior being shown on screen were not those that were followed, even in the most Islamically modest of households. The fact that women always had to be shown dressed for being in public (with their hair covered and in loose outer clothing), even when represented as being in private (at home with family or inside with other women only), meant that the artifice of the representation was highlighted. Sometimes the frisson of contradiction could be avoided by setting scenes in public spaces, although this in itself called into question the expectation that women's

31 Some of the more resolutely Islamic filmmakers, like Hatamikia, take up a reflexive approach less in regard to filmmaking, than toward the Islamically appropriated topics of the Iran–Iraq War and veterans' experiences. Hatamikia's *The Glass Agency* (1999) is especially forthright in its questioning of expected attitudes and conventions of deference to sacrifice.

roles were primarily private or domestic.[32] But even when filming in open streets or common courtyards, the best filmmakers took up the challenge of visible artifice by addressing it headlong, directly incorporating and surprising the expectations of the audience within the representational frame.

A brilliant, overlooked early example of the productive uses of this creative tension, juggling the legal requirements of *hejab* with the visual expectations of the audience to great comic effect, is the almost unknown film *Pickpockets Don't Go to Heaven* (Abolhassan Davoodi, 1992).[33] It's a light comedy about a good-hearted but poor hero who gets involved in a bank robbery to raise money for his equally poor but deserving sweetheart and her widowed mother, who are threatened with eviction because they cannot pay their rent. Although the plot is unexceptional, the comic direction is not, and relies on a deft sense of visual timing, including a very overt give-and-take between the recognized requirements of the visual modesty codes and the cinematic expectations of the film audience. The film includes a number of scenes that play with the tension between expectation and representation, but two are particularly noteworthy. As the plot develops, the heroine, her substantial mother, and a sympathetic male friend need to pursue some bad guys; they approach a motorcycle equipped with a sidecar, but then there is a slight moment of hesitation. Cinematic expectation of the globally conventional seating arrangement – young man driving, young woman sitting behind while holding on tight, and mother in the sidecar – is confounded by the local film code restrictions on physical contact. The tiny pause is a moment of audience suspense: Will the scene be able to play itself out as we conventionally expect it to, or will there be an awful, awkward break from the natural representation of the real (meaning a jarring interruption of the conventional representation of the cinematic)? What to do? Instead of cutting away from the problem, the director solves it to great comic effect by having the

[32] See Norma Claire Moruzzi, "Women's Space/Cinema Space: Representations of Public and Private in Iranian Films," *Middle East Report* 212 (Autumn 1999), 52–55.

[33] My discussion of *Pickpockets* here is based on a longer discussion of the film in my article "Women's Space/Cinema Space," 54. Other than that essay, I have been able to find only one other quick mention of this film in the extensive literature of Iranian cinema (Reza-Sadr in Issa and Whitaker, *Life and Art*, 39). Many film scholars have never even heard of it.

mother, a large, older woman in a traditional flowered *chador*, stride ahead and mount the bike. She will drive! Her daughter climbs on behind her, and the man hops into the sidecar as the audience laughs at its own limitations: the scene works because it overtly tweaks the audience's cinematic expectation that in a romantic melodrama, only a man can drive a motorcycle.

In the film's final scene, after a bank robbery has been foiled and the hapless hero has been snagged by the justice system, the camera tracks him in close-up as he walks down the courthouse hall with his sweetheart. Their heads are close together, and they are murmuring promises of mutual devotion. As their heads draw even closer, the audience senses the classic cinematic buildup to a screen kiss, made even tenser by the knowledge that it cannot happen. The buildup makes the kiss inevitable; the modesty codes make it impossible: What will the young couple do? As the camera pulls back, the hero whirls round and plants a big smooch on the prison guard, who is revealed to be shackled to his other side. The audience has the release of the film kiss, plus the delight of a surprise; the censors have no complaints, because there's no heterosexual physical contact. The joke is shared, because it's on the artfulness of cinema itself: the convention of cinematic realism only works if everyone involved – director, censor, and audience – is complicit.

## Kiarostami and Makhmalbaf: Different Takes on the Reflexive Project

In 1991, both Kiarostami and Makhmalbaf begin a sustained period when they each make a series of linked films that are explicitly about filmmaking. They establish themselves as the masters of reflexive cinema and its possible techniques, but their reflexive focus is different.[34] For Makhmalbaf, cinema is inextricably linked with society, and reflexivity is a means to fold and integrate competing, plural perspectives into the same representational frame: it is a fundamentally

[34] Jonathan Rosenbaum is one of the most perceptive writers on the comparative efforts of Kiarostami and Makhmalbaf. See his many very thoughtful essays first published through the 1990s as film reviews in the *Chicago Reader*; for instance, "Iranian Sights [Life and Nothing More]," in *Chicago Reader*, October 23, 1992, and on JonathanRosenbaum.com.

political project.[35] For Kiarostami, who breaks open the possibilities of cinematic form with *Close-Up*, reflexivity is primarily an interrogation of the artifice of filmmaking itself, and the closed autonomy of any narrative construct in relation to any other. If the point of Makhmalbaf's multiple representations is to get the perspectives all tangled up, Kiarostami's point is that all those multiple perspectives remain parallel lines, each one a straight narrative trajectory unto itself.

Kiarostami consolidates his reputation as the master of reflexive method with the Koker trilogy: *Where Is the Friend's House*, a classic of the children's cinema genre; *And Life Goes On* (1992); *Through the Olive Trees* (1994).[36] All three films are set in or around the northwest Iranian village of Koker, and the two later films explicitly reference or remake scenes from each of the previous films. *And Life Goes On* is the most serious, a road trip through the destruction of the 1990 northwest Iran earthquake, which is not incidentally the regional location of *Friend's House*. In terms of the development of the reflexive genre, it is important because Kiarostami incorporates a character as himself, the director (and auteur). It is this film, with its intertextual references to the earlier, simpler children's story and its gently scathing presentation of the middle-class filmmaker and son on their well-meaning but worse than useless travel adventure into locations of devastation and disaster, that truly establishes reflexive filmmaking as an Iranian genre.[37] Searching for the actors from the earlier film, residents of the region most heavily damaged by the earthquake, Kiarostami casts a

[35] I want to thank Anahita Ghazvinizadeh for her brilliant analysis of the "folded" perspectives in Makhmalbaf's films.

[36] Kiarostami's *The Wind Will Carry Us* (1999) shares a number of visual and narrative themes with the Koker films; it is a similar reflexive inquiry into parallel realities of a cinematic construction, both more scathing and funnier in its depiction of the self-involved would-be director than the Koker trilogy.

[37] It is also the film that closes the circle with prerevolutionary Iranian political filmmaking. For both *Close-Up* and *And Life Goes On*, Kiarostami borrows tremendously from the techniques explored by prerevolutionary documentary filmmaker Kamran Shirdel in his masterpiece *The Night It Rained* (1967): following up an odd incident from the news (a village boy who stopped a passenger train from proceeding over a washed-out bridge; Makhmalbaf's would-be filmmaker impersonator); incorporating the filmmaker and the filmmaking project as central to the film project; setting the whole film as a search after an elusive truth (who stopped the train; what has happened to the young actors from *Where Is the Friend's House?*) centered on a little boy; the fragmentation of that singular truth into multiple strands of observation linked to the individual perspectives of multiple bystanders.

sympathetic actor to play his own role but calls the whole production into question. The filmmaker is well intentioned but quixotic; his son is cute but spoiled and annoying. They are tourist interlopers, caught up, like the audience, in a self-referential search for tokens of their own cinematic experiences scattered through a ruined landscape. In the meantime, the locals have their own agendas, ranging from the necessary tasks of getting on with living, which include removing debris, carrying supplies, and washing dishes, to the very immediate goal of global connectivity, which means rigging a makeshift antenna in order to listen to an important live match of the World Cup.

For one *And Life Goes On* young couple, the necessary tasks of daily life apparently included getting married; this small temporal fiction becomes the entire focus of the third film of the trilogy, the 1994 *Through the Olive Trees*. The unlikely off- and on-screen courtship is drolly suspenseful, and *Through the Olive Trees* is the most comic and the most moving of the three films. It also makes explicit the larger pattern that links all three films into a series: each film reveals a story unto itself, a parallel construct to the version that went before, overlaid one onto the other to provide a deeper and more confused vision of the same, while each individual version remains dedicated to its own representation of the truth. As the final film in the series, *Olive Trees* seems to be the definitive narrative account: we explicitly see that the "director" of *Life Goes On* is really an actor; that the seemingly "real" human stories encountered after the earthquake were made up. Or were they? By the time he makes *Olive Trees*, Kiarostami is internationally famous enough so that most audiences who see all three films will already know what he looks like. They will recognize that the "director" in *Olive Trees* is again an actor who is not Kiarostami, and the "real" story of the youthful romance in the face of family disapproval is another version of the "fiction" of the previous film. The script has shifted. Is it now real? Is the final characterization of "Kiarostami" as the jovially benevolent father figure gently stage-managing the lives around him, the "real" director? For Kiarostami, these questions are beside the point. The construction of the cinematic artifice becomes its own parallel immediate truth, a reflexive reality that is always being called into question and sustained by its own structure of familiar references.[38]

[38] Others have written more extensively about what I am defining as the reflexive aspects of Kiarostami's films, although they may describe these dialectical

## Parallel vs. Plural Narratives: Reflexivity in Cinema and Politics

While Kiarostami's films layer over each other like a palimpsest, Makhmalbaf's films are individually more pluralized, with multiple versions of any singular narrative intersecting wildly within the shared space of the representational frame. During the same period of the early 1990s as Kiarostami's Koker trilogy, Makhmalbaf makes a series of films that move from representing the politics of Iranian cinema (*Once Upon a Time, Cinema*) to representing cinema as politics (*Salaam Cinema; Moment of Innocence*), to representing the formal possibilities of aesthetic representation (*Gabbeh*).[39] In his version of reflexive cinema, the intimate details of personal and national histories, of Iranian cinema and politics, are all inextricably linked and folded into each other, the past and the present intercutting to prevent any single view or voice from claiming formal hegemony.

They are very different films. Makhmalbaf's *Once Upon a Time, Cinema* (1992) is no less than a black-and-white cinematic love letter to the history of Iranian filmmaking, lyrically poetic at some points and surprisingly funny at others. It is a loose depiction of the origins of Iranian cinema, including the deployment of the first film camera imported to Iran and put to use by the Qajar court (some of the most fascinating scenes are archival footage, including fully veiled court ladies going on an outing, inserted into the narrative flow of the film). The most comic elements, and the most self-reflexive on cinema as representation, involve the escape into the film of the heroine from *The*

relations between film and audience and among the films themselves in somewhat different terms. See particularly Casey Williamson, "Art Matters: The Films of Abbas Kiarostami," in Issa and Whitaker, *Life and Art*, 90–104, and the chapter on Kiarostami in Hamid Dabashi, *Close Up: Iranian Cinema, Past, Present and Future* (New York: Verso, 2001), 33–75.

39 *Gabbeh* (1996) is the film Makhmalbaf seems to have had in mind when he made the casting call that resulted in both *Salaam Cinema* and *Moment of Innocence*. It is a remarkable fable of image, storytelling, and geography, as complexly visual as *Once Upon a Time, Cinema* (1992), but in saturated color rather than pristine black and white. In *Gabbeh*, Makhmalbaf pushes the possibility of symbolic narrative into the realm of Sergei Parajanov, creating a lush visual poem of exacting images and ambiguous narratives. *Gabbeh* is probably Makhmalbaf's most formally experimental film, but it sidesteps overt political issues and so remains more of a beautiful digression in his oeuvre, rather than a significant trend.

*Lur Girl* (1933), the first Iranian talkie.[40] Playing the tribal peasant Lur girl, Fatemeh Motamed-Aria runs into and out of palace scenes, desperately searching for the hero, disrupting the plans of court officials and the royally appointed camera man, and shrilly calling "Ja'far, Ja'far" (the name of her beloved), her famous line from the original film. She is a young woman on the loose, incidentally wreaking havoc on the apparent order of the proceedings. Instead of the official (cinematic) version of events being sanctioned by the (Qajar) state, we get an exuberant montage of familiar but unexpected faces, diverse voices, and divergent desires, all held loosely together by the plural project of new form of representation, whether formally cinematic or implicitly political. Even the final, more melancholic scene of an absent reflection in a mirror hints at further questions of inclusion or invisibility in the vision of the (national) self that appears in the cinematic frame.

Makhmalbaf follows *Once Upon a Time* with two films in which the political undercurrent of the Iranian reflexive cinema comes to the surface: *Salaam Cinema* (1995) and *Moment of Innocence* (1996).[41] *Salaam Cinema* almost seems to be a conventional documentary, a tribute to the enthusiasm of the postrevolutionary national audience, made in honor of the centenary of cinema.[42] An apparently accidental film, it is prompted by the overwhelming popular response to an open casting call for a new Makhmalbaf film: thousands of Tehranis show up and almost mob the site. In response, Makhmalbaf institutes mass auditions: groups are brought in, a few or a dozen at a time, and asked to cry, fall down dead, jump into the air, and otherwise show the

[40] Abdolhossein Sepanta's *The Lur Girl* was made in India, but for Persian language audiences primarily in Iran. See Reza Tahami, "Iranian Women Make Films," *Film International* 2(3) (Summer 1994), 4–13.

[41] In 1996, he also releases *Gabbeh*, the film it seems he intended to make before he was caught up in the process of the other two, but which remains a mostly separate filmic project, more concerned with issues of aesthetic representation than with political ones.

[42] *Salaam Cinema* also functions as a gentle reminder of the reflexivity of the very first Iranian feature film, Ovanes Ohanian's *Haji Agha, Cinema Actor* (1933): a film director clandestinely and comically films an ordinary Iranian who is morally opposed to cinema, and who is converted by his own experience of being in the film. Makhmalbaf himself points out, in the documentary *Iran: A Cinematographic Revolution* (Nader Homayoun, 2007), that the ordinary Iranians mobbing the gates in *Salaam Cinema*, desperate to be in a film, are essentially the same ordinary people who burned down cinemas at the start of the revolution. Many thanks to Hamid Naficy for enabling me actually to view a print of *Haji Agha, Cinema Actor*.

director that they can "act." Sitting behind a desk, Makhmalbaf watches them impassively. The film has been criticized for exposing Makhmalbaf as a dictatorial martinet, except that it is Makhmalbaf making the film, and therefore managing the exposure.

So what is being exposed? A supposedly authentic, unmediated view of the authoritarian director at work? Or a very intentional revelation of charismatic leadership, popular adulation, and individual self-interest? Within the context of the postrevolutionary Islamic Republic, this particular set of relationships cannot escape their political significance, even if formal politics are never explicitly addressed.[43]

Makhmalbaf began his film career as an Islamically committed, polemically political director, but he quickly evolved a more complexly engaged personal style. Even while he distanced himself from his more pedantic initial efforts, early films like *The Bicyclist* (1987) and *Marriage of the Blessed* (1988) established him as a filmmaker dedicated to representing the emotional realities of the lives of the *mostazafan*, the revolutionary term for the oppressed and downtrodden, deserving poor that became the ideological rallying cry for the Islamist factions of the Revolution.[44] The crowds seen mobbing his casting call in *Salaam Cinema* were responding to his ability to seem to embody the national political persona and its evolution, before, during, and after the Revolution. They wanted to be a part of his postrevolutionary representation, and Makhmalbaf includes them, even as he begins to demystify his own popular persona by also including himself in the representational frame. Particular individuals who audition in *Salaam* turn up again in other films: the lout who wants to play a hero turns up as the sympathetic policeman/actor in *Moment of Innocence*; the young woman who confides that she wants to act so that she can travel to international festivals and visit her out-of-country boyfriend returns as the heroine in the internationally acclaimed *Gabbeh*. Makhmalbaf himself appears and reappears: the

43 Makhmalbaf identifies his reflexive filmmaking as "documentary," explicitly connecting his work with the prerevolutionary genealogy of politically engaged Iranian documentaries. The key figure in this lineage, in which the observation of small and apparently unpolitical actions provides an indirect representation of larger institutional power relations, is Kamran Shirdel.

44 The most complete overview of the relations between Makhmalbaf's filmmaking and films and the evolution of Iranian political development is probably Eric Egan, *The Films of Makhmalbaf: Cinema, Politics & Culture in Iran* (Washington, DC: Mage Publishers, 2005).

enigmatic authority figure of *Salaam Cinema* becomes the bemused instigator of memory and action within *Moment of Innocence*.

If there was any remaining doubt that Makhmalbaf had embraced the reflexive cinematic model that Kiarostami had initiated, but developed it in a more pointedly postrevolutionary political direction, it should have been banished by *Moment of Innocence*. *Salaam Cinema* challenged film viewers to ask, what is the "real" nature of the performance(s) we are watching, or enacting? How far are we each responsible? But in *Moment of Innocence*, Makhmalbaf asks these questions of himself, not only as a filmmaker but as a political actor. The director who had best enabled Iranians to identify with what they saw on-screen, so much so that so many of them wanted actually to be on the screen, Makhmalbaf embodied the trajectory of the nation, from revolutionary Islamist activist to postrevolutionary public citizen. By collapsing the distance between the "real" (documentary) and the "original" (feature), he posed similar challenges to his audience and himself regarding questions of authority and narrative in both cinema and politics. But by offering an internally contested representation of the story of his own political history – and therefore explicitly putting into play the question of its authority and representation – he allowed the Iranian audience to reconsider their own participation, individually and collectively, in the divisive events of the past decades.

*Moment of Innocence* is funny, charming, generous, and very, very serious.[45] It is seemingly prompted by the brief scene from *Salaam Cinema* in which an enormous and rather thuggish-looking man admits he would typecast himself as a bad guy, but longs to play a romantic hero. At that moment, he is just another would-be actor in a mass audition. Although it is not acknowledged in *Salaam Cinema*, the moment is an abrupt instance of reversed déjà vu. In 1974, the would-be actor was a young policeman who was stabbed by a young Islamist radical. The culprit (revolutionary hero? violent criminal?) went to jail for his crime and grew up to be a famous postrevolutionary film

[45] *Moment of Innocence* is a rather arbitrary English title for *Noon-o Goldoon*; the literal translation from the Persian would be "Bread and Flowerpot." Apparently the film's French distributor realized that retaining the poetic alliteration of the original title might be more important than its literal meaning; hence "un instance d'innocence" becomes "Moment of Innocence." See Hamid Dabashi, "Mohsen Makhmalbaf's *A Moment of Innocence*" in Issa and Whitaker, *Life and Art*, 115.

director. The director is now holding mass auditions, in which he encounters his victim: the man who knows he looks like a villain but longs to be recognized as a good guy. Cinema brings the two young antagonists back together as middle-aged versions of themselves, and allows them the chance to rediscover their own story through the making of a further film: a political story that also, in the best romantic tradition, includes a lovely girl.

*Moment of Innocence* is about the effort to represent this small history on film, and about how the questions of representation open up other possible versions of the story.[46] Was the original encounter a botched political action, or a possible love story that went wrong? Everyone's perspective is their own: the policeman, offered the chance to cast himself, wants to choose a very obviously diffident, entitled rich kid, rather than the sweet-faced but more working-class innocent who does get cast; the woman who was the original romantic interest won't even appear on film, although she permits her daughter to play her younger self. The intersection of old and new viewpoints changes the trajectory of the original story: the young actors, asked to recreate history, relive it on their own terms. The past is always with us, but to the extent that we share it with each other, it is plural, fluid, and contingent. So is it true? Is it possible, is it even desirable, to keep separate the stories we tell from the reality of (the) experience?

[46] The complex ambiguity of the film is well captured in Nasrin Rahimieh's "Capturing Cultural Transformation on Film: Makhmalbaf's *A Moment of Innocence*," *Edebiyat* 12 (2001), 195–214. Rahimieh's focus is on the tension between the fixity of the remembered past, and the unpredictable choices of the present. Even so, in her efforts to document the film's shifting individual viewpoints, she occasionally misses the plural references and perspectives maintained within its construction. This is especially noticeable in her discussion of the role of the former policeman. In the scene in which he must cast a young actor to play his younger self, Rahimieh points out the unknowable gap between the truth of the photograph of himself the policeman holds but the camera never sees, and the insistence by everyone else that the policeman's first choice of actor is not a good one. Rahimieh seems caught by the concealed authority of the photograph, missing the wider (and funnier) significance of the scene. The policeman wants to be represented by a conventionally handsome, arrogantly upper-class kid, the matinee idol version of himself, while disdaining the gentle working-class youth standing next to him. The scene is not only about memory but also about class; even the audience can discern, without reference to the historical evidence of the photograph, that the policeman's choice of would-be actor has little to do with authenticity and memories of the past, and everything to do with desire and representations in the present.

Both Kiarostami and Makhmalbaf address this problem, but they pursue it differently. Kiarostami relies on a more formalist, auteur model of cinema as autonomous aesthetic innovation, and his subsequent work moves away from the immediacy of Iranian material experiences and toward a more metaphysical problematic of being and narrative. Ironically, this has made him more globally accessible: the French, and the international cinema cognoscenti, adopted him as the acknowledged heir of the French New Wave (Catherine Deneuve's 1997 Cannes kiss providing the seal of approval). Kiarostami's ability to assimilate into this widely recognized modernist tradition is a sign of his distance from the specifically Iranian origins of his work, and from the immediate source of its innovation within the localized material and social context of the Revolution. Without the sharply reflexive connection to the representation of contingent Iranian histories, his filmmaking has become more predictably "original": apparently random road movies on the poetically meaningless nature of life like *Taste of Cherry* (1997) or *Ten* (2002), or scripted features about the unreliability of narrative truth like *Certified Copy* (2010). The interpellation of cinema and reality becomes a formalist style, more than a dynamic question.

Despite his highly personalized vision, Makhmalbaf's filmmaking has always been embedded within the more interconnected relations of a collective political project.[47] This has led him in different directions of wider engagement: mentoring the films of others, especially the women in his family; highlighting the misery nearby but not necessarily in Iran, especially in Afghanistan; positioning himself as the political spokesman-in-exile for the silenced candidate (and presumed election winner) Hossein Mousavi during the first hectic days after the contested June 2009 Presidential election. For Makhmalbaf, the supposed line between political action and cinema has always been an intentional blur: self-reflexivity as participation in the heady plural endeavor of cultural and social politics. Makhmalbaf's reflexivity opens up the possibility that creativity is an organic process that transcends the cinematic frame and can never speak with a single voice. The "truth" of Makhmalbaf's representation is its insistence on the

[47] Although I am hesitant to use these terms as identifiers, it could be said that Kiarostami is a more modernist filmmaker, while Makhmalbaf is more postmodernist.

possibility of multiple truths and divergent perspectives, although unified by the republican commitment of the postrevolutionary narrative.

Given his more explicit involvement with the dynamics and representations of Iranian internal political developments, Makhmalbaf came to represent the opposite aesthetic position from Kiarostami: more grounded in the specific complexity of the local, and therefore more susceptible to the blockages in Iranian national politics. Both filmmakers had to situate themselves at some distance from events in Iran: Makhmalbaf in apparent creative exile outside the country; Kiarostami having been able to travel in and out, but seeming to base his filmmaking efforts outside, even if he maintained a low-profile presence in Iran as a teacher and mentor.[48] They remain influential figures, but the radically creative cinema they sponsored has been taken up by other figures offering a slightly different reflexive view.

## Getting Off the Bus: Women Step Forward

By the late 1990s, a new postrevolutionary generation was increasingly present in Iranian public life. This shift in perspective is evident in a comparison of two films from 1997, Kiarostami's *Taste of Cherry*, and Panahi's *The Mirror*, for which Kiarostami wrote the screenplay. *Taste of Cherry*, an existential meditation on the meaning of life, is a classically philosophical inquiry shared entirely among men, and won the *Palme d'Or* at Cannes. *The Mirror*, a story about a little girl making her way home through the busy urban streetscape of Tehran, seems initially to be a reversion to the children's film genre. But then *The Mirror* breaks through the frame, in the scene quoted at the beginning of this essay, and the children's genre suddenly becomes the route for the continuing explorations of reflexive cinema.

When Mina pulls off her *hejab* and insists she won't act anymore, the audience is again thrust into the doubled perspective of reflexive cinema: Is it "real" or is it scripted; is it a documentary or is it "original"? Other postrevolutionary Iranian filmmakers had already introduced strong on-screen women protagonists, developed the genre of children's films, or explored the possibilities of reflexive films about

[48] Kiarostami continued to mentor rising young Iranian filmmakers, but he kept his distance from the political travails of former protégées. (He was noticeably reticent about Jafar Panahi's situation.)

filmmaking. But *The Mirror* combines all of these: it puts into question the authority of the filmmaker and the reality of the representation, while introducing a new set of reflexive protagonists – often girls and women – and a new reflexive focus – the postrevolutionary individual at large in the spaces of modern social experience. Usually, but not always, these spaces are urban. They are always contested: by claims to tradition, family, individual freedom, and collective solidarity.[49]

When Mina gets off the bus, she sits down on the curb and changes her shoes: she makes herself at home in the public space of the street. Then she gets up and marches off on her own. After a hasty reorganization of the film project, the camera and crew, including the director, follow her. The remainder of *The Mirror* sticks with the general convention of the Iranian children's film in that the most dramatic struggles are still resolutely mundane; there is no kidnapping, shocking accident, or other spectacular occurrence to threaten the adamant little girl. In fact, the film continues to follow the same story as it set out to. The difference is the question of who is in charge: The grown-up male director, or the small but independent-minded youthful heroine?

As a children's film, *The Mirror* is simple enough. As reflexive cinema, with its established emphasis on foregrounding questions of authenticity and perspective, the film displaces the focus from the interactions between cinematic authority figure and subject to the autonomy of the subject herself. Panahi as director gets out of the way. When Mina gets off the bus, the audience watches the next generation begin to take off on its own.[50]

[49] Marzieh Meshkini's *The Day I Became a Woman* (2000) would seem to break with the urban focus, as its three segments are set in the relatively isolated spaces of Kish Island. But all the spaces of the film are saturated with modernity: the first segment takes place in and around a village where a little girl clings to her autonomy despite the demands of tradition; the second segment of a young woman takes place while she rides a bicycle along the very modern space of a built bike path; the third segment of the old woman is almost overwhelmed by up-to-date consumer commodities.

[50] Rasul Sadr Ameli's *The Girl in Sneakers* (1999) is another example of a film following a young female heroine making her way on her own through the city. But the urban environment is much more threatening for Sadr Ameli's teenage subject than it is for Panahi's child protagonist; a young adult woman's experience of navigating through society is very different from a little girl's. Although his films do not engage the most representative strategies of reflexive cinema (films about filmmaking; films that break the fourth wall; films that blur the distinction between on-screen and off-screen reality), both Sadr Ameli's *Girl in Sneakers* and his *I Am Taraneh, Fifteen* (2002) allow the narrative of a young

The generational shift was less about age than perspective: agency being claimed by upstart voices and subjectivities, requiring new techniques of representation.[51] By the late 1990s, an increasing number of Iranian films were focused on the subject of women's lives and were being made by women directors, including Rakhshan Bani-Etemad (born 1954), Tahmineh Milani (born 1960), Marzieh Meshkini (born 1969), and Samira Makhmalbaf (born 1980).[52] In taking up the challenge of representing serious adult social relationships on-screen, directors inevitably had to focus their creative visual strategy on the problem of representing women's social interactions realistically while abiding by the required filmic modesty codes. Milani, the most explicitly feminist director, sidestepped the representational issue by emphasizing women's relationships with each other and the political context, and women's distance, both psychological and physical, from the men in their lives. But filmmakers who wanted to demonstrate the ambiguities, rather than simply the tensions, of Iranian domestic life had to incorporate some of the same techniques of negotiation with the audience's visual expectations of gender and *hejab* as Davoodi's *Pickpockets Don't Go to Heaven*, but to more serious effect.

woman's difficulties making her way through the modern, urban society of contemporary Tehran to reflect upon the gendered barriers to autonomy – not always Islamic or exceptionally traditional – that continue to structure postrevolutionary experience.

51 A foreshadowing of this eruption by a young woman into the representational frame occurs in Makhmalbaf's *Once Upon a Time, Cinema*, when Fatemeh Motamed-Aria as the Lur girl starts running in and out of scenes and interrupts the intentionality of the masculine-controlled narrative. Makhmalbaf knows what he's doing with this inclusion of apparently uncontrolled feminine agency, but he doesn't let it go far enough for Motamed-Aria to run away with the film.

52 Both Bani-Etemad and Milani were already well-established filmmakers with a focus on women's lives: Bani-Etemad made several films in the late 1980s and achieved popular success and critical acclaim with *Nargess* (1992); Milani came to prominence as an explicitly feminist filmmaker with *Legend of a Sigh* (1991), but achieved Iranian superstar status (and equivalent negative state attention) with *Two Women* (1999). But by the late 1990s, Iranian films about and by women become almost a new genre in themselves. This development was aided through the support of some prominent male directors: Dariush Mehrjui consistently addressed issues related to women's social experiences; Mohsen Makhmalbaf mentored the filmmaking careers of both his wife (Meshkini) and his daughter Samira. It was also aided by the more open cultural policies supported by the administration of the newly elected president Mohamad Khatami administration, as pointed out by Ziba Mir-Hosseini, "Iranian Cinema: Art, Society and the State," *Middle East Report* 219 (Summer 2001).

The representational problem of reconciling the internal tension between the on-screen modesty codes (no heterosexual touching even between supposed family members; no uncovered women's hair or bodies even when supposedly in private and at home) and the audience's awareness of their artificiality (the cinematic fourth wall always in jeopardy) encouraged some directors to push postrevolutionary Iranian films about urban women to a new level of visual creativity. The experienced master craftsman Dariush Mehrjui (1939–2023) became particularly expert at choreographing scenes with actors performing ordinary tasks of domestic labor, allowing them to provide for character development or social intimacy, while unobtrusively restraining from any actual physical contact between the men and women involved.[53] In *Sara* (1993), the heroine determinedly sews and embroiders, enveloped in sensual billows of fabric that are lush despite the black and white photography; in *Leila* (1996), multiple scenes rely on a subtheme of domestic food preparation and exchange, smoothly incorporating the essential material lubricant of any Iranian social interaction as a substitute for other forms of physical relation.[54] Rakhshan Bani-Etemad, already an established filmmaker known for socially aware neorealist stories about strong women characters, found equally innovative techniques for representing domestic intimacy

[53] One of the preeminent filmmakers of the prerevolutionary Iranian New Wave, Mehrjui continued to find innovative techniques to represent his ongoing concerns with issues of injustice, exclusion, and social continuity. Although living a quiet life with a low public profile, in March 2022 Mehrjui publicly denounced the state restrictions on screenings of his 2019 film *A Minor*. In a very emotional video statement, the 83-year-old director denounces the state's arbitrary repression of his film and cinema as an art form, stating "I cannot stand it. I will protest at the Culture Ministry with my assistants. I won't give up until I get my right ... Kill me, do whatever you want with me ... destroy me, but I want my right." On October 14, 2023, Mehrjui and his wife were stabbed to death in their Tehran home. Their deaths are widely regarded to be suspicious (rather than the deed of their unhinged gardener, the original story of the state authorities).

[54] Mehrjui will revive the theme of food preparation as a social function to great comic effect in *Mama's Guests* (2004), one of the only really funny Iranian light comedies other than Davoudi's *Pickpockets Don't Go to Heaven*. Mehrjui was exceptional in the breadth of his subject matter and his willingness to adapt Western literary and film classics in order to convey resolutely local contemporary Iranian issues: *The Lady* (1992) adapted from Luis Bunuel's corrosive satire on morality and avarice *Viridiana*; *Sara* (1993) from Ibsen's classic feminist play *A Doll's House*; *Pari* (1995) from J. D. Salinger's *Franny and Zooey*.

despite the modesty codes, and while reminding the audience of the limits of their own expectations. In *The Blue Veiled* (1995), the cross-class romantic union of the unlikely couple is satisfyingly confirmed by a late shot of their feet coming close together, hers bare, as he steps to her doorway. In *The May Lady* (1998), the middle-class professional heroine torn between private fulfillment and social expectation enters her apartment, talking with her son and dropping her bag, and starts to pull off her headscarf; the scene cuts just as she walks through a doorway, and just at the moment when the scarf would be expected to come off.

Like *Through the Olive Trees* and *Moment of Innocence*, *The May Lady* is a reflexive film about filmmaking, but from the perspective of a woman filmmaker and focused on the combined question of both being and representing a woman's proper social role. Like Kiarostami's film, the main character is a film director very much like the actual director, whose actual previous films are integrated within the current project. Like Makhmalbaf's film, the outcome of the film (rather than the characters) is in doubt and depends on the filmmaking experience itself. But Bani-Etemad's subject is the postrevolutionary gendered subject, and specifically the feminine subject whose proper realization is not self-evident until discovered through the self-reflexive process of the film. In the Islamic Republic, where postrevolutionary women's role was reassigned to the domestic sphere, what does it mean to be a woman filmmaker? To make a film about finding a model (through one's films) of a good mother? And what does it mean to make a film about such a film? Representation documents the possibilities of experience; experience and identity can be acknowledged as real through their representation.

At the other end of the professional generation is Samira Makhmalbaf, whose film *The Apple* (1998) is a small gem of Iranian reflexive filmmaking. Like *Close-Up*, it is a recreation of a publicly documented event: residents in a poor neighborhood in south Tehran reported to the authorities that a neighbor had never allowed his two daughters to leave the house. The authorities investigated and the press covered the case: the father was unemployed, the mother was blind, and the two children could not even speak. The film seems to be a documentary, but then not: how could real life be so spontaneously poetic? In the beginning of the film, the two girls seem to be mentally, as well as socially and physically, immobilized, and when their father again locks them up, he seems to be a villain. But like *The Mirror*, *The Apple* pushes through genre boundary to something new: a documentation of the quiet possibilities of freedom for unexpected agents in postrevolutionary Iran. The father and mother are assuaged of their fearful assumptions; the girls leave the confines of home to explore the neighborhood and make friends. An apple dangles just out of reach: knowledge not as sin, but as collective adventure; filmmaking not as an original artifact, but as itself a contingent participant in the everyday real.[55]

## Life Is Here/Life As Elsewhere

For twenty years, from 1986 to 2007, Iranian cinema was probably the most dynamic in the world. This was also the period when the most positive results of the 1979 revolution were becoming clear: a healthier, better educated, more integrated, youthful population increasingly understanding themselves to be citizen participants in a national project with collective political and individual social ramifications.[56] The creative energy that was so present in Iranian films was a reflection of the dynamism present in the society, with cinema being one of the main venues for the public exploration of previously hidden social questions and problems. Reflexive filmmaking provided an unspoken dialectic of mutual self-recognition between filmmakers and audience, establishing a sense of intimacy and shared participation in the excitement of new endeavors. Even conventionally made films with storylines that might have been considered mildly thoughtful in other national contexts were often thrillingly forthright in Iran:

[55] For more developed discussions of *The Apple*, see the interview with Samira Makhmalbaf by Sheila Johnston, "Quietly Ruling the Roost," *Sight and Sound*, 9(1) (1999), 18–20, and Moruzzi, "Women's Space/Cinema Space," 54–55.

[56] As is pointed out in Chapter 4, "Food as a Social Relation," at the time of the revolution the majority of the Iranian population was illiterate, with a large statistical gap between male and female literacy rates, and an enormous difference existed between urban and rural levels of social and material development. For a detailed overview of changes in women's social development over time and distinguished by geographical region, see Azadeh Kian-Thiébaut, "From Motherhood to Equal Rights Advocates: The Weakening of Patriarchal Order," *Iranian Studies*, 38(1) (March 2005), 45–66, and Sepideh Yousefzadeh Faal Deghati, *Childhoods Embargoed: Constructing and Reconstructing Multidimensional Child Poverty in Iran, 1984–2009* (Maastricht: Boekenplan, 2013).

Mehdi Fakhimzadeh's *The Spouse* (1994), about a wife promoted over her husband in the business where they both work (and including a memorable car chase with a redoubtable policewoman in full black *chador*), and Fareidun Jayrani's *Red* (1999), about domestic violence and a wife's forceful efforts to resist, are two prime examples. Every film was a possible revelation, not just in cinematic terms but of the expanding daily possibilities of life itself.

This was as true for films that attempted to reveal the grim realities of injustice, inequality, or deprivation: the freedom to do so, even in the face of government pressure, was itself a fervent new sensibility of shared recognition. This postrevolutionary fervor was more social than political; a society coming to terms with itself and its possibilities. Life was difficult, and the authorities might be arbitrary, but there was no more exciting place to be than here at home. Iranian filmmaking seemed to be leading the way by acknowledging the initiative of the independent-minded Mina; films documented the difficult social truths of an energetically plural modern nation, grounded in a very local sense of place, claiming an identity of their own.

Perhaps it was inevitable that this trajectory of promise would decline. In 1986, Beyzaie opened up a whole range of representational possibilities, both cinematic and national, with *Bashu*. In 2006, Massoud Bakhshi presented *Tehran Has No More Pomegranates!*, a film about the impossibility of making a film about the city and the people of Tehran, a film made theoretically impossible not by the residents (identified from the beginning as historical thieves and criminals, as quoted by a thirteenth-century Persian historian), but by the official conundrums of its postrevolutionary contradictions.[57]

*Tehran Has No More Pomegranates!* is wryly black-humored, affectionately skeptical of Tehran's realities and dreams. It is a shaggy-dog story of a film, an apparently haphazard urban journey that is an adult version of the episodic quest films of the earlier children's film genre. If the children's films usually presented an innocently naïve perspective on the turmoil of life around them, *Pomegranates!* is all grown up but

[57] The film opens with this quote, from the thirteenth-century geography *Asar al Bilad*: "Tehran is a large village near the city of Rey, full of gardens and fruit trees. Its inhabitants live in anthill-like underground holes. The village's several districts are constantly at war. Tehranis' main occupations are theft and crime, although the king pretends they are subject to him. They grow excellent fruits, notably an excellent pomegranate, which is found only in Tehran."

still intent on finding its way home, even if it can't get the requisite permits. The film claims its own nonexistence (its narrator – the director – describes it through voice-over as a documentary that couldn't get made), but it won't let go the reflexive cinematic embrace of the city as historically absent-minded construct and contemporary contradiction. Bakhshi has a sharp eye for absurdity, to be found both among ordinary Tehranis and in official authority. Although there is a strong current of irony that flows through most Iranian jokes, it has been mostly absent from the serious, sincere endeavors of postrevolutionary filmmaking.[58] But the sincerely skeptical humor is essential to *Pomegranates!* It sustains both its commitment and its diffidence, and especially its keen affection for a city that is now full of traffic and air pollution instead of fruit trees.

Without humor, the response to absurdity points in the other direction: over the hills and far away. After *Pomegranates!*, a whole series of Iranian feature films revolve around their middle-class protagonists' dreams of exile: life as elsewhere.[59] For mid-century avant-garde Central European novelists like Milan Kundera, "life as elsewhere" was a scathing reference to the banal middle-class escapism (whether artistic or romantic) of mediocre sensibilities, blind to the ramifications of actual choices and actions in the postwar (rather than postrevolutionary) society around them.[60] Cinematic representations of Iranian dreams of escape come all too close to being a caricature of their earlier Central European counterparts, but without the black humor: middle-class visionaries staking their futures on a fantasy of elsewhere, oblivious to what lies beyond the immediacy of their own - self-preoccupation. There are glimpses of other possibilities, be they in reference to class, ethnicity, or aesthetic sensibility. But the

58 Two noteworthy exceptions are the aforementioned *Pickpockets Don't Go to Heaven* and Mehrjui's sharp-eyed social comedy *Mama's Guests* (2004).

59 In *An Accented Cinema: Exilic and Diasporic Filmmaking* (Princeton, NJ: Princeton University Press, 2001), Hamid Naficy utilizes the concepts of *fernweh* (nostalgia for elsewhere) and *heimweh* (nostalgia for homeland) to capture the international phenomenon of displaced positionality among exile or diaspora filmmakers; the striking thing about so many local Iranian films is the extent to which this nostalgia of displacement functions while they are apparently at home, in the here and now.

60 Milan Kundera, *Life as Elsewhere*, trans. Aaron Asher (New York: Harper Collins, 2000), first published in Czech in 1973.

protagonists' vision is myopic; they just can't seem to see the complex panorama that insistently surrounds them.[61]

The limitations inherent in this sincere escapism are quite evident in two of the Iranian films that garnered huge international critical and popular attention: Bahman Ghobadi's *No One Knows about Persian Cats* (2009) and Asghar Farhadi's *Nader and Simin, A Separation* (2011). *Persian Cats* is a film that is in every way the inverse of *Tehran Has No More Pomegranates!*, including its rapturous international reception compared to the relatively minimal response to Bakhshi's film. If *Pomegranates!* was a late example of reflexive cinema and a self-deprecatingly ironic meditation on the kinetic energy of contemporary Tehran, *Persian Cats* is seemingly reflexive by accident. Made by Ghobadi without a permit, it was a brilliant survey of the vibrant Tehran underground music scene, stapled around the minimal plot of touchingly young "rock" musicians of questionable talent who will do anything unto death (although this is clearly part of the scripted feature rather than the documentary aspect of the film) to get out of the country. Their quest is for a visa; their dream is to perform at an English music festival. The wonderful irony of the whole project – that the immensely variegated Tehran music environment offers a richer set of opportunities to local musicians, most of whom would be lucky if they are successful enough abroad to be consigned to a tiny slice of the world music niche – seems lost on the director, the actors, or the audience.[62]

[61] Increasingly, some of the most striking and provocative Iranian films directly addressing these issues of perspective and representation are classic documentaries, as though the most powerful thing a director can do is to provide a forum for the revelation of an experience that would otherwise be present but all too often overlooked. A striking example is Mahnaz Afzali's *The Ladies Room* (2003), which is filmed entirely in a women's restroom in a Tehran public park; in a marginal space, marginal women sit in a circle and chat among themselves about taboo experiences of homelessness, addiction, prostitution, and family abuse. Some of these documentaries can be surprisingly moving despite their clunky efforts at dramatic editorializing; Hassan Rastgar's *Alas Nice Days* (2007), about an HIV-positive working-class couple and their fears over the wife's pregnancy, is extremely poignant in spite of the baroquely melodramatic music that often surges up from the background.

[62] A somewhat similar version of the youthful life-as-elsewhere dilemma, but made by a diaspora Iranian-Australian filmmaker, is the feature *My Tehran for Sale* (2009) by Granaz Moussavi. The opening scene of the film cuts between the rock music of an illegal rave at a farm outside Tehran, and the folk music being played by a family gathering of the Afghan farm workers. Both groups get

Ghobadi's film would seem to be slyly reflexive: the intermingling of the representation of original and real material through the blurring of the genres of feature and documentary; the narrative that plays off the nonprofessional identities and experiences of the actors. The film would seem to offer a quixotic narrative quest through a fabulously real musical landscape. But the didactic storyline takes over; rather than merging reflexively with the representational structure of the film, it is imposed on it. Ghobadi is determined to respect the absolutist sincerity of the life-as-elsewhere fantasy and provide it with some extra political support: innocence martyred by state repression (the hero jumps out a window – to his death – when the security police raid a noisy party).[63] The film pulls back from its own multiple reflexive possibilities: the politics become predictable; the narrative becomes melodrama; the musical context is reduced to background picturesque. Life as elsewhere, indeed.

In contrast, Farhadi's *A Separation* treated the life-as-elsewhere dream as one strand of a complex and multilayered story. Farhadi's films are nuanced portraits of the crosscutting relations among classes, genders, and social groups. They are ambivalent explorations of the implications small personal choices can have on the delicate web of individual connections that make up any social network, carefully crafted and beautifully acted. When *A Separation* won the 2012 Academy Award for Best Foreign Language Film, the event marked the institutional acceptance of an Iranian film as part of mainstream global cinema. It was a relief for the audience, inside and outside Iran, to see something familiar on-screen, a representation of recognizable middle-class characters and stories that almost could have been made anywhere. But it is precisely this achievement of conventional familiarity, including a strict return to the expected techniques of original

raided, but from then on the film forgets the Afghans, while following the travails of its middle-class heroine, a theater actress rather than a musician. She gets away and hopes for love and a visa from a visiting Iranian-Australian; by the film's end, she's in Australia, HIV-positive, and in detention as an illegal immigrant. We never find out what happened to the Afghans.

63 Kundera's hero catches a mortal case of pneumonia because he insists on freezing outside on the balcony rather than returning to a party where he has just embarrassed himself. But the hero's tragic pose is undermined by Kundera's subsequent extension of the reader's perspective to another character who had been secondary; all was not as it had seemed; the real tragedy was in the frame but previously out of focus.

feature filmmaking (i.e., tight control of script and shooting by the director, a realist narrative convention that doesn't question the fourth wall) that marks a turning away from the dynamic mirror of reflexive filmmaking. Beginning with *About Elly* (2009) and including the Spanish language *Everybody Knows* (2018, costarring Javier Bardem and Penelope Cruz), Farhadi's films often depend on unexpected plot revelations, their suspense more in the narrative tradition of Hitchcock than the reflexive project of the Iranian New Wave or even the earlier neorealist tradition.[64] Farhadi is an accomplished, thoughtful filmmaker. But his films are a return to cinematic tradition, and a retreat from the radical promise of both postrevolutionary Iranian cinema and the social politics that this cinema has struggled so originally to reflect.

## Film as the Mirror of Possibilities

The reflexivity of Iranian postrevolutionary cinema has been as much a pragmatic response to contextual necessity as an original creative strategy. Filmmaking itself became part of the process of political self-reflection under duress, in that films enabled an active self-recognition, by filmmaker and audience, that enabled further possibilities for individual and collective agency. Mohsen Makhmalbaf, in the documentary *Iran: A Cinematographic Revolution* (Nader Homayoun, 2007), explained that postrevolutionary reflexive (what he calls documentary) cinema provided Iranians with a recognizable self-representation and self-reflection, a release from the rigid mask of ideological conformity that had been imposed on national identity. "These crowds [referring to *Salaam Cinema*] manifested this desire to be seen. Ideology had blinkered us, stopped us seeing ourselves, as if we were blindfolded. When you take off the blindfold, you're relieved: 'This is who I am!'" Film had become a mirror in which the filmmaker and audience could see themselves, while recognizing and reflecting back the dynamic multiplicity of a self-image at odds with official strictures.

As a postrevolutionary cultural representation, Iranian cinema loosely tracked the emerging social possibilities and ongoing political

[64] Adam Eisenberg, in his review for the Tribeca Film Festival, makes the connection with Hitchcock's suspense in his review of *About Elly*. See Adam Eisenberg, "Tribeca Review: *About Elly* Brings the Iranian Middle Class Center Stage," April 27, 2009, www.flavorwire.com/18391/tribeca-review-about-elly.

tensions in the Islamic Republic. But by the summer of 2009, the tense balance between Iranian state and society, always complicated by the fragmented reality of both, was broken. The strongly contested outcome of the June Presidential election, and the government's very open use of force, shocked the population.[65] Since that critical break, all forms of representation – political and aesthetic – have been more heavily repressed. Certainly, state repression had been increasing before 2009. But the questing negotiation that had characterized the relations between state and society for the previous twenty years was changed. For cinema and society, the reflexive inquiry of coded self-recognition gave way to more direct questions and definite statements. Having lost its authority, the government has resorted to increasingly more bluntly authoritarian tactics. The probable winner of the 2009 Presidential election – Mir-Hossein Mousavi – was put under indefinite house arrest. Mohsen Makhmalbaf has been living outside Iran since 2009. Jafar Panahi, the director of *The Mirror* and an outspoken supporter of the 2009 Green Movement, was jailed and then placed under house arrest and banned for twenty years from making films, communicating with media, or leaving the country; he was later allowed more freedom of movement, but his passport was not returned. In 2022, Panahi was arrested again while following up on the situation of another arrested filmmaker; he went on a hunger strike and several days later was released to house arrest. In 2023, Dariush Mehrjui, one of the enduring masters of both prerevolutionary and postrevolutionary Iranian cinema, was murdered with his wife in their home, an attack that many (whether justly or unjustly) attribute to shady state sponsorship.

In 2014, Reza Mirkarimi's film *Today* provided a relatively unremarked but important contribution to the genre of Iranian reflexive filmmaking. The film is a low-key narrative about a taciturn, impassive taxi driver waiting in and around a hospital for news of his passenger, the reactions of those he encounters, and the brusquely efficient head nurse who observes him. The plot involves the taxi driver's passenger, an abused and endangered pregnant woman. But the film revolves around the audience's reactions to the (mostly mistaken) reactions of

[65] A more thorough discussion of the significance of the 2009 Iranian Presidential election contest and its ongoing implications is provided in Chapter 8, "Women, Life, Freedom."

others. The pace is slow enough for the audience to begin to take for granted the moral positions of the protagonists, and our own audience perspective. We think we have it figured out: who is right; who is wrong; who should know better. But as the complexities of the story stretch themselves out, we begin to question, even as we ourselves silently disapprove of most characters' mistaken projections onto the frustrating *tabula rasa* of the main character's stoic silence, if we are similarly judging a fragment of a story that we have impatiently taken to be complete?

As spectators, we bristle at the condemnations of the innocent driver as domestic abuser, even as we must admit to ourselves that those doing the condemning are nonetheless enacting an ethical attitude (against a man who would beat a vulnerable pregnant woman) we would probably endorse. We catch ourselves rejoicing in the human sympathy extended to the driver by those who are actually indulging violent domestic abuse. Toward the end of the film, a young male doctor vents his frustration by hitting and kicking the taxi driver, whom he assumes to be the perpetrator of the woman passenger's tragic fate. We watch, horrified and strangely satisfied, as the disabled old man is pushed to the floor: horrified that his innocence is so wrongly abused; satisfied that the young doctor would react so righteously to the violent victimization of a pregnant woman. At that moment, our doubled reaction becomes our own self-reflection: we recognize the ethical implications of the on-screen burst of satisfyingly righteous anger. In giving in to his own violence, the doctor has become what he was condemning: an abuser, a perpetrator of the same kind of self-indulgent, impatient (in)justice by the strong against the weak that he was presumably punishing. And in that moment, as we simultaneously identity with virtuous retribution and recoil at brutal injustice, the audience must ask itself: to what extent might we have been doing the same?

## But Life Goes On…

Mirkarimi's *Today* demonstrated that reflexive filmmaking could still implicate the audience's viewing experience with the representational complexities of contemporary Iranian daily life and its historical underpinnings. But the filmmaker who has most clearly continued to expand the potential of reflexive filmmaking has been Jafar Panahi.

Panahi has been banned from leaving the country or making films since 2010.[66] Since then he has made an average of a film every two years, all illicit and all dealing explicitly and self-reflexively with the constraints of forbidden filmmaking. Over time, the perspective of these films has evolved. The video documentary *This Is Not a Film* (2011) and the feature *Closed Curtain* (2013) are both claustrophobically confined, as Panahi was, to the private space of the home, even if *Closed Curtain* insists on a larger view.[67] *Taxi* (2015) reprised the format of Panahi's mentor Kiarostami's *Ten* (2002), in that it all takes place within a taxi driving around Tehran. But Panahi is the driver, and the interactions provide glimpses of the range of choices (ethical, personal, ideological, and practical) that are happening indirectly and directly around us all the time. The film *3 Faces* (2018) got further out of the city, creating a road trip movie with overtones of Kiarostami's *And Life Goes On* (1992). Then in 2022 Panahi completed *No Bears*, a film that plays with fragmented, cross-cutting filmmaking stories, the implicated resonances of his own and others' earlier reflexive films, and the tragic, absurdist contradictions of life, art, and ethics in Iran today.

*No Bears* cuts between the two filmmaking stories. The first follows an Iranian refugee couple stuck somewhere in Turkey who are trying to obtain the false passports necessary for them both to leave for Europe; Panahi is directing the film, even though he is stuck in a border village in Iran. The second story observes Panahi's travails with his crew in Turkey, and the village community where he is

[66] Iran is not the only state that has restricted Panahi's travel. In 2001, while changing planes in the JFK airport on his way from Hong Kong to Buenos Aires to attend a film festival, Panahi was detained by US security officials. They wanted to fingerprint and photograph him; he refused on the grounds that he was not a criminal. He was denied a phone call or interpreter and was detained in handcuffs until the following day, when he was returned to Hong Kong rather than allowed to proceed on to Buenos Aires. (Iranian security authorities also make use of the intermediate no man's land of airport passport control to detain individuals without recourse to legal or social support.)

[67] Bakhshi's *Tehran Has No More Pomegranates!* and Ghobadi's *No One Knows about Persian Cats* both dealt with the subject of lack of official permission but were made out and about in Tehran. While Ghobadi's story is a melodramatic escape fantasy attached to a vibrant music documentary, Bakhshi's is in some ways a lighthearted, earlier version of Panahi's *This Is Not a Film*. Both films are explicitly premised on the official prohibition against their existence, but while *Pomegranates!* can afford to treat its situation as an absurdist existential joke, Panahi's film and his situation are all too serious.

staying; his interactions with these apparently separate groups nonetheless implicate each other. Post-pandemic, directing a film by video conferencing doesn't seem as outlandish. Yet Panahi's regular search through the first third of the film for an adequate internet signal (mobile phone held up overhead on the terrace, on the roof, and up a hill) comically resonates with similar scenes in Kiarostami's *The Wind Will Carry Us* (1999), in which a frustrated director stuck in a village waits for the events of his film to happen (and keeps searching for a signal). *No Bears* is a film haunted by other films, and other filmmakers.[68] But it is resolutely its own, plural story and individual statement.

The crosscutting is (intentionally) confusing. Initially, Panahi is preoccupied with keeping track of what is happening with the Turkish film (is it a documentary? a representation of filming a documentary?), its cast and crew. There are details (regarding passports, smugglers, and personal motivations) to which neither we nor Panahi are fully privy. On the Iranian side of the border, the village seems a picturesque local backdrop; Panahi snaps random photos. Initially, the two stories cut back and forth at extended intervals. In Turkey, everything hinges on a passport that might be too fake to be useful. In Iran, Panahi drives for a clandestine nighttime meeting with his assistant director. Their interaction, in which Panahi is almost, but then not, persuaded to cross over the national border, pivots the movie and reorients it to the unexpectedly messy, mutual reality of what is happening in Iran. The border is under our feet; the choice is in the moment. Panahi chooses: he marches back down the hill. Life is not elsewhere; life is here.

And life is messy. On the drive back into the village, a young woman abruptly runs before the car, begging Panahi for help. She is blurting something about a photo; neither we nor Panahi are clear what she is talking about. Back in his rented rooms, Panahi looks through his camera memory; perhaps he deletes something. Neither the supposed photo nor the scene it apparently represents are ever seen; the photo is a myth, whether or not it ever existed. Yet it becomes a fought-over symbol, the documentation that will settle individual claims and

[68] *No Bears* (2022) also has extraordinary resonance with *Hit the Road* (2021), the film about a family transporting their elder son to smugglers on the Turkish border, made by Jafar Panahi's son Panah Panahi.

resolve social contradictions. Panahi is repeatedly called to account by shifting groups of villagers who insist that he supply the photo and appreciate the strangeness and significance of "our traditions." Panahi is polite, if a little rueful. All the negotiations are full or *ta'arofs* – this is *ta'arof* as weaponized politeness rather than mutual acknowledgment. The villagers resist his protestations of innocence; he is involved in whatever this (masculine) argument is (after her first irruption into the nighttime frame, the desperate young woman Gozal does not appear again). They demand that Panahi swear to his truthfulness and innocence in a ceremony that is another tradition. Yet on the way to the confrontation, Panahi encounters wise advice and (no) bears.

In the meantime, we and Panahi have almost lost track of what is happening in Turkey. The backdrop story of the backward villagers (self-described as superstitious and traditional) is the locale where the intersections of contradictory experience are most immediate: between tradition and modernity, old and young, men and women, self and other. In Turkey, the scene that should be the culmination of the exile story – the refugees' departure for the airport and the flight to Europe – becomes an adult version of the scene with Mina in *The Mirror*. The professional actress (Mina Kavani) playing the woman member of the refugee couple suddenly turns and begins to speak to the camera, addressing the viewer on the other side who is both the director Panahi (who is supposed to watch through a video link) and the audience (watching the scene on screen). She scrubs with her hand at the lipstick on her mouth, pulls off the wig covering her hair, and refuses to follow the script. The scene uncannily resembles the child Mina's ripping off of her *maghneh* and refusal to remain in character; lipstick and hairstyle a grown-up, secular version of a girl child's accommodation to a (school) uniform and conventional feminine self-representation. It seems there was an issue with a passport, although neither we nor Panahi know the details. In Turkey, the film narrative of the modern, urban couple seeking escape has collapsed. In Iran, the villagers' lives are even more imbricated in each other's and in Panahi's than we had realized, and Panahi himself is urged to leave. He does so, driving off in his car. And then he stops. Considers. Hesitates. And pulls the brake.

Both stories end in tragedy, but that is not quite the ending of the film. The authorities – of both state and community – hover, their strictures shaping the conditions of lives (and sometimes deaths). Yet within the film, the absence or presence of a passport or a photo is a diversion. The fundamental issue remains the choices we make of how to live together, and with ourselves. The mirror may have cracked, but the multiplied fragments reflect the mosaic structure of our lives, and the recognition that we are in this mess together. Panahi keeps making cinema. Life (in Iran) goes on.

# 8 *Women, Life, Freedom: One Movement out of Two Legacies*

I am not political, I have no talent in politics. But I was ready to die; it was shocking to myself. This was an extreme situation. There are situations when you feel you have to die; you are ready to die for your cause.

Before that I couldn't imagine how some people go to war, how people are ready to die for a cause. I thought this was empty talk. But last year there was this situation. Last year, for the first time in my life, I lived in the present, a very temporal time.

Every day we went in the streets, I took a shower, put on some make-up and nice clothes and I am ready to die. And I told my husband, you should look nice when you are ready to be killed. I was writing my will every night. Everyone was like this, more or less. It was very dangerous.

I am telling you this, because I am personally not a very brave person. But the situation was leading us to be heroes. It was good, because we were defending the suppressed, leading against injustice.

*M, university student, referring to the street protests following the disputed 2009 Presidential election*

## Forging Bonds of Citizenship: Women, Life, Freedom

In September 2022, a young Iranian Sunni Kurdish woman, Mahsa Jina Amini, was visiting Tehran in the company of her brother when she was detained by the morality police (known as the Guidance Patrols, the *Gasht-e Ershad*). Days later, she was pronounced dead in a hospital. The government stated she had preexisting health conditions (which her family denied), and these had led to a heart attack; witnesses to her treatment while in custody stated that she had been physically and verbally abused in the police van and had collapsed in the police station, from where she had been transferred to the hospital (an initial hospital statement stated that she was brain dead upon arrival).[1] The

[1] The two women journalists who initially covered Amini's arrest and condition in hospital, the security responses to protests outside the hospital, and her burial

combination of believable witness statements; leaked medical records of bruising, bleeding, and possible bone fractures; public skepticism of state denials of responsibility; and images of Amini wearing what most Iranians would understand to be quite modest dress and proper *hejab* led to the eruption of widespread, sustained protests, first in Tehran and then spreading broadly to other cities and regions.[2] Coalescing around the slogan "*Zan, Zendegi, Azadi*" ("Women, Life, Freedom"), a new social movement was born, with women at its symbolic and activist heart.[3]

Amini's arrest and death in September had followed closely on the case of another young woman, initially from the provinces, whose arrest because of a dispute with the Tehran Guardian Patrol had led to widespread condemnation of the state's heavy-handed enforcement of its authority to police women's bodies.[4] In July 2022, Sepideh

were themselves arrested in September 2022 and detained in prison for over a year until their release on bail in January 2024. While in prison, they were both actively doing outreach work with fellow prisoners. As soon as they were released, they were both subject to new charges filed for appearing in improper *hejab* in their release photos. See Veera Nikkilä and Helsingin Sanomat, "Iran: IPI Welcomes Temporary Release of Journalists Niloofar Hamedi and Elaheh Mohammadi while Appealing Convictions," *International Press Institute*, January 17, 2024.

2 Several researchers have created an empirical data set of the differences in national regional, ethnic, and sectarian community participation in the Women, Life, Freedom protests, as well as details of the specific kinds of protests engaged in. See Mohammad Ali Kadivar, Saber Khani, Vahid Abedini, and Samira Barzin, "The Contingency of Structures: Triggers and the Social Geography of Revolutionary Episodes in Iran 2018–2022" (Working Paper, 2024).

3 The slogan originates with the Kurdish autonomy movement and is particularly associated with the writings of Kurdish-Turkish dissident Abdullah Öcalan. The Kurdish version is usually written as "*Jin, Jîhan, Azadî.*" The slogan resonates with Mahsa Jina Amini's Kurdish name, giving it an additional significance in the Iranian context, both to commemorate her death and to include minority and marginal identities within a collective national project. For an Iranian feminist view of the significance of the mobilizations, written during the early weeks of the movement, see Fatemeh Sadeghi, "From Women's Revolution to *Jiyanist* Democracy," trans. and ed. Setareh Shohadaei, *Journal of Middle East Women's Studies* 19(3) (November 2023), 458–468.

4 The 2022 cases followed accumulating concerns about the use of physical and sexual abuse as an intentional tool of repression in Iranian prisons. In 2003, Canadian-Iranian journalist Zahra Kazemi's death in Evin Prison prompted national and international condemnation because of conflicting official statements claiming accidental death from a stroke, and medical reports indicating she had been raped and beaten. Credible reports of women (and men) being sexually abused and/or beaten by prison authorities as punishment for

Rashno, a twenty-eight-year-old student, artist, and editor from Khorramabad in western Iran, appeared on Iranian state television to confess to having violated mandatory *hejab* laws. A few days earlier, a video of her arguing on a Tehran bus with a woman attempting to enforce strict *hejab* compliance had gone viral; although the other woman had been ejected from the bus by passengers, she had filmed Rashno and threatened to send the footage to the Revolutionary Guards. Rashno was later arrested in her home and disappeared for several days before appearing on state television to make a short public confession, accusing herself and apologizing and asking forgiveness of her harasser. But she showed indications of physical abuse and was reportedly moved directly to a hospital after the television appearance, and then returned to prison. Her arrest, televised self-abasement, and continued disappearance prompted popular sympathy and an online campaign of support asking "Where is Sepideh?" Rashno was released on bail in late August 2022. Amini was arrested and died a little over two weeks later.

Televised public confessions are not new in Iran, but they are no longer considered credible by most of the public. Sepideh Rashno's public humiliation was widely regarded as disproportionate to her offense: summer is hot, Tehran air is polluted, and many women seasonally expand the boundaries of state-imposed modesty standards. Summer pushbacks against strict mandatory *hejab* and the accompanying state crackdowns have been a regular push-and-pull standoff for years. The much more intensive enforcement by President Raisi's hardline administration came after a series of other crises of the state's political legitimacy: excessive Covid deaths blamed on the state's resistance to accepting Western vaccines; ongoing economic and environmental crises. Televised confessions had usually been reserved for oppositional political activists or notorious criminals; a young woman's apparent torture and forced confession for the crime of bad *hejab* seemed like a new state breach of a fraying social contract. Sympathy for Rashno was based on popular shock that such a stark public punishment has been meted out for a common and what many regarded as a trivial infraction: if such a thing could happen to her, then how easily could it happen to me or my sister/my daughter/my

participating in protests emerged after the 2009 Green Movement, as well as during the 2022 Women, Life, Freedom movement.

wife? Then Mahsa Jina Amini was arrested for a similar and even more minor *hejab* infraction, but she wound up dead, and popular anger and frustration exploded into what became "Women, Life, Freedom."

During the autumn months of 2022 and the winter months of 2023, mass protests and demonstrations seemed to sweep the country.[5] Women were at the symbolic center of the new movement, and often its active public faces. Many women publicly cut their hair and openly threw off their *hejab*. Ordinary people rallied to the support of young women being harassed on the street for supposedly immodest dress. Now people knew that it wasn't enough to push a vehement critic out of the bus as they had in support of Sepideh Rashno; defending women's personal bodily freedom was in fact a matter of life and death. For many women, the protests – whether by masses in the street or individual women appearing publicly with their hair intentionally uncovered – were about women's right to bodily autonomy and self-determination. Yet for others, resistance to state authority remained a matter of personal patriarchal honor: only a close male member of the family (not the state) had a right to protect and enforce the *nomous* (reputational and sexual honor) of a family's women, since women's honor was also the honor of a family (and its men).[6] Even as many celebrated the centrality of women as equal political subjects within the overarching framework of the aspirational slogan "Women, Life, Freedom," slogans and protests against the Islamic Republic's theocratic institutions and its representative political leadership led to expectations of imminent regime change.[7]

[5] Kadivar et al.'s research demonstrates that although protests did occur around the country they were unevenly distributed, including striking differences of participation among provincial areas and ethnic groups.

[6] This retained presence of patriarchal moral codes within a women-centered protest movement has sometimes been overlooked in the celebration of men's apparent solidarity. See, for instance, the affirmation of the protest chant "I will kill, I will kill, whoever killed my sister" in the otherwise sharply insightful inquiry into the question, "*What does transnational feminist solidarity look like at this moment?*" (emphasis in original) in Hanieh Molana, A. Marie Ranjbar, and Sahar Razavi, "Woman, Life, Freedom: Decoding the Feminist Uprising in Iran," *Political Geography*, 103 (May 1, 2023), 102834.

[7] Peyman Jafari characterizes the Women, Life, Freedom uprisings as "revolt with a revolutionary perspective" and argues that they have "facilitated the emergence of a revolutionary subjectivity" and reclaimed the concept of revolution from its historical appropriation by the conservative authorities of the Islamic Republic. Yet the "WLF revolt" followed the model of most of the aborted Arab Spring uprisings by failing to integrate economic grievances with politics demands:

Iranians inside and outside Iran were giddy with the sense of revolutionary potential; many Iranians outside, as well as some of those inside, were narrowly insistent that this, now, finally was the new revolution, and anyone not celebrating regime change and not denouncing everything and anything associated with the Islamic Republic since 1979 was a political suspect. But revolution for what, and by whom? Despite unprecedented levels of protest across much of the country, and gleeful predictions by external and diaspora observers of the imminent fall or overthrow of the current regime, it wasn't clear what would or could come next. Another version of an old-fashioned monarchy? Civil war and state collapse (accompanied by the collapse of the state's capacity to provide public goods like electricity and running water)? All too much like the 1979 Revolution that so many now confidently rue as an overreaction to a corrupt and repressive regime, the 2022 protests were more against an out-of-touch authoritarian leadership than they were clearly in favor of a specific institutional creation. Women, Life, Freedom was a movement claiming a new and expanded political subjectivity: both women and men's right to full participatory citizenship and membership in a shared national polity. But the existing state responded with intensified repression and violence. Some state tactics were familiar from previous protest uprisings: Sharif University was raided and put under siege (like the violent incursions into Tehran University in 1999); nonviolent protesters and even bystanders were shot in the streets, arrested and tortured with open impunity (as had happened in 2009).

The state and its apparatus of domination remained in place. By the time the active protests dissipated in late winter 2023, many observers considered that despite whatever changes had taken place in society, the street, and the family, the continuing existence of the authoritarian structures of the Islamic Republic meant the movement had failed.

I think this is a mistake. The Women, Life, Freedom movement didn't come out of nowhere; it emerged from a longer series of similarly "failed" but accumulating collective experiences of building shared political solidarities, awareness, and participation. Taking the

politics and economics as separate spheres, rather than mutual aspects of a political economy. See Peyman Jafari, "Revolt with a Revolutionary Perspective," *Iranian Studies*, 56(3) (July 2023), 569–575. I would argue that the revolutionary perspective has been continuous since the 1979 Revolution, but has evolved through both more latent and more active periods.

state is not always an unambiguous mark of success, and social movements can nonetheless succeed in expanding popular conceptions of citizenship. Women, Life, Freedom emerged from the integration of two distinct political genealogies: the genealogy of postrevolutionary protests to demand accountability from the state, and the genealogy of collaborative interventions to expand women's political subjectivity and engagement. Only by recognizing this shared inheritance can we see what Women, Life, Freedom has accomplished, and where it might be leading.

## Chronic Crisis: Two Steps Forward, One Step Back

Iran always seems to be in crisis or on the verge. Workers, students, women, voters, and ordinary people of all ages and conditions have been talking, organizing, striking, and protesting at frequent intervals since the 1979 Revolution and before. Sometimes they have been able to unify in mass collective actions over shared goals; sometimes in smaller or more cohesive groups organizing around their own specific frustrations. Sometimes these groups have intersected and overlapped, leading to major national upheavals, significant for what these actions represented about popular expectations for political representation and social and economic justice, even if they rarely achieved their goals. From the beginning of the Islamic Republic, students and workers – the vanguard and the backbone of the revolution – were especially targeted for control, and willing to organize for their shared interests.[8] Labor strikes are protests too, even if not always regarded as directly political: organized public, collective actions against what are perceived to be unfair or inadequate shared conditions, they are

[8] Sustained labor strikes in the Iranian oil sector helped bring down the Pahlavi monarchy and have recurred intermittently in the Islamic Republic. Although independent labor unions are banned since the revolution, many workers have organized themselves through syndicates and associations that coordinate collective negotiations and labor actions, including strikes. The June 2021 national Iran workers strike, known as Campaign 1400, began among temporary and contract oil, gas, and petrochemical workers in southern Iran, but spread nationally. The strike mirrored a similar set of labor actions in August 2020. For a sense of the many Iranian industrial actions that have become prominent enough to gain some international attention, see the section on Iran on the IndustriALL Global Union's website, https://www.industriall-union.org/search?query=iran&language=en.

challenges to relations of authority and have implicit, and sometimes explicit, political significance. Labor strikes by Iranian miners, teachers, and bus drivers, among others, have been recurrent and widely supported, both within the country and outside; labor leaders, especially those who have been more effective organizers, have been systematically and often violently repressed.[9] Generations of students have thrown themselves into support for political change, been disillusioned, and gone back to their private concerns a little older, grimmer, and more skeptical. But always, even in the most depressing interim periods of apathy and cynicism, there was a sense of possible change. The economic situation is dire, the political spaces are closed, and social life is constrained. And then there is a spark. This is what the status quo fears, and why there is repression. A society that has created a revolution is postrevolutionary, and that lived experience of transformative collective action changes the structure of expectations even when everyone is most bemoaning their national fate. The emancipatory impulse can become dormant, but it is always latent.

Sometimes from inside the country, often from outside, I have observed Iranians go through major crisis periods of protest, even if looking back they always seem less significant than whatever is the

[9] The Syndicate of Workers of Tehran and Suburbs Bus Company (SWTSBC), a prerevolutionary union, reemerged as an independent workers' organization in 2004 under the leadership of Mansour Osanloo. The SWTSBC coordinated bus operators' collective actions during 2004 and 2005, which were then heavily repressed. Osanloo and other activists were fired from the United Bus Company of Tehran in 2005, and Osanloo was arrested. He was released but detained again in 2006 (possibly by *Ansare-Hezbollah*, the neofascist paramilitary group unofficially linked with the most conservative elements of the regime), beaten, and sent to Tehran's Evin Prison (the prison associated with political prisoners). Released after public outcry, in 2007 he was sentenced to a five-year prison term, but sent to Rajaee Shahr Prison in Karaj rather than Evin, because he had helped Evin prison guards organize their union. In August 2010, Mansour Osanloo and his brother Afshin Osanloo were both arrested on the charge of "collusion and assembly with the intent to act against national security"; Mansour was sentenced to a year in prison, while Afshin was sentenced to five years in prison and died in Rajaee Shahr Prison in 2013 under suspicious circumstances. Mansour Osanloo continues to organize and mobilize for workers' rights. Both brothers seem to have been targeted for more violent repression because of their effectiveness as organizers, and their cases have received widespread support from international labor and human rights organizations (Amnesty International, Human Rights Watch, International Labour Organization, IndustriAll, International Brotherhood of Teamsters, International Transport Workers' Federation, etc.).

current crisis situation of the moment. For many years, I consistently described Iran as a situation of two steps forward, one step back: a dynamic, politicized society that was continually moving forward in terms of its own self-consciousness and democratization, while the authoritarian factions of the government regularly cracked down on individuals, groups, and movements. One had to look to less formally political, everyday indicators to recognize how Iranians kept developing their political aspirations and expectations, building on their previous struggles even as they seemed to be blocked at every effort and thrown back from some. Formal government statements were rhetorical indicators, often intended either to shore up competitive positions within internal political (usually conservative) rivalries or to annoy Western observers.[10] That a state's public pronouncements and policies are not reflective of people's consent would seem to be obvious under conditions of authoritarianism; you can't trust a government to reflect popular sentiment when the government doesn't trust its own people. I trusted Iranians, the Iranians inside the country, who were living in a postrevolutionary society and making do with each other's realities as postrevolutionary citizens and subjects. But even I would get jaded. Maybe that comes with age. It was always easy to blame the younger generation. "They're not political," we would say. "They're spoiled by their parents" (who feel guilty about bequeathing their offspring a tarnished dream and a disappointing reality). "They only think of themselves." And then something would happen; every ten years or so the spark, and I would bite my tongue and look on in awe as a new generation rediscovered the promise of the revolution by acting together on their own collective frustration, and their deep-seated expectation that nation and state could be, must be, more than the current experience.[11]

[10] This was especially true under President Ahmadinejad, who was an effective provocateur, if an erratic, unsteady leader.

[11] Several months before the Women, Life, Freedom protests began, imprisoned journalist and political dissident Keyvan Samimi suggested that "From wherever anyone is standing, take one step forward." See S*, "Anger Piled Atop Anger: Iran Diary," *Bidoun*, January 12, 2023, https://www.bidoun.org/articles/anger-piled-atop-anger. Writing in the midst of her experiences of the early months of the Women, Life, Freedom movement, S*, the young Tehrani woman author of the article (which is organized as diary entries), mentioned that Samimi's words hadn't meant anything to her until she found herself in the middle of an effort to make change. Samimi, a former head of the Iranian Writers Association and

## Student Protests in 1999: Inchoate Rebellion in the Universities

After the end of the Iran–Iraq War, when life began to normalize in the 1990s, students and intellectuals were the core of support for the *Do-e Khordad* (Second of Khordad, or May 23, 1997, the day of Mohammad Khatami's election to the Presidency) Reformist movement and politically and practically invested in the success of President Khatami's Reform project and administration. This was not only an ideological commitment to opening up public space for critical engagement. One of the ongoing insecurities for regime critics had been the "chain murders," a series of killings of dissident writers and intellectuals that went on for ten years (1988–1998). Supporters of a Reformist position felt (and sometimes were) targeted for assassination by shady and unaccountable elements of the state.[12] Khatami sponsored the renewal of the independent press, and multiple new and independent newspapers suddenly emerged, presenting guardedly critical commentary on national politics (television remained national and a mouthpiece for the conservatives).[13] Morning and evening, our household (like so many others) made sure someone went to the corner store to purchase a selection of these publications. They were avidly read and passed hand to hand; then one or several of the titles would be shut down by the conservative Judiciary for having gone too far, only to reopen within days under a new name, but with the same publisher, journalists, and editorial position. Newspapers, like films of the time, suddenly presented Iranians with a recognizable, shared

editor of (banned) independent publication *Iran-e Farda*, is in his 70s, a longtime activist who has been imprisoned multiple times before and since the 1979 Revolution, including for activities connected with the 2009 Green Movement and in 2019 for participating in a peaceful protest in Tehran on International Workers' Day. He was released in January 2023 but arrested again in April 2023.

12 The impunity of attacks on prominent critics continued even after the chain murders were resolved. Saeed Hajjarian, one of the most important strategists of the Reformist movement and among President Khatami's advisors, was shot in the face by a motorcyclist in March 2000. He survived with severe health complications that impeded his political activities. At the time, motorcyclists, singly or in a group, wearing an unofficial uniform of dark pants and a light or white shirt, commonly and publicly harassed and attacked students and prominent political critics. The attackers were assumed to be members of the conservative paramilitaries (either the Basij or Ansar-e Hezbollah).

13 See Kaveh Ehsani, "'The Conservatives Have Misjudged': A Conversation with Ahmad Bourghani," *Middle East Report* 212 (Fall 1999).

reflection of themselves and their concerns, even if that view was refracted through an allusive language that was always negotiating the heavy constraints of state regulation and censorship. If films were the coded representations of daily life, newspapers were the public voice that could focus attention.

In 1998 and 1999, the independent newspapers were instrumental in investigating the chain murders and revealed increasing evidence that the murders had been sponsored by the Intelligence Ministry.[14] Pressured by President Khatami, in January 1999 the Intelligence Ministry announced that "rogue elements" within its ranks had committed the murders, but that they had been arrested and imprisoned. In June, it was announced that Saeed Emami, one of the "rogue elements" (and under twenty-four-hour prison watch), had committed suicide the previous night by drinking hair remover in the prison bathroom. Much of the independent press, public, and the families of the victims viewed Emami's death as a cover-up of wider, and higher level, involvement.

During this febrile period, in early July the Iranian parliament narrowly passed a new, even more repressive press law. On the eve of the vote, the independent newspaper *Salaam* published an internal government report indicating that the new press law originated with Saeed Emami, the disgraced, dead, former intelligence vice-minister who had been held publicly responsible for the chain murders. *Salaam* was closed down on July 7, and University of Tehran students organized peaceful protests against the closure.[15] That evening, July 9, the university campus and dormitories were raided, invaded by hundreds of riot police and armed paramilitaries who attacked students in their dormitories; several students were injured and one was killed.[16]

[14] For an overview of the January to July 1999 events and their significance, see Kaveh Ehsani, "Do-e Khordad and the Specter of Democracy," *Middle East Report* 212 (Fall 1999).

[15] See Sha'banali Bahrampour and Ramin Karimian, "Iranian Press Update," *Middle East Report* 212 (Fall 1999).

[16] Iranian university campuses are enclosed and require identification to be admitted to the campus space. This restriction on public access is intended as a guarantee of the autonomy of the university space, rather than an enclosure of those within it. Since 1953, police and military had been banned from entering campuses (in response to the on-campus shooting of students by the army). The mass invasion of the University of Tehran campus by the paramilitaries was regarded as a direct challenge to the integrity of university life, and a flaunting of a national regulation that had endured through governments and versions of the state.

The shock of the attacks prompted more protests, in other universities and other cities. The student protests were not the first widespread uprisings after the postwar recalibrations – political and economic – of the Rafsanjani years. Immediately after the revolution and during the Iran–Iraq War, the internal political struggles and public protests were over the nature and control of the state. After the end of the war in 1988, protests were more often over civil issues and the moral economy of the revolution.[17] Ordinary Iranians had supported a revolution and overthrown a government in order to achieve a vague promise of social justice. That promise had often been made in the rhetorical language of Islam, but its substance was not merely religious. People had fought for a political promise of a just society symbolized for many by Islam; within the context of the complicated dual-natured theocratic/republican state structure of the Islamic Republic, people have been protesting for civil issues of land tenure and property rights; family law and women's rights; wages, working conditions, and workers' rights; and environmental safeguards and ecological sustainability.[18] Initially these protests had usually been quite particular and relatively confined to people with direct interest in the problem. The 1999 student protests were the first since the Reformist faction, with Khatami as President, had won some governmental power. Khatami's surprise landslide election victory had unexpectedly reminded ordinary people that they shared aspirations with their fellow citizens and were not alone in their frustrations. The students were protesting over press freedom, intellectual freedom, and also government accountability: accountability of the state to the people, and to their elected representatives. The people had elected a President; the President had opened up a sphere of public engagement through the new newspapers and called the hard liners' "rogue elements" to account. In response to the revelation of "rogue" Saeed Emami's continued influence, the conservatives had

[17] See Kaveh Ehsani and Arang Keshavarzian, "The Moral Economy of the Iranian Protests," *Jacobin* (January 11, 2018). I am indebted to both authors for their insights into the function of the "moral economy" of the revolution. For discussion of how recurring protests are integral to a crisis of representation for Iranian postrevolutionary state and society relations, see Arang Keshavarzian, "Protests, Participation and Representation in an Improvisational Polity," in Mehran Kamrava, ed., *The Sacred Republic: Power and Institutions in Iran* (London: C. Hurst & Co., 2023), 47–65.

[18] See Ehsani and Keshavarzian, "The Moral Economy of the Iranian Protests."

forged ahead with his policy and shut down *Salaam*, the newspaper responsible for the revelation. The students had protested; the ongoing and open factional rivalry within the state between the electoral and appointed branches of government, and the unaccountability of the unelected conservative powers, had culminated in the shock of the "tragedy of the university dormitory," and upheavals across the country.[19]

But what next? Every day, there were violent clashes and protests of resistance and solidarity around the universities. Every night, there were big, long discussion meetings among the students on the campus. Many slightly older people who had connections with the university, the students, or were known for their critical engagement – professors, publishers, translators, and activists – visited the meetings. Since the campus entrances were now being resolutely patrolled by the students, visitors had to be trusted to be admitted. There was a sense of immense possibility, and threat. The adults came back frustrated. Themselves often former members of the highly organized student groups before and during the Revolution, they were appalled that in this urgent moment, among the "children of the revolution," there was no plan, no platform, not even an emerging set of common goals. Observers described endless ongoing discussions involving one person after another taking the floor to make unrelated speeches about their individual grievances and frustrations; a total lack of organization, and worse, a lack of shared vision. "They don't know what they want," these older would-be mentors kept reporting. "They don't know how to come together." At the same time, credible accounts were coming through that the conservative ministries and leadership had drawn up detailed plans for retaliation that involved precise calculations of how much violent repression, in how many cities, over how many days, could be sustained while establishing order. The students were exasperated by President Khatami's restrained support. The Reformists, with ties both to the student movement and to other factions in the government, were terrified that there would be a bloodbath.

[19] For first-person accounts of the students' experience, see "MEE Correspondent" (anonymous), "Iran's 1999 Student Protests: The Hot Summer that Shook Tehran," *Middle East Eye* (July 8, 2019); Kaveh Ehsani, "'Our Letter to Khatami Was a Farewell': An Interview with Saeed Razavi-Faqih," *Middle East Report* 212 (Fall 1999).

Khatami was given an ultimatum by the military; the student protests ended.[20] Life calmed down, with seemingly little having changed. What was there to show for all that, except a slightly clearer reveal of the unequal balance of power between entrenched authority and popular legitimacy? But in the war of position within Iran, the 1999 student movement provided an important postrevolutionary point of reference. The authoritarian state had made clear that success at the ballot box did not guarantee government power. The factions in power had not succeeded in pacifying and privatizing a politicized society, let alone a younger generation assumed to have been shaped since the revolution by official state ideology.

## Thinking about Politics: A Shared Space of Freedom

In the Spring of 2007, I taught a graduate seminar on Hannah Arendt. Although I have taught individual Arendt texts before in both undergraduate and graduate courses, this was my first opportunity to teach a full course with an explicit focus on Arendt's writing and ideas. It was a normal graduate course: we didn't have time to read everything, so I selected the readings according to certain interrelated conceptual trends among her arguments. The students wrote weekly analytical papers, and a final seminar essay. There were about a dozen students enrolled, with a few extra auditors, and a core group of three really dedicated and gifted individuals (one woman and two men). There was one not especially gifted but self assured student who tended to talk too much and annoyed the other students. We met weekly, plus additional hours for individual consultation, and I was always a bit rushed on the days I was teaching to be sure that I was fully prepared, had organized my notes, taken care of student details, and managed to eat lunch before walking into the classroom in mid-afternoon. In other words, according to my experience, a very normal course. The only exceptional thing about this course was where it was: in the Iranian Institute of Philosophy in Tehran, Iran.

The *Moasaseh-ye Pazhooheshi-ye Hekmat va Falsafeh Iran* (the direct translation is the Iranian Institute of Metaphysics, Wisdom and Philosophy, but the official translation is the Iranian Institute of Philosophy or IIP) is an independent academic institute affiliated with

[20] See Bahrampour and Karimian, "Iranian Press Update."

but independent from the University of Tehran, which is the oldest and the most prestigious humanities and social sciences university (as opposed to the science, technical, and engineering schools) in Iran. Every major academic discipline at the university has a separate affiliated research institute, housed and funded independently, with an explicit mandate to encourage scholarly exchange, original research, and intellectual inquiry. When Habermas, Rorty, and other foreign philosophical dignitaries came to Iran, their lectures were given at the IIP. Often, these lectures were overflow, standing-room-only events. A few years earlier, when I had gone to the Institute to hear Habermas speak, the lecture room, the verandahs, and the grounds were so packed that even with the French doors wide open and a loudspeaker system, we couldn't get close enough to understand anything and made do, like many others, with hanging out in the farther reaches of the Institute gardens, talking philosophy and politics in a picnic-like atmosphere.

Some of the Institutes, like the IIP, also run small, very selective doctoral programs. Some, but not all, of my seminar students were enrolled in degree programs at the Institute, but most of them used the Institute for its other intended purpose: as an affiliated resource that can provide a more open environment for less politicized, that is, less controlled, teaching and discussion. Although good work still comes out of the major Iranian universities, both students and faculty are under constant surveillance, and the atmosphere is always more pressured. Precisely because the Iranian universities have always been a source of student resistance and opposition to the state, both before and after the revolution, the universities have often been sites of awkward cohabitation between intellectual and student critics of the authorities, and loyalist administrators and student pressure groups who enforce correct ideological positions.[21] This is the significance of

[21] This tension became more pronounced after the first election of President Ahmadinejad in 2005. He supervised a new, quieter purge (compared to the postrevolutionary closure of the universities from 1980 to 1983) of faculty and administrators who were seen as inadequately Islamic according to the views of the most hard-line elements of the regime. In the repression after the contested June 2009 Presidential elections, pressure on universities, students, academics, and intellectuals became even greater, including on the Institute of Philosophy. A regime spokesman even ascribed the intellectual organization of the Green Movement to maneuvers by Richard Rorty, Jurgen Habermas, and several of the other international speakers who had given speeches and seminars over the years

the Institutes' combined affiliation and independence from the university system; the Institutes have been legitimate places of restrained but authentic academic freedom in what is otherwise a highly restricted institutional environment. During periods when "filtering" (i.e., censorship) of the internet was particularly intense, and ordinary public and university servers couldn't even access the *London Review of Books*, the computers in the Institute library were rarely blocked. The main problem for Institute students, faculty, and visitors was not the usual Iranian state controls, but the access controls Western university libraries and journals put on their own materials; if you don't have the membership password, you can't get in. As paradoxical as their tolerated freedom in the midst of social and political crackdowns can seem, the Institutes have a logical role in the organization of the Islamic Republic: if you are an ordinary university student or overworked faculty member, the government makes your life difficult and restricts your ability to explore ideas and educate yourself about alternative possibilities. But if you are a really serious student or intellectually dedicated faculty member, the kind who will be more trouble than you are worth if you can't dig out a particular article about neoliberalism or Emanuel Kant, the state provided you with a small but available outlet where you can read and talk about ideas to your heart's content. This is where I taught my seminar on Hannah Arendt.

I taught in the same room where Habermas spoke, but we only occupied the front table and first rows, instead of overflowing into the garden from what had been the main salon of a small but jewel-like nineteenth-century urban mansion. The Institutes' privileged status is reflected not only in their internet access but also in their real estate; they tend to be housed either in elegant mid nineteenth-century mansion compounds in the old downtown (like the Fine Arts and Philosophy Institutes) or late twentieth-century estates in the cooler, greener northern foothills of the city (where Political Science is

at the Institute of Philosophy. Since the 2022 Women, Life, Freedom protests, what academic freedom that remained within the universities has been increasingly curtailed by expelling and suspending both students and faculty considered suspect. These faculty are being replaced by political appointees, often without academic credentials. See Shafigeh Shirazi, "IRAN: Campus Persecutions Ramp Up as Protest Anniversary Looms," *University World News*, September 6, 2023.

located). Always walled, the Institutes, especially those downtown, are literal oases of serenity in the midst of a very polluted, noisy, and overcrowded urban landscape. But the IIP neighborhood is particularly evocative. Around the corner and down the street are the Vatican Embassy and a neighboring Catholic Church; parallel to the *kucheh* (alley or small street) entrance to the IIP is the Kucheh Prof. Henri Corbin. The neighborhood is a remnant of one version of the "old" Tehran: the late nineteenth- and early twentieth-century city of urban cosmopolitanism and art deco architecture, a dream of social hybridity (before the term was fashionable) that incorporated indigenous and borrowed cultural traditions. It's now shabby and somewhat forsaken, but it's still there. I had been traveling to Iran for a number of years, doing research and working with students and colleagues there, and I had felt comfortable in the culture for some time. But finding this neighborhood, working in it and passing through it on a regular basis, shopping for shoes there, and teaching Hannah Arendt at the Institute to dedicated if skeptical students, this is what made me feel at home.

## Teaching Arendt in Iran: Politics as Action

There is an intensity about studying philosophy in Iran that is different from studying philosophy, or even political theory, in the US. Ideas matter, not only as an intellectual avocation but sometimes as a matter of literal freedom or incarceration, autonomy or subjugation. It is exhilarating to teach in Tehran. But it is also a further responsibility. The Iranian Institute of Philosophy was a sphere of relative freedom, but teaching a seminar on Arendt, including Arendt's work on anti-Semitism and Adolf Eichmann, in a politicized context in which the then-current President liked to make very provocative statements on the historical veracity of the Holocaust, was a somewhat daunting prospect.

Along with selected articles and essays, we read four books: *On Violence*, *The Human Condition*, the three volumes of *The Origins of Totalitarianism*, and *Eichmann in Jerusalem*. We didn't read *On Revolution*, which in some ways would seem to have been the obvious choice. Even in President Ahmadinejad's Iran, I knew we would have no official problems reading and discussing a book that takes as its premise (for all the controversy of its specific argument) the historical and moral reality of the Holocaust. But I was hesitant to teach a book that explicitly argues that there are two stages to a fully successful revolution and that it is quite possible to succeed at the initial project of liberation while failing to succeed at the subsequent project of the foundation of a new political polity.[22] In fact, the text that provided the sharpest insights, for myself and my students, was the one that might have seemed to be least controversial: *The Human Condition*, Arendt's meditation on the possibilities for truly public, political life in the context of the Greek (meaning Athenian) city-state, the *polis*.

I hadn't thoroughly considered *The Human Condition* for years, and while I found Arendt's distinctions among labor, work, and action provocative, her positing of the polis as the free space of political action and being seemed historically problematic and overly idealistic. But the book produced unexpected resonances, in surprising directions, when considered in the Iranian context. Our seminar discussions of Arendt's hostility to the social gained a different significance when connected with the nonpolitical, absolute cultural authority often deployed within the private (familial) sphere. You could argue with government laws or religious edicts, but when presented with familial demands for obedience in the apparently always minor but nonetheless encompassing matters of doing things according to "our tradition" (always presented in the singular), the social became recognizable as the main forum for individual repression (especially for young women). There was possible leverage against any other temporal authority. But faced with the supposed cumulative investment of generations, any one individual's preference not to do things the way (it was claimed) they had always been done was inevitably experienced and narrated as an assertion of shallow self-indulgence in the face of massed implicit, and sometimes explicit, expectation. Expectation is not the same as demand, which can be argued against or resisted. But the expectations of the social brooked little resistance, in that the category of resistance was not recognized in matters so minor as daily social practices. In the postwar West, one sign of Western identity has been the relaxation of familial generational ties and the emancipation (or alienation) of the individual from traditionally defined social obligations. But in postrevolutionary Iran, where family ties were

22 I may have been overly cautious. But this was the period when the government had arrested a series of high-profile binational Iranian-American academics and researchers, several of whom I had worked with.

practically and emotionally extended into a network of constitutive social and material relations, Arendt's resolute recognition of the implacable and confining expectations of the social suddenly made sense.

Despite my surprise at the shift in perspective that reading *The Human Condition* in an Iranian context provided for my own conceptual understandings, I was not prepared for the intensity of my students' response. They were not especially concerned with the issues that are most often critically targeted in that book: the exclusion of women and slaves from the sphere of freedom; the consignment of labor and work to a subsidiary role in human experience; the hostility to social or economic analysis. No. What really bothered them was Arendt's (Aristotelian) conception of political action as speech. Vehemently, they took up and argued against this definition, and its apparent implication that real politics was not street politics; real politics was the kind of talkative persuasion they associated with a frustrated Reform movement and its inability to challenge an authoritarian regime.

Hannah Arendt's political theory emphasizes the political quality of speech, the transformative experience of action, and the plural nature of power. According to her theory of revolution, the vertigo that accompanies the leap into a new political future can only be counterbalanced by the claim that it is really a grounded return to an historical past. For most readers of Arendt, these are familiar concepts but abstract experiences. Arendt inspires her readers in part because most of us so rarely encounter the revelatory, constitutive political reality she describes.

Yet the students in my seminar found Arendt provocative but frustrating for exactly these reasons: the combination of her inspiring political concepts and the lacunae in their own postrevolutionary lives of the actual experience of political action. Arendt's wariness of mass street protest as politics, and her prioritizing of the slow process of speech over the immediate gratification of confrontation, were deeply frustrating to a younger generation of Iranian citizen readers. Having grown up after the revolutionary period of the 1970s and during the blocked reforms of the Khatami Presidency, remembering the fervor and fizzle of the 1999 student university protest movement but having been for the most part too young to participate, these students had experienced neither the adrenalin of mass uprising nor the tepid satisfaction of the kind of local street march many in the West have participated in almost without thinking. In the Spring of 2007, the students in my Iranian graduate seminar on the political philosophy of Hannah Arendt fetishized street action (without ever having experienced it) and disdained political talk (having experienced too much of it).

These were philosophy students who longed for a theory of uprising. Adamantly committed to a democratic view of politics, they were viscerally opposed to the authoritarianism and arbitrary abuses of power so prevalent in the government they experienced. Born after the 1979 Revolution and having grown up under the Islamic Republic, they were themselves intensely frustrated by the lock on governmental power being maintained by what was obviously a very small faction of the political community. They were further frustrated by the Reform movement's apparent unwillingness to challenge the regime directly, and its focus on press freedom and intellectual argument and other forms of talk. These were philosophers who wanted action, and having a political theorist (whether me or Arendt) argue that the highest form of political action was a collective process of self-disclosure through speech – in other words, more talk – did not make them happy.

Yet of course this was discussion in a seminar, where speech was taken absolutely seriously. No one confused speech with jargon, whether when speaking among themselves or attending to the public pronouncements of political and administrative authorities. The students were remarkably free of the academic lingo that can be so seductive to some burgeoning intellectuals, and later in the course they were appreciative of Arendt's argument that Eichmann prevented himself from thinking about his actions because he had immersed himself in a language of noncommunicative bureaucratese. Their frustration with their own political landscape was not that public officials said or revealed nothing in their statements, but that the statements, rather than being action, seemed to prevent it.

The Arendtian give-and-take of mutual persuasion, policy negotiation, and stable political change, all of which could arguably have been recognized to have been occurring during the Khatami Presidency and Reform period under which they had grown up, seemed as nothing to them. They were trapped by the legacy of the Revolution: political action as absolute liberation, even if the foundation of the new (Islamic) Republic got rather stuck. Despite their serious, scholarly commitment to the conceptual argument, and the fact that a number of students were involved in various ways with student activism, they didn't want to talk; they wanted to do something. Doing something (political) meant moving into the street.

## The 2009 Green Movement: Collective Action in the Streets

Being part of a march – the epitome of street politics – is a phenomenon familiar to Iranians, even those too young to have experienced it. The Revolution was built from strikes and street politics. Strikes and street politics liberated the country from the Shah, but the subsequent conditions of national and civil wars shaped the institutional reality of the new state and consolidated the transition from one authoritarian executive regime to another. In 2007, the power and restraint of collective action was a conceptual possibility for my students but not an experienced reality; as citizens, they had little direct familiarity of either institutional mobilization or grass-roots organization. Children of the Revolution, they didn't romanticize violence, but they longed for the drama and immediacy of street politics: action as confrontation, the manifestation of democratic power and agency in the public realm. By the summer of 2009 (after the contested election of June 2009 and the subsequent mass protests and emergence of the Green Movement, as well as its suppression), their experience had been transformed. Having experienced both the pluralist unity of collective political action, and the absolutist negation of public political power through state violence, their internal landscape, both intellectual and national, had been revolutionized.

The 2009 Green Movement began as an election protest after the unexpectedly quickly completed final vote count and announcement of an overwhelming numerical victory for incumbent president Mahmoud Ahmadinejad. One of my seminar students, an unusually thoughtful but previously not political young woman, explained,

> The morning of the election, I believed it [the results]. But that evening I saw police attacking people violently in the street, and I knew something was wrong.

From Paris, the filmmaker Mohsen Makhmalbaf (translated by graphic novelist Marjane Satrapi) reported that leading opposition Presidential candidate Mir Hosein Mousavi's campaign headquarters had been closed down and key personnel arrested; that Mousavi had first been informed by the Ministry of the Interior that he had won, and then seen the subsequent official announcement claiming the vote for Ahmadinejad. Mousavi himself refused to accept the official result; he and Mehdi Karroubi, the other opposition candidate, both rejected the formally announced election numbers and outcome. Widespread popular disbelief was supported by news of unbelievable local results, including missing and uniformly marked ballots and the exceptional, supposed loss of Mousavi's home region to Ahmadinejad.[23] Even as primary Reformist strategists and campaign organizers were arrested, ordinary people began demonstrating in the streets, and new layers of loose organization kept emerging from the campaigns of both Mousavi and Karroubi, providing a weak but real structure to the popular response. The color green, which had been associated with Mousavi's campaign, became a symbol of democratic expectation and legitimacy; the Green Movement emerged, even though no one knew exactly what it was.

Within days, there were massive, peaceful, silent marches across the major cities. I realized that my seminar students had finally gained their experience of street politics, and the euphoria of collective action.

> There was a big rally on 25th of Khordad, Doshambeh [June 15, Monday, the enormous peaceful march of several million in Tehran and other cities three days after the election]. It was very hot. We were so happy, so proud of ourselves. We had heard the police would shoot, and seven people died. That day, I felt I was doing action, something meaningful. This was the first political action of my life.[24]

But instead of the dream of immediate confrontation my students had seemed to cherish, they were displaying something else. Ironically, those massive, silent green marches were not the rowdy protests of the revolutionary era that my students had seemed to have in mind and so desired. Silent and almost leaderless but coherent in their presentation of a collective political agency, the marches presented street politics as speech, with a multiplied single voice *not* speaking while clearly enunciating a clear message: "Where is my vote?"

[23] For an immediate overview of the significance of the 2009 events as they were occurring, see Kaveh Ehsani, Arang Keshavarzian, and Norma Claire Moruzzi, "Tehran, June 2009," *Middle East Report Online (MERO)*, June 28, 2009.

[24] Former seminar student, conversation with the author.

Can silence be a form of speech? Can *not* speaking together be a form of (Arendtian) action?[25] My students seemed to think so.

I felt that my political life was beginning at that moment. That day, 25 *Khordad*, the big rally, we did something that day. I feel we shared something, and we are proud of it, even people older [the generation of the Revolution]. My generation, and younger, girls and boys in their twenties – they are very disobedient, rational, and brave ... In the street I saw very young girls, leading a group of people, in protesting.[26]

Yet over the tumultuous events of next several months, inside and outside Iran, there were concerns that the Green Movement was either only a narrow candidate protest or a radical rejection of the entire Islamic Republic; that it was being manipulated by disgruntled losing candidates or that it was an amorphous mass with no leadership at all; that it was the long-awaited Iranian counterrevolution or nothing of consequence.[27]

We had our doubts. Some of my friends said, maybe this is like the revolutions.

[Author: You mean in a bad way?]

Yes. We didn't want violence, oppressing minorities. We wanted democracy, freedom, basic human rights. But when we saw the government lying, we became morally committed. When you see injustice, you should do something.[28]

The Green Movement was not the revolution. It was something else: massive, collective civil disobedience. Writing about civil disobedience in the context of 1970s US civil rights and anti-war protests, Arendt characterized civil disobedience as a form of political action that

[25] I am not the only one to make the connection between the postelection Green Movement and Arendt's political theory. See Nima Emami, "The Consolation of Philosophy: Hannah Arendt and the Green Movement," in the online journal *Tehran Review*, May 21, 2010/30 *Ordibehesht* 1389 (no longer available) and *Rozenberg Quarterly: The Magazine*, https://rozenbergquarterly.com/the-consolation-of-philosophy-hannah-arendt-and-the-green-movement/.

[26] Former seminar student, conversation with the author.

[27] The combined atmosphere of thrill, disbelief, anxiety, and wishful/jaded projection, both inside and outside Iran, was similar for both the 2009 Green Movement and the 2022 Woman, Life, Freedom movement. Both were massive, spontaneous, notably youthful mobilizations after a shock injustice, and both provoked similar questions about exactly what the mobilizations signified: (another) revolution, or not.

[28] Former seminar student, conversation with the author.

emerges only when citizens (not subjects) presume a norm of (democratic) government accountability and represent that norm back to the state.[29] Her characterization of civil disobedience as a genuinely political response to delegitimized state authority is strikingly relevant to the 2009 Iranian Green Movement. Arendt is precise: civil disobedience must not only be performed in public, but it must be part of a public enaction of nonviolent participatory politics. "Civil disobedience arises when a significant number of citizens have become convinced either that the normal channels of change no longer function, and grievances will not be heard or acted upon, or that, on the contrary, the government is about to change and has embarked upon and persists in modes of action whose legality and constitutionality are open to grave doubt."[30] In the Iranian postelection context of 2009, the massed, silent, peaceful citizens' protests were representing democracy back to a state that had failed to uphold what the citizens expected of it: to abide by the prescribed legal process for the electoral transition of power, according to the rules the state itself had set out. And they were doing even more.

## "*Allah-o Akbar*": Reclaiming the Democratic Potential of the Revolution

Civil disobedience can also entail reworking the accepted significance of recognizable ordinary practices in order to shift a contested balance of both power and hegemony within the local framework. During the Iranian Revolution, the evening rooftop calls of "*Allah-o Akbar*" (God is Greatest) signified an encompassing moral unity and the righteousness of sacral authority against the temporal, secular claims of the monarchy. But in summer 2009, the same rooftop chants signified the reappropriation of the popular democratic potential of the revolution, against the formal religiosity of the theocratic state.

> I can say that we reacted to the government, many of us, not because of political reasons but for moral reasons. It was a matter of justice and injustice. When we shouted "*Allah-o Akbar*" from the rooftops, many of

[29] Hannah Arendt, "Civil Disobedience," in *Crises of the Republic: Lying in Politics, Civil Disobedience on Violence, Thoughts on Politics, and Revolution* (New York: Harcourt Brace Jovanovich, 1972), 49–102.

[30] Arendt, "Civil Disobedience," 74.

us meant that God is bigger than your deceitfulness, than your lies. It meant that there is some moral, spiritual power in the world that is bigger than your guns and your forces.

It is a very colorful movement, so we for the first time experience on the streets of Iran pluralism and tolerance. We were side by side with *chadori* women. Religion in Iran is a very important factor in identifying yourself, your identity. But last year it wasn't the decisive factor. Just our social goals was the important factor. It didn't matter if you were a Muslim, atheist, or whatever. We were unified by our cause.[31]

Together in the streets, they were signaling a refusal of the Islamic state's authority to set the meaning of revolutionary symbols, and insisting on recalling a shared national inheritance: the liberatory, democratic, ethical promise of their own revolutionary history.[32]

Other religiously inflected postrevolutionary practices were similarly reclaimed within a shared national framework of political signification. The politically important, state-sponsored Tehran Friday prayers had continued to be held in a hall on the campus of the University of Tehran.[33] Hotbeds of revolutionary fervor (both Islamic and leftist and of various combinations) before and during the revolution, the universities had become postrevolutionary centers of Reformist student activism and were under suspicion as nurturing-grounds of intellectual critique (and had of course been at the center of the student uprisings of 1999). Despite this, the Tehran Friday prayer sermon had remained a national platform for institutional conservatism and hardline positioning, and its location on the university campus only emphasized the contested ideological and institutional legacy of the Revolution: a combined recognition of the radical power of organized student and

[31] Former seminar student, conversation with the author.

[32] We can again take note of Arendt's comments. "The civil disobedient shares with the revolutionary the wish 'to change the world', and the changes he wishes to accomplish can be drastic indeed – as, for instance, in the case of Gandhi, who is always quoted as the great example, in this context, of nonviolence. (Did Gandhi accept the 'frame of established authority', which was British rule in India? Did he respect the 'general legitimacy of the system of laws' in the colony?)" Arendt, "Civil Disobedience," 77.

[33] The state took years building an enormous Tehran Friday prayer mosque; completed, it has been used for trade shows because it is far too big for the regular Friday religious congregation. See Kaveh Ehsani, "The Politics of Public Space in Tehran's International Book Fair," unpublished paper delivered at the Middle East Studies Association, 2006.

popular movements, and a heavy-handed reminder of the presence of established authority.

On July 17, 2009, Hashemi Rafsanjani, the former President and present leader of both the powerful Assembly of Experts and the Expediency Council,[34] gave the Friday prayer sermon at the University of Tehran. Rafsanjani was considered a wily pragmatist rather than a principled Reformer and was at times one of the most universally hated national political figures, a status that heavily contributed to the election success of Ahmadinejad in 2005 when the two competed as Presidential candidates. But the blatant inconsistencies accompanying the official 2009 election results, the severity of the repression mounted against the peaceful protesters (including young woman bystander Neda Agha-Soltan's death on June 20, caught on a phone camera and widely transmitted), and the apparent consolidation of the government around a very narrow and exclusive faction connected with the Supreme Leader Khamenei, President-elect Ahmadinejad, and the Revolutionary Guards, meant Rafsanjani's insistence on leading the prayers, and therefore delivering the public sermon from the biggest national platform, was regarded as an important challenge from within the mainstream of the government against the new extremism, and in guarded support of the legitimacy of the Green Movement.

Access to the campus was restricted, but the audience for the sermon was huge, filling the campus, streets, and neighborhood surrounding the entire university.[35] This was a tense moment for the regime: the Friday prayer sermon is an official institution, closely associated with the conservatives, but in this case was also an opportunity for the Green Movement protesters to come back into the streets legitimately.

[34] The Assembly of Experts is an elected body formally responsible for electing and if necessary dismissing the Supreme Leader; the Expediency Council is an administrative assembly appointed by the Supreme Leader to mediate between the Parliament and the Guardian Council; the Guardian Council is the appointed assembly of jurists who determine if parliamentary laws are constitutionally Islamic and vet candidates for election according to their Islamic credentials. Although there are sharp rivalries between factions within these bodies, membership in any one is an indication of insider status within the clerical nomenclature of the state.

[35] Estimates are that this was the most widely attended Friday sermon since the Revolution, with possibly one million persons filling the streets and area around the university.

There was a heavy police presence, but the state certainly couldn't openly dissuade people from attending an official event, especially a religious one.[36] In this context of suddenly reappropriated religious meaning, young women and men who might not otherwise observe the prayers, let alone practice them publicly, turned the shared space of the streets into a collective forum for civil disobedience by praying together, side by side.

In Iran, women as well as men attend public prayers at the mosque, but they are physically separated, usually with the men at the front and the women at the back or to the side. (Foregrounding the women's bodily prostrations would presumably distract the men from their proper concentration.) But the prayer space of the streets was fully integrated. Men and women stood side by side listening to Rafsanjani, and they prostrated themselves side by side in the collective movements of Muslim religious devotion.[37] On that Friday outside the Tehran University campus, shared public prayer became a recognizable form of peaceful protest against the violent authoritarianism of the theocratic state: within the context of the Islamic Republic, public prayer as civil disobedience.

Like silence, ritual prayer does not usually count as speech. But as civil disobedience, both collective silence and collective prayer can count as action. And action, according to Arendt, is precisely that which is open-ended and plural, rather than instrumental or hierarchically fixed. It is by nature unpredictable and creative, and therefore especially threatening to those who want to restrict change, whether in terms of the social organization of public prayers or the democratic accountability of the state. Those public prayers were not innocuous, and the repressive elements of the state did not mistake them as such. As soon as the sermon and the prayers were finished, police and

[36] A similar dynamic has occurred on other official, state-sanctioned public holidays occurring during periods of widespread unrest, including Al-Quds/ Palestine Day and the mourning festival of *Moharram*.

[37] Despite the widespread modern assumption that religion (especially Islam) is inherently traditionalist rather than socially or politically progressive, religious identity and religious spaces have often provided the main resources for democratic political mobilization. For the incorporation of religious spaces into the "free spaces" of political activism, see Sara M. Evans and Harry C. Boyte, *Free Spaces: The Sources of Democratic Change in America* (Chicago: University of Chicago Press, 1992). "Free spaces are never a pure phenomenon. In the real world, they are always complex, shifting, and dynamic . . .," 19.

members of the paramilitary *Basij* began dispersing the crowds with batons and teargas.

Action creates the free space of the political, and the community of individual political actors who share it. But in Arendt's conception, action is always ephemeral; its public appearance is what constantly makes and remakes the shared context in which it can appear. The ongoing struggle is to establish a more stable basis for that context: the institutional supports that enable the possibilities of political action as democratic citizens' plural, public engagement. This didn't happen in Iran in 2009. The Green Movement was heavily repressed; the government consolidated further around a delegitimized but entrenched hard-line coterie; my Iranian philosophy students went on with their lives. And as in so many other periods after a period of crisis and repression, the democratic potential of the Iranian Revolution again seemed to become dormant and even to disappear.

## Women as Participatory Citizens: Divisions and Collaborations

As subjects and citizens, Iranian women have been mobilizing for social emancipation for more than a century, and for political and civil freedoms since well before the Islamic Republic.[38] Women were part of the revolution and the Reform movement, the university protests in 1999, and the Green Movement in 2009.[39] In the mid twentieth century, after the Constitutional Revolution (1905–1911) but before the 1979 Revolution, the Pahlavi regime's legal reforms gave women near-equal political rights. But in a state context of near-absolute rule, neither women nor men were full citizens, and social organizing was

[38] Iranian women have never simply accepted attempts to exclude them from the modernization of the political and social spheres; the modern history of women's activism and organizing begins in the nineteenth century and continues in the twenty-first. The most comprehensive historical analysis of the Iranian women's movement is Parvin Paidar, *Women and the Political Process in Twentieth Century Iran* (New York: Cambridge University Press, 1995).

[39] Women's participation in radical anti-government organizations before and during the revolution, whether secular or Islamist, challenged more than the legitimacy of the monarchical state. For insight into how profoundly women (and their male comrades) had to adapt the social expectations of their private roles in order to remain publicly active, especially in the more covert activist groups, see Naghmeh Sohrabi, "Writing Revolution as If Women Mattered," *Comparative Studies of South Asia, Africa and the Middle East* (*CSSAAME*), 42(2), (2022), 546–550.

often co-opted by the monarchy. The large majority of women were illiterate, and the realities of their lives made these formal legal rights often unknowable and unattainable. Certainly, some women found it possible to live full lives as engaged public subjects under the Westernizing monarchy. But the category of feminist identity and activism became associated with secularism, adherence to Western social practices, and a model of legal reform (adjudicating from the top down) rather than social mobilization (transformation from the bottom up).[40]

After the revolution, "feminism" became even more identified with secular cultural identity, and religiously identified women activists were usually skeptical of "feminist" identity, which could sometimes seem to represent little more than a fashion rejection of state-mandated *hejab*.[41] More religiously identified women activists often preferred to identify themselves as "gender-justice activists" and were often affiliated with the Reform movement of the Khatami era. They were often referred to by secular women, rather dismissively, as "Islamic feminists," although in the Iranian context the more appropriate terms would be "Reformists."[42] Paralleling the secular-religious divisions

[40] This top-down appropriation of women's issues does not necessarily bear a close relation to the multifaceted reality of twentieth-century Iranian women's activism over gender issues, and the modern history of Iranian feminism's uneasy relation with an imposed or assumed Western or secular identity overshadowed by a royalist elite has been well documented. See Nima Naghibi, *Rethinking Global Sisterhood: Western Feminism and Iran* (Minneapolis, MN: University of Minnesota Press, 2007), and Afsaneh Najmabadi, "Hazards of Modernity and Morality: Women, State and Ideology in Contemporary Iran," in Deniz Kandiyoti, ed., *Women, Islam and the State* (Philadelphia, PA: Temple University Press, 1991), 48–71.

[41] When I first started going to Iran, I privately referred to this apolitical claim to feminist identity as "mini-skirt feminism," after observing multiple instances of women and especially men claiming a feminist identity when all that meant was a preference for Western-style dress and superficial social mingling.

[42] This tension between secularly identified and religiously identified women's issue activists has not been unique to Iran. In Part 3, "New Discourses" of *Women and Gender in Islam*, Leila Ahmed chronicles the tensions between two twentieth-century generations of either secularly or religiously identified Egyptian women's status activists, despite clear overlaps in their concerns. Individual women activists chose how to frame their arguments, and who they were addressing with them, depending on the cultural framework within which they had received their own early mentoring and education. See Leila Ahmed, *Women and Gender in Islam: Historical Roots of a Modern Debate* (New Haven, CT: Yale University Press, 1992). This tension between Iranian secular

between other democratic elements, feminists and gender justice activists found it difficult to collaborate. Yet postrevolutionary activist women's groups, whether identifying themselves as feminists (like the Million Signature Campaign) or as gender justice activists, helped change laws and raise awareness.[43]

When they did collaborate together, the results could be strikingly effective. Between 1992 and 2008, Shahla Sherkat published and edited *Zanan* (*Women*), a groundbreaking independent women's magazine that gained journalistic respect and a wide readership by covering formerly taboo topics, from women's right to child custody to the rise of plastic surgery, the issues of domestic violence, the transmission of AIDs, and the challenges faced by girl runaways.[44] Sherkat also established a uniquely plural atmosphere in the magazine's editorial offices and on its pages: one of the only spaces where secularly identified feminists and Reformist gender justice activists mingled their opinions and their efforts. Sherkat herself was quite intentional about this

and Islamist oppositional (left) mobilization was not confined to women's groups. See Maziar Behrooz, *Rebels with a Cause: The Failure of the Left in Iran* (New York: I. B. Tauris Publishers, 1999).

43 The Million Signature Campaign was a darling of Western observers and media, but its effectiveness inside Iran was meager. Modeled on the successful efforts to reform the Moroccan constitution, the Campaign was initiated shortly after the first election of President Ahmadinejad and immediately subject to heavy repression. But it lacked either a heavy-weight state sponsor (as Moroccan women's groups had in the monarchy) or a manageable, clearly defined feminist project (like Iranian mothers' lack of the right to pass Iranian citizenship on to their children, a cross-class issue affecting both privileged middle-class diaspora families and working-class women married to male Afghan migrants and refugees). By insisting on a project of large-scale constitutional reform and mobilizing at the beginning of a period of intensified state repression, the Campaign was always of more significance outside rather than inside Iran. Yet inside Iran, networks of professional and activist women continued to work effectively within and through the system to change laws (regarding child custody, age of marriage, and rights during divorce) and improve women's social condition.

44 For a fuller discussion of *Zanan*'s significance, both through its emphasis on women-centered interpretation of religious law and texts, and its ability to provide a platform to encourage cross-activist collaboration, see Afsaneh Najmabadi, "Feminisms in an Islamic Republic," in Joan W. Scott, Cora Kaplan, and Debra Keates, eds., *Transitions, Environments, Translations: Feminism in International Politics* (New York: Routledge, 1997), 390–399; Asef Bayat, "A Woman's Non-movement: What It Means to Be a Woman Activist in an Islamic State," *Comparative Studies of South Asia, Africa and the Middle East*, 27(1) (2007), 160–172.

project of boundary crossing, in the magazine's offices and on its pages.[45] Having grown up in a religious family but having gone to secular schools, Sherkat had early learned to negotiate between two cultural communities while working within both.[46] She founded *Zanan* after being dismissed from the semiofficial national women's publication, *Zan-e Rooz* (*Today's Woman*) where she was previously editor (a publication that had existed since before the Revolution and had been repurposed after to address the needs and interests of the appropriately postrevolutionary Iranian women).

Without hesitating, I set out to publish *Zanan* (*Women*) magazine for which I became the license holder ... Now I was in the arena of maximum expression of views and desires of women no matter their ideology, perspective, taste and approach. And our magazine welcomed them, not just a minority of women who had official legitimacy and whose thoughts and needs coincided with commonly prescribed standards ...[47]

Sherkat fully appreciated that this provision of a plural feminist platform of discussion was as much of an intervention as any of the articles that *Zanan* published.

At *Zanan*, we practiced collective work, democracy and tolerance for opposing views. Our governing principle was the elimination of sexism and the gaining of understanding of the problems facing women working in double shifts in public and private spheres ...

This intimate, unified and collaborative family worked – or better put, lived – together for 16 years ... Anyone who did research on women's issues benefitted from hundreds of articles, stories and interviews that were featured in *Zana*. And the magazine served, too, as an indicator of the progress made by Iranian women ...[48]

Despite or because of having modeled a successful democratic working practice for years, *Zanan* was closed down in 2008. Sherkat tried to

[45] In Iran, a publisher is legally (and financially) accountable for editorial decisions; publishers have their freedom and livelihoods on the line at least as much if not more than writers and editors. See Haleh Esfandiari, "Iranian Women Please Stand Up," *Foreign Affairs* (October 21, 2009).

[46] Conversation with the author. Sherkat's view of the atmosphere and plural participation in *Zanan* was also reflected in the author's contemporaneous interviews with several *Zanan* journalists.

[47] Shahla Sherkat, "Telling the Stories of Iranian Women's Lives," *Nieman Reports: Nieman Foundation for Journalism at Harvard* (Summer 2009).

[48] Sherkat, "Telling the Stories of Iranian Women's Lives."

reopen, but she and the magazine had been targeted as part of the increased repression under President Ahmadinejad, and the magazine staff and their collective project dispersed.

Yet in the months leading up to the June 2009 election, and after experiencing the harsh repressive policies and attitudes of the first Ahmadinejad administration, thirty-four Reformist and secular women's activist groups had come together to form the Women's Movement Convergence. Both gender justice and feminist groups realized they had to overcome their mutual distrust and work together to defend their accomplishments and to achieve their goals. This was the first time women's groups had been able to mobilize together on a larger scale; their collaboration also provided the first public example of collective secular-Reformist mobilization within the Iranian social and political landscape.[49] The Convergence successfully put together a common platform, and they interviewed representatives of the opposition candidates to determine which candidate would be most consistently committed to women's rights. After reviewing the candidates' responses, the Convergence approved both Karroubi and Mousavi as acceptable candidates, but stated that Mousavi's positions regarding women were better and more comprehensive. Mousavi's campaign was also notable for the very public, active presence of his wife Zahra Rahnavard, a university professor and then chancellor of Al-Zahra (Women's) University, who had been a political advisor of former president Khatami. Both Rahnavard and Mousavi were associated with the prerevolutionary sociologist and radical social critic Ali Shariati.[50] Mousavi himself stated that interactions with the Convergence had made him realize that he needed to incorporate women's concerns more fully into his campaign platform; they pushed

[49] On May Day in 2010, ten independent Iranian labor organizations representing different reform strategies presented a joint public resolution stating shared demands. This was the first example in the independent labor movement of a similar collaborative public platform among different political factions, but it followed the Women's Convergence initiative. See Farhad Nomani and Sohrab Behdad, "Labor Rights and the Democracy Movement in Iran: Building a Social Democracy," *Northwestern Journal of International Human Rights*, 10(4), (Summer 2012), 212–230.

[50] See Nasrin Alavi, "Iran: A Blind Leap of Faith," *Open Democracy* (June 2, 2009).

him to define his leadership on women's issues more explicitly.[51] It seemed that women's voices and issues were finally going to become fully part of mainstream Iranian political discourse and explicitly integrated into common democratic struggles. But then the postelection process exploded into the Green Movement, and this noteworthy precedent of women's cross-faction oppositional cooperation was overwhelmed in the urgency of a general political crisis.

This had happened before. At other historical junctures, just when it seemed that women's collective demands would finally become more fully incorporated into national political awareness, the moment got lost in the crisis of events. But generations of activism accumulate a sediment. They build a foundation, slowly, almost unnoticeably, but there underneath. Each struggle in itself may seem to fail, sometimes crushed, sometimes dissipating. But a quiet revolution is not only made up of private personal choices; it is also shaped by the effects of generations of activism within individual lives and across societal expectations.[52]

## Shaping a Feminist Consciousness: Women's Autonomy and Agency

The twentieth-century history of struggles for Iranian women's full participation in national social and political life was a tug of war between competing visions of women's citizenship, viewed variously through a secular or religious lens. Although "feminism" is associated with secular identity, and anticlerical and secular identity are associated with feminism, this has never been a straightforward relationship. Throughout the century, leading secular (male) reformers

[51] See the English language feminist website *Meydaan* and their online archives for good coverage of the cooperation among groups and the development of the Convergence joint platform before the election.

[52] Asef Bayat's concept of "quiet encroachment of the ordinary" is an insightful explanation of how the accumulation of individual choices can add up to a "nonmovement" that nonetheless achieves large-scale social changes, for instance, by women to pursue higher education, employment, delayed marriage, etc. But it is not an adequate explanation of social change. See Bayat, "A Woman's Non-movement: What It Means to Be a Woman Activist in an Islamic State"; Asef Bayat, *Life as Politics: How Ordinary People Change the Middle East* (Stanford: Stanford University Press, 2013).

often explicitly considered women to be unsuited for public life.[53] Ahmad Kasravi (1891–1946) was Iran's most significant anticlerical secular thinker and is considered the intellectual godfather of modern Iranian secular identity. A scholar and writer, he was alternatively critical and guardedly supportive of Reza Shah's modernizing national reforms.[54] Kasravi opposed veiling and supported women's education, but he did not support women's political or professional participation in roles of public authority.[55] Kasravi's position on women's appropriate social role situates them firmly in the domestic sphere as homemakers, wives, and mothers. Like many modernizing intellectuals and policymakers of his generation in Iran and elsewhere, he believed women needed to play a significant role in raising a modern generation of national (male) citizens and supporting a (male-defined) modernizing nationalist agenda, while nonetheless remaining outside of direct public participation.[56]

53 Women did not simply accept their exclusion from the modernizing political and social spheres. The long and continuing modern history of women's activism and organizing begins in the nineteenth century and continues in the twenty-first.

54 Reza Shah is widely credited or blamed for banning women from wearing traditional *hejab* (*chadors* and face coverings) while requiring Western dress (with hats rather than scarves covering hair) in public. However, the 1935 directives targeted women who were either government employees (for instance teachers) or the wives of government employees, and were presented as the modernization of properly Islamic dress within a larger project of state-directed social modernization. The higher officials in the central government were wary of overextending state authority, emphasized a process of education to change attitudes, and were concerned that coercion would lead to a backlash against the larger modernization project. Nonetheless, local police and municipal officers were reported to be violently enforcing unveiling in the streets on ordinary women, despite the more restrictive specifications of the national campaign. See Jasamin Rostam-Kolayi and Afshin Matin-Asgari, "Unveiling Ambiguities: Revisiting 1930s Iran's *kashf-i hijab* Campaign," in Stephanie Cronin, ed., *Anti-Veiling Campaigns in the Muslim World: Gender, Modernism and the Politics of Dress* (New York: Routledge, 2014), 121–139.

55 See Zohreh T. Sullivan "Eluding the Feminist, Overthrowing the Modern? Transformations in Twentieth-Century Iran," in Lila Abu-Lughod, ed., *Remaking Women: Feminism and Modernity in the Middle East* (Princeton, NJ: Princeton University Press, 1998), 215–242; Camron Amin, *The Making of the Modern Iranian Woman: Gender, State Policy, and Popular Culture, 1865–1946* (Gainesville: University Press of Florida, 2002), 215–245; Paidar, *Women and the Political Process in Twentieth-Century Iran*, 112–117.

56 In his eclectic combination of nationalism, hostility to traditional Islam as a backward social force, and paternalistic attitude toward women's appropriate role in a modernizing society, Kasravi's position is quite close to the Egyptian Qassim Amin's. See Ahmad, *Women and Gender in Islam*, chapter 8, "The

Religiously oriented modernizing thinkers often held views similar to Kasravi's regarding women as primarily responsible for the domestic and family aspects of a modernizing national project. Both Ayatollah Morteza Motahari (1920–1979) and Ali Shariati (1933–1977) are considered leading intellectual figures in the project to develop a recognizably modern, Islamic identity for Iranian women. But Motahari's analysis is recognizably an updated justification of male privilege, framed as benevolent guardianship and protection in a modern stylistic frame (he incorporates paternalistic opinions from the professional field of psychology as well as from theology).[57] Shariati is unique: an anti-colonial, anti-capitalist Islamist modernizer influenced by Marx and Frantz Fanon, and instrumental in inspiring a generation of young revolutionaries – men and women – toward a vision of an inclusive, egalitarian version of participatory Islam.[58] Shariati explicitly advocated female agency, while leaving open the details of how women themselves would determine the specific decisions of their life choices.

Unlike Motahari, Shariati was not a formal religious leader, and his legacy sits uneasily with the more conservative, theologically and socially orthodox factions that now dominate the authoritarian power structures of the Islamic Republic. He trained at secular rather than theological institutions and received a BA from the University of

Discourse of the Veil," 144–168. There are also parallels with the contradictory dynamic between "The Nation and Its Women" and "Women and the Nation" described by Partha Chatterjee, *The Nation and Its Fragments: Colonial and Postcolonial Histories* (Princeton, NJ: Princeton University Press, 1994). Zohreh Sullivan, in her insightful discussion of the contradictions in Iranian male reformers' views of the proper role for modern women, points out the continuing prerevolutionary parallels with Chatterjee's analysis of contradictory visions for women's appropriate role within a modern, independent Indian nation. See Zohreh Sullivan, "Eluding the Feminist, Overthrowing the Modern? Transformations in Twentieth-Century Iran," in Lila Abu-Lughod, ed., *Remaking Women: Feminism and Modernity in the Middle East* (Princeton, NJ: Princeton University Press, 1998), 215–242.

57 See Motahari's various writings on women and women's issues, including Morteza Motahari, *The Rights of Women in Islam* (Tehran: World Organization for Islamic Services, 1980); *The Islamic Modest Dress* (Qom: Dar us Seqafe, 2013); *Sexual Ethics in Islam and in the Western World* (Qom: Bethat Islamic Research Center, 2016).

58 "Shariati preached what may be termed a liberation theology, which combined a reinterpretation of Islamic belief with modern sociopolitical thought." See the "Foreword" by John Esposito in Ali Shari'ati, *What Is to Be Done: The Enlightened Thinkers and an Islamic Renaissance*, ed. Farhang Rajaee (Houston, TX: The Institute for Research and Islamic Studies, 1986), xi.

Mashhad and a PhD from the University of Paris. He worked outside of formal religious establishments, lecturing primarily at a *hoseiniyeh* (a Muslim public lecture or ceremony hall), and many of his audience were university – not seminary – students.[59] His influence was fundamental to a vision of the Iranian Revolution as liberatory, egalitarian (and Islamic) political project, and deeply influenced many of the more religiously identified women who went on to make change in the formal conditions for Iranian women after the Revolution.[60]

Shariati's writings on Iranian women's modern role can appear contradictory. In his most famous lectures on women, collected as *Fatima Is Fatima*, he seems to celebrate the more passive, quietist, family-centered role of Fatemeh, the Prophet's daughter, wife of Ali (the first Shi'a Imam), and mother of Hasan and Hosein (the second and third Shi'a Imams), rather than some of her more publicly active relatives (for instance, her more outspoken daughter, Zeinab). Yet *Fatima is Fatima* is not a simplistic reduction of Muslim women to their domestic role and male lineage identities (as in fact I have done to her in the previous sentence). Even the title attempts to place under

59 Shariati lectured primarily at the Hoseiniyeh Ershad, located toward the northern end of a busy north–south shopping street named Qadim-i Shemiran (Old North Quarter or Neighborhood), and many of his students were university – rather than seminary – students. The Hoseiniyeh Ershad is still there, and after the Revolution the street was renamed Shariati. But his publications, with their explicit critiques of both religious orthodoxy and the cultural, societal, and individual costs of modern capitalism's consumer-oriented social promise, emerging from an Islamist religious perspective, contradict the ideological emphases, both political and economic, of the more powerful state factions.

60 Zohreh Sullivan describes Shariati as "an antecedent of hope and the road not traveled" and likens the postrevolutionary rightward shift in the new state's ideology and governance as a "squandering of an opportunity to transform Iran on the basis of a secular idealism that keeps the faith with Islamic traditions even as it activates those traditions as agents of a partnership with the humanistic imperatives of a liberal modernity." See Zohreh T. Sullivan, *Exiled Memories: Stories of Iranian Diaspora* (Philadelphia, PA: Temple University Press, 2001), chapter 3, "Revolution: Narrating Upheaval," 126. Discussing Shariati as an important influence on Foucault's changing conceptions of revolution as well as on continuing emancipatory revolutionary political movements, Drucilla Cornell and Stephen D. Seely point out that "Shariati's work continues to inspire generation after generation of revolutionaries throughout the global south." See Drucilla Cornell and Stephen D. Seely, *The Spirit of Revolution: Beyond the Dead Ends of Man* (Cambridge: Polity Press, 2016), 59.

question any reduction of women's identity to familial relations.[61] Shariati is saying Fatima is herself: Fatima.[62] He is avoiding the identity trap of primarily identifying Fatima through her role as daughter, wife, and mother of Islamic leaders, by insisting that she is fundamentally an individual unto herself, and therefore worthy of emulation in terms of her own personality and accomplishments. But what exactly are those? It is the disconcerting lack at the center of the question of Fatima's identity – who *is* Fatima, even as we acknowledge that she is *herself* – that opens up the full potential of Shariati's challenge to Iranian women's self-realization of their own modern identity.

## Shariati's (Writings about) Women

The question of who Shariati's Fatima is, and therefore who the modern Iranian woman should herself be, is initially addressed through a critique of what then contemporary Iranian society was. Shariati is scathing about society's ignorant religiosity, the monarchy's model of modernity as shallow secular materialism, and the religious establishment's irrelevant and antiquated clerical leadership; they all combine to support an outmoded and entirely unproductive attitude toward women's social development as fully realized thinking and acting beings (as opposed to demographic indicators or theological followers).[63] Like young men, young women want to be modern, to contribute to society, to live fulfilled and meaningful lives. But they are

[61] Shariati further displaces the tendency to reduce women's relational identities to a subsidiary position by emphasizing that one of the nicknames for Fatima as "*umm al-abiha*," [sic] "the mother of her father." This is the spelling for the phrase as it is used in the Shariati Foundation translation (online). The usual Arabic transliteration would be "*umm'u abeeha*" or "*ummu abeeha*." See also Shariati, chapter 9, "Islam Revolutionizes the Position of Women," in Laleh Bakhtiar, ed., *Fatima Is Fatima* (Chicago: ABC Group International, 1996), 162.

[62] Iranians spell the name of the Prophet's daughter as Fatemeh, but the English translations of Shariati's text spell her as Fatima (the Arabic version). This may be an indication of the significance of his writings beyond the Iranian national/Persian linguistic communities. Within the Iranian context, Fatima is Fatemeh. In order not to be too confusing, I have chosen to use the spelling used in translations of Shariati's text. Yet this indeterminacy of her name – Fatima is (also) Fatemeh – is an extension of the problem of limiting identity to a category (linguistic, familial, or otherwise) that Shariati is describing.

[63] See Shariati, chapter 4, "What Should Be Done?" in *Fatima Is Fatima*.

frustrated, and their frustration is the result of the failure of their elders to offer them serious role models.[64] Although his discussion in these sections has often been mischaracterized as anti-Western, that is a misreading: Shariati is emphatically against the type of Western, supposedly modern feminine identity that has been made available as a model for Iranian women, even as actual Western women have achieved so much more. By name and description, he admiringly cites specific examples of strong, accomplished Western women (including Angela Davis) who are contributing as activists, scholars, scientists, and translators, but who are not the models on offer by either the religious or secular establishments for Iranians to emulate or admire.

The foreign woman has progressed to the point of becoming the embodiment of an ideology, of a country, of salvation and of the honor of a generation. But we have no right to know her.

We only have the right to know fashion models and beauty queens. We have only the right to know movie sex goddesses in cheap exploitation films, the Queen of Monaco and all of the seven female guards around James Bond. Such women are the sacrifices made to European production. They are the toys and wind-up dolls of the wealthy. They are the slaves of the houses of the new merchants.[65]

As opposed to a future as an objectified Western-style doll or a repressed local lump, Shariati offers his urban, educated, Muslim readers a reconstructed alternative: the new Fatima.

Shariati practically wills Fatima into existence as a modern woman, but the central question of who she is remains in tension.[66] He gestures

[64] See Shariati, chapter 6, "What Role Did Women Play in the Attack?" in *Fatima Is Fatima.*

[65] See Shariati, the section on "Women We Cannot Know" in chapter 5, "Which Mold Do They Fill?" in *Fatima Is Fatima*, 118–120.

[66] Part of what is at stake is Shariati's determination to present the ideal Muslim family as based on mutual partnership marriage and nuclear singularity rather than the hierarchies of polygamy. By centering attention on Fatima, Shariati can model the Muslim family as monogamous. Shariati's family narrative presents Khadija as the devoted, respected, but aging and sick wife of the Prophet; Fatima as the lonely youngest daughter who accompanies, supports, and learns from her father; Aisha as the new wife whose arrival after Khadija's death allows Fatima to relinquish responsibility for her widowed father's household; and finally Fatima as the devoted wife of Ali and hard-working mother of the next generation. Throughout, the focus is on the couple in its nuclear singularity; the complicating fact of the Prophet's polygamy (for the model of the new woman) is almost entirely absent from the text.

toward Fatima's capacity for revolutionary responsiveness to the world around her; toward her exceptional ability to be fully herself in each radically changing circumstance of her existence and her world.[67] This is indeed a religious understanding of the possibilities for becoming a fully realized being, but a conception of religion that is premised on emancipatory, continuing self-transformation. Shariati understands Fatima as completely responding to God's ongoing call, even as that call always finds her located within a worldly context of familial relations. But what is her answer? Her faithful responsiveness to her own potential as an active being within those immediate relations and circumstances makes her, for Shariati, an appropriate model of emulation for the modern Iranian (Shi'a) woman. Contemporary observers, including Shariati's own students, can sense a lack of pragmatic specificity: in being herself, who *is* Fatima, as herself (other than the familial lineage roles Shariati says she transcends)? Shariati doesn't exactly answer the question.[68]

## Shariati's Women (Students)

At least, he doesn't seem to answer it in his writings; there is no directive about exactly how the modern Iranian woman should become who she is supposed to be. Certainly, Shariati's women students were not expected to take Fatima's example literally, in terms of being part of a family group that founds a new religion, and he provided a lot of indication of what the modern Iranian woman should not become. His women students found this inadequate.

[67] In *Fatima Is Fatima*, Shariati makes Fatima the central woman in the new project of Islam, which is presented as a social renewal through religion (not just social renewal as a result of religion). Further, Fatima is the true partner of her father the Prophet; not his wives, not his son-in-law or other male followers, whether of his lineage or not. "Two people were selected to carry out this plan [of renewal]. The Prophet (the father) must carry the leavy load and Fatima (the daughter) must reflect within herself the newly created revolutionary values." See Shariati, *Fatima Is Fatima*, 153.

[68] Despite appreciating that Shariati opened up the possibility of valuing Fatima as a woman with agency in herself and not only as a mourning figure (for dead men) or a relative (of men), his women students expressed frustration that she doesn't do more. "I have a question: why she didn't she do better than this? What did she do after that? These are my questions always." Author's conversation with one of Shariati's women students.

When I heard the lectures [*Fatima Is Fatima*] and when it was published and came out I bought it and read it again ... It's not enough, I think it's not enough.[69]

Often the women listening to Shariati were already committed to making changes in the day-to-day conditions of Iranian society: in the family, in the conditions of work and home, in the structures of social relations. These interventions could be as apparently simple as establishing accessible day care centers, kindergartens, or education centers for children with different kinds of disabilities. While such actions may not be formal politics, they radically transform the possibilities for societal and political contribution, especially for women.[70]

What Shariati offered to these women was an open-ended question, rather than a simple negation and its replacement with a new directive. Instead, there is a critique and a collective possibility of a new direction. The glory of Shariati's Fatima is that she is herself a proffered but unanswered question, a possibility to be responded to individually and anew by each woman who would emulate her. Fatima isn't a history of admirable actions like her more energetic daughter Zeinab. Fatima is the representation of the possibility of response to the call to become who she can and should be; to be her full self, active in her context and her time. Times and contexts change. Shariati's message to his (women) students was: Fatima is Fatima. You are you. You figure out your response.

This open-ended gesture, this lack of a specific answer only works as a constructive pedagogy if space is made, literally and figuratively, for the individual to hear the invitation and respond. Shariati did that: he literally made space in the lectures in the *hoseiniyeh* so that his women students were included, and not only confined to the balcony at the back of the hall.

We heard Dr. Shariati and his discussions in the Hossiniyeh Ershad and he is a very critical man about the Shah and why things are as they are. We went there. Always he was late. Always. More than 100 women and men are sitting downstairs, upstairs, all of the spaces are full of people, but he never comes. We don't know if he was arrested, we don't know if he was asleep, we don't know! But then he came. When he came, he started. He makes people like a *sehr-o jaadou* (magician), mesmerized. He was a fluent speaker with a

69 A woman student of Shariati's, conversations with the author.
70 A woman student of Shariati's, conversations with the author.

very beautiful voice. He used very effective titles. For example, *Areh, inchenin bood baradar*, "Yes, it was like this my brother" [sic]. Or talking about *Fatemeh Fatemeh hast* (Fatima is Fatima) it was like this.

When I listened, it was very different from many things I had listened to before. It was new.[71]

As text alone, Shariati's Fatima is frustrating, and this same student was both inspired and frustrated when she heard it and then read it. Only by noting Shariati's pedagogy with his women students, and their own energetic responsiveness (including their frustration) to his call, can we recognize a dynamic invitation for Iranian women to make their own way, rather than follow a singular voice of instruction.

Shariati's prerevolutionary vision of a renewed Muslim identity and Iranian society, conveyed through lectures, writings, and smaller regular discussion groups, galvanized many young people who were exposed to it, whether or not they identified themselves as especially religious. This shared commitment to social and self-renewal, through both collective action and individual pursuit, is part of what drew Shariati's students to him. For women particularly, he conceptualized an alternative of the possible and provided the beginnings of an expansive community in which to create it. Although not himself a feminist, Shariati shaped and encouraged a generation of women and men toward social critique and activism, including through a gendered lens. Then he died suddenly (under the euphemism of mysterious circumstances) in London in June 1977. The events that marked the beginning of the uprisings that became the Iranian Revolution began in January of 1978. And women's concerns were again subsumed within the maelstrom of national upheaval.

Shariati's students, women and men, helped make the Iranian Revolution, and many of them then helped shape the more participatory, egalitarian aspects of Iran's postrevolutionary society. But they were a minority among the religious trends that came to dominate the postrevolutionary state. New waves of democratic reform and dissent washed through the Islamic Republic, shifting the sands of expectations and accumulating strata of experience for women and for men. In 1999, in 2009, in 2022, the waves of protest surged upon widespread frustration with the status quo, but then crested and fell back. They failed to destroy the edifice of the theocratic state. But none

[71] Shariati's woman student, conversations with the author.

was a failure, if we recognize the extent to which democracy as collective and individual emancipation is a long and continuing process, based on a revolutionary vision of shared social justice, participatory citizenship, and political freedom.

## Building a Shared Political Community, One Small Step at a Time

After the 2021 election of President Ebrahim Raisi, Iranian society seemed to sink into another period of public apathy and private preoccupations. The economic situation continued to deteriorate; even people still able to make ends meet worried constantly about prices and the cascading effects of shortages and economic insecurity. Political conditions seemed to preclude organized dissent or opposition; everyone complained, most people were resentful, but there seemed less and less space for collective action. And then again, there was a spark. Mahsa Jina Amini died, and people responded by coming into the streets to protest and to demand something better: Women, Life, Freedom as political aspiration and institutional possibility.

The 2022 movement grew out of a genealogy of protest: generational waves of political action that accumulated shifts in national expectations and awareness. The striking difference was the centrality of women as actors, women's concerns as essential to the movement, and women's political subjectivity being symbolically positioned as representative of collective national political subjectivity. Women, Life, Freedom may or may not have been a feminist movement, depending on locally understood definitions of feminism. It did not overturn the state. But it further shifted the political ground, not only at the public and national levels but also in the more private spheres and daily spaces.

Like generations before them, young Iranians in 2022 were willing to risk violent state repression and even their lives. But they also began shifting their own sense of the right to determine individual behavior within mutually shared space, both private and public, and innovating small but hugely symbolic interventions in participatory practices. One of these was the phenomenon of offering public hugs. During these months of upheaval, someone, often a young woman, would stand on a busy public sidewalk or street corner, arms spread wide, offering a quick physical embrace to any passerby, female or male, young or old.

The hugs were brief, anonymous, and given and received with smiles. They were intended to share joy, to create social solidarity, and to break down the cultural barriers to public demonstrations of physical affection between unrelated persons of different genders.

Iranians habitually greet intimate friends and family by kissing each cheek, but at least in public these cheek-to-cheek contacts are reserved for those of the same gender unless noticeable age differences indicate clear kinship relations. The public hugs that emerged with the Women, Life, Freedom movement were something else: they were about transforming and expanding the model of kinship to a societal relation of mutual recognition and support. "Let me offer this to you," they seemed to say, and by accepting the hug, a stranger effectively answered back, "I see you, I recognize you, and I return the offer." Like the best forms of democratic *ta'arof*, this random public hugging established horizontal relations of equality, mutuality, and shared obligation. The public embraces also created a quietly radical, non-religious extension of the Islamic Revolution's model of comradely kinship. If Islamists had appropriated the terminology of (religious) "brother" and "sister," the anonymous huggers were creating a network of egalitarian connection and kinship that rested on shared recognition and intentional generosity rather than orthodox ideology. "For insight into the complex interrelations of models of kinship and governance, see Ihsan Mejdi, "The Nexus Between Kinship and Politics During Times of Democratic Crisis in Tunisia," paper delivered at the Middle East Studies Association meeting, 2023. In doing so, they were creating the social fabric of a shared democratic polity, and carrying through the implicit promise of the revolution as providing both liberation from a previous regime and foundation of a new political and social contract, now based on a recognizably expanded and inclusive political subjectivity.

Revolutions, unlike coups, rest on extended waves of transformation in the quotidian power relations of daily life. Normative hierarchies of age, gender, and status are disrupted by new imaginaries of autonomy and agency; accepted cultural taboos of gendered propriety and acquiescence are open to challenge. This is why even if the immediate political aim of a revolution may apparently fail, its emancipatory project may continue. On the 2023 anniversary of Mahsa Jina Amini's death, young Iranian women discussed the ongoing ramifications of the 2022 events as continuing to change their intimate relations in the neighborhood and the family, and their own sense of increased agency in an expanded social realm. Women, Life, Freedom galvanized a change in national and individual political consciousnesses about women's roles as citizens and subjects. It built on the genealogies of protest that had developed the emancipatory promise of the revolution in abbreviated but significant ways and expanded collective understanding of the rights to its inheritance. According to Iranian (Islamic) law, women's family inheritance is less than men's: sisters inherit only half of what their brothers do. The Women Life, Freedom movement overturned that presumption of diminished right, at least in regard to political subjectivity; women were acknowledged to be as central to the national political project as life and freedom, and to be as fully entitled to be participant citizens.

The repressive elements of the Iranian state may continue to contest this more expanded conception of national citizenship, for women as well as men. But the political equation of two steps forward, one step back, still indicates forward movement. The Women, Life, Freedom movement did not overturn the state or immediately dislodge its repressive apparatus. But continuing the emancipatory, inclusionary process of Iranian citizens' postrevolutionary national political development may matter even more.

# 9 Being a Public Woman: Streets, Cars, Crimes, and the Shifting Calculus of Moral Accountability

For Mahsa Shekarloo

## A Secure Claim Version 1: Traditional, Islamic Space and Identity

Walking through the bazaar in Yazd, an ancient provincial city in southern Iran, I saw a small group of three women in black *chadors*, pushing forcefully through the crowd, shopping bundles bulging in all directions. Because the traditional Iranian *chador* is a sort of loose cape that rests on the head but doesn't have sleeves or fasteners, it has to be held together to keep it in place. The historical alternative has been to wrap it around the body, almost like a sari, but this is now considered an extremely old-fashioned rural or outmoded working-class practice and is rarely seen in public urban settings. *Chadors* worn in this wrap-around fashion are also often made of the colorful floral print fabrics that are also rarely seen now in public urban spaces. Iranian women wearing a conventional black *chador* in the usual modern style will necessarily hold it closed and in place by clutching the fabric with one hand under the chin. But this leaves only one hand free, so a busy practical woman will often grip the fabric between her teeth, enabling her to use both hands to do whatever is necessary. When a *chador* is held properly closed in front, it should drape closed over the arms, so a *chadori* (a woman who wears a *chador* by choice) with packages will usually hold them under her *chador*, enlarging her silhouette at odd angles.[1]

[1] In order to deal with the obvious practical problems of managing a *chador* while managing to do anything else that requires two hands, a version of the "Arabic chador" incorporating subtly tailored sleeves (and sometimes an elastic fastener at the head) has been endorsed by state authorities and redubbed the "national chador" (*chador melli*). But it remains a minority choice; most women opt either for the more straightforwardly sleeved alternative of a *manteau* (overcoat) or the

The three women I noticed were youngish middle-aged, and not extraordinary in any way except for the authoritative way they strode forward, opening their way through the crowd despite their bulk and ungainly, package-laden shapes. They were not official in any way and were probably what they seemed: ordinary women doing their family and personal shopping in a shared outing to the bazaar, where prices are almost always cheaper than in small neighborhood shops. What was noticeable about the women was their bodily confidence, and the assurance of their mobility and deportment: their *chadors* functioning almost like a protective carapace, enabling movement without hesitation through the crowded public space.[2]

Without a *chador*, and even in the most modest form of *manteau/magneh* (overcoat/pullover hood) *hejab*, a modern woman trying to move through any dense crowd usually has to make certain feminine bodily accommodations.[3] This is not a question of lack of entitlement but a technique of physical self-containment: a slight sideways adjustment, leading with the shoulder, and perhaps lifting the elbow and forearm slightly to preserve space in front of the body. It is a practically unconscious trick to manage the press of bodies, and especially to defend the breasts from unwanted or untoward physical contact. But these *chadori* didn't need to do that. They strode straight ahead, parting the sea of bodies before them and making space for themselves and their bulkily enlarged corporeality. Yazd is a fairly traditional city, and the women were not exceptional in their dress or their presence. No one made way for them from a sense of religious obligation or political acquiescence. Rather, it was the assurance of their embodied agency that freed them to claim space unabashedly. Covered by the enveloping *chador*, no matter

classic authority of a conventionally cut *chador*. See N. C. Moruzzi, "Trying to Look Different," *CSSAAME*, 28(2) (2008), 225–234.

2 Both women's and men's sense of bodily comfort in the public space of the bazaar is part of what has kept the bazaar itself a sustainable space of economic and social relations. See Zahra Shirani, Parvin Partovi, and Mostafa Behzadfar, "Spatial Resilience in Traditional Bazaars; Case Study: Esfahan Qeisariye," *Bagh-e Nazar* 14 (October 2017), 57–68.

3 *Manteau*, the French word for overcoat, has been adopted as the Farsi term for the overgarments (jackets/overcoats/capes) worn by more secular-minded Iranian women in order to fulfill the requirements for public *hejab*; the same garment is sometimes also called a *roopoosh*. A *manteau* can be outerwear worn on the street, or a more fitted jacket worn indoors as professional dress. A *maghneh* is a pullover hood that falls to the shoulders and can be worn instead of a headscarf; it is part of the required girls' uniform for elementary through high school students.

how ungainly its management, these women did not have to negotiate the conventional physical enactment of uncovered modern modest public deportment. The *chador* was not a defense against being seen; it was a means enabling an adamant physical presence.

The classic black *chador* is the officially sanctioned Iranian version of Islamic feminine public identity, and the bazaar is the classically defined form of Islamic public space. It is also considered the epitome of traditional space, and *chadori* are the epitome of women's approved traditional identity. The slippage between "Islamic" and "traditional" is problematic but ubiquitous; *chador*-clad women moving through the public space of the bazaar are assumed to be symbols of both Islamic and traditional life. But the assimilation of "traditional" with "Islamic" assumes several other characteristics for women: an emphasis on private spaces and roles, a deportment of reticent, almost passive, modesty. Yet these three women were striding boldly through public space, embodying a version of "traditional" feminine agency and identity that lay secure claim to its own active mobility.

## A Secure Claim Version 2: Hyper-Modern, Global-Cosmopolitan Space and Identity

Mahsa Shekarloo (1970–2014) was my student, friend, and mentor. Our relationship spanned Chicago and Tehran, and a mutual dynamic of ongoing exchange. Mahsa was born in Iran but grew up in Chicago. Her family were active in the diaspora cultural community, but I first met her in my university office as a returning undergraduate, determined to follow an independent path. After graduation, that path took her back to Iran, and the possibility of finding a place and making a contribution in a transforming society. Mahsa was a smart and sensible feminist; figuring out what she had to offer, she recognized the value of her excellent English as a transnational skill to be put at the service of the local activist community. Persian-speaking Iran was never formally colonized, meaning it did not suffer the successful widespread imposition of a single modern imperial language (whether English, French, Russian, or Turkish).[4] Many Iranians spoke at least

[4] Twentieth-century Iranian nationalism was built in part on a state-sponsored disavowal of the cultural and linguistic heritage of the Arab-Islamic conquest. Although the Pahlavi state never denied the Muslim religious identity of the majority of the Iranian population, it celebrated Iran's pre-Islamic past, and

one other language, but there was no single widely shared national second language, and until satellite TV and the internet made foreign language learning much more accessible, even the intelligentsia struggled to transmit their ideas and the vibrancy of local argument to the wider, non-Persian-speaking world.[5] With a friend, Mahsa cofounded *Bad Jens*,[6] an online English-language feminist journal based in Iran that was dedicated to providing a platform for anyone writing on Iranian women's issues and defending gender equality, regardless of ideological stance. She collected and translated the Persian-language articles into English, enabling Iranian feminists to speak to interlocutors outside the country during a period when they felt most isolated, and affording those outsiders insight into developments in Iran.[7] *Bad Jens* quickly gained respect and attention, being picked up by the BBC and other reputable global news outlets long before social media had become a commonplace route to public attention. Mahsa made herself useful in further ways: as a member of a local feminist cultural NGO; as the assistant to human rights lawyer (and eventual Nobel Peace Prize winner) Shirin Ebadi and translator of two of her books into English; and as the Women's Empowerment

implicitly, the endurance of Persian as a national language. Since Persian became the court and legal language of much of the extended Islamic dominions, Iranians didn't experience their linguistic autonomy as autarky until their confrontations with the new powers of the modern age of imperialism.

5 Geographical, historical, religious, ethnic, and class differences all have determined and fragmented Iranian linguistic communities. In northwest Iran, Turkish is a common second language; in southwest Iran, Arabic is more common; Armenian Christian communities have maintained their language. Through much of the twentieth century, the most prestigious elite language of Western education was French; only in the last few decades has English become widespread. For discussion of the modern (nineteenth century) transmission of ideas through Persian language publications between linguistic communities in Iran and India, see Mohamad Tavakoli-Targhi, *Refashioning Iran: Orientalism, Occidentalism and Historiography* (New York: Palgrave Macmillan, 2001).

6 The title of the journal is a play on words. "*Jens*" means gender, nature, or type, and "*bad*" means bad, but "*badjens*" (spelt as one word) means disreputable/sly. "*Bad Jens*" spelt as two words play off the overlapping meanings of "bad gender," "disreputable/sly," and "disreputable/sly gender"; in other words, women. See the *Badjens* Sixth Edition December 2003. The journal website is no longer active, but limited access is available through some library and NGO websites.

7 As an example of her collaborative work, explicitly positioned as a public intervention, see Jelve Javaheri, Mahsa Shekarloo, and Navid Keshavarz, "News and Views [Interview with Jelve Javaheri, Iranian Feminist]," *Feminist Studies* 34(½) (Spring–Summer 2008), 329–342.

Project Officer for UNICEF in Iran.[8] And she made a life for herself: falling in love, getting married, having a baby, and with her partner Sohrab, making their small north Tehran apartment home a salon of sorts for music, conversation, and creative activism.

And her clothes were always fantastic! In or out of *hejab*, her style was always comfortable, chic, and avant-garde (she got married in sneakers before sneakers were a fashion thing); always more original and less studied than the ubiquitous, risqué *badhejab* outfits of so many aspirational young Tehrani women. Mahsa had the confidence that comes from being a member of a cosmopolitan, transnational creative elite. The apparent opposite of the Yazdi women in the provincial bazaar, she was secure in her sophisticated modernity and global in her identity as an active internet citizen with a visible presence in virtual public space. She also had the self-doubts that are inseparable from creative, critical, reflexive engagement, especially when linked with the diaspora childhood of a refugee. But those questions were individual and personal ("am I a good enough writer to be doing this?"), rather than structural and gendered ("should a woman be doing this?").

As different as their modes of dress and mobility may have been, both Mahsa and the Yazdi women strikingly embodied a forthright feminine public presence, including the ability to move effectively through different versions of public space. Whether "traditional" or (hyper-)"modern," they demonstrated modes of feminine agency that can only be admired and regarded as examples for emulation. But most of us are not Mahsa, and even if the bazaar is still usually the central urban space of Iranian cities, it is no longer the most significant public space. We might visit the internet or the bazaar, but to get to where we're going, most of us need to go into the street.

## Moving through Public Space with Less Security: Stepping into the Street

Whenever I arrive in Tehran, I have to learn to cross the street all over again: relearning the courage to step out into moving traffic, trusting

[8] See the obituaries in *Middle East Report* 272 (Fall 2014), 48; *Feminist Studies* 40(3) (2014), 722, and the extended discussion of Mahsa's contributions in "Mahsa Shekarloo: Women's Rights Activist, Internet Pioneer" on the website of international civil society NGO *Arseh sevom (Third Sphere)*, https://www.arsehsevom.org/en/2014/09/mahsa_shekarloo/.

that the cars will make room and accommodate a new object in their midst. This generally happens, the cars parting like schools of fish around a foreign body. Except when there are signals that they won't. One summer, doing research in Oxford before flying to Tehran (and nervous about the wrong-side-of-the-road problem), I was so slow stepping off the British curbs that I realized cars were habitually blinking their lights at me, giving me a polite invitation to "please, go ahead." Then I got to Tehran and noticed cars blinking at me from a distance. It was quickly apparent that the meaning was different; in Tehran, a car blinking its lights at you from a distance is signaling that "I see you, and if you don't move, I'm going to run you down."[9] Given the local traffic, this is understandable. In Oxford, cars blinked while sedately stopped at intersections, waiting for their turn to go. In Tehran, cars only blink when they are a long way off and they have a rare clean shot and no traffic in the street between you and them; the opportunity to cruise even a few blocks without stopping or swerving is so unusual that it's reasonable to warn pedestrians to get out of the way. Usually, the street traffic is packed like sardines, crowded together without apparent linear rationality or measured lanes but functioning with an organic logic of its own. Crossing the flow requires stepping out and in; a car won't stop for you until you are literally in front of it and then will move on as you pass in front of the next one, and so on and so forth, until you get to the other side. This is so intensely nerve-wracking for anyone not habituated to Tehran traffic, and so counterintuitive to all the learned rules of North American traffic safety, that I can only initially cross by positioning myself close by another pedestrian, preferably a respectable-looking elderly person whose venerable demeanor will elicit a modicum of respect from the apparently heedless current. Of course, it isn't

[9] Under slightly different traffic conditions, blinking car lights in Tehran can also mean "Do you want a ride?" It is then up to the pedestrian to figure out if this is an offer of transportation from an unmarked taxi or a sexual invitation from a private driver. See articles regarding the relation between taxis, sexual encounters, and crime by journalist Roya Karimi Majd in the Iranian feminist journal *Zanan*, 1379–1381 (2000–2003). Karimi Majd also investigated the Mashhad serial murders by "the Spider," Saied Hanafee (whose crimes occurred in relation to the ambiguity of street and transportation interactions); that case is discussed in more detail later in this chapter.

heedless and after a few days I learn again to cross on my own. But it always takes a little while.[10]

Access to public space is freedom and modernity, for women as well as men, and the need to get out and about is enough to get one out of the house. But the everyday stress of crossing the street as a pedestrian isn't necessarily solved by relying on motorized transport: buses, shared taxis, reservation taxis, private automobiles, motorcycles, and the subway.[11] Although there are an immense number of cars on the streets, for most people moving around the city means relying on some form of public transportation, with the irksome accompanying negotiations of crowds, delays, and security concerns (pickpockets). Everyone complains about traffic (and pollution). For women, there are additional annoyances and security issues: unwanted physical mingling, unsolicited corporal attentions, and intrusive state surveillance of dress and behavior. Women's public insecurity pivots in two directions, confronting unpredictable levels of threat from both society and the state.[12] In order to move through public space with a sense of security, many women prefer segregated space.

[10] Like any other apparently specialized skill, this learned ability to step into traffic can come in unexpectedly handy. Visiting the old pluralist city of Antakya in 2011 with Turkish friends used to the big city rules of Istanbul and Ankara, my friends were appalled by the free-form flow of rush hour traffic in the single main downtown intersection. While they huddled on the curb, I knew what to do. Recognizing this as a mild version of Tehran traffic rules, I pulled them with me and we set forth. Sure enough, the cars made way for us, one at a time, and we crossed over (almost) like locals.

[11] Horse-drawn carriages (*droshkies*) only began to appear in Tehran in the mid nineteenth century, and even then the city roads were impassable except in the northern suburbs: most people walked. See Chahryar Adle and Bernard Hourcade, *Téhéran, capital bicentenaire* (Paris: Institut français de recherche en Iran, 1992), 58–59. Now they only exist as urban transport in tourist destination areas of scenic cities like Shiraz and Isfahan.

[12] For women, unwelcome bodily attention can come from the sexual harassment of ordinary passersby and/or the imposition of more stringent dress code requirements by official morality police, and either of these sources of threat can unpredictably become violent. Mahsa (Jina) Amini's September 2023 death in custody for supposed infractions of proper *hejab*, and the nationwide protests that erupted in response, reflected the perceived arbitrariness and lack of accountability of the state's claims to be securing both public and private virtue. Although the *Gasht-e Ershad* (Guidance Patrol) target both men and women while enforcing public respectability in terms of heterosexual interaction and alcohol, they particularly focus on women's bodily decorum and maintenance of changing versions of proper (conservative) *hejab*. See Azam Khatam, "The

## Safe Space Is Segregated Space: Gender

The main problem with Tehran buses is that there aren't enough of them: they are almost always crowded, and they pass along limited routes. They get stuck in traffic, so they can be slow, but you can look out the window and see where you are going. And they are relatively calm. Buses in Tehran are gender-segregated: men enter and sit in the front; women (and children, including young boys) enter and sit in the back; the two halves are divided by a metal bar that people occasionally squeeze under or over.[13] Despite the inevitable US association of segregated buses with the notorious American history of racial segregation and its blatantly false claims to "separate but equal," many Tehrani women appreciate the reserved space in the buses: no matter how crowded, women are spared unwanted physical attention by the male passengers.[14] This sense of sexual security has made public buses an unproblematic space for women and has encouraged women's urban mobility.[15] The relatively new Tehran metro (subway) cars are mostly mixed, although from the beginning there was always at least

Islamic Republic's Failed Quest for the Spotless City," *Middle East Report* 250 (Spring 2009).

13 In recent years, some of the new line of Bus Rapid Transit (BRT) express buses that run in dedicated bus lanes have reversed the spatial order, seating women in front and men in the rear, although some still seat women in the rear and men in the front.

14 There was some sporadic gender segregation of Iranian buses shortly after the revolution, but it took several years for a consistent policy to be established. An indication of the ambivalence they initially provoked can be seen in a small political caricature published in an exile leftist student publication dedicated to women's issues: on a gender-segregated bus, a lone woman in *hejab* sits smiling contentedly in the back, while the overstressed male passengers fill the entire space of the front half, floor to ceiling and hanging out the windows. See *Women & Struggle in Iran: A Publication of the Women's Commission of the Iranian Student Association (ISA-US, supporters of O.I.P.F.G.)*, No. 3 (Summer 1984), p. 6 (O.I.P.F.G. stands for Organization of Iranian People's Fadayian Guerrillas). The caricature is interesting not only for its early appearance but also for its location: the political perspective of the publication is Marxist (Leninist) and resolutely hostile to the Islamization of Iranian society. (Note that *Women & Struggle* went through several iterations of political identity; numbers 1 and 2 (both 1982) were identified as "A Publication of the Women's Commission of the Iranian Students Association in the U.S." The name change is indicative of the multiple sectarian fractures that occurred within the Iranian leftist student organizations, both in Iran and in exile.)

15 For a careful examination of the women passengers' experiences and the policy history of the Tehran gender-segregated buses, see Nazanin Shahrokni, *Women*

one car reserved for women, and then two; one in front and one at the end. Women ride the other cars as well, but the reserved cars can be a relief during rush hour or other periods of extreme crowding.[16] They also provide a space of women's entrepreneurial initiative; many women peddle small items of household or feminine utility (kitchen goods, scarves, makeup) within the relatively protected confines of the (women's only) metro carriages.[17] The metro was extremely popular as soon as it opened, but neither metro nor buses can meet the public transportation needs of the city's male and female citizens.[18] National policy has supported local automobile production, and cars have become more affordable (to a noticeable negative effect on air quality and traffic). Although there are many more private cars on the road, many Tehranis still rely on taxis.

## Safe Space Is Segregated Space: Class

An *agence* is an individual taxi that must be reserved and will take you from your point of pickup to your destination for an agreed-upon fee. The privileges of solitude and control offered by an *agence* – the ability to ride only with whom you want to and to be driven exactly where you want to go – is a luxury most Tehranis cannot afford. An *agence* is much more expensive than an ordinary taxi, which is a shared car that follows a general direction and picks up and discharges multiple

*in Place: The Politics of Gender Segregation in Iran* (Oakland: University of California Press, 2020).

16 The women-only metro cars become spaces of diverse identity creation as well as mobility. See Nazgol Bagheri, "Tehran's Subway: Gender, Mobility, and the Adaptation of the 'Proper' Muslim Woman," *Social & Cultural Geography*, 18(5) (August 2017), 304–322.

17 Women metro vendors make up an employment category in themselves, distinct as an identity and in terms of spatial practice from (women) street peddlers. See Roksana Bahramitash and Jennifer Olmsted, "Choice and Constraint in Paid Work: Women from Low-Income Households in Tehran," *Feminist Economics*, 20(4) (2014), 260–280; the chapter "Low-Income Female Workers, Micro-Entrepreneurs, and the Informal Sector," in Roksana Bahramitash, *Gender and Entrepreneurship in Iran: Microenterprise and the Informal Sector* (New York: Palgrave MacMillan, 2013), 101–148.

18 The first underground line of the Tehran metro system opened in 2000; an aboveground commuter rail line had begun running in 1999. Subway and light rail lines in Shiraz and Mashhad came next, and then in Isfahan, Tabriz, and Karaj. More cities have similar projects in the planning stage.

passengers along the route.[19] Sometimes these cabs are registered and may be recognizable by the colored stripe over the top or a taxi light on the roof. More often they are informal and look like any other passing automobile; for years, they were primarily different models of the Paykan, the ubiquitous Iranian-made passenger sedan modeled on the British Hillman Hunter. Taxis have no meters; the cost for a trip tends to be fairly standardized by distance but can legitimately be slightly above or below the norm, according to the traffic, weather, condition of the car, or the whim of the driver. A passenger will murmur that they are ready to get out and hand over an estimated sum; the driver will hand back change or not, depending on the calculation. There is no tipping, and rarely an argument: you just have to be familiar with the local rules.

## Women in Public: Women in the Street

Hailing one of these taxis means standing partway in the road and peering at oncoming cars if they are not already full to the brim with passengers. For decades after the revolution, a full taxi carried five passengers: three in the narrow back seat, and two sharing the front passenger seat, squeezed in next to the driver. Increased police enforcement of driving regulations has meant that a full load is now only four passengers: three in the back and one in the passenger seat. If a car is a taxi and still has room, it will slow down, and the pedestrian would-be passenger leans farther forward and murmurs the name of their desired destination, usually the name of a major intersection. Depending on the judgment of the (usually male) driver, the car will stop or not; sometimes the passenger's destination is too close, or the driver's intended route veers off in a different direction.[20] If the taxi stops,

[19] During the period of my fieldwork, there were no app-based rideshare services, although now Iran has its own national internet-based service, Snapp. An *agence* (private taxi) had to be reserved or called in advance. Shared taxis are hailed in the street or collect multiple fares while waiting curbside at the busy traffic exchanges that are the start of multiple routes. Shared taxis (*savaris*) can also be requested as private taxis (*dar baste* or closed door) if there are no other passengers, and for a higher fare. Otherwise a taxi is considered *na dar baste* (not closed door) and is available for anyone the driver is willing to pick up.

[20] There are some women taxi drivers, and some women-only taxis; the experience for both drivers and passengers is noticeably different from taxis with male drivers. See Reza Banakar, *Driving Culture in Iran* (London: I. B. Tauris, 2015)

the current passengers often make a quick rearrangement of seating: people will sometimes change seats so that a woman isn't sandwiched between two strange men in the back, or in the old days, so that two women, rather than an unrelated woman and man, would have to sit on top of each other in the front passenger seat. But this gendered accommodation doesn't always happen, and sometimes it can seem that the crowding by unrelated men against women passengers is intentional.[21]

Although it is often impossible to recognize a taxi from a private car, it is impractical to try to travel only in recognizable official taxis, and there aren't enough buses. So a woman who wants to get somewhere on public (as opposed to private) transportation must stand in the street and solicit.[22] If a taxi does stop for her, she is expected not to mind sitting among male strangers; before the capacity regulations, she could find herself sitting literally in the front seat lap of a male stranger and be expected not to find this a reason for complaint or particular embarrassment. Women of all ages and most classes go through this experience all the time in Tehran and other major Iranian cities. Women are expected to be out and about; they need to do the shopping, get to school, go to work, get home to look after the children. Because women's public mobility is now accepted in Iran,

for interviews with women taxi drivers about their experiences (it is not always clear if the women drivers only carry women passengers, or if they also sometimes convey mixed loads). Like the other interview subjects in the book (male taxi drivers, lawyers, medical doctors, etc.), the women drivers tend to bemoan the lawlessness and lack of collective respect in "Iranian driving culture."

21 Shahram Khosravi enthusiastically mentions that he "frequently heard stories from young men about how they enjoyed the erotic moments of physical contact with a strange female body that, outside the taxi, would be separated from them and inaccessible," S. Khosravi, *Young and Defiant in Tehran* (Philadelphia: University of Pennsylvania Press, 2007), 147. For an alternate female perspective on this commonplace experience, see Mahsa Shekarloo, "Publicly Intimate Tehran: Desiring Subjects in Buses and Cabs," unpublished paper presented at the conference "Private Lives and Public Spaces in Modern Iran," St. Antony's College, University of Oxford, July 2005.

22 In discussing "public" as opposed to "private" transportation, I am now using the terms to refer to whether or not the spaces of transportation are shared, rather than to ownership. Thus an *agence* or a car driven by oneself or a friend of a family member is "private" because the passengers can assert private control over sharing the space, while transportation shared with strangers – whether a bus, metro, or shared taxi – is "public." Private transportation, whatever the type, is always more expensive than public.

and because taxis are so necessary for mobility, the fact of riding in a crowded taxi is not considered an immodest action, no matter how uncomfortable the experience. But the fact that Iranian women are habitually out in public, and that they accommodate themselves to public insecurity, only makes their identity as public women more ambiguous.

## Women in (the) Public: Being a "Public Woman"

What does it mean to be a woman in public, a public woman in a modern, urban society? The term "public" cuts here in two directions. In one case, it stands for the public sphere of citizenship and civic participation, as well as the public spaces of daily appearance and representation. But its other meaning is more gendered. By using the term "public woman," I am intentionally referencing the genealogical association between women in public and their lack of private virtue: a woman's identity was her sexuality; a woman in public was a privacy exposed. In English, a "public woman" is an old term for a "woman of the streets," "a streetwalker," or a "woman of ill repute": historically, being a "public woman" has meant being a whore.[23] And a "whore" is sometimes explicitly a woman who exchanges sex for payment, but sometimes simply a woman who is being accused of an encompassing lack of propriety.[24] A "public woman" is a woman in public whose virtue is suspect, in part because of the very fact of her public presence.

23 Historical elaborations of the use of the term "public woman" and its sexual implications in Britain and the US are developed in *Radical Femininity: Women's Self-Representationin the Public Sphere*, Eileen Janes Yeo, ed. (Manchester: Manchester University Press, 1998). See Eileen Janes Yeo, "Some Paradoxes of Empowerment," in Yeo, *Radical Femininity*, 1–24; Michelle de Larrabeiti, "Conspicuous before the World: The Political Rhetoric of the Chartist Women," in Yeo, *Radical Femininity*, 106–126, and Eileen Janes Yeo, "Protestant Feminists and Catholic Saints in Victorian Britain," in Yeo, *Radical Femininity*, 127–148, in which Yeo quotes nineteenth-century reformer Josephine Butler referring to the situation of "the despised 'public women'" in reference to the Contagious Disease campaigns, 139.

24 Before becoming the US-based public face of the Iranian neoconservative expat community, muckraking journalist Masih Alinejad was targeted by conservative Iranian commentators for her exposé journalism and her "My Stealthy Freedoms" women-without-hejab Facebook site. Some of the accusations explicitly condemned her propriety (as a public woman) rather than her arguments (as a public critic): conservative Iranian television commentator Vahid Yaminpour used his own Facebook page to argue against some of her

The contemporary inheritance of public and private spheres divided into disputed realms of proper masculinity and femininity, although it has been easily mapped back onto traditional Muslim (and classical Greek) spatial and social distinctions between outsiders and family, is a construction of Western modernity.[25] It is specifically linked to the modern process of democratization as a continual struggle to enlarge access to citizenship. As the form of political representation moved from the singular body of the sovereign to the plural body of the people, from the being of the monarch to the ability of the state, it could retain a recognizable outline only by claiming a limited corporeal identity.[26] Class, race, and gender, as well as religion and ethnicity, have all been invoked as absolute limits to political participation and citizenship.

In a parallel development to ongoing political changes, the organization of power in the social world moved from rigidly elite stratifications organized around families rather than individuals, to more mobile autonomous agents who must be men.[27] Women's proper

critics by explaining that "Masih Alinejad is a whore, and not a heretic as some people claim her to be. We shouldn't elevate her to the level of a heretic." See Masih Alinejad, "Iranian State Television Faked My Rape," *Time* (June 4, 2014), .

25 Elaheh Koolaee, "Iranian Women from Private Sphere to Public Sphere, with Focus on Parliament," *Iran and the Caucasus*, 13(2) (2009), 401–414.

26 The limits to proper modern political identity also had to be appropriately performed: proper "condescension" (graciousness to inferiors), improper "impudence" (back-talk to superiors), and thoughtless "insolence" (taking advantage of a position of supposed superiority to lord it over supposed inferiors) all held implications in the maintenance of social order through a period threatened by new Enlightenment possibilities of political equality. See Don Herzog, *Poisoning the Minds of the Lower Orders* (Princeton, NJ: Princeton University Press, 1998), especially the section on "Contempt," 202–402.

27 The first recognizably modern public feminist arguments for women's equal political citizenship were provided by radical women writers (Mary Wollstonecraft, Olympe de Gouges) supporting the new democratic project of the French Revolution and appalled that their male fellow radicals (Jean-Jacques Rousseau) would nonetheless explicitly exclude women from the philosophical project of democracy as well as its practice. Abigail Adams may have written apparently similar arguments in 1776 in response to the potential of the American Revolution and the founding of the new US ("Remember the ladies ..."), but she wrote privately in letters to her husband John. Both De Gouges and Wollstonecraft wrote and published publicly and in direct response to significant public texts presenting the democratic project as exclusively male: de Gouges' 1791 *The Rights of Woman* (also known as

exclusion helped define the space of public participation, both literally and conceptually, and the "woman question" became the pressing need to establish the boundaries of that exclusion, which were continuously in question. These social and political changes occurred in a context of increasing urbanization. As cities swelled with new urban migrants from the countryside, the traditional community linkages of family and neighborhood became strained. Family and community often set conservative limits on women's agency, but they also can provide a relational network that establishes individual identity as dynamically embedded in a temporal and spatial location.[28] If I am known as the daughter of my family and if my family is recognized by its local residence, then there is less room for the modern urban anonymity that signifies individual freedom, but that can also allow a woman in public to be mistaken for a public woman.

The representational problem of the public woman is exactly that although her virtue is suspect, she may be virtuous; for the woman herself as well as her social observer, there is danger in her being mistaken for what she is not. Unless, in a problem of categorization, she is what she is mistaken for by the very fact of having been mistaken for it.[29] A woman in public is all the more suspect of being a public woman if she is apparently loitering, if she is apparently of a class whose general morality is considered inadequate, if she is apparently

*The Declaration of the Rights of Woman and the Female Citizen*) in response to *The Declaration of the Rights of Man and of the Citizen* (written in 1789 but the preamble to the French Constitution as of 1791); Wollstonecraft's 1792 *A Vindication of the Rights of Woman* was subsequent to her own 1790 *A Vindication of the Rights of Men*, itself in opposition to Edmund Burke's 1790 *Reflections on the Revolution in France*.

28 See James C. Scott, John Tehranian, and Jeremy Mathias, "The Production of Legal Entities Proper to States: The Case of the Permanent Family Surname," *Comparative Studies in Society and History*, 44(1) (January 2002), 4–44.

29 Joan Scott discusses this problem in terms of French *femmes isolées*: women who could be either unlicensed prostitutes (women not working from a registered bordello) or independent women wageworkers (seamstresses, dressmakers) not employed in another's establishment. See "*L'ouvrière!*," in Joan Wallach Scott, *Gender and the Politics of History*, revised ed. (New York: Columbia University Press, 1999), 142. In Britain, working-class women might have moved informally in and out of prostitution, but resisted being identified as prostitutes precisely because it confined them from an otherwise negotiable social identity. See Judith Walkowitz, *Prostitution and Victorian Society: Women, Class and the State* (New York: Cambridge University Press, 1980).

independent of respectable male guardianship.[30] All of these accumulating demerits to her character are issues of external perception. But a woman in public has to manage both the external representation and the intimate physical experience of her public mobility, including its ongoing contradictions.

This is the issue of feminine appearance. But "appearance" itself incorporates two modes: appearance as visibility (which includes questions of external perception and self-representation) and appearance as physical entry (which includes questions of the personal experience of corporeal mobility).[31] To appear in a doorway is both to be seen and to move into previously empty space. And it is a political issue: appearance links questions of physical mobility (whether women can bodily enter into and move through public space) with questions of social and cultural meaning (how their public presence is viewed and interpreted). It encompasses the problems both of being present and of being seen as a woman in public.[32]

A reductionist notion of modern women's public role is that no respectable woman should have one: no woman should have any business to be alone in public without a male chaperone or guardian. This attitude has not been confined to Islamic societies; nineteenth-century Western history is a long story of women's efforts to negotiate an acceptable public role and to find a way to move through public

[30] For a brilliant analysis of the problem of women's public presence, as well as a defense of all women's right to be in public, to claim public space, and to enjoy being in it for frivolous ("fun") reasons as well as serious ones (work, school), see Shilpa Phadke, Sameera Khan, and Shilpa Ranada, *Why Loiter: Women & Risk on Mumbai Streets* (Haryana: Penguin Books, 2011). For an interrogation of the class and gender contradictions of loitering as utopian promise, see Susan Buck-Morss, "The Flaneur, the Sandwichman and the Whore: The Politics of Loitering," *New German Critique*, No. 39, second special issue on Walter Benjamin (Autumn 1986), 99–140.

[31] Fanon addresses these two aspects of women's appearance in his discussion of both the external perception and internal experience of Algerian women during the Algerian Revolution. See the chapter "Algeria Unveiled," in Frantz Fanon, *A Dying Colonialism* (New York: Monthly Review Press, 1965), 35–67.

[32] Some of the most provocative theoretical writings on the linked issues of representation and observation have been produced by feminist film theory, particularly its development of the theory of the (male) gaze as productive of women's (self)representation. See Laura Mulvey, "Visual Pleasure and Narrative Cinema," *Screen* 16(3) (1975), 6–18; Mary Ann Doane, "Film and the Masquerade: Theorizing the Female Spectator," *Screen* 23(3–4) (1982), 74–88.

space without physical or reputational risk.[33] The real difficulty arises when there is a preliminary acceptance that women have a legitimate public role as autonomous subjects and/or citizens; when the question is no longer whether women should be in public but how they should appear and be present.[34]

Women's freedom to appear in public (spaces) elicits a sense of danger: that she is in danger; that she is a danger. Underlying this fear is a concern that a woman in public is a public woman: a woman available; to be commented on; appropriated. Being a public woman can be uncomfortable. Or it can be deadly.

## Public Women: Violence and (Im)Morality

In 2001, Saeed Hanaei, the notorious Iranian "Spider Killer," admitted to killing sixteen women in the city of Mashhad between 2000 and 2001; he identified his victims in the street and offered them a ride on his motorcycle. (He was arrested in 2001 and executed in prison in 2002.) He claimed he targeted prostitutes ("street women"), and the women knew why he "lured" them to his home. During this period, motorcycles were a common working-class form of shared transport; although they were not used as taxis, multiple passengers and sometimes whole families (an adult man and a woman and several children) would share a single machine. It was assumed that a woman riding with a man must know him, but the anonymous physical intimacy expected in shared taxis meant that the moral and physical propriety of public transportation, and transportation in public, couldn't be taken for granted. Any woman seeking a ride was vulnerable; Hanaei's wife had herself been mistaken in the street for a prostitute while soliciting a

[33] There is an enormous literature on this topic. As a sample: for discussion of the representational problem of urban women's insecurity, both as themselves posing a sexual threat and the sexual threat they faced, see Judith Walkowitz, *City of Dreadful Delight: Narratives of Sexual Danger in Late-Victorian London* (Chicago: University of Chicago Press, 1992). For discussion of the experiential problem of women moving through public space, see Patricia Cline Cohen, "Safety and Danger: Women on American Public Transport, 1750–1850," in Dorothy O. Helly and Susan M. Reverby, eds., *Gendered Domains: Rethinking Public and Private in Women's History* (Ithaca, NY: Cornell University Press, 1992), 109–122.

[34] In *Why Loiter?*, the authors discuss in specific detail how Mumbai women of different neighborhoods, religious communities, class backgrounds, and levels of privilege negotiate public access, appearance, and identity.

taxi. After he was arrested, Hanaei stated that he had begun his killing spree in retaliation for the error of his wife's moral (mis)categorization; his wife stated that women who ride on motorcycles with strangers deserved to die.[35]

Hanaei's case garnered immense attention inside Iran and opened a national dialog on the morality of women's honor in public and men's relation to it: a dialog on the question of women in public and public women. Most of the public, the media, and representatives of the government condemned the crimes. But Hanaei and his lawyer argued that the women victims, as prostitutes, were "sinners" and therefore "a waste of blood."[36] His family members defended his moral righteousness; in interviews, his brother asserted that Hanaei wasn't a murderer because whores aren't human, and his young son explained that his father had been purifying the Islamic Republic of

[35] Two well-regarded films have been made about the case: the documentary *And Along Came a Spider* (Maziar Bahari, 2002) and the feature *Holy Spider* (Ali Abbasi, 2022). The investigative journalist Roya Karimi Majd covered the case and interviewed Hanaei and his family members; unexpectedly, she was also able to be present at his execution. She is featured in Bahari's documentary and is the basis for the woman journalist character, Arezoo Rahimi, in Abbasi's *Holy Spider*. In a 2022 interview with *Radio Farda*, Karimi Majd discussed her experience working as a legal reporter for the independent (Reformist) newspaper *Nowruz* and her investigation and coverage of the Hanaei case, first published in the independent women's journal *Zanan*. She also discusses her collaborations with Bahari, Abbasi, and Ebrahim Irajzad, the director of *Killer Spider*, a more muted 2020 Iranian feature film also based on the case and released in Iran (interview in Persian, available online through YouTube), www .youtube.com/watch?v=FPz2zT_Ltow. For other discussions of Karimi Majd's role in the case and the films, see Dan De Luce, "The Beast of Mashhad," *The Guardian* Monday, August 18, 2003; Diksha Sundriyal, "Is Holy Spider's Arezoo Rahimi a Real Life Journalist? Where Is She Now?," *The Cinemaholic* (April 8, 2023); Samaneh Ghadarkhan, "Iran's 'Spider Killer' Is Re-Dramatised Two Decades after Original Documentary," *IranWire* (May 23, 2022). *IranWire* is the online news website founded in 2013 by Mazian Bahari (the director of *And Along Came A Spider*). The artist Khosrow Hassanzadeh created the poster image for Bahari's film (lined up headshots of the victims, most of them police mug shots) and went on to create a painting series entitled *Prostitute* dedicated to the victims. See the artist's website, www.khosrow-hassanzadeh.com/works/prostitute/. Hassanzadeh is also one of the artists involved in the 1990s collective art projects discussed in the chapter 11, "We Are More Than One, When We Speak Together."

[36] This is a vague category of Iranian Islamic law; the death of some sinners would be a "waste of blood" (and therefore also a waste of blood money), but the sins themselves are unspecified. The trial judge was emphatic that such judgments cannot be lightly made and that Hanaei's judgment was inappropriate.

the corruption hidden under *chadors*.[37] A significant faction of the hard-line conservative media celebrated Hanaei as a moral crusader (even though he admitted to having had "improper relations" with his victims before killing them), and the shadowy political pressure group *Ansar-e Hezbollah* warned starkly that women's increasing immorality could lead to similar crimes in Tehran.[38] Since paramilitary groups with equally shady ties to conservative elements of the state had been linked to other extrajudicial killings, including the "Chain Murders" (a series of assassinations of prominent intellectuals in 1998), this was considered a none-too-veiled threat wrapped in a pseudo-paternalistic warning.

Hanaei's self-proclaimed moral righteousness provided a symbolic alternative for conservative elements wanting to push back against President Khatami and the elected reformist government. Whatever his actual motives, Hanaei was available for appropriation by the hard-line conservatives because he presented himself as a solitary moral crusader avenging the (feminine) vice of modern urban society. But he was by no means the only serial sexual criminal active during the period, or the only one who took advantage of the ambiguities of women's public mobility and presence.[39]

## Women in Public: Violence and (In)Security

Between 1999 and 2001, six young men working together and styling themselves as the "Black Vultures" gang (*Karkas-hayeh Siah*) were responsible for perhaps two hundred cases of rape in the Tehran Pars

[37] Hanaei, who claimed that most of his victims were drug addicts, admitted to having himself become "addicted" to the killing, and that the victims weren't human beings to him, that he would have felt "sorrier for an animal." His mother asserted that "these morally corrupt women" (working-class women who are possibly addicts and/or sex workers) shouldn't think that "now they're free and can be happy" (interviews in *And Along Came a Spider*).

[38] Hanaei later claimed that he had been pressured to admit to sexual impropriety. Ansar-e Hezbollah is an Iranian neofascist paramilitary group that has no relation to the Lebanese political party Hezbollah.

[39] Perhaps because Hanaei's case was so publicized and politicized, the issue of "forgiveness," whether by the victims' families or the society, was not resonant; Hanaei was either regarded as an inhuman monster (the "Spider") or a righteous vigilante. For discussion of the formal role forgiveness plays in capital offense murder trials, see Arzoo Osanloo, *Forgiveness Work: Mercy, Law, and Victims' Rights in Iran* (Princeton, NJ: Princeton University Press, 2020).

region.[40] They were caught in 2001, and five were publicly executed in 2002; one was given a twenty-year prison sentence. Their professed leader was a thirty-two-year-old who had been working in Japan, but the rest were in their twenties, young men (including a university student) whose lives seemed mostly unremarkable until they were caught, tried, and executed.[41] Initially, they simply paid for sex with actual prostitutes (women who exchanged sex for cash), but the leader warned them that from prostitutes they could catch VD, and one of them did get gonorrhea. Convinced that "prostitutes" were more likely to be diseased than other women, the gang began to target runaways for sex. Runaway girls could be "paid" for sex through barter or even housing; they might be public women and sex workers, but they were not considered "prostitutes," and therefore not associated with the same risk of sexual infection. But runaways carried their own risk. During this period, unmarried couples who were caught together by late-night Guidance Patrols could be punished by being required to marry. For some clandestine dating couples, formalization of the relationship through marriage might not be unwelcome. But the Black Vultures didn't want to have to marry runaways they had picked up in the street.[42] After they were caught with some runaway girls, the police gave them a warning, but the young men were afraid that the

[40] Discussion about the Black Vultures case is based on personal interviews conducted by the author with local women university student researchers investigating serial sexual crimes; these student researchers conducted their own interviews of the families of some of the gang members. Although they did not mention her, their audacious investigations of the attitudes of the family and social milieu of the killers were similar to the work of Roya Karimi Majd, the woman reporter who followed the Saeed Hanaei case and who is presented as the heroine of the feature film *Holy Spider*. Hanaei himself stated that he wished his ideas would be discussed in universities; he probably did not have in mind the approach of these young university women student researchers.

[41] Their ages were 21, 23, 24 (the student), 25, and 28, and the leader was 32.

[42] The involvement of the gang with runaways was described to the author by the women student researchers. In *Passionate Uprisings* (197–198), Pardis Mahdavi describes an upper-class north Tehran boy and a more working-class south Tehran girl who are caught together at a sexually open party, arrested, and faced with an obligatory marriage. Mahdavi does not acknowledge the class tensions that prompt the girl's (but not the boy's) ambivalent attitude toward the punishment. My own impression was that most unmarried couples harassed by the police were not threatened with forced marriage; "courting couples" (couples who seemed to be in a relationship rather than a more anonymous sexual pickup) were less at risk, possibly since for many of them marriage might not have been so much of a threat.

next time they would face forced marriage. So they came up with an alternative: late at night, they would stop women driving in lonely areas in their own private cars, probably coming home on their own from parties. They would identify themselves as enforcers of the morals police and insist the women go with them. Then they would threaten them with knives and rape them.[43]

The gang used two SUVs to block passenger sedans, then assaulted the women in the cars or took them to parks, stripped them, and left them (alive). Some of the women hung themselves in the park, and the police found their bodies; one married woman who was raped and left naked in a park went home and told her husband, who dropped dead of a heart attack.[44] Many reported their attacks to the police, and at least four testified in the court proceedings. Eventually, the student gang member was caught during a routine nighttime traffic check for contraband or improper gender mingling; while driving his Paykan, he was found to have a large container of alcohol in his trunk and was arrested for illegal liquor possession. But the police had put together a composite sketch from the victims' reports, and he was matched to the suspect sketch and arrested for the sexual attacks. The police quickly arrested another gang member, but only after a year of imprisonment and torture did the first two suspects confess; the other four were subsequently arrested, tried, and convicted in 2002. The charges were mostly for sexual crimes; most of the women had lived, and it seemed that the few who had died had bled to death or committed suicide; their murders were inadvertent rather than intended. Only one of the accused (identified as the least violent since he was often the driver and didn't always rape) received a sentence of imprisonment rather than execution.[45]

[43] Some of the public media coverage of the case said the men also robbed the women; according to the student researchers who interviewed several of the men's families, the gang only ever stole a video recorder from a mother and daughter; otherwise their attacks were purely sexual. The media reported that the gang was prosecuted for perhaps ten rapes, but the student researchers believed they had been responsible for approximately 200 assaults in the Tehran/Pars region.

[44] Information from the student researchers. Whether this death was factual or "urban legend," the Black Vultures were publicly identified as a gang of rapists, not murderers.

[45] The executions were widely covered in the local and international press (www.news.bbc.co.uk/2/hi/middle_east/2287381.stm) and were characterized variously as deserved (www.victimsfamiliesforthedeathpenalty.blogspot.com/2012/07/

Before the executions, three of the men protested their death sentences to the media; one claimed that the women they attacked were prostitutes who had no grounds to file complaints; another asserted that in any case the women "did not resist our demands"; the third acknowledged that they deserved punishment but not to be executed.[46] These statements seem to have been made after the trial in order to rally public sympathy against the executions. But the trial judge had already denied that the victims were prostitutes, although he added that the "fading of spiritual values, the type of make-up and inappropriate appearance of some women provokes some youth and hence brings about certain difficulties."[47] In contrast to Hanaei's case, and despite their late claims about their victims' sexuality, the Black Vultures were widely portrayed as criminals rather than moral crusaders, and the executions themselves were public, prolonged, and widely perceived as just.

It made a difference to public perception that the crimes had targeted women in more middle-class areas of the city and that the women had been stopped in their own vehicles rather than picked up in the street. Their more middle-class identity adequately covered them with the veil of feminine respectability, and the ability to rely on their own private transportation conveyed their authentic, if compromised, private feminine virtue. As legitimate victims, the women had a right to state justice. They were not seen as public women, but as (middle-class) women in public who had been unjustly targeted by violent, immoral (working-class) criminals who were themselves a grave threat to public security. But the case did not do much to clarify the question of Iranian women's public (in)security, and class and gender continued to structure social responses to issues of women's public presence. At the family mourning ceremonies for the young men, women family members railed at the regime and lamented that the boys had no jobs, no prospects, and no chance to marry. One of the fathers turned on a young woman student researcher, standing next to a woman journalist, and said that his son "did good, I wish he had done it to you too."[48]

black-vultures-of-iran.html) or as human rights violations (www.iranrights.org/memorial/story/-4802/payam-amini) (www.amnesty.de/umleitung/2002/mde13/016).

46 www.iranrights.org/memorial/story/-4802/payam-amini

47 www.iranrights.org/memorial/story/-4802/payam-amini

48 Author's personal interview with student researchers.

## Public Fear: Societal Security

Iran's city streets didn't necessarily become safer after the Vultures' arrests and convictions. Newspaper coverage of organized, violent attacks on women taking various kinds of street transportation would cause a certain amount of general hand-wringing over the insecurity ordinary women faced when present in public, and especially when attempting to move through public space, but attitudes didn't really change.[49] Ordinary people, both men and women, blamed the poor economy for the delayed age of marriage, and for young men resorting to rape out of sexual frustration.[50] If anything, media coverage of sexual crimes made women more insecure. The Black Vultures had been unusual for targeting Tehran women driving their own cars. But most women had their own unpleasant stories regarding public transportation, especially the informal shared taxis, and in multiple cities. The overcrowding and surreptitious groping were bad enough. But women feared worse: there were plenty of accounts of taxi drivers coordinating with other men to trap unknowing women passengers. A driver with an empty car could pick up two women and, then five hundred meters later, pick up two men who were actually accomplices of the driver. Even if a woman was the lone passenger of an *agence* taxi, a driver late at night, or in a lonely area, could take an alternate route, speed up, and hope the woman would be too frightened or confused to do anything but sit in the back rather than throw herself out of a moving vehicle.[51]

[49] Another Tehran gang seemed to have learned a lesson from the capture, conviction, and execution of the Back Vultures: that no witnesses should be left alive. Since the Vultures had been identified through victims' reports that provided the information for suspect sketches, the Wolves (*Gorgha*) decided that the solution was to preclude possibilities for identification by killing their victims: combining rape with murder (author's interview with student researchers). In subsequent years, media coverage identified a number of other gangs that committed serial sexual assaults (and sometimes murder) in other major cities, including *Bermoda* (2012) and the Yellow Wolves/*Gorg-hayeh Zard* (2015) in Mashhad, and Fear/*Vahshat* (2013) in Kerman.

[50] The student researchers conducted a survey among university students about attitudes toward sexual crimes; both men and women hesitated to condemn male sexual criminals (including the Black Vulture gang), although women condemned them slightly more (author's interview with student researchers).

[51] Some of these accounts were second hand ("the daughters of a friend of my grandmother's"). But some of the most disturbing and intimidating were

Even younger women who seemed relatively fearless in terms of claiming their entitlement to public mobility as a social right to the city had become individually hesitant. It was one thing to argue for women's right to traverse urban space securely. It was another thing to walk in the street alone at night, to solicit a taxi, or enter a car without being accompanied by a reliable man (and who was reliable?). Women needed to be able to move securely through public space, and society supported their mobility. But no one knew quite how to secure their security. Closer regulation of public transportation was slow and contradictory: the buses were already gender-segregated, as was the metro to some degree; the taxi system (both taxis and *agence*) was too informal and unlikely to become uniformly formalized. Taxis of any kind were simply too integrated into the structural realities of Iranian urban life: too necessary for many ordinary people as an available means of informal transportation; too necessary for many ordinary people as an entrepreneurial source of informal income.

The problem of public insecurity was disturbing to everyone but seemed resistant to available policy solutions. Yet it could be approached another way; as a general problem of moral security faced by the entire society. Understood from this perspective, the issue was less the physical insecurity Iranian women faced in public, and more the social insecurity presented by the face and appearance of the Iranian public woman. But who was she? Was every woman in public a public woman? Saeed Hanaei had based the argument for his own vigilante crusade on the moral distinction between his wife's self-evident-but-publicly-mistaken private virtue and the compromised public character of his victims. Public opinion uneasily balanced concern for legitimate feminine fears (physical and social threats to women in public) and criticism of women's illegitimate presence and behavior (the moral and social contagion of public women). No one wanted to argue that all women in public were public women, and few dared to argue that any woman in public, whatever her private virtue, deserved to be secure. The problem of women in public depended on the perceived direction of the threat: toward women or from women. In either case, the state was obligated to ensure security, but against what, and for whom?

first-hand accounts told to the author, over a number of years and covering several major cities.

## Public Women and Women in Public: The Role of the State and the Right to the City

The term "social security" (*amniyat-e ejtamai'i*) began to be used by Iranian government security officials in the summer of 2007, at that time referring almost exclusively to the sexual threat women's public immodesty posed to the well-being of society: the generalized threat of Iranian public women.[52] The term linked issues of public security (risk) and questions of private morality (virtue): the intersection of public and private concerns within the context of the wider social environment. The "Plan for Societal Security" (*Tarhe Amniyat-e Ejtama'i*) targeted women's immodest dress and behavior, certain forms of provocative male youth street fashion, and the public manifestation of apparently improper heterosexual relationships (couples holding hands, couples sitting too close together in coffee shops and parks).[53] It was then expanded to include more working-class youths who were identified as "*Arazel o Obash*" (gang-bangers and drug-dealers), a category that specifically targeted young (unemployed and under-employed) working-class men in south Tehran neighborhoods whose street presence (loitering on corners, hanging out in small groups) was

52 *Amniyat-e Ejtama'i* can best be translated in English as "societal security," although the literal translation is "social security." The problem with the literal translation is that it is too close to the English translation of *T'amin-e Ejtema'i* (the national Social Security organization that provides pensions, etc.). Both terms use the same Farsi word for "social" (*ejtema'i*), but different words for "security": security as the enforcement of disciplinary safety vs. security as the provision of material support.

53 During Winter 2006/Spring 2007, some young Iranian men for the first time embarked on the kind of radically provocative fashion styles that had for years been the exclusive province of young women. While young women's *badhejab* had ceased to become especially noteworthy, in that it continued to make quantitative rather than qualitative changes in a fairly standardized dress style (ever shorter and tighter jackets, lots of exposed hair, heavy makeup), the hairstyles of boys in this period suddenly exploded. This was almost literal: gelled and spiked, the hair of the young men on parade in the upscale shopping areas of north Tehran often stood out several inches above and around their heads. This was not merely styled long hair, but a particular fashion innovation (a kind of punk look without the grunge attitude, sported by would-be yuppie clubbers) that was indigenous to Tehran, although slightly less extreme versions could be spotted in other parts of the country. The boys' rather abrupt entrance into the street competition for *badhejab* distinction meant that the social security campaign against unIslamic appearance and behavior was not targeted only at women.

considered a potential social threat, even if their personal appearance was not.[54] But in 2008, Ahmadreza Radan, the Deputy Chief of the Tehran Police, explicitly expanded the consideration of "social/societal security" to include the insecurity women faced when present in public, rather than only the insecurity their public presence presented. In a televised interview, Radan asserted that the police were not focused on controlling women but the men who threatened them, especially men in cars (*mozahemate khiyabani*). Taxis were a particular concern, although Radan avoided any direct implication that Tehran's urban transportation system was systemically a problem for women (he specifically stated that there was not a problem of a lack of taxis). Rather, Radan asserted that "badly dressed" women faced street threats four times more than other women.[55] Radan specifically used the term "badly dressed" (*bad-pooshesh*) rather than *badhejab*, a significant distinction in the context of Iranian arguments about women's public appearance. Any woman can be badly dressed: managing the social codes of clothing is always a tricky business. But in the Iranian political context, *badhejab* is a moral category as well as a sartorial description; being *badhejab* means being compromised in feminine appearance and virtue.[56] Because "*hejab*" refers both to the articles of (appropriately modest) clothing that cover the hair (a hat that completely covers the hair is not necessarily considered good *hejab*), as well as the more expansive notion of modest behavior, decorum, and self-management, the categorization of women as *badhejab* identifies their provocative public immodesty as a threat to societal security. They are women publicly displaying dubious dress that is presumed to be revealing dubious morals; they are public women. Badly dressed women are women in public who unfortunately haven't paid adequate attention to their representation and appearance.

[54] The simultaneous "societal security" crackdown on *badhejab* elites and working-class youths ("thugs") seems to have been part of the same wave of youth repression, although the public threat was differently identified and differently treated. There were rumors that working-class youths who were arrested for "social insecurity" were then given the option of joining the unofficial street militias that enforce Islamic/political observance and are more feared (and more violent) than the official police.

[55] See www.tabnak.ir/fa/pages/?cid=10993 (May 19, 2008) and www.farsnews.com/newstext.php?nn=8602250358.

[56] Thus, being a *badhejabi* is the feminine moral opposite of being a *chadori*.

As a moral and policy categorization, whether a woman is identified as "badly dressed" or "badhejab" has implications for how she should be treated as a social agent. When Radan, speaking as a government authority, changed his terminology, he implied a different possible relation between the state and its badly veiled citizens than the confrontational hostility that had been the norm. "Badly dressed" women presumably were owed some acknowledgment by the state that they were entitled to efforts to ensure their public security, even if they were still unnecessarily putting themselves in harm's way. In contrast, "badhejab" women were still regarded as being in direct challenge to the state's efforts to ensure social security, and as a category might therefore remain a target of enforcement. Radan's statements didn't specify any definite changes in the implementation of the societal security policies. But they definitely indicated a shift in the usual balance of moral and political responsibility between the state and its citizens.

A few years later, a similar discursive and policy shift was targeted at another troublesome version of women's public presence and identification. In 2011, Ahmad Roozbehani, the Chief of the Tehran morality police (the Guidance Patrols), announced a new effort to classify "street women" (referring not to homeless women but to women-of-the-street, i.e., public women) into two separate categories of sexual impropriety: "those who sell their body for money" and "those who are wealthy but promiscuous." He stated that poor women who engaged in prostitution out of financial need would be offered guidance; their financial straits identified them as implicitly socially damaged even if morally suspect, and they deserved some level of social support. Women who were not/did not need to be actual prostitutes – those who were publicly immodest without even a class justification to defend their compromised private virtue; women in public who insisted on being public women even though they didn't need to – would be dealt with more severely.[57]

The distinctions between badly dressed and *badhejab* women, and between prostitutes and the sexually promiscuous, were similar attempts to maintain the difference between women in public and

[57] See "Moral Police in Tehran to classify 'street women'," *Kodoom* (January 4, 2011), http://features.kodoom.com/en/iran-culture/moral-police-in-tehran-to-classify-street-women/v/2420/

public women, and the variations in the state's obligations to its worthy or errant women citizens. But by pluralizing the categories of problematic women in public, both Radan and Roozbehani were acknowledging that the moral borders were blurring. The state still claimed its right to regulate and repress designated public women, especially those who flaunted convention without apparent remorse. But it was also acquiescing to public sympathy for hapless women caught up despite themselves in the state's uneven policing of societal (in)security: for the "badly dressed" women who found themselves the target of orchestrated sexual violence; for the poor women who sold their bodies to feed their children. Women's entitled claims on the state – for the public security of safe streets and the social security of economic support – were being grudgingly acknowledged.[58]

## Public Woman, Public Man, Public Citizen

Rhetorics of identification both reflect social understandings and help shape them: whether an individual is perceived as intentionally flouting society's moral and legal norms (a delinquent) or a legitimate claimant on the state's obligations and resources (an entitled citizen) can make the difference between official repression or social support.

During the same period, there were other significant changes in Iranian discourses of social regulation and responsibility. But these were calculated interventions rather than accommodations. By 2011,

[58] This slow process – of women getting the state to acknowledge its responsibility to making public space (and specifically the space of the street) safe for women citizens – is not unique to Iran either spatially or temporally. See, for instance, historian Emily Remus' account of similar efforts by turn-of-the-twentieth-century Chicago women to raise public awareness of street harassment and obligate police to secure public space for women's presence. The development of the process in Chicago is strikingly similar to that in Iran: street harassment only becomes accepted as a generalized public problem after high-profile assaults on unescorted (respectable) women make clear that private feminine virtue cannot secure women's public safety. Remus points out that historically, securing public safety for women only becomes an urgent municipal problem (demanding a response from both social and institutional actors) when urban public space is being reconfigured by a modern culture of mass consumption (as both practice and display). Before that transformation, any unescorted woman in public was explicitly "thought to be a 'public woman', her body available for sale." See Emily Remus, *A Shoppers' Paradise: How the Ladies of Chicago Claimed Power and Pleasure in the New Downtown* (Cambridge, MA: Harvard University Press, 2019).

social work, medical, and public health researchers inside Iran were using a new and apparently unique categorization for what elsewhere might be termed "at risk" behaviors and populations: "socially damaged" (*aseeb-dideh-ye ejtema'ee*). They used this not only in internal research publications and debates but began to introduce it within international publications as well.[59] Deploying a Durkheimian conception of the socially constructed individual, researchers and practitioners working with the Organization for Rehabilitation under the Health Ministry, and those dealing with policy issues involving morally denigrated categories of gender and sexuality (drug addiction, sex work, transgender and transsexuality, runaways and vagrancy, illegitimate children) attempted to shift the dominant discourse from individual to societal responsibility, and from a legal and policy conceptualization of social deviance (*monharef-e ejtema'ee*) to one of social vulnerability.[60]

The researchers were intervening in the rhetorics of moral culpability in order to change public perception and public policy. Their effort was an attempt to open space for public sympathy and policy support for taboo populations that were often implicitly gendered: addicts, sex

[59] For a brief explanation of the conceptual, legal, and policy framework of the terms, see Gohar Mohammadi, Sedigheh Amiraliakbari, Ali Ramezankhani, and Hamid Alavi Majd, "Poor Reproductive Health among a Group of Socially Damaged Middle Eastern Women: A Cross-Sectional Study," *International Journal of Women's Health* 3 (2011), 399–403. Thanks to Azam Khatam for bringing this source to my attention.

[60] Some Iranian researchers disapprove of the term, regarding it as an evasive euphemism that avoids explicit identification of women as sex workers or addicts (the classification usually refers to women). Nonetheless, it became prevalent in the relevant scholarship published by Iranian researchers, whether publishing in Iran or in international English-language journal publications, although the meaning of the term has often been opaque to their global colleagues. See Leila Allaqoli, Zhila Abeed Saeedi, Ali Azin, Sepide Hajaan, Hamid Alavi Majd, and Nader Molavi, "Socially Damaged Women's Perceptions of Sexually Transmitted Infections: A Qualitative Study," *Life Science Journal* 11(4s) (2014), 244–250; the ensuing confusion among non-Iranian researchers over the use of the term "socially damaged," prompting a series of posts during spring 2014 on a global research listserv on health/sexuality issues and policies within the MENA region (author's archive). For an example of how different categorizations ("lumpenproletariat," "dangerous classes") of homeless addicts as a social group influence a research perspective, see Maziyar Ghiabi, "Under the Bridge in Tehran: Addiction, Poverty and Capital," *Ethnography*, "Tales from the Field", 21(2), (2018) (DOI: 10.1177/1466138118787534), 1–25.

workers, and vagrants.[61] Words matter. If not all badly dressed women are *badhejab*, perhaps not all women of the street are to be condemned. If not all women in public are public women, then perhaps the public woman herself has become a different political character. The denigration of the "public woman" rests on the question her public appearance throws over her private virtue. But the "public man" is an exemplary participatory citizen. It may be too much, too soon, to regard public space and the public sphere as freely accessible and gender neutral, whether in Iran or anywhere else. But Iranian women's claim to public appearance – understood plurally as physical presence (mobility through public space), political participation (agency in the public sphere), and social representation (construction of the body and the self) – is firmly established.

In 2002, some young women university students responded to the Black Vultures' attacks and trial by deciding to research attitudes toward sexual violence. They further decided to extend their research beyond their local public (their university peers, other researchers, and journalists) and to include the milieu of the attackers' families. These were the young women who were told by a father at the mourning ceremony, "I wish he had done it to you too." By inserting themselves within the private setting of the mourning ceremony, a ceremony that is also the family forum for public grief, the women disregarded the implicit restraints that define respectable social behavior, especially for women. In doing so, they did indeed assert themselves as public women. In turn, they were castigated as such by an aggressive family man. But they also staked a claim: to be present; to be in public; to be a woman. To be a public woman, indeed.

[61] Filmmakers had already been exploring unorthodox approaches to the representation of these stigmatized issues and identities. Mahnaz Afzali's *The Ladies Room* (2003) finds the representational space for a sympathetic portrayal of marginal women's lives by locating them in the marginal space of a women's public toilet facility; the double stigma of space and subject combine to cancel each other out, enabling an intimate and empathetic view of subjects otherwise unspoken and unseen.

# 10 *Shopping for Shoes: Consumer Identity, Commodity Fetishism, and Gender as a Brand*

## Objects of Desire

During the Spring of 2007, when I was teaching at the Iranian Institute of Philosophy, I tried to buy a pair of shoes. This was an extended process. Twice a week, on my way to the Institute, I walked past the shoe shop; I was usually too preoccupied on my way to class to dawdle and gaze. But after class, I would consider my options. I could sit in the walled Institute garden for a time and breathe in the green peacefulness; the serenity of the space made the more intensely immediate by the barely distant rush of the car traffic and pollution. I could make my way down to Jomhuri Avenue, through the busy throng of early evening shoppers, and wander by the somewhat timeworn shops selling regional specialties (olives, smoked fish) or odds-and-ends of old-fashioned household notions (umbrellas, ladies underthings, tobacco pipes). Or I could go back to the shoe shop and try to buy shoes.

I knew exactly which shoes I wanted: the brown version of the sleekly sturdy black fisherman's sandals sitting in the window. They were out of my size, but the workshop was right next door; the workshop the same compact size as the shoe shop, the individual workmen sitting at their benches, working leather into the shoes and bags that were set out for display on the other side of the wall. But the shoes that I wanted would always be ready "next week." After several weeks, I put down a deposit. After several more, I put down the rest. Some time later, I collected my shoes.

I don't think the shoe salesman or the shoemakers were unwilling to sell shoes to me. But I don't think they felt very urgently the need to accommodate me, either. Although the model was on display, someone had to make those shoes for me; one of the workmen next door had to put his hand to that craft. I had to pester the salesman enough to insert myself into the process of production, to make it worthwhile for all of them to make the shoes in order to sell them to me. What a petty and demanding consumer! And yet after all, all I wanted to do was buy a pair of shoes.

The problem was precisely that the shoes I wanted – the shoes that were tantalizingly on display but not actually obtainable – were not a disconnected, sanitized, cleanly available commodity. It was not only that they needed to be produced, to be made by one of the men next door. To become a material reality – to become shoes available for me to purchase – they required social and economic negotiation: between me and the salesman; between the salesman and the shoemakers. They were embedded in an immediate geography of making, of production rather than simply consumption. As objects of elusive desire and tangible materiality, those shoes were a nexus of visibly interconnected social relations.

I loved the downtown shoe shop, including the extended project of getting my shoes, because the process of buying them inserted me into an entire social landscape and forced me beyond a smoothly impersonal commodity exchange. Beyond the shoes and the store itself, the street did that: *Nofel Loshato* (or Neauphle-Le-Château), named for the municipality where Ayatollah Khomeini spent his French exile, and intersecting with Avenue Henry Corbin, named for the French philosopher, scholar of Persian Islam, and longtime winter resident of Tehran. It was an abbreviated length of quietly forgotten cosmopolitanism, a mix of purpose and identity: some small shops (including the shoe shop); some remnants of communitarian diversity (the venerable Armenian Club, the Vatican embassy); some well-tended older apartment buildings and a few walled 1930s modernist villas, pristine in their neglect.[1] But I was regularly in the neighborhood not only for reasons of nostalgia, or shopping. I was there to teach a lively new generation of students who understood theoretical analysis to be

[1] The "modern" villas on the street (as opposed to the more traditional styles in the compound of the Philosophy Institute) were preserved icons of blocky art deco modernism. Mina Marefat provides descriptions and illustrations of this new style of building that appeared in Tehran in the 1930s. Making use of reinforced concrete faced with cement, and designed by architects rather than builders, these modern garden villas often incorporated curving entrance porticos and upper-story open porches, combining the traditional indoor–outdoor spaces of the older courtyard homes with a streamlined geometric aesthetic. See Marefat, text and illustrations for chapter 3, "Private Architecture: The Construction of Values," in M. Marefat, *Building to Power: Architecture in Tehran 1921–1941*. PhD diss., Massachusetts Institute of Technology, 1988.

directly linked to contemporary political choices and events. The Philosophy Institute was housed in the garden compound of a late Qajar estate. But its library hosted unfiltered access to the internet, and its students were more up-to-date on intellectual and cultural global trends than I was. So the shoes, the shop, the street, the Institute, and the students were all part of the ongoing life of the neighborhood: social relations in process and in contradiction, past and future equally present and recalcitrant and productive of possibility, day to day.

During that same period, I saw some other shoes: "Clark" shoes in a trendy, brand-new store uptown. That shoe store had sleek open shelving and careful lighting; the opposite of my downtown haunt, with its crowded window display of funkily elegant merchandise, the outdated accumulation of decades of artisanal design, never revised, never abandoned. In the uptown store, the young saleswoman could barely bring herself to speak to me, and the shoes were set out and spotlit like treasures. They were expensive, and obviously counterfeit; slapped together with luck and glue, they cost four times as much as my coveted downtown sandals. But they had a brand: the "Clark" label stuck to the inside of the shoe and affixed to the outside of the store. "Why would anyone buy these?," I kept asking. Why would anyone pay so much money (a bit pricey by US standards, they seemed fabulously expensive at that time in Iran) for shoes that were unashamed fakes, and such a rip-off? Why didn't everyone want the wonderful shoes from my downtown shoe shop, shoes that were well made and well designed and local and cheaper?

## Shopping for Oneself

Since the revolution, Iran has been isolated by economic sanctions of various kinds. State policy has veered between the production of national self-sufficiency (of automobiles, of sugar) and tolerating national binges of imported consumer goods; the same shadowy state-linked economic actors are often in control of both tendencies.[2] But the political and economic isolation of the postrevolutionary

[2] For analysis of how the postrevolutionary Islamic Republic has created a large (and economically and politically expectant) national middle class through inclusive social welfare policies (thus moving to a biopolitical governance model), see Kevan Harris, *A Social Revolution: Politics and the Welfare State in Iran* (Oakland: University of California Press, 2017).

decades has bred a popular romance of the global, especially the global brand. Like national populations in the late days of the former Soviet Union, Iranians yearn for the shiny, clean commodities of the global market, the brands that will convey their participation in a recognizable and universal modernity, whatever that now is.[3]

By its nature, an international brand is a connection to an established external reality, a sleek modernity guaranteed by participation in a global norm of consumption and exchange. Even if it's a fake, buying the brand means buying into a global community and thereby negating the limits of one's provincialism. But in a country that has never signed any agreement with the WTO, a brand name doesn't mean much without a personal relation to back it up. There were reputable distributors in Tehran for major imported consumer brands, from household appliances to cars and cosmetics. And there were individual sellers who had brought in an item or a few on their own, and whose wares you could trust. But you could also buy spools of luxury brand labels at dedicated stalls in the bazaar, or ask a producer to insert a more generally recognized brand or stamp in your purchase of their house product, if you wanted a little of that extra cachet. Irony of ironies, on the Iranian market, actual made-to-measure local consumer goods – the skilled creative outcome of a tangible fabric of social relations of production – were less privileged in the shopping hierarchy than mass-made global imports and even badly made knockoffs of big-name luxury brands.

As an expatriate from the metropole, I didn't have to worry about my association with modernity. I took it as a given, only problematized to the extent I wanted it to be (did a modern identity imply an identification with modernism? with postmodernism?). My own privileged shopping experiences in Iran were often akin to my shopping for shoes, although most of them did not take as long and did not require such a determined commitment. I was happiest when my shopping excursions

[3] The irony is that global retail commodity brands are now adapting themselves away from the anonymous clean commodity model by highlighting (tiny) efforts to certify respectful economic relations at the originating points of production, whether agricultural or industrial. Savvy consumers want to be assured their item of purchase doesn't come with a bad conscience about desperate conditions along the supply chain; global brands don't want the bad publicity. The economic need for assurances about the sustainability of procurement and production means "the age of commodities [is] dead." See David Pilling, "The Real Price of Vanilla," *The Financial Times*, Wednesday, June 6, 2018, 7.

were saturated with evidence of human involvement: finding a few bars of British Vinolia soap ("the only soap in the first-class cabins of the Titanic") on the shelves of our local grocer, side by side with and for the same price as the similarly imported global Dove, was a sure sign they had both arrived informally in someone's suitcase.[4] That was early on, when any import was hard to come by, and we would bring in single bottles of Worcestershire to jazz up local tomato juice. Later, when the brands on the busier grocer's shelves were becoming the same brands familiar from anywhere, I began more determinedly to seek out local heritage: the Iranian "palm-olive" soap on the shelves of the other, smaller local grocer, with the drawing of the palm tree on its crumpled paper wrapper;[5] the locally compounded skin cream from the corner pharmacist that was the only thing in summer that kept my hands from peeling; dried vervain leaves to make *tisane* (not tea; tea was *chai*, black tea only), bought in season from the traditional herbal apothecary; sweet-sour date vinegar to make a tangy salad dressing. I became a smug and happy consumer, delighted with the small details and social histories of my neighborhood purchases.

Of course, what this really meant was that I had managed to replicate my own familiar consumer identity, adapted to the Iranian market. Confident in my established cosmopolitanism, I sought out the local, the artisanal, the obscure; like so many who can afford to take the abundant replicability of consumer items for granted, I was captivated by evidence of heritage, or a provenance narrative. I eschewed the global brands that were from everywhere and nowhere; I was proud of finally being able to fit in and distinguish myself on local terms. Despite my best

[4] For discussion of "smuggling" and the blurring of illicit and licit commodities and import practices (whether by individual "suitcase" smugglers or well-organized institutional commercial mafias), see Narges Erami and Arang Keshavarzian, "When Ties Don't Bind: Smuggling Effects, Bazaars and Regulatory Regimes in Postrevolutionary Iran," *Economy and Society* 44(1) (February 2015), 110–139.

[5] I've never been clear exactly what or if the relationship is between the "palm-olive" soap I could find in the modest local grocery in Iran, and the global Palmolive soap brand. The imported, global Palmolive brand soap is an entirely different size, shape, and smell from the local version, but Palmolive did historically export to the region. See the discussion of the Palmolive soap 1922 Egyptian advertising campaign in Mona Russell, "Marketing the Modern Egyptian Girl: Whitewashing Soap and Clothes from the Late Nineteenth Century to 1936," *Journal of Middle East Women's Studies*, 6(3) (Fall 2010), 19–57.

efforts – because of my best efforts – to avoid the soulless trap of interchangeable, impersonal commodity culture, I had found my Iranian identity through what I could and would buy. (Are we all neoliberals now?)

## Buying (into) Modernity: Girls and Makeup

In the early twentieth century, consumer goods and changing feminine roles combined to create the "Modern Girl," an international phenomenon that appeared simultaneously in recognizable but localized forms "around the world" in the 1920s and 1930s.[6] She was young, adventurous, attractive, and distinct from slightly earlier versions of the New Woman, who had been a more serious being. The New Woman had challenged a previous generation's expectations of feminine accommodation, and she may even have gone out to work without compromising accepted notions of respectability; even the Gibson Girl (an American version of the genre) in her practical shirtwaist and simple skirt was often assumed to be a Business Girl with a job.[7] But the

[6] Throughout this section, I am intentionally referencing the Modern Girl Around the World Research Group and their published volume of essays chronicling the emergence of this new early twentieth-century feminine identity; see Alys Eve Weinbaum, Lynn M. Thomas, Priti Ramamurthy, Uta G. Poiger, Madeleine Yue Dong, and Tabi E. Barlow, eds., *The Modern Girl around the World: Consumption, Modernity, and Globalization* (Durham, NC: Duke University Press, 2008). Essays in the volume chronicle the Modern Girl's nearly simultaneous appearance in multiple and unexpected places: in the big city capitals of the US and Western Europe (France and Germany); in the provincial outposts of settler colonialism (the Caribbean, Australia, India, and South Africa); and in the urban centers of nation-states that cautiously engaged the imperialism of the global market while avoiding outright colonialism (the Soviet Union, China, and Japan). Russell's 2010 study of consumer marketing to early twentieth-century Egyptian women and the local construction of a consumer "Modern Girl" explicitly references Weinbaum et al.'s project.

[7] The late nineteenth-century social construction of the "New Woman" was closely related to the "Woman Question," that is, the question of women's suffrage and public participation. If the New Woman was not necessarily a suffragist or suffragette, she was nonetheless associated with the determined expansion of women's social roles, opportunities, and participation. This included everything from shifts in dress to allow for greater mobility, to bicycle riding (for similar reasons), to new workplace opportunities. The "Gibson Girl" was a reference to the ubiquitous late nineteenth/early twentieth-century drawings of Charles Dana Gibson, of young women who epitomized the ideal of active, attractive modern femininity. Gibson Girls tended to wear neatly tucked shirtwaists (blouses) and skirts and to wear their long hair piled high on their heads; they might be portrayed riding a bicycle or working in an office at a typewriter, but their figures

Modern Girl was less interested in the Woman Question or workplace negotiations; as embodiment and representation, she was the confirmation of modern identity as not just an extension beyond, but as a break with cultural traditions, both physical and moral.[8] She could be elite or working class, but the Modern Girl was always recognizably "modern": emancipated from narrow strictures of responsibility, and resolutely accommodating herself to the ever-fleeting pleasures of consumer capitalism. Compared to the family-based domestic identities of the past – the reproductive roles of daughter, wife, and mother – the Modern Girl embodied individualized autonomy and narcissistic excess as an aspirational ideal.[9] Although the details of her stylistics varied according to local conditions, the practices that made the Modern Girl recognizably who she was depended on an intimate relationship with a retail market of imported or locally produced, but globally recognizable, consumer goods.[10] In particular, the Modern

were always corseted and their features composed. Gibson Girls were the turn-of-the-century American epitome of the New Woman; the Modern Girl was essentially the Gibson Girl's runaway daughter.

[8] Kathy Peiss and others have examined the leisure practices of a slightly earlier generation of working-class young women who identified becoming modern as fitting in with middle-class New Women models of dress and behavior. Immigrant urban working-class women in late nineteenth-century big cities like New York and Chicago wanted to be able to dress like their middle-class "American" counterparts (with a hat on their head, not a shawl over it) and be able to do things like go out dancing, to the theater, or to an amusement park. See Kathy Peiss, *Cheap Amusements: Working Women and Leisure in Turn-of-the Century New York* (Philadelphia, PA: Temple University Press, 1986). The shift in emphasis from "Working Women" to the "Modern Girl" is from an identity attached to practices, to one attached to representative consumer goods. For another national example, see Mary Louise Roberts, "Making the Modern Girl French: From New Woman to *Éclaireuse*," in *The Modern Girl*, 77–95.

[9] In the US context, the classic representation of the Modern Girl is probably in the early short stories of F. Scott Fitzgerald. See for instance "The Last of the Belles" (1929), whose heroine so completely embodies the desirable alternative to domestic, reproductive femininity that she transcends her marital prospects. By retaining her Modern Girl autonomy, she becomes by the end of the story a paradoxical feminine self-contradiction: a successful coquette who is also an old maid.

[10] The Modern Girl emerged as a new icon of feminine desire – both subject and object – through practices of consumer-based self-construction that were appropriated and extended beyond the dominant racial and ethnic communities, whether as market-making producers like Madam C. J. Walker or as retail consumers of corporate advertising campaigns who were both celebrated and disparaged for their participatory presumptions. Although she does not use the term "Modern Girl," Kathy Peiss' groundbreaking study of the development of

Girl's use of commodified (rather than homemade or bespoke) beauty products and cosmetics identified her as the epitome of feminine consumer-driven self-transformation, authenticated by the proper use of the proper brand.[11]

The Iranian version of the Modern Girl definitely made her early twentieth-century appearance, even if she wasn't especially noticed by her global sisterhood. In his essay "Importing 'Beauty Culture' into Iran in the 1920s and 1930s: Mass Marketing Individualism in an Age of Anti-Imperialist Sacrifice," Camron Amin traces the rise of "modernity in a jar" in the Iranian context.[12] Starting in 1926, Amin tracks the emergence of advertising for consumer goods, especially women's clothing and toiletries, in the pages of the main Iranian general interest daily newspaper *Ettel'at*. In the 1920s, no photographs of women were being printed in Iranian newspapers, but advertisers used drawings of women with uncovered arms, legs, and hair (long and

US beauty culture in the 1920s and 1930s tracks this early twentieth-century comingling of feminine identity and consumer culture. See *Hope in a Jar: The Making of America's Beauty Culture* (New York: Metropolitan Books, 1998).

11 For a rare example of inchoate feminist resistance to the modernized self-commodification epitomized by branded retail cosmetics, see Fatima Mernissi's description of her mother's explicit rejection of expensive imported store-bought cosmetics ("made by scientific men in clinical laboratories"), which her husband brings her as a present after disappointing her hopes to attend adult literacy classes. Mernissi's mother, forcefully supporting her daughter's right to go to school (like her boy cousins), struggles to claim the possibility of literacy that represents the emancipatory possibilities of modernity. Frustrated in that hope, she adamantly rejects the bribe of feminine consumer modernity and insists on retaining self-control at least of her own (homemade) beauty practices: "If men are now going to rob me of the only things I still control – my own cosmetics – then they will be the ones who have power over my beauty. I will never allow such a thing to happen. I create my own magic, and I am not relinquishing my henna." See Fatima Mernissi, *Dreams of Trespass: Tales of a Harem Girlhood* (Cambridge, MA: Perseus Books, 1994), 232–233. For parallel references to accepting "modernity" (or "hope") "in a jar," note the following discussion of Amin (and Peiss).

12 The "modernity in a jar" quote is from Camron Michael Amin, "Importing 'Beauty Culture' into Iran in the 1920s and 1930s: Mass Marketing Individualism in an Age of Anti-Imperialist Sacrifice," *Comparative Studies of South Asia, Africa and the Middle East*, 24(1) (2004), 79–95, quote from p. 82. Although most of Amin's references in *Beauty Culture* are Iran-specific, for the phrase "modernity in a jar" he cites Peiss' *Hope in a Jar*. Peiss herself provides one of the concluding essays in *The Modern Girl*; see Peiss, "Girls Lean Back Everywhere," in *The Modern Girl*, 347–353. Amin's essay, written in the same spirit as Weinbaum et al.'s international Modern Girl project (2008) and Russel's Egyptian study (2010), was published first in 2004.

flowing or short and bobbed) to advertise imported English women's clothing and French "soap" (*sabun*, but apparently meaning face cream) for prospective local customers. In 1936, the same year that Reza Shah Pahlavi initiated national dress reform (for women and men),[13] photographs of women began appearing in newspaper news stories as well as in advertising, both combining new workplace roles (as typists and office workers) and new make-up techniques (powdering your nose in the office).[14] The implication was clear: both office typing and applying makeup could symbolize the achievement of a laudably modern feminine identity.

The shock to local convention of a fashionably modern Iranian woman's appearance, unveiled and in the tailored Western clothes of the 1920s, may have been quite similar to the shock prompted in her own social circles of the same period by her American flapper equivalent, appearing without a corset or the rigidly structured, upright physicality it had provided. The Iranian Modern Girl, like her counterparts elsewhere, challenged traditional expectations of feminine identity and decorum: new styles of dress and makeup were the outward indications of new modes of feminine self-creation that existed in relation to new

[13] Reza Shah's dress reforms were probably the most notorious aspect of his cultural modernization programs, especially the state-feminism unveiling policies associated with the "Women's Awakening" project of 1936–1941. For an analysis of the Women's Awakening as a struggle over styles of "male guardianship" rather than an intervention in favor of women's autonomous emancipation, see Camron Amin, *The Making of the Modern Iranian Woman: Gender, State Policy, and Popular Culture, 1865–1946* (Gainesville: University Press of Florida, 2002). For analysis of whether Reza Shah's anti-veiling initiatives were actually mandatory or only encouraged by the central government, although often implemented with heavy-handed discretion by local officials, see Jasmin Rostam-Kolayi and Afshin Matin-Asgari, "Unveiling Ambiguities: Revisiting 1930s Iran's *kashf-I hijab* Campaign," in *Anti-Veiling Campaigns in the Muslim World: Gender, Modernism and the Politics of Dress*, ed. Stephanie Cronin (New York: Routledge, 2014). For a general historical overview of the Iranian women's movement, see Parvin Paidar, *Women and the Political Process in Twentieth Century Iran* (Cambridge: Cambridge University Press, 1995).

[14] Amin, "Beauty Culture," 87–88, including notes on 97. Like Peiss and the *Modern Girl* authors, Amin is a historian who is focused on the material evidence of advertising, imports, and purchases, in their national and transnational iterations. Other authors have focused more on the discourse of beauty and its intersection with the cultural permutations of imperialism; see Mimi Thi Nguyen, "The Biopower of Beauty: Humanitarian Imperialisms and Global Feminisms in an Age of Terror," *Signs* 36(2) (2010), 359–383.

social possibilities, not least in modern consumer culture, rather than older domestic, reproductive, and familial conventions. Everywhere she appeared as a possible identity, the Modern Girl may have been an ideal more readily available to young trend-setting elites than most ordinary women.[15] But her relation to constitutive products, available through the public realm of the retail market to whoever had the money to buy, gave her a new sheen of accessibility. Nonetheless, these young heroines needed some kind of outside authority to back up their highly individualistic, performative identity projects.[16] Iranian beauty culture, like

15 But social ideals and innovative new practices are not only the domain of elites. In the late nineteenth century, the active, athletic image of the New Woman was often represented riding a bicycle, and white middle-class women reformers extolled the virtue of the bicycle as a dramatic new opportunity for women's physical and spatial mobility. Frances Willard, the most influential leader of the Women's Christian Temperance Union, wrote a book in praise of women's bicycling as a route to mobility and independence (and to her personal bicycle, "Gladys"). See Frances Willard, *A Wheel within a Wheel: How I Learned to Ride the Bicycle, with Some Reflections By the Way* (Evanston, IL: Frances Willard Historical Association, 2014, originally published 1895). But other women – including working-class women of color – also cycled. See the William Bullard photograph, No. 45, "Portrait of Rose Perkins Posing with Her Bicycle," 1900, in Nancy Kathryn Burns and Janette Thomas Greenwood, *Rediscovering an American Community of Color: The Photographs of William Bullard, 1897–1917*, catalog for the exhibition of the same title (Worcester, MA: Worcester Art Museum and Clark University, 2017), 94. Other exhibition photographs of community men posing with their bicycles or in recognizable cycling gear, along with the accompanying texts, make clear that for this turn-of-the-century, working and lower-middle-class, urban African-American community, bicycling was a popular pastime that was proudly associated with new possibilities for (physical and social) mobility and emancipation: with being modern and being free.

16 The obvious reference for recent discussions of gendered (especially feminine) performativity is to Judith Butler's writings, especially *Gender Trouble: Feminism and the Subversion of Identity* (New York: Routledge, 1990). But although Butler popularized the concept of "performativity" for the US audience, her conceptualizations built on the theories of the French feminist psychoanalytic theories that explored femininity as embodied artifice. See especially the essays in Luce Irigaray, trans. Catherine Porter and Carolyn Burke, *This Sex Which Is Not One* (Ithaca, NY: Cornell University Press, 1985, originally published in French by Editions de Minuit, 1977), and Joan Riviere, "Womanliness as Masquerade," in *Formations of Fantasy*, ed. Victor Burgin, James Donald, and Cora Kaplan (New York: Methuen, 1986), 35–44; originally published in *International Journal of Psychoanalysis*, 10 (1929), 303–313. Butler's theoretical analysis also for the most part ignored the more historical studies of modern femininity constructed as a performance, especially through recognized (and often commodified) leisure activities.

American, looked to European products and practices to confirm newly emerging models of feminine sophistication.[17] At the same time, feminine beauty began to be more explicitly connected to then new but now familiar standards of health and hygiene, endorsed by the authority of medico-scientific experts, and requiring the knowledgeable application (and removal) of combinations of purchasable (not homemade) beauty products.

In Iran and around the world, the early twentieth-century Modern Girl was a fleeting historical presence.[18] The coming decades of political upheavals and economic pressures, at both national and global levels, left little space for such apparently superficial feminine self-constructions. Before the Revolution, Ali Shariati chastised a version of the Iranian Modern Girl in *Fatima Is Fatima*; instead of aspiring to a trivial, derivative femininity (personified by the objectified babes in the Bond films), young Iranian women should get serious and discover their intellectual and political potential. After the Revolution, the ideal Iranian woman was celebrated by the state for the rigor of her Islamic commitment and the modesty of her *chador*.[19] But the puritanical asceticism of state-sponsored postrevolutionary Iranian civic identity set up a social dynamic in which consumer self-indulgence was at once an apolitical general option and a sign of supposedly independent individual achievement, publicly performed. In the twentieth-century context of Iranian modernity, the Modern Girl provides a key

[17] Amin clearly argues that the development of Iranian beauty culture occurred parallel to the same phenomenon in the US. See Amin, "Beauty Culture," 94.

[18] In the 1950s, the commodity purchase (or fantasy of commodity purchase) most associated with the confirmation of an ideal, modern feminine identity became the home appliance. These newly desirable, mass-market identity-commodities similarly signify a resolutely modern (and admirably hygienic) social identity, but located firmly back within the confines of a privatized domestic sphere and space. Kristin Ross identifies the preoccupation with national hygiene as a (gendered) signifier of proper identity within the flux of postwar decolonization and competitive (inter)national repositioning. See Kristin Ross, "Starting Afresh: Hygiene and Modernization in Postwar France," *October* 67 (Winter 1994), 22–57.

[19] Both Shariati and the postrevolutionary Iranian state identified Fatemeh as the ideal model of (modern) Islamic-Iranian womanhood. But their construction of her defining characteristics was very different: Shariati's Fatemeh embodied self-actualization through her responsiveness to the call of living a faithful life in fraught times; the state's vision seems to have been for passive acquiescence to traditional feminine loyalties as daughter, wife, and mother (the antithesis of Shariati's effort to distinguish Fatemeh as a self-defining individual).

transition figure to recognizable forms of more contemporary, consumer-influenced, gender identity. And in Iran, she is popularly present as never before.

## Consumer Spectacles: Boys in Cars

During the same spring that I was in weekly, private pursuit of my stubbornly sought-after shoes, some avid young consumers put on a more public display. On Friday afternoons, a weekend promenade of imported luxury vehicles (brand-new Mercedes and BMWs, Range Rovers, and Land Cruisers) crawled up and down a few of the most fashionable north–south shopping avenues, especially the Jordan/Africa Boulevard and Vali-Asr Street.[20] Most of the drivers were young men; all were driving shiny new cars that were assumed to belong to their fathers. During this period, imported cars were subject to a 100 percent or higher import tariff, making these vehicles fantastically expensive, whether reckoned comparatively on the local economy or simply by price. The high import tax meant that a Honda was a local extravagance comparable to a BMW, but the promenade vehicles topped out at the high end of performance luxury. Up and down a half-kilometer stretch of hillside asphalt, boys in cars inched along in the bumper-to-bumper traffic, north up one side, south down the other, and then circling back again. They clearly weren't getting anywhere geographically. So what were they driving at?

Stuck in Tehran traffic, these performance cars were all about competitive associational display. Their power was through their status as branded commodities, as advertisements for the social relations of both production and consumption congealed in their purchase price.

[20] Many of the major streets in Tehran and other cities were renamed after the Revolution. Street signs list the postrevolutionary names, but the local population often still uses the prerevolutionary references, especially for very popular streets. "Africa" is the postrevolutionary name; "Jordan" is the prerevolutionary name, after the American Presbyterian missionary who founded one of the first modern high schools in Tehran in the 1930s. One of the most pointed renamings (and one where the new name has stuck) is of the street where the British Embassy is located in downtown Tehran; after the revolution, it was renamed Bobby Sands. Similarly, the Egyptian Embassy's street has been renamed Khaled Istanbuli, after President Sadat's assassin, even though he was a Sunni radical and vehemently anti-Shi'a. See the chapter "A Street Called Revolution," in Asef Bayat, *Life as Politics: How Ordinary People Change the Middle East* (Stanford, CA: Stanford University Press, 2010 edition).

Privileged scions of the well-connected, these youths spent Friday afternoons crawling their cars along a route chosen to best display the exchange-values of their imported four-wheeled commodities (German, British, and Japanese), since their use-values as high-performance vehicles were functionally nonexistent in a congested city located in a country with one of the highest rates of road accidents (fatal and nonfatal) in the world. Daddy might hesitate to risk the car on an ordinary commute, and it was rare to see these vehicles in weekday traffic. But there they were, on display, and clearly being put to use.

The weekend promenade was a peak performance luxury spectacle; the aim was to become as closely connected as possible to the seductive power of the car, preferably as a driver, secondarily as a passenger (especially in the front seat), or finally even as anyone outside the car (whether on the sidewalk or in another vehicle) but touched by its privileged aura, having been taken notice of by those seated within. Convertibles were especially covetable, providing full viewing potential in all directions. The promenade cars always held a minimum of two people; the passengers were usually all young men, occasionally all young women; rarely did a heterosexual couple bother to join the public scene. A trophy girl(friend) seated next to a boy amid the promenade traffic was almost an advertisement for the instability of the couple; this was an exhibition of narcissistic desire, not of the radiant pleasures of satisfaction. Iran's urban auto pickup culture has been well documented: young people chatting each other up through passenger windows, tossing across scraps of paper scrawled with phone numbers, eying each other's hookup assets amplified or discounted by the symbolic commodity frame of the cars in which they sit. This scene has often been interpreted as a display of (hetero)sexual agency, and even as antiauthoritarian personal liberation.[21] But the girls admiring the boys (driving the cars) and the boys admiring the boys (driving the cars) were all in thrall to the associational glamour of the cars. If this was sexual agency, it was also an aggressive pursuit of the patriarchal bargain refracted through the actual object of desire: the branded commodity; the commodity as fetish.

[21] Pardis Mahdavi's *Passionate Uprisings* presents an especially celebratory, and uncritical, discussion of Tehran's car pickup culture as a sphere of "freedom."

## Commodity Fetishism: Patriarchal Desires

It was mostly boys who drove the cars in the weekend promenade: sons who had the most direct line to the heritable power of the father.[22] But within a legal structure that explicitly privileges men, and the economic role of sons over daughters, girls had a more mediated relation to the patriarchal power embedded in this public commodity display. Young men who drove the luxury brand vehicles flaunted themselves as sons of the fathers, as the younger generation in line to inherit male privilege. Their patriarchal bargain was to wait and eventually come of age, to bide their time until they could assume the mantle of patriarchal (psychoanalytic, social, and economic) authority as the senior male head of a family. Girls couldn't just passively wait, satisfied that it was enough simply to display themselves as recipients of generational favor. Girls had to construct themselves as subjects appropriate to masculine attention from boys themselves distracted by the compelling attractions of spectacular commodities, congealed social meanings on competitive display.

The commodity dances autonomously and seductively in front of us, luring us to believe that our needs and desires can be summoned and satisfied in the right pair of shoes, or a fast set of wheels.[23] These cars,

[22] Iranian family law prioritizes male inheritance (sons receive more than daughters), on the assumption that men are in line to become economic actors and providers for their families, while women receive their economic position and support through the family. The system assumes that daughters' and widows' inheritance is essentially a marriage-portion and that their major economic support will come from the men in their (marital and natal) families. Even though this system may not work in modern practice (if it ever did), boys are still legally better positioned than girls to inherit paternal economic capital.

[23] Karl Marx used the example of the "dancing table" to illustrate the arbitrary projection of autonomous powers onto the commodity; it seems fairly clear he was also referencing occult experiments in "table turning" (the infamous, mysterious, and presumably cynical knocking and wobbling under the table of nineteenth-century séances). See Karl Marx, trans. Ben Fowkes, section 4 on "The Fetishism of the Commodity and Its Secret," in chapter 1, "The Commodity," in *Capital: Volume 1* (New York: Penguin Books, 1990), 163–164. Jacques Derrida picked up on the playful and/or grotesque image of the dancing table to highlight the "spectrality" of Marxian thought and its elusive power; see Jacques Derrida, trans. Peggy Kamuf, *The Specters of Marx: The State of the Debt, the Work of Mourning and the New International* (New York: Routledge, 1994). Derrida's use of the dancing table metaphor has been picked up on extensively in Queer Theory; see, for instance, Samuel Weber, "Piece Work," in *Strategies for Theory: From Marx to Madonna*, ed. R. L.

and the young people seated in them, were the ultimate local display of the clean commodity, of the effacement of the messy realities of material and social relations and their reification onto tangible shiny display.[24] The commodity as fetish effaces the social relations of its material production, the creative and physical work that goes into putting together the outcome of the final product. But the fetish effect of the promenade was so powerful because it cut two ways: economic and sexual. The luxury cars, with their youthful drivers and passengers, displayed a tableau of modern ease; they also functioned as a sexual fetish that redirected a trajectory of patriarchal authority through its willing youthful agents. This was a choreographed spectacle of desire, effacing the social relations of familial patronage that positioned some favored scions in the driver's seat. These were daddy's cars, bought with daddy's money. The cars were a double fetish, an apparent performance of blatant preening that danced around transgressive sexual possibilities even as it reified multiple permutations of patriarchal power. The drivers were themselves a fetish object for the refracted power of the head of the family; male or female, everyone in the promenade circulated around patriarchal desire.[25]

Rutsky and Bradley J. Macdonald (Albany: State University of New York Press, 2003), 3–22; Jordana Rosenberg, "The Molecularization of Sexuality: On Some Primitivisms of the Present," *Theory and Event* 17(2) (2014), https://muse.jhu.edu/article/546470.

24 Walter Benjamin provides the key analysis of the commodity (as fetish) on display; Susan Buck-Morss provides a concise summation of his insights. The *Passagen-Werk* entries cite the relevant passages from *Capital* on the fetish character of the commodity, describing how exchange value obfuscates the source of the value of commodities in productive labor. But for Benjamin, whose point of departure was a philosophy of historical experience rather than an economic analysis of capital, the key to the new urban phantasmagoria was not so much the commodity-in-the-market as the commodity-on-display, where exchange value no less than use value lost practical meaning, and purely representational value came to the fore. Everything desirable, from sex to social status, could be transformed into commodities as fetishes-on-display that held the crowd enthralled even when personal possession was far beyond their reach. Indeed, an unattainably high price tag only enhanced a commodity's symbolic value. See Susan Buck-Morss, *The Dialectics of Seeing: Walter Benjamin and the Arcades Project* (Cambridge, MA: MIT Press, 1991), 81–82.

25 Like the commodity fetish, the phallus (the psychoanalytic representation of the ultimate of ownership of power and desire) represents all that we think we want and can have. It offers a dream of satisfaction, autonomy, and power, dancing in front of us, just out of reach. No one ever securely has the phallus; it's a myth of projected desire. But it can seem that someone has it, especially when they seem

Given the state of the private and public sectors of the Iranian economy, it was inconceivable to think that any of these young drivers had earned their luxury transport through their own economic efforts (it may have been occasionally true, but it was inconceivable). The purchase price made the cars outrageously conspicuous status displays, symbolizing the wealth of a family rather than a single individual. Whether the fathers were simply successful *bazaaris* (traditional merchants) or involved in the lucrative construction trade as *besaz o befroosh* ("builder-sellers" or speculative developers), they clearly had privileged access to business opportunities, including to the shady, highly lucrative, and nontransparent parts of the economy. Such dramatically successful business connections were usually assumed to indicate comfortable relations with conservative elements of the regime, and therefore more traditional moral and cultural ideologies, evident in appropriately modest Islamic public presentations.[26] But whatever the fathers' modes of dress and comportment, they were apparently happy to have their sons, and sometimes their daughters, act as family representatives of conspicuous consumption and leisure, a vicarious role that the Western bourgeoisie has more usually assigned to women. The promenade was a patriarchal spectacle of fetishized desire: for the economic power congealed in the commodity; for the sexual power referred hierarchically up through the cars and the drivers to defer finally to the elder men, the fathers of the families, who might not drive the cars but bought and paid for them and the whole spectacular collective performance.

## Happy (Dancing)(with) Commodities

The spectacle of commodity fetishism through consumer culture can be more or less mediated. There are the big-ticket items, and the phallic shadows that loom behind them, combining psychosexual and economic powers. But there are also more lighthearted, easy-going

to fit the patriarchal mode: the old man, the head of the family, the one who controls the purse strings.

[26] For an analysis that undermines the assumption that the *bazaaris* are the backbone of the regime, see Arang Keshavarzian, "Regime Loyalty and *Bāzārī* Representation under the Islamic Republic of Iran: Dilemmas of the Society of Islamic Coalition," *International Journal of Middle East Studies*, 41 (2009), 225–246.

versions, and when successful, these can actually be much more charmingly convincing: the effect of *sprezzatura*. The term, originating in Baldassare Castiglione's early sixteenth-century *Book of the Courtier*, means an apparently effortless mastery of complex social manners and practices.[27] In our contemporary market society – the global norm despite widespread and varied local resistances – *sprezzatura* means graceful, gracious consumer display, casual enough to be naturalized within the trending energies of market culture. *Sprezzatura* – the fluid ease of the performer, the courtier, or the contemporary influencer – now means knowing how to dance to the tune, of the right global brand.

Pharrell Williams' 2013 pop song "Happy" was a light, ebullient melody with a boppity-bop rhythm and pleasantly repetitive, singable lyrics. It became a global sensation because of its music video: the music single was released with a web version of "24 hours of happy," a twenty-four-hour music video of various people dancing to all or part of the four-minute song in various locations in and around Los Angeles. The original website announced itself as "the world's first 24-hour music video" and opens to a twenty-four-hour clock that sets to the local time and opens with the dancing sequence performed to that moment.[28] The video dancers include Pharrell, some of the animated minion characters from the movie *Despicable Me 2* for which the song was originally written, and a few celebrities, but are mostly anonymous locals. All dance exuberantly along to the music, some doing slick choreographed routines, some apparently dancing to their own tune, many simply bopping down the streets, sidewalks, and semipublic places of LA: parks, mountain trails, the train station, schools, churches, diners, supermarkets, movie theaters, bowling allies. The participants are noticeably a mix of races, ethnicities, ages, and body types; it is clearly meant to be a spectacle of diverse participation, including people and spaces of the city not usually celebrated for their glamour. This message

[27] The ability to display *sprezzatura*, whether under that name or not, is the time-honored requisite for success in public life, whether for the Renaissance Italian courtiers or Classical Roman statesmen; Castiglione's recommendations for mastering the niceties of social interactions and display are surprisingly parallel to Cicero's recommendations to his son (and the entire younger generation of would-be public servants in the last expiring days of the Roman Republic) in *De Officiis* (*On Duties*), written in 44 BC.

[28] www.24hoursofhappy.com/

of inclusivity is brought home in the official four-plus minute video edit that was released on YouTube: intercuts from the longer project of Pharrell and a motley selection of the dancers, with a definite emphasis on the joyfulness of dancing to the beat and down the street in some of LA's grittier locations, along with a few more polished interiors.[29] Including the fat and the skinny, the very young and the quite middle-aged, the athletic and less abled, the short video is a triumph of infectious camaraderie. It celebrates the charm of the ordinary and the uncool and makes everyone in it a collaborator in the shared party.

No wonder "Happy" tribute performance videos became a global phenomenon. People all over the world made their own versions of a music video dancing along to Pharrell's song, named it for their location (usually their city), and sent it out into the world through postings on YouTube. A spring 2014 map of where the videos had been shot showed most were located in Europe, but there are dots in unexpected places too.[30] By that summer, there were lots of "Happy" videos of ordinary people, male and female, bopping along in public streets, parks, and stairwells, in parts of the world not usually thought of as very happy, or as much given to public dancing: *Happy Nablus, Palestine*; *Happy Khartoum, Sudan*; *Happy We Are From Yemen*. Even the two sex-segregated Saudi Arabian videos shared the engaging spirit of the other Happies: the (male) *HAPPY (We Are From KSA) Saudi #Happyday*, and the (shorter, female) *Happy We Are From KSA. #Saudi #Happyday (Hijabi girls version)*. But the most notorious "Happy" tribute video was probably one made in Iran, because unlike almost anywhere else (and also unlike other Iran "Happy" tribute videos made during the same period), the participants got arrested.

The full title of the video is *Happy: Tehran Pharrell Williams' Fans*, and – rare among the "Happy" videos – it is preceded by a credit ("SOL Production presents") and a copyright statement at the bottom of the screen.[31] The six young Iranians performing in the video – three men and three women – are all energetic and rambunctious, dancing

29 Pharrell Williams – Happy (Official Music Video), www.youtube.com/watch?v=y6Sxv-sUYtM.

30 www.bbc.com/news/blogs-trending-26889726. The map was apparently taken from a French site that had tried to upload all the international videos, but that site later listed the locations without a map (as of July 24, 2017). www.wearehappyfrom.com/

31 www.youtube.com/watch?v=tg5qdIxVcz8

on the roof, through the stairways, and then in an apartment of what seems to be a single mid-rise brick apartment building. Each dancer presents as a distinct personality – the guy with the bandana who likes to smoke; the curly-haired girl with the sense of humor; the bald guy in the duster; the pretty girl in red with the gold jewelry; the guy with the bushy beard and the ironic military jacket; the girl always with her camera – although in the credits, which are identified by performer first name and named character, it's not quite clear who is who. Who is "Pharrell"? Who is "Detective"? Who is "Happy"?[32] All the performers are roughly the same age-fit, and attractive. Their outfits are all fashionably avant-garde, and none of the women wear anything close to a mandatory public *hejab*. They all look alike; variations on a theme. They all look cool.

At least, they all look like the conventional cool of the popular kids clique. In Tehran, as in many other places, that kind of cool now means aligning yourself with the global brands of Western popular culture. It means making clear you have spending money and that you are an upstanding member of the consuming (middle) class with a certain lifestyle adherence to secular values (i.e., consumer self-indulgence unfettered by pious moralizing).[33] After all, the right brands, the right commodities – dancing or otherwise – are often the beckoning route of access to consumer modernity, and both women and men are eager to join the dance. In 2007, being young and cool in Tehran may have meant simply buying "Clark" shoes, or maybe driving daddy's fancy car. In 2014, it meant not just being happy, or dancing along to Pharrell Williams' happy song; it meant publicly positioning yourself as a Pharrell Williams "Happy" fan, a bona fide member of the global audience actively consuming and then loyally enlarging upon, popular culture.

## Being a Fan, Buying (into) the Brand

A good location helps with being cool: the *Happy: Tehran Pharrell Williams' Fans* video is entirely set in the kind of north Tehran building

[32] The credits are for the characters of Pharrell's Wife, Pharrell, Detective, Happy, Firecracker, and Firecracker's Partner. They appear just after the fourth minute of the video and remain onscreen during the outtakes.

[33] See the multiple essays in Rachel Heiman, Carla Freeman, and Mark Liechty, eds., *The Global Middle Classes: Theorizing through Ethnography* (Santa Fe, NM: SAR Press, 2012).

that has become ubiquitous as the default middle- and upper-class residential address. But cool can be most reliably demonstrated by a well-choreographed display of appropriate stuff. The video is full of artfully careless props: fancy sunglasses, some hefty gold jewelry, an expensive camera, and a casual cigarette. Other props seem almost accidental: a shiny new iMac sits on a desk in the background of some playful indoor scenes. But this is not all simply impromptu. At the conclusion of the video, there's a screen full of credits, including director, art director, cast, and costume designer, and a final message to the audience, complete with a repeat of the copyright statement at the bottom of the screen. "We have made this video as Pharrell Williams' fans in 8 hrs, with iPhone 5S. 'Happy' was an excuse to be happy. We enjoyed every second of making it. Hope it puts a smile on your face." Just to make sure of the smile, the video ends with a couple of comic outtakes.

The smiles didn't last. On May 20, 2014, the arrests of *Happy: Tehran Pharrell Williams' Fans'* performers and director became public. Both Pharrell Williams and Iran's president Hassan Rouhani tweeted sympathetic responses: Pharrell linked to the *New York Times* news story and commented "It's beyond sad these kids were arrested for trying to spread happiness." Rouhani, whose election was not supported by the hardline conservative faction that controls the judiciary (and therefore the arrests), tweeted an excerpt of his June 2013 victory speech, "Happiness is our people's right. We shouldn't be too hard on behaviors caused by joy."[34] Major news outlets all over the world carried stories about the poor kids in Tehran who got arrested just for dancing, just for being happy, just for being fans.[35]

There was another Iranian "Happy" video that spring that didn't receive the same kind of public attention, inside or outside of Iran. *Pharrell Williams – HAPPY (from TEHRAN)* is much more like most of the other global "Happy" videos: lots of different people, different body types, outside in streets, parks, and public places, wearing

[34] Williams tweeted on May 20, 2014; Rouhani tweeted on May 21, 2014: www.abcnews.go.com/blogs/politics/2014/05/pharrell-iranian-president-react-to-tehran-happy-arrests/

[35] An incomplete list of news outlets covering the story includes the BBC, *The Guardian*, *CNN*, *NPR*, *New York Times*, *LA Times*, *USA Today*, *People*, and *Al Jazeera*. These were the top stories that appeared in a Google search for "happy Iran" on July 31, 2017.

seemingly ordinary street clothes, the women in that season's loose-letter-of-the-law-but-not-the-spirit of Iranian urban youth's version of mandatory *hejab*, which in 2014 meant that their scarf might well fall off (and remain off) while happily continuing dancing.[36] There are a couple of dogs, some little kids, some people working while they dance, others simply out and about. There is a clear mix of classes, spaces, and body types. Except for some car interiors (of drivers and passengers bopping along to the music), a barbershop, and a quick view of a barista in a café, every shot is in public space. This version of being happy in Tehran, like most of the other "Happy" tribute videos, displays a possibility of happiness as a collective public project, something to be shared freely and creatively as a popular good. Everyone can participate: the street seller, the fat kids, the group of young women playing with a water hose in a park. Everyone is cool. And no one got arrested.[37]

So why were *Happy: Tehran Pharrell Williams' Fans* targeted? After all, weren't they just being happy? And when they went to all that trouble to keep their dancing, and their display, discretely private – on and in a residential building – rather than taking to the streets? But then they uploaded their private performance to the shared public space of the global internet, carefully making sure to identify themselves by name: to claim their brand. They were cool enough to get noticed but then received too much of the kind of unwanted attention that is always a possibility from a state that heavily, if somewhat arbitrarily, polices the public performance of morality. You'd think that such savvy global consumer participants would have been aware of the local political risk, not of dancing to a pop song, or even dancing in public to a pop song, but for striving for public celebrity for dancing to a pop song. Apparently not.

No one should get arrested for making an innocuous, apolitical music video. The young team involved in making *Happy: Tehran Pharrell Williams' Fans* seem not to have had a political agenda but were rather working within the assumption that (global consumer)

[36] www.youtube.com/watch?v=4OWYCgGOSMA

[37] *Pharrell Williams– HAPPY (from TEHRAN)* seems to have been posted online around the same time as the other video. Both videos were up in May 2014; the performers and creators of *Happy: Tehran Pharrell Williams' Fans* were jailed on May 18, 2014. www.people.com/celebrity/iranians-jailed-for-happy-dance-video/

culture is both (politically if not materially) free and at the same time inherently resistant to dominant local political norms. Local cultural producers, whether of music, literature, or cinema, are usually of necessity keenly aware of formal institutional political constraints on their actions. But the *Fans* team seems to have assumed that by positioning themselves as iconic local consumers of a global brand – the Tehran fans of Pharrell Williams – they could claim the mantle of liberal (economic) values without paying the cost of fighting for the politics. All they wanted was to be "Happy."

The *Happy: Tehran Pharrell Williams' Fans* team distinguished themselves from the *Pharrell Williams – HAPPY (from TEHRAN)* group precisely because the *Fans* were intent on claiming the public credit for the private achievement of their "Happy"-ness. Most of the "Happy" tribute videos have been joyfully amateur; part of their charm was that the people in them were sometimes wonderful dancers, and sometimes somewhat ridiculous, and often both; the point was the shared ebullience. But the Tehran *Fans* video was trying to do something else, and serious enough about it to copyright the project; since Iran does not observe international copyright law, this may have been more a claim of artistic aspiration than a legal right. Theirs was not meant to be a presentation of the inclusive, embodied varieties of (being) happy in Tehran.[38] The *Fan* video was instead an exclusive claim to being the Tehrani personification of a Pharrell fan: a claim to being part of a community of global modernity, of global consumer fandom, of personal identification with and through the celebrity of a global brand.[39]

## Commodifying Ourselves

Most young Iranians have not courted international celebrity as unfortunately as the Tehran *Fans*. But everybody feels the obligation to

[38] In this aspect, the 2014 "Happy" display performed and shared (under questionable copyright) by the youthful dancing Pharrell fans in the *Happy: Tehran Pharrell Williams' Fans* video was the opposite of the 2022 effort to create and share happiness by offering public hugs in the context of the Women, Life, Freedom movement. See Chapter 8, "Women, Life, Freedom."

[39] One of the *Fans*' video actors has gone on to develop the visual public association with celebrity as a successful career. Once she came out of prison, Reihaneh Taravati became a recognized photographer of celebrities. Unlike the conventional paparazzi, she is known for including herself in the photo frame.

maintain "face": *aberou*, a term meaning having and maintaining face as public self-respect, requiring a careful attention to public self-presentation.[40] In cases where the materially unavoidable choice of the necessary is asceticism as style and practice, religious rhetoric can be usefully deployed. But the most popularly approved local social identities often exhibit an intense preoccupation with achieving a precise transnational identity image, including appropriate use of accessory commodities. The Modern Girl may have been a passing historical trend, but her Iranian descendants seem to be everywhere, heavily but carefully made up and, like the Pharrell *Fans*, displaying the requisite consumer accessories.

In Iran, fashionable accessorizing extends to the body. For both young men and women, having the right look is tantamount to having the right social identity, and the right social identity means the proper inhabitance of the relevant social codes. Clothes are codes, but so is the body itself. Years ago, after a very pleasant but long day driving around polluted and dusty summer Tehran in the back of an open pickup truck, several of us spent a fruitless hour trying to convince a group of visiting young Swiss artists that it was more important to go home, clean up, and change clothes for a party being given in their honor, than it was to arrive at the host's home "on time." Explanations that "everyone" would arrive late, and that "Tehran time" meant that delays were expected and promptness was not especially a virtue, made no impression. For the Swiss, artists or not, punctuality was key to social and self-respect. The rest of us exchanged glances. For Iranians, we knew that the exact arrival time was less significant than what you looked like upon arrival. Making the right appearance was a question of embodiment. And embodiment is always a question of both experience and performance.

For trend-conscious young Iranians, the performance of "face" is often about the nose, and especially the recognizably surgically diminished button nose that has made Iran one of the global hotspots of

[40] The Iranian preoccupation with *aberou* as face-saving has often been denigrated as evasive and duplicitous, but for more insightful approaches, see the extensive discussion of face in Manata Hashemi, "Waithood and Face: Morality and Mobility among Lower-Class Youth in Iran," *Qualitative Sociology* 38 (2015), 261–283, and more briefly in Asef Bayat, *Street Politics: Poor People's Movements in Iran* (New York: Columbia University Press, 1997), 13.

cosmetic plastic surgery.[41] A postrevolution, postwar expanded middle class has staked its future on participation in global consumer culture, and young people growing up in this context are eager to display their worldly sophistication. Before the revolution, upper-middle-class Iranians connected to or aspiring to the (Westernized) fashion standards of the Pahlavi court got their (too big, too Persian) noses fixed.[42] The transformative ideal was to modify "from a large eggplant to a small pepper."[43] But since the revolution, nose jobs have become a much more mass-market phenomenon, and in themselves a sign of class status.[44] The question of the nose itself – whether an eggplant or a pepper – can be sidestepped by focus on the shopping bag – the facial bandages that (should) signify nasal surgery. Young Iranians proudly and publicly display the bandages across the face that are a sign of having had a nose job (which usually involves techniques of breaking, cutting, and reshaping the nose). If attaining the fashionable outcome of a surgically improved nose is impossible (too expensive, out of reach), then just wearing the facial bandaging can at least temporarily perform the spectacle of the desired surgical intervention.

41 As has been the case elsewhere, the development of national expertise in plastic surgery was prompted by the experience of war. In Iran, the Iran–Iraq War led to expansion of hospital-based plastic surgery centers, and eventually the development of an academic plastic surgery department at the leading medical school (Shahid Beheshti University of Medical Sciences in 1992) as a national training center. See Abdoljalil Kalantar-Hormozi, "A Brief History of Plastic Surgery in Iran," *Archives of Iranian Medicine*, 16(3) (March 2013), 201–206.

42 See Didier Gazagnadou, "Diffusion of Cultural Models, Body Transformations, and Technology in Iran: Iranian Women and Cosmetic Nose Surgery," *Anthropology of the Middle East*, 1(1) (Spring 2006), 106–111. For the export of the prerevolutionary Iranian diaspora preoccupation with too-big Iranian noses and the social naturalization of nose jobs, see Persis M. Karim, "In Praise of Big Noses (Personal Reflection)," in *Global Beauty, Local Bodies*, ed. Afshan Jafar and Erynn Masi de Casanova (New York: Palgrave MacMillan, 2013), 51–58.

43 Comment to the author by a Tehrani man (with a definite Iranian nose but uninterested in a nose job) about the aesthetics of Iranian rhinoplasty.

44 Although the number of annual rhinoplasties (nose jobs) in Iran cannot be verified, in 2006 the Iranian Medical Council claimed there were more than 3,000 plastic surgeons performing nose jobs in Iran and 35,000 to 70,000 rhinoplasties in Tehran alone. See Sara Lenehan, "Nose Aesthetics: Rhinoplasty and Identity in Tehran," *Anthropology of the Middle East*, 6(1) (Spring 2011), 47–62, notes 1 and 2 on page 47. Deborah Young's review of the documentary *Nose Iranian Style* (*Variety*, July 10, 2006, 28) mentions that the estimate of nose jobs in Tehran alone is from 35,000 to 70,000.

In either case, with or without actual surgery, the facial bandages are often worn as a trophy. They are a sign of progress along the approved aspirational consumer route: an upscale accessory.[45] If what remains under the bandage is still an eggplant, without direct intervention toward the tasty pepper, at least the evident bandage indicates the vegetable owner's proper respect for the value of maintaining a proper (fashionable, standardized) face.

Everywhere that it is globally popular, elective cosmetic plastic surgery (as opposed to reconstructive plastic surgery) relies on the desires and insecurities of its consumers. The justifications for surgical interventions are that these improvements will make the postsurgical individual happier, more self-confident, and self-satisfied. But why is that? What is the cost of assuming that visible accommodation to a (public) norm will resolve the internal ambiguities of the (private) self?

Because of the prevalence of plastic surgery in Iran, both social science and medical scholars have taken note.[46] Perhaps unsurprisingly, they have found that surgical interventions are not always the shortest paths to happiness, and patients often report dissatisfactions with not only the surgical outcome but also the preliminary context of

[45] See Sara Lenehan, "Nose Aesthetics: Rhinoplasty and Identity in Tehran," *Anthropology of the Middle East*, 6(1) (Spring 2011), 47–62. Lenehan is careful to align her work with other national studies that analyze cosmetic surgery and rhinoplasty as "a symbolically meaningful practice that is part and parcel of a more fluid and globalized consumer culture" (Lenehan, "Nose Aesthetics: Rhinoplasty and Identity in Tehran," 51–54). Lenehan also relates the desire and pressure to undergo rhinoplasty as part of the Iranian concern with "face" ("*aberu*") as social status and public self-respect, but she does not directly link the term "face" with the physical facial preoccupation.

[46] For examples of medically focused scholarship on Iranian plastic surgery, see Mohammad Javad Fatemi, Fateme Rajabi, Seyed Jaber Moosavi, and Majid Soltani, "Quality of Life among Iranian Adults before and after Plastic Surgery," *Aesthetic Plastic Surgery*, 36 (2012), 448–452; Zahra Farshidfar, Reza Dastjerdi, and Fateme Shahabizadeh, "Acceptance of Cosmetic Surgery: Body Image, Self Esteem and Conformity," *Procedia – Social and Behavioral Sciences*, 84 (2013), 238–242; Marita Mohammadshahi, Abolghasem Pourreza, Parvaneh Heidari Orojlo, Mahmood Mahmoodi, and Feizallah Akbari, "Rhinoplasty as a Medicalized Phenomenon: A 25-Center Survey on Quality of Life Before and After Rhinoplasty," *Aesthetic Plastic Surgery*, 38 (2014), 615–619; Ramin Zojaji, Hamid Reza Arshadi, Mozhdeh Keshavarz, Morteza Mazloum Farsibaf, Fatemeh Golzari, and Mostafa Khorashadizadeh, "Personality Characteristics of Patients Seeking Cosmetic Rhinoplasty," *Aesthetic Plastic Surgery*, 38 (2014), 1090–1093.

their choice to undergo surgery.[47] Cosmetic plastic surgery is expected to be a simple and obvious choice, the thing to do for both appearance and self-respect. But the aftereffects are not so uncomplicated, either physically or psychologically. Patient dissatisfaction is all-inclusive; it is not particularly that the medical establishment utilizes its authority to bring pressure to bear, but that one's social milieu encourages surgery as a quick-fix route to improved well-being and a successfully achieved and approved social identity.[48] Some young Iranian women who had their noses done in their twenties because it seemed the thing to do – a sort of rite of passage to socially approved public adulthood – wondered, a few years later, why they had accommodated so easily to social pressure to alter themselves.[49] A little older, a little wiser, a little more mature in understanding their range of options for creating an individual social self, young women in their thirties questioned why, a decade earlier, their critical energies had been so adamantly targeted at their own faces. They had been and still were frustrated with Iranian social norms and expectations, especially for women. But whereas their earlier choice had been to alter their face to fit the ideal, now they were more skeptical of the implicit promises on offer in becoming the Modern Girl. Now regarding themselves as women rather than girls, but more secure in their modernity, the nose job no longer seemed like a shortcut to self-achievement but more like a cul-de-sac. Its accessibility was a trap, making it a too-easy distraction from whatever making of their modern Iranian (feminine) identity still needed to be done.

## Gender as a Brand

Simone de Beauvoir famously said that "[o]ne is not born, but rather becomes a woman."[50] But can gender, identity, and happiness, like

[47] Omid Salehi, interviewed by Negar Esfandiary, "Make Me Beautiful," *Reproductive Health Matters*, 18(35) (2010), 103–105, copyright to *Index on Censorship* No. 1, 2010.

[48] See Lenehan, "Nose Aesthetics"; Salehi, "Make Me Beautiful."

[49] Author's conversations. See also the unpublished dissertation by Ghazaleh Haghdad Mofrad, "(Sur)vivre et naviguer entre deux eaux. Histories de ruse, de résistance et de 'par-être' chez les femmes téhéranaises," Universite catholique de Louvain, Belgium, 2015.

[50] Simone De Beauvoir, *The Second Sex* (New York: Vintage Books, 2011, originally published 1949), vol. 2, "Lived Experience," Part One "Formative Years," chapter 1 "Childhood," 283.

almost everything else, now be reduced to and achieved by a simplified and alienated commodity transaction: stripped of the evidence of its laborious process of creation; sanitized of the inherent contradictions of its value; fetishized as the reified objectification of displaced human relations? One is not born a woman; one does not become a woman; gender, like shoes, now can be purchased ready-made.

Certainly, it is always nice to have a choice. The freedom to have a choice has become the political and personal rallying cry of the liberal order, so well assimilated to righteous understanding of modern identity that its hegemony crosses ideological divides and therefore is able to pass almost unquestioned. The private consumer is the modern public hero, freely pursuing their chosen path to material and existential satisfaction. The happy consumer is one who can choose their brand. Or at least such is the fantasy appeal. One must still get accustomed to and through the new commodity: step into the shoes, learn to walk the walk, dance to the appropriate music. The brash consumer performance of the *Happy: Tehran Pharrell Williams' Fans* video was lauded as cultural activism because it had called down the wrath of state authorities. But the Iranian state has its own uneasy relationship with its citizens' identities, and particularly with gender. Keen to avoid the disruptive energies of social and political reform, the regime has guardedly embraced consumerism as a panacea for other frustrations. Much of the economy may still be under the murky control of state actors, but citizens are encouraged to find themselves as consuming subjects. Under these (and similar) local conditions, is gender identity now experienced as a consumer choice? Is gender a brand? And in the state-sanctioned contemporary Iranian version, does it come in (only) two choices?[51]

Iranian religious, legal, medical, and social norms privilege heterosexuality as practice and institution, and marriage remains a social goal and a moral imperative. Gender identity is expected to be thoroughly amalgamated to heterosexual identity, and to be securely constructed on a conventional binary of feminine and masculine social

[51] This situation of embodied identity being accommodated to the social authority of capitalist cultural values (which can quite easily be made to coexist with pious traditional morality) is not unique to Iran. See Silvia Federici, *Caliban and the Witch: Women, the Body and Primitive Accumulation* (New York: Autonomedia, 2004), especially the chapter on "The Great Caliban: The Struggle against the Rebel Body," 133–161.

practices. The androgyny of earlier Persian cultural models is out; the ambiguity of desire has been transcended.[52] At least, this is the official policy. But apparently conservative state policy is sometimes managed in unexpected directions, especially when responding to the health challenges of social issues that might be considered taboo.[53] Same-sex desire, let alone sexual practice, is not religiously, legally, or socially accepted, and individuals whose appearance confuses gendered conventions are often harassed by security forces. But in collaboration with medical authorities, gender problems can be resolved. Is your body at odds with your gender? Are your desires for the wrong

[52] Persian cultural references (including literary and visual culture) before the twentieth century often celebrated androgyny and emotionally intimate same-sex relationships (that were not always sexual). See Afsaneh Najmabadi, *Women with Mustaches and Men without Beards: Gender and Sexual Anxieties of Iranian Modernity* (Berkeley: University of California Press, 2005).

[53] In the late 1990s, policy shifts made contraception and information on reproductive health more widely accessible than in the US. Individually wrapped condoms were openly displayed for sale in bowls on the counter of pharmacy stores in the Tehran downtown bazaar, a shopping location that is considered relatively conservative and traditional. Comparative researchers identified that "Only Tunisia and Iran can be said to have truly national governmental programmes on young people's sexual and reproductive health." See Jocelyn DeJong, Rana Jawad, Iman Mortagy, and Bonnie Shepard, "The Sexual and Reproductive Health of Young People in the Arab Countries and Iran," *Reproductive Health Matters*, 13(25) (2005), 49–59, quote on p. 51. In the mid-2000s, Iran's high regional rates of HIV infection were attributed to social decline, whether because of the absence of Westernized social behaviors (leading to repression) or the presence of Westernized social behaviors (leading to corruption). Yet public health researchers inside and outside the country consistently pointed out that rates of infection depend on reliable epidemiological documentation, and many international public health researchers considered only Iran and Israel to have reliable national statistics on HIV/AIDS. Unlike other regional states that denied they had an infection problem, casual observers in Tehran could notice public health posters highlighting the risk of HIV and encouraging safe sex and safe needle exchange prominently displayed in the Tehran airport and on main city streets. In a research journal special issue devoted to "HIV/STI Research in MENA," four out of the twelve articles were case studies of Iranian at-risk populations (five other articles were country-based studies, three were general research overviews, and the editorial was general). See "HIV/STI Research in MENA," *Sexually Transmitted Infections*, 89 (Suppl. 3) (November 2013). See also Mohammad Karamouzian, Maryam Nasirian, Abbas Sedaghat, and Ali Akbar Haghdoost, "HIV in Iran," *The Lancet* 383 (March 22, 2014), 1040; the publications evaluating regional responses to the epidemic are available on the website of the World Health Organization, Regional Office for the Eastern Mediterranean, http://applications.emro.who.int/library/Databases/wxis.exe/Library/Databases/iah/.

other, and even for a different self? Don't worry, and certainly don't think about contesting the underlying social structures or cultural assumptions that may be contributing to your alienation. Your gender can be (ex)changed.

Unfortunately, the clean model of the commodity transaction gets messier when it is reduced to an identity choice off the shelf. Despite the apparent transactional ease, consumer choices from a narrow brand selection are not always more satisfactory than making it yourself. But the Islamic Republic has created a hostile climate for feminist mobilization or queer activism, and under conditions of intense social pressure, without a critical community of solidarity, the lonely individual faces the choices on offer – those endorsed by the leading religious, medical, and legal authorities – without much support. Under these conditions, what does it mean to encourage individuals to exchange gender, rather than critically engage it? If there is no institutional acknowledgment of any need to contest the structural provisions of the relations of gender production, what does it mean to treat gender as a brand? And how does this branding intersect with the state's encouragement of its citizens to consider themselves as acquiescent consumers of the options on offer, rather than a plurality of active producers of social relations?

## Two Doors, One Choice

The history of transsexuality in Iran has already received extensive attention from scholars, the media, and among activists in the US and elsewhere.[54] In the early 1980s, the founding father of the Islamic

[54] In this section, I am concerned with transsexuality as a philosophical (and therefore political) construction within the popular culture of contemporary Iran; how it is constructed as a medical/legal/religious option that fits within the state and society dynamics of an authoritarian and increasingly neoliberalizing state. I am not addressing the individual experience of transsexuals and transgendered persons. In taking this approach, I am inquiring into what Iranian transsexuality, as representation and policy, tells us about the paradigm of identity within modern consumer culture, and gender as a brand. Although Michel Foucault's *History of Sexuality: An Introduction* is often mistakenly read as a celebration of studying sexuality unto itself, Foucault makes clear that the text is in fact an introduction to a much more extensively structured genealogy. His model of how to study sexuality as an aspect of social practice enmeshed within an encompassing regime of cultural meanings – political, moral, physiological, and philosophical – is presented in volume two, *The Use of*

Republic Ayatollah Khomeini issued a *fatwa* (a religious edict) that "changing sex with a doctor's approval is not prohibited," and legal and medical decisions developed from there.[55] As other national debates over the public policies and personal politics relating to transgender and transsexuality became increasingly controversial, Iran's relatively supportive state policy toward transsexuality caught international attention. The religious, legal, and medical establishments were accommodating, and state-approved insurance programs would pay for surgeries. Compared to the situation in much of the more apparently liberal world, the Islamic Republic seemed to offer a paradise of gender choice. These initial external accounts were often fairly superficial, highlighting the paradox of a supposedly sexually repressive Islamic society/Islamist regime extending such tolerance toward sexual identity issues. But starting in the mid-2000s, more nuanced analyses began to appear in different formats, including ethnographically informed scholarship, documentaries, and feature films.[56] Many of the more recent studies

*Pleasure*, his study of ancient Greece. Foucault situates Greek sexual attitudes, practices, and relations within a political (democracy) and ethical (moderation) context. I am trying to do a brief version of something similar, within an Iranian context that situates modernity uneasily within Islamic Republic and consumer culture.

55 Afsaneh Najmabadi, *Professing Selves: Transsexuality and Same-Sex Desire in Contemporary Iran* (Durham, NC: Duke University Press, 2014), 165, quote by Mulk-ara. Some of the earliest critical scholarship on Iranian transsexuality came from two senior historians of Iranian women, gender, and sexuality. Janet Afary touched on transsexuality in the concluding section of her book *Sexual Politics in Modern Iran* (New York: Cambridge University Press, 2009). Najmabadi's previous historical research on homosociality, homosexuality, and feminism in Iran led her to question the Iranian government's apparent support for transsexuality and continuing hostility toward homosexuality. See Najmabadi, *Women with Mustaches*; "Mapping Transformations of Sex, Gender, and Sexuality in Modern Iran," *Social Analysis*, 48(2) (Summer 2005), 54–77; "Truth of Sex: While Trans-sexuality in Iran Is Made Legitimate, Homosexuality Is Insistently Reiterated as Abnormal," January 12, 2005, *Iranian.com* (accessed June 8, 2017); "Transing and Transpassing across Gender Walls in Iran," *Women's Studies Quarterly*, 36(3&4) (Fall/Winter 2008), 23–42; "Verdicts of Science, Rulings of Faith: Transgender/Sexuality in Contemporary Iran," *Social Research*, 78(2) (Summer 2011), 533–556; "Genus of Sex or the Sexing of *Jins* in *International Journal of Middle East Studies*, 45 (2013), 211–231; much of this work culminated in *Professing Selves*.

56 An incomplete list of significant public (rather than strictly scholarly) works on transsexuality, and sometimes transgender issues, includes documentary films (*Trans-Sexuality in Iran*, Amir Amirani, 2005; *The Birthday*, Negin Kianfar and Daisy Mohr, 2006; *It Happens Sometimes*, Sharareh Attari, 2006; *Transsexual*

are sensitive ethnographies of the experience of transsexuals in Iran, or careful investigations of the uneasy relation among religious edicts, medical diagnoses, and social attitudes toward heterosexuality, deviance, and transsexuality as an appropriate diagnosis or reform.[57]

As more detailed work on transsexuality in Iran appeared, including evaluations of the historical development and contemporary state of medical and legal policies, and accounts of individual social experiences of transsexuality over several decades, a contradiction emerged. The Iranian state, Iranian medical authorities, and even Iranian society may be guardedly supportive of transsexuality. But transsexuality is distinct from transgender. And transgender is another story.

Within contemporary academic analyses and popular discussions, the terms "transsexuality" and "transgender" are sometimes used interchangeably but have come to be identified with two different

*in Iran/Be Like Others*, Tanaz Eshaghian, 2008; *Sex My Life/Tedium/Khastegi*, Bahman Motamedian, 2008; *Iran's "Sex Change" Solution*, Ali Hamedani, 2014); an acclaimed feature film (*Facing Mirrors*, Negar Azarbayjani, 2011) and related publications (Shima Houshyar, "Queer and Trans Subjects in Iranian Cinema; Between Representation, Agency, and Orientalist Fantasies" in online journal *Ajam Media Collective*, May 11, 2013); and policy reports (*We Are a Buried Generation: Discrimination and Violence against Sexual Minorities in Iran*, Human Rights Watch, 2010; *Human Rights Report: Being Transgender in Iran*, OutRight Action International, 2016).

57 Although Najmabadi grounded *Professing Selves* in contemporary ethnography, much of the book is historically focused. In contrast, much of the more recent critical work is primarily ethnographic and comes from a generation of new transnational scholars. See Raha Bahreini, "From Perversion to Pathology: Discourses and Practices of Gender Policing in the Islamic Republic of Iran," *Muslim World Journal of Human Rights*, 5(1) (2008), Article 2, 1–49; Fatemeh Javaheri, "A Study of Transsexuality in Iran," *Iranian Studies* 43(3) (June 2010), 365–377; Elhum Shakerifar, "Visual Representations of Iranian Transgenders," *Iranian Studies*, 44(3) (May 2011), 327–339; Sahar Sadjadi, "The Endocrinologist's Office – Puberty Suppression: Saving Children from a Natural Disaster?" *Journal of Medical Humanities*, 34 (2013), 255–260; Farrah Jafari, "Transsexuality under Surveillance in Iran: Although Clerical Control of Khomeini's Fatwas," *Journal of Middle East Women's Studies*, 10(2) (Spring 2014), 31–51; Rochelle Terman, "Trans[ition] in Iran," *World Policy Journal*, (Spring 2014), 28–38; Shima Houshyar, "LGBT Rights in Iran,"*MERIP Blog in Middle East Research and Information Project* (October 21, 2015); Zara Saeidzadeh, "Transsexuality in Contemporary Iran: Legal and Social Misrecognition," *Feminist Legal Studies*, 24 (2016), 249–272, and "Understanding Socio-legal Complexities of Sex Change in Postrevolutionary Iran," *TSQ: Transgender Studies Quarterly*, 6(1) (February 2019), 80–102.

positions. Transsexuality implies the desire/process to change sex/gender and presumes a binary scale, even if individuals, at stages of their transition, inhabit intermediate identity categories. Transgender implies a more disruptive relationship with the gender binary, such that individuals can be less easily categorized, by themselves and others, as either "sex." Transgender is often mobilized as a category to expand gender identities, including more androgynous models, and provide for less normative sexualities. Transsexual, especially in the Iranian case, is often mobilized as a category to emphasize the absolute binary of a (heteronormative) opposite-sex identity model.[58] Within Iran, transsexuality is a medical diagnosis supported by the clerical authority and state institutions. Transgender is not. And neither is homosexuality.

The paradox of Iranian "trans" policy is that transsexuality has been diagnosed as the solution to transgender, with same-sex desire subcategorized as a primary indicator of gender misidentification.[59] Too-masculine girls and problematically effeminate boys can solve the problem of their (inadequately binary) gender identity by pushing through to the formal destination of gender resolution: as appropriately masculine men and conventionally feminine women. Iranian young people who are uncomfortable with their gender and choose to pursue a transsexual identity enter a complicated medical and legal process in order to be diagnosed as transsexual, and therefore cleared of suspicion of gendered or sexual deviance. The medical diagnosis means they can receive the legal identification papers (as a transsexual) of the opposite gender. With the papers, if and when they are stopped by security forces who disapprove of their unconventionally

[58] Despite the explosion of interest in and writing about transgender and transsexuality, there has been remarkably little that makes serious use of psychoanalytic theory. Patricia Gherovici's work is a rare exception. Working from a Lacanian analytic perspective, Gherovici contextualizes contemporary transgender experience within the history of transsexual medical diagnostics, rigid psychoanalytic paradigms, and the encompassing consumer culture in which all of our sexual and gender identities are now being constructed. See Patricia Gherovici, *Transgender Psychoanalysis: A Lacanian Perspective on Sexual Difference* (New York: Routledge, 2017) and *Please Select Your Gender: From the Invention of Hysteria to the Democratization of Transgenderism* (New York: Routledge, 2010).

[59] The documentary *Transsexual in Iran/Be Like Others* highlights this dichotomy in its first seconds. On the opening black screen, one statement appears, immediately followed by a second. "In the Islamic Republic of Iran, sex change operations are legal." "Homosexuality is punishable by death."

gendered appearance or behavior, they can demonstrate their legitimacy and (supposedly) be allowed to proceed. But the transsexual diagnosis commits them to the medical process of changing genders. With the medical diagnosis and the legal papers, apparent deviance from gender norms is formally acceptable, because it is accommodated as a temporary stage in the resolution of gender ambiguity: the religiously authorized, medicalized achievement of one's properly binary gender identity.[60]

Among those who have chosen the possibility on offer of transsexuality as a means of resolving gender contradiction/conflict, the messy, personal, psychosocial dreams of desire – for the self, for the other(s) – can be channeled toward a stringent heteronormative ideal. With pride, a young Iranian trans man describes being a very jealous and controlling boyfriend, and therefore properly masculine; a trans woman literally puts on femininity (hair, clothes, and makeup) to enact the classic courtship scenario of being taken out to dinner on a nice date.[61] Girls like makeup; boys like cars. Women want babies; men want jobs. To be (a) feminine (woman) is to want to be admired, to take pleasure in being taken care of, and to accommodate to the desires and demands of others, especially men. To be (a) masculine (man) is to be in control, to be controlling, and to assert one's autonomy of desire and agency, especially over women.

So far, so "Freudian."[62] But a psychoanalytic engagement is always immensely complicated, contradictory, and full of paradox: gender as a relational process, a becoming of immense complexity and risk (of relational confusion, of thwarted and misrecognized desire). The French psychoanalytic theorist Jacques Lacan even provided a helpful little drawing of the apparently stark (but actually deeply ambiguous) binary of gendered identity and desire: an image of two doors,

[60] The most complete account of the history of transsexual policy in Iran, and of the very often extraordinarily moving accounts of individuals going through the process, is Najmabadi's *Professing Selves*.

[61] See *The Birthday*, 2006.

[62] This is a caricature of Freudian theory, but so is much of what is popularly assumed to be "Freud." Freud's great contribution was the development of psychoanalytic method: the attention to the coded meanings the self enunciates in an internal balance of screaming clarity and attentive self enunciates. But "Freudian" interpretations by analysts of the material provided by analysands in the analytical context are often unfortunate lessons in the reductive conventionality of the analyst's own projection and repression.

appropriately marked "Ladies" and "Gentlemen." The doors are separate – one for each gender. But they are also identical; there is no apparent distinction between them.[63] In Lacan's illustration, the two signifiers (the words) for Ladies and Gentlemen are different, but the conceptual image of the signified (the doors) is the same. How can that be? Is gender difference just a linguistic sign? Are the two doors of gender identity nothing more – nor less – than conveniently fixed entrances to realms of social meaning, closed representations until we open them to reveal what we ourselves have hidden on the other side? Lacan spares us the abstraction of essential gender difference in its familiar stick figure representation. His wit is in using images that represent the everyday practice of gender auto-distinction: passing through the familiar, arbitrary doors of the "necessary."[64] Yet who has not some time transgressed their specified entrance in a moment of urgency? The closed doors leave us with a puzzle and an invitation. Is the problem a choice between two doors? Or is it what we see presented before us when facing them, and what we presume to find behind them, if and when we pass through?

Iranian transsexual policy offers two doors, clearly marked. For those who find themselves awkwardly (dis)located in relation to their designated gender, it promises to shortcut the psychosocial journey of self-becoming by diagnosing the shortest medicalized route to the destination of gendered identity arrival.[65] Yet no subject can ever be entirely as one with its own identity, just as no name can ever entirely

63 Jacques Lacan, trans. Alan Sheridan, "The Agency of the Letter in the Unconscious or Reason since Freud," in *Écrits: A Selection* (New York: Norton & Co., 1977), 151. Lacan's two doors appear on the page directly underneath a drawing of a single tree, Lacan's reference to and break with the classic illustration of structural linguistics by Ferdinand de Saussure. Saussure's image of the tree is supposed to indicate an exact relation between the signifier and the signified, between the signifying word "TREE" and the abstract concept represented as an image. For Lacan, the two-door illustration demonstrates that no concept (either "LADIES" or "GENTLEMEN") exists without relation to others, and the meaning of the concepts depends on social usage, necessary contingency, and inevitable mistake.

64 In *The Human Condition*, Hannah Arendt theorized the realm of "the necessary" as that inseparable from the needs of the body and its daily physical maintenance, a necessity marked as feminine, corporeal, and laboring. But "the necessary" is also an archaic New England term for the toilet.

65 For a discussion of how Lacan's two-door image is connected to its accompanying origin story of two children on a train misrecognizing what they see in the station, see Virginia Blum, "Ladies and Gentlemen: Train Rides and

capture the subject it would represent.[66] Lacan's illustration is of the contingent, relational construction of any social choice, rather than any essentially given distinction between the identity choices. The doors are structured within a genealogy and a geography of power, both mobile and fixed; they are blank images on the page, already saturated with invested meaning.

There are Iranian individuals who are attempting to navigate a transgendered path between, without being forced to arrive at, a binary sex/gender destination.[67] But Iranian transsexuals who have chosen to pursue the singular destination of their desired binary sex/gender may find they get stuck en route. Religious, medical, and legal authorities may condone transsexuality; social reality can be another matter. The medical process of transition is expensive, and financial and emotional resources can be scarce. Ordinary social relations – of finding and keeping a job, of finding and keeping a partner – are compromised when one's present gender identity is at odds with the informal social network of known kinship relations that encompasses any individual in Iranian society. With anguish, some young transsexuals describe their painful estrangement from their natal families, who cannot accept their child or sibling's transition. This seems to be particularly true for families who feel they are losing a son (male transition to female) rather than those who find they are gaining one (female transition to male).[68] Transsexuality may provide a change,

Other Oedipal Stories," in *Places through the Body*, ed. Heidi Nast and Steve Pile (New York: Routledge, 1998), 263–280.

66 Lacan indicated this tension through the symbol S/s, in which the Subject is itself divided by its experience as a being always constructed and experienced through the excess of language: the small subject always overshadowed by the dominance of the discourse – the naming – through which it experiences itself.

67 See (Farhad) in *Transsexual in Iran/Be Like Other* (2008) and (Donya) in *Iran's "Sex Change" Solution* (2014). The ethnographic documentaries made about transsexuality in Iran often visit the same well-known Tehran clinic, the Mirdamad Surgical Center. This means that even though they are made over a span of years, their subjects are drawn from the same patient population over time. It is noticeable that over the time span of the documentaries, the number of interview subjects who enunciate a transgender rather than transsexual identity (the decision to accommodate themselves within a nonbinary, nonheteronormative gender identity rather than to pursue a medical change to the opposite gender) has grown, and the enunciation has become clearer as a constructive choice that is critical of existing structures and conventions (both of gender and transsexuality).

68 See *The Birthday* (2006); *Transsexual in Iran/Be Like Others* (2008).

but it does not necessarily undermine the twinned structural hierarchies of masculine privilege and heteronormativity.

## Questions and Answers

Faced with obstruction – closed doors; rigid hierarchies; political, personal, and sexual repression – what is to be done? This question can (most famously) be answered on the state level. But it has also – and more originally – been posed at a scale both more intimate and more collective.[69] Especially under conditions of state repression, now combined even more effectively with the diversions of consumer culture, choice is not necessarily freedom. It depends on what the choices are. Instead of the spurious either/or of two formal doors, anyone searching for productive – let alone radical – alternatives for personal, social, or political transformation may need to look past the available limited options.

As social beings, our trajectories of identity and desire – sexual, social, and political – are refracted through the prism of our shared imaginary. For better or worse, this is now mostly the fraught landscape of globalized market modernity. Accommodation to its ready-made consumer models for self or society can be a respite, but the horizon of productive desire bends toward perfect satisfaction: toward utopia. Nothing frustrates that possibility more than the solipsistic

[69] The common association with the phrase is with Lenin's pamphlet "What Is to Be Done? Burning Questions of Our Movement" written in 1901 and published in 1902, enunciating a strategy of a revolutionary party vanguard necessary to foment political revolution and take the state. But the earlier revolutionary reference that Lenin was quite aware of is to Nikolai Chernyshevsky's 1863 novel *What Is to Be Done?* Chernyshevsky's text narrates the maturation of a middle-class young woman in her private life: her natal family, her suitors, her marital domestic arrangements, and her working life. Published and popular under the heavy censorship conditions of tsarist Russia, the novel provides a quiet blueprint for personal self-transformation and the construction (and deconstruction) of the institutions required to build a new society: the first stage of a political revolution, starting at the personal and social level. See Nikolai Chernyshevsky, trans. Michael Katz, *What Is to Be Done?* (Ithaca, NY: Cornell University Press, 1989). A later reference with its own implicit acknowledgment of Lenin's essay, but conceiving a very different set of revolutionary possibilities, is a collection of lectures (several with that title) Ali Shariati delivered in the 1970s: Dr. Ali Shari'ati, ed. Farhang Rajaee, *What Is to Be Done? The Enlightened Thinkers and an Islamic Renaissance* (Houston, TX: The Institute for Research and Islamic Studies, 1986).

logic of the commodity, which is always founded and refounded on displacement and lack.[70]

Whether we are asking questions or looking for answers, we need to find some different doors.

[70] Analyzing Walter Benjamin's unfinished study of space, identity, and political possibility under capitalism, Susan Buck-Morss writes, "Erotic desire, instinctual nature itself, and also those forces of fantasy-life that might imagine a better society, are cathected onto commodities. Trapped within capitalism, they become its enthusiastic source of support." See Susan Buck-Morss, "The Flaneur, the Sandwichman and the Whore: The Politics of Loitering," *New German Critique*, 39 (1986), 99–140, p. 121.

# 11 *We Are More Than One, When We Speak Together: Collective Art, Plural Possibilities, and the Horizon of Utopia*

All revolutions go down in history, yet history does not fill up.

Guy Debord, *Panegyric* (1993)

Where violence and law had failed them, they had recourse to art.

Carlo Levi, *Christ Stopped at Eboli* (1947)

## Spaces of Possibility: Art (in) House(s)

Some time in the early 1990s, I walked through another door. Actually, I don't remember the doorway; I remember the building. It was a rundown private family villa in north Tehran, the property emptied of residents and awaiting its future as the building site of a new apartment tower. The sale of the property, and the high-rise construction that would soon appear there, would presumably secure the economic and housing futures of its former resident owners. That was in the early days of the speculative shift from single-family homes with courtyard or garden areas to vertical apartment towers. It was still shocking to see a perfectly good house be consigned to the process, to be replaced by a looming vertical mass that would tower over its context and that (in those days) didn't seem to fit the low scale or the neighborhood fabric of the city. In the meantime, the location had been turned over to a younger generation. The home had been abandoned, the house an already derelict ruin, but the place had been appropriated as a space to make art. The entire house had been turned into a collective art installation.

I remember walking around corners and through doorways, entering a room, a foyer, or a storage space that was full of surprise. Various interior spaces had been worked on by individual artists in completely different styles: installations of graphic design, broken crockery, taxidermy, and murals. It had been an expansive but not enormous single-family home; now it was a plural initiative and response. Different rooms held different encounters, approaches to materials, and relations to light. I remember dead stuffed crows in what might have been a small storeroom, detritus (accidental? intentional?) on the floor of a passage. Were there kites on the floor? It was evening and already dark; the whole place was dilapidated. But then there was a room of vibrant color, light, and invitation. Upstairs, in what may once have been the main salon, there was a continuous wall mural of a dinner party, brilliant colors brightly lit. The painted table extended along all sides of the room, the diners seated behind it, facing us, the newest guests. It was a scene of sociability and abundance as had perhaps often taken place within that room. Now it was hosted only by the fixed enclosure of the walls; it was welcoming and convivial and also deeply melancholy. All those faces, and no one home. Were we invited, or were we interlopers? Who could tell (us)?

The whole place was now temporary; the power of the art was the contradiction between the implied permanence of a home (and a fine, solid bourgeois villa at that) and the transience of the market, the commodity, and the effort involved. It would all be torn down; it would all be destroyed. The entire house was an installation, precious and precarious in equal measure. The wall mural dinner party, so movingly hospitable to the interlopers' gaze, was already as fatally lost as everything else. Everything – (material) form and (aesthetic) content – would be demolished.

That's what I remember.

## Places of Possibility: Memory, Myth, Making

What did I remember? Those images stayed in my mind for decades, vivid and confounding. I knew they were from early in the time when I began going to Iran, when I really didn't know much of anything about anyone or anywhere. Yet they remained with me, a touchstone for something, I wasn't quite sure what. They were explicitly statements about loss, but they were also profoundly about making something with and from that forfeit. I didn't know, or didn't remember, who the artists were, or where the house had been. I didn't see references to it in the standard discussions of postrevolutionary Iranian modern (and postmodern) art. I almost thought it had been a dream.

It wasn't. Once I started looking, I found traces. But they were confusing, multiple, and contradictory. It was hard to find any reference to what I remembered, and then when I did, different dates were mentioned: 1378, 1371; 1999, 1991, 1992. The slippage between the Persian and Gregorian calendars made it all the more confusing: since the Persian new year begins in March with the Spring Equinox, an Iranian year bridges two Gregorian year numbers.[1] It seemed there had been two, maybe three abandoned houses in the 1990s that had been made use of as art installations. The projects were worked on by a loose collaboration of experimental artists whose individual names sometimes came up in association with one project, sometimes another, and occasionally both. There were the mentions of the different dates, and it was hard to find images.

Asking foolish questions (I didn't know exactly when; I didn't know exactly where; I had only my own distant recollections), I got confirmation from Sohrab Mahdavi, a friend, editor, journalist, and respected cultural producer of a collective installations project in a to-be-demolished house in north Tehran. Mahdavi identified the project as the "Experience of 78" (*Tajrobeh-ye 78*) and also confirmed its significance, writing that the project was "a milestone in art in postrevolutionary Iran. It changed the relationship of the artist with her/his environment – it brought art into public space from the confines of 'white cubes'."[2] The "Experience of 78" seemed to refer to the year

[1] I first went to Iran in March 1992, meaning that the earliest Persian year I would have seen something in Iran was the very end of 1370 into 1371. I later realized that some of the confusion among possible dates (for me and for others) may also have been because it might be easier to misremember 1370/1371 as 1991 rather than 1992.

[2] Author correspondence with Sohrab Mahdavi, 2018. Mahdavi's recollection is that the contributing artists included Bita Fayyazi, Sadegh Tirafkan, Khosrow Hassanzadeh, and others. Sohrab Mahdavi was the cofounder of the influential bilingual (Persian and English) online website/journal *Tehran Avenue*, an Iran-based forum for cultural critique and dialog that was unique at the time. With his wife, Mahsa Shekarloo, Mahdavi also provided a social nexus (and a kind of old-fashioned salon) for critical intellectuals, social activists, artists and musicians, and generally those interested in the urban experience of Tehran as a place of unexpected vibrancy and possibility. See Media Farzin and Sohrab Mahdavi, "It Went Green and Then It Went Red," in the issue on Iran of *ArteEast: The Global Platform for Middle East Arts*, Spring 2012, https://arteeast.org/quarterly/it-goes-green-and-then-it-goes-red/?issues_season=spring&issues_year=2012. For a discussion of *Tehran Avenue's* (and Mahdavi's) "embedded urbanism" and commitment to creating and maintaining open public space (including in a virtual

1378 (1999/2000), but Mahdavi was also working from memory. He remembered some of the artists involved but hadn't actually seen the installations, and even more surprisingly, he couldn't find any online references to it.

Tracking these artists, several of whom had become quite well known inside and outside of Iran, I found a 2004 published interview with installation artist Bita Fayyazi about the origins of the public art movement in Iran. The article discussed what seemed to be the same project I remembered and Mahdavi identified, but referred to it as "The Art of Demolition" and as having taken place in 1998.[3] The article also mentioned an earlier group project in 1992, involving a different group of artists, as well as a third art house installation organized in 1994 by a single artist, Houman Mortazavi.[4]

I was still confused, but I was able to contact some of the artists. Houman Mortazavi confirmed there were three projects in abandoned houses, "yet the first one was the most memorable." He identified the first group project as the *Khaneh Kolangi* ("To-Be-Demolished House"), and the "featured artists" as Sassan Nassiri, Shahrokh Ghiasi, Farid Jahangir, and Mostafa Dashti. Mortazavi and other artists including Yousef Rezaei had "chipped in to make it happen," but Mortazavi himself had not exhibited any work and had instead mounted a 1994/1995 solo installation in another abandoned house ("Life Accessories"). Mortazavi also confirmed that "some of the original team at *Khaneh Kolangi* joined new artists and repeated the experience a second time," but he himself had not been in Iran for the

realm), see Babak Elahi, "Crossing Tehran Avenue," *Cultural Studies*, 26(6) (November 2012), 956–981.

3 See Antonia Carver, "Dead Dogs: A Decade of Public Art Experiments in Tehran" in the journal *Bidoun*, (1) (2004), "We Are Spatial," www.bidoun.org/articles/dead-dogs. The term "Art of Demolition" is used in the interview article and by Fayyazi in correspondence to refer to the 1998 project (author correspondence with Bita Fayyazi, 2019). *Art of Demolition* is also the title of Maziar Bahari's 1998 documentary film on the construction and deconstruction of the same project.

4 "Fayyazi dates the first experimental public art project in Tehran to 1992, when a group of then younger artists – Mostafa Dashti, Sassan Nasiri, Farid Djahangir and the late Shahrokh Ghiasi – took over a five-storey house, producing original work for exhibition. (A second show in a dilapidated villa in north Tehran, organized by the (now US-based) artist Houman Mortazavi, took place in 1994; although this is described as impressive, it was unfortunately not documented or reviewed.)" See Carver, "Dead Dogs."

second group project.[5] I was able to contact Sassan Nassiri to ask about the houses, and he sent me some images.[6] I saw the art house installations I remembered: I saw the detritus on the floor; I saw the dinner party painted on the walls. But this wasn't the house of 1999 (or 1998): the "Experience of 78," or the "Art of Demolition." The art house and the images I remembered were from the first of the installations, the "most memorable" To-Be-Demolished House, the *Khaneh Kolangi* from 1992, the first year I went to Iran.

Even with the talisman of the images, sent as jpg files, it was still hard to determine exactly who had been involved, in which project, and in what location. The differences in transliterating the years, the various spellings of the artists' names, and the apparent informality of the group didn't help.[7] I remembered the detritus on the floor: Sassan Nassiri covered the kitchen floor, countertops, and windowsill with broken crockery and listed his participation on his gallery website as "Group Conceptual Show, Tehran, Iran" for the year 1991.[8] I remembered the dinner party: the "Last Supper" dinner party wall mural was documented in Sassan Nassiri's photographs of the first *Khaneh Kolangi*, painted by Farid Jahangir, and listed on Jahangir's website as "1992: 'Contemporary Free Art Group' exhibition – Conceptual Art Demolishing House 1."[9] I remembered the crows on crates: I found images I recognized of crows on crates, signature work by Bita Fayyazi, but placed outside in the courtyard of what is identified on her gallery website as the "Experiment 98 An Exhibition of

5 Author correspondence with Houman Mortazavi, 2018.

6 Author correspondence with Sassan Nassiri, 2018.

7 The artist Shahrokh Ghiasi, who was also an actor, died young in an accident on a film set. His unexpected and untimely death is one reason the spellings of his name are especially varied (since he did not have a chance to establish a preferred transliteration). Mortazavi uses one of several different spellings: Shahroukh Gheyasi vs. Shahrokh Ghiassi or Shakrokh Ghiasi. Throughout this discussion, I am spelling individual artists' names as they spell them on their own or their gallery's websites, unless I am quoting directly from correspondence referring to them while using an alternate spelling. The multiplicity of possible spellings reproduces the confusion of establishing who was who and who was involved.

8 Sassan Nassiri artist entry on Saatchi Art, www.saatchiart.com/sassanassiri. The entry lists the artist participants in that show as Sassan Nassiri, Farid Jahangir, Mostafa Dashti, and Shahrokh Ghiassi. There is also an entry for a 1998 "Group Conceptual Show, Tehran, Iran" that doesn't list participants.

9 Farid Jahangir website home page (including the list of the artist's work) on www.farid.jahangir.com. There is also an entry for "1998: 'Contemporary Free Art Group' exhibition – Conceptual Art Demolishing House 2."

Ephemeral Art," Tehran 1998.[10] Fayyazi states she was not directly involved in the 1991/1992 house project.[11] I remember crows, inside that dark small room. I recognized the images of Fayyazi's work, but they were outside and perched on a much more massive pile of crates.

As I found more comprehensive documentation of the second collaborative art house (the "Art of Demolition" of 1998) and the artists and the artworks installed in that project, I recognized the style of some of the artists who overlapped with the 1992 project.[12] But I recognized none of the work, except for Fayyazi's crows and crates, which were nonetheless out of place: photographed in 1998 in an outdoor courtyard; positioned in my memory of 1992 in a small enclosed room. I am certain (can I be certain?) I never saw the 1998 art house. I am sure I saw the 1992 *Khaneh Kolangi* installation. That is what I remember.

What do I remember? What did I find.

## Fragmented Memory: Ephemeral Objects

There is a slippage in my own memory, and even the collective memory, of these projects. The sign of the slippage is the presence and absence of the crows, there in my recollection of the earlier project, but not in the artist's own claim or the documentation I have been able to find for the first To-Be-Demolished House, the *Khaneh Kolangi* of 1991/1992.[13] The missing documentation is a research issue, a lack that haunts what I write as well as what I remember. But it is also something else: a lacuna of possibility inherent in the work(s) of the art house(s) and the artists involved.

The To-Be-Demolished art house I saw in 1992, at the corner of Pasdaran and Dowlat streets, featured the work of four artists: Sassan Nassiri, Farid Jahangir, Shahrokh Ghiasi, and Mostafa Dashti. Others

[10] Bita Fayyazi entry, "Crows," Gallery Isabelle van den Eynde (Dubai). Downloaded by the author 2019.

[11] Author correspondence with Fayyazi.

[12] Bahari's *Art of Demolition: Ephemeral Art in Tehran* (1998) shows the entire (second) art house project, from construction, to exhibition, to demolition, and lists the artists involved as Bita Fayyazi, Ata Hasheminejad, Khosrow Hassanzadeh, Farid Jahangir, and Sassan Nassiri. Several of the artists provide extensive interviews; the film specifically states that Fayyazi, the only woman, refused to be interviewed on film.

[13] The filmmaker Rakshan Bani-Etemad apparently made a documentary of the 1992 *Khaneh Kolangi*, but I have not been able to view it.

were also involved; others who were not involved remember it or remember of it. The installation has taken on the power of a myth: while its legacy had been hugely significant, its tangible details have been extremely difficult to track down, and contradictory (hence the evident confusions). There were at least two, or possibly three, similar art installations in empty, soon-to-be-demolished residential houses, depending on whether one is focused on the houses as collective group work or including Mortazavi's individual project. There had been a loose grouping of artists who knew each other and worked on overlapping projects, individually and together, over a few years. There was little formal documentation, and the documentation that does exist, whether on websites, documentary films and clips, or other means (including individual recollections), provides multiple titles, different participants, and different dates for the same project(s).[14]

Fundamental to both the 1992 and 1998 *Khaneh Kolangi* installations was the constant awareness that the sites and the works were inextricable and mutually foreclosed: the art and the houses would all be torn down and destroyed together. The projects were constructed as interventions in the present that commented at once on both the past and the future by emphasizing the losses of both. The more permanent seeming the pieces were – the exemplary dinner party wall painting – the more assuredly their fate was linked with the rest of the house. They would be demolished. The individual artworks and the collective art house projects were intentionally ephemeral; both Fayyazi's website and Bahari's documentary use that term explicitly for the 1998 art house project, and it applies as well for the original *Khaneh Kolangi.* "Ephemeral art" is a loose but specific term for an art project that is

[14] An example of this is the overlap and contradiction between the artists' website entries. Collating and comparing the various references makes clear that Nassiri and Jahangir are both identifying their participation in the same group collaborative project of 1371/1992 although identifying it by different years, and by slightly different names: "Group Conceptual Show, Tehran, Iran" (1991) for Nassiri; "'Contemporary Free Art Group' exhibition – Conceptual Art Demolishing House 1" (1992) for Jahangir. The short film clip on Jahangir's website is one of the only sources of publicly available documentation that mentions both To-Be-Demolished Art House projects and clearly distinguishes between them. Mortazavi, who clearly remembers the collective ethos and specific details of the various projects although his work was not featured in either of them, nonetheless wrote "Our documentation of our efforts sucked … even by Iranian 90s standards … Guess we are terrible in documenting and archiving our history." (Author correspondence with Houman Mortazavi.)

intentionally temporary and cannot be sustained as a lasting object; it often but not always involves aspects of performance and is site specific.[15] By definition, ephemeral art leaves a light trace, an aftereffect in those who saw or experienced it rather than a formidable material piece. The art house works' only permanence exists in some snapshots, in documentary film(s), and in the fallibility of memory.[16] But in being created as willfully impermanent, and freed from the formal confines of the gallery space – and the potential commodification that is intrinsic to the gallery exhibition – the art and the art house projects have become a more significant and lasting aesthetic legacy than any of their temporary individual art-works-as-objects might imply.

The destruction of the art and the art house spaces was intrinsic to their creation. The houses were available only because they were already gone for speculative development (and because in all cases the artists had personal connections with the owners). The installations as a whole shared important aspects with the street art movement, including a commitment to radical impermanence.[17] But this

15 "Ephemeral art," "performance art," and "site-specific" art are all art terms and categories in themselves, often involving some overlap. Ephemeral art in particular often "carried subversive messages out into the world." See the Tate Gallery's online glossary of art terms, the entry for "Ephemeral Art": www.tate.org.uk/art/art-terms/e/ephemeral-art.

16 Nassiri's photos, Jahangir's film clip, and Bahari's documentary all clearly show the destruction of the houses and the art, partly carried out by the artists themselves. The films are themselves hard to access. Bani-Etemad's I haven't been able to track down. Bahari's *Art of Demolition* is listed on his website (under Films), but the link is inactive; I was able to view a copy of the film by requesting it. The website also lists a documentary, *Paint! No Matter What*, on Khosrow Hassanzadeh, one of the 1998 *Art of Demolition* artists, which is also difficult to access. Hassanzadeh died unexpectedly in July 2023.

17 Street art is not quite the same as commissioned public wall murals, a form of public art that has been quite common in postrevolutionary Iran and has been well documented. Street art, especially graffiti, has traditionally been clandestinely but freely applied – without permission or price – to available surfaces in public space, regardless of whether those surfaces are themselves publicly or privately owned. Sometimes this was considered vandalism; sometimes it was considered public art, especially if the design work had the permission of whoever had formal authority over the wall space, whether private or public. The applications rarely stood the test of time; they were painted over, tagged over, covered up, and knocked down. But street art has often avoided commodification because it couldn't be brought to market. The pieces didn't last long enough; some artists disclaimed ownership and insisted their street work (as opposed to their gallery work) was part of a free creative community of public making and seeing, rather than a private object for sale and

was not street art; the houses were not public space.[18] Because the villas were and remained private property, there was no question of the wall paintings meeting the perverse fate of some Banksy-style graffiti: the installations were site-specific, but they were not vulnerable to the usual degradation of the commons through being surreptitiously extracted and transported to the (art) market.[19] The Tehran art house works had been created in private space, but they were not for sale, and their material existence was premised on their immediate, terminal context; they were protected from endurance as generalized art objects because they were consigned to the mortal limits of specificity.

The *Khaneh Kolangi* I saw in 1992 was a creative critical commentary on the process of urban redevelopment that was beginning to overtake Tehran, and the social and political changes that implied. The project was a sly plural response to the transformation of a durable use object – a house as a home – into an expendable commodity only of use for its speculative exchange value. Because so many Iranians had undergone versions of this postrevolutionary, postwar experience, the reflexivity of the interventions was viscerally accessible.[20] After having survived the small- and large-scale material threats

ownership. Street art in the graffiti tradition could not easily be commodified, because installations were so difficult to sell on: cutting out the side of a building or a subway car is a daunting task, especially if it must be accomplished surreptitiously. The essentially clandestine nature of street art applied without formal permissions meant that its removal for private appropriation also took place without (the artists') permission.

18 One of the best-known and most provocative Tehran-based Iranian street graffiti artists, Black Hand (who like many other Iranian street graffiti artists has remained anonymous), made their own version of a *Khaneh Kolangi* in 2014, installing their work in a historically protected single-family home in central Tehran that was going to be destroyed for municipal development. Black Hand, who has been called "the Banksy of Iran," makes artwork that evades straightforward commodification through the art market while gaining enormous significance through publicity over social media. See Pamela Karimi, "Tourism, Voyeurism and the Media Ecologies of Tehran's Mural Arts," in *Murals and Tourism: Heritage, Politics and Identity*, ed. Jonathan Skinner and Lee Jolliffe (Oxford: Routledge, 2017), 75–92.

19 See the documentary *Saving Banksy* (Colin M. Day, 2017) for an account of the difficulty of saving street art without trying to monetize it.

20 In Bahari's 1998 documentary *Art of Demolition* about the second *Khaneh Kolangi*, this aspect of memorialization of the loss of homes and the displacement of populations by larger forces is made explicit, especially by Sassan Nassiri (who was involved in both house projects).

of the previous decades (the economic degradations of the postrevolutionary international sanctions, the physical destruction of the bombing of the cities during the Iran–Iraq War), it seemed an insult to the house and those who had experience of it as a home that it would be sacrificed to a building boom. Yet that was the point of the art, to take a seemingly arbitrary personal loss and collectively create a plural intervention.

The recognizable fragility of the *Khaneh Kolangi* as an art object was integral to its immediate power as a larger shared metaphor. By virtue of its radical impermanence, the art house installation as an entirety succeeded in resisting the possibility of becoming an (art or exchange) object, and therefore of becoming an art commodity. It remained instead a fragmented memory and a shared legacy. The collective achievement of the art house was the plurality of its effect: a project that subtly shifted its implications over time, changed its parameters according to the memories of its participants, and opened up the possibility for doing something new. Art, even a most eloquent wall painting, when self-consciously separated from its capacity for material endurance, becomes less significant as an object. But if ever art was conceived and performed as action – as a plural intervention, rather than an individual achievement to be revealed for a consuming public in a closed-off, theatricalized, dedicated (gallery) space – this project, so difficult to pinpoint, so variously described even by those who were its direct participants, is it.

## Fragmented Memories: Collective Art/Collective Action

But artists, no matter how idealistic, have to make a living, so art enters the market of exchange, even if it's not monetized. Stories are told, or (mis)remembered; reputations are made (or forgotten); citations go up on websites, even if some of the citations contradict each other. The American contemporary art scholar and curator Nato Thompson invited the (first) 1991/1992 *Khaneh Kolangi* group project artists to be "collaborators" with *Living as Form (The Nomadic Version)*, the 2013 international collective exhibition. *Living as Form (The Nomadic Version)* included retrospective as well as new work and described itself as "an unprecedented international project exploring over 20 years of cultural works that blur the forms of art and everyday life, emphasizing participation, dialogue and community engagement."[21]

The *Living as Form* web page for the Iranian artists included a photo of Farid Jahangir sitting in front of his dinner party wall mural, and eloquently described the project, including details of the works, the collaboration, and the shared emphasis on material decay and temporal impermanence.

In 1991, five Iranian artists – Farid Jahangir and Sassan Nassiri, Bita Fayyazi, Ata Hasheminejad, and Khosrow Hassanzadeh – took over an abandoned house in Tehran, Iran, and used it both as a studio space and found object – a place to collaborate, and also explore the physical and political meaning of urban architectural detritus. They spent two months creating various projects in the house, including paintings, installations, and sculptures, An installation of wallpaper peeled away from the walls in long strips, broken vases spilled over countertops and out of cabinets, and atmospheric projections of images like El Greco's Curial of Count Orgaz filled the relatively spare rooms of the house.

At the end of the two-month period, they opened the project to the public, as well as other artist collaborators. During the artists stay, the house maintained its status as abandoned property – no effort to renovate it occurred – while it also evolved into an active, lived space. After the run of the show, the artists demolished the house, carrying out its original, intended fate.[22]

But the names are wrong: Jahangir, Nassiri, Fayyazi, Hasheminejad, and Hassanzadeh are the group involved with the second, 1998 house. Sassan Nassiri has confirmed that Thompson got the names of the

[21] From the *Living as Form (The Nomadic Version)* project description by curator Nato Thompson, on the website and exhibition materials on Independent Curators International (ICI), https://curatorsintl.org/exhibitions/living_as_form_the_nomadic_version. The website includes a complete list of all artists involved.

[22] From the project catalog: Nato Thomspon, ed., *Living as Form: Socially Engaged Art from 1991–2011* (New York: Creative Time Books, and Cambridge, MA: The MIT Press, 2012), 152–153. The same description, dated June 29, 2013, is repeated in the *Living as Form* description for TheCube Project Space, Taipei, Taiwan. See https://thecubespace.com/en/living-as-form/farid-jahangir-and-sassan-nassiri-bita-fayyazi-ata-hasheminejad-and-khosrow-hassanzedeh/.

1992 artist group wrong, even if he got the works and the project exactly right.[23]

One of the artists Thompson mentions as part of the 1992 house, who was not involved with that project but was one of the group for the 1998 house, is Khosrow Hassanzadeh. Speaking in the documentary *Art of Demolition* about the 1998 art house project, Hassanzadeh emphasized the significance of the project as collective, plural work.

> Creation of this exhibition in this building is an important movement with no comparisons before or after the revolution in Iran. It's unprecedented that a group of artists from different backgrounds gather in one place and work together. It's against the norm. Artists usually work by themselves and have a monologue rather than a dialogue and exchange of ideas. We've never had such group works in Iran except for some artificial and informal exhibitions. But here for the first time a group of artists have come together and are able to observe the creative moments when a work of art comes to life. It's not important whether the work is technically good or bad. It's the movement that's significant.[24]

Although Hassanzadeh was only involved in the second To-Be-Demolished House, his words are both accurate in describing the lasting significance of the art house project(s) for offering a possibility of collective work and plural action, and indicative of the slippage of origin stories among multiple sites of innovation. The significance Hassanzadeh identifies with his 1998 experience was precedented in the 1992 house, with which he wasn't involved (although he is credited for it by Thompson). Even Sohrab Mahdavi (mis)remembered the dates of the art house as precedent. The two collective house projects blurred into a shared, singular intervention. It was as though the first To-Be-Demolished house, the *Khaneh Kolangi* of 1992, became a latent memory that was only activated as a recognizable precedent, only became significant as change in form and action, with the recurrence of a collective To-Be-Demolished art house project in 1998.

[23] Sassan Nassiri confirmed that Nato Thompson contacted him about including the 1991 *Khaneh Kolangi* in *Living as Form* collective, but misidentified the artists as those associated with the later 1998 To-Be-Demolished art house (author correspondence with Nassiri).

[24] Khosrow Hassanzadeh speaking in Maziar Bahari's documentary film *Art of Demolition: Ephemeral Art in Tehran*. Hassanzadeh worked with Bahari again, designing the poster for the documentary *And Along Came a Spider* (2002).

Where is an origin located, except in the moment when an object or an action has become familiar enough to be recognized as original?[25] Does it matter that the credits (the individualization of institutional documentation) are wrong: accurate about the form, content, and intention of the project; wrong about creative ownership? Both house installations were collective projects, and collective projects are never singular claims. It is a shame the *Living as Form* curatorial notes don't quite get the artists right, but at least the significance of the work was noticed beyond the insular, cosmopolitan art world of Tehran. Is that enough? It is a shame Hassanzadeh ignores the first iteration of the *Khaneh Kolangi* as a collective working process, but at least he enunciates the significance of the dynamic collective aspect. Is that enough? A plural experience, let alone a plural initiative, presents a challenge to our habitual assignments of authority and authenticity. But whose work was this? Whose initiative, whose recollection? Who defines the past, and with it, the questions of accountability in the present, and the implied potentials of the future?

Tracking down the details of a collective, collaborative, plural art project, the *Khaneh(-ha-ye) Kolangi*, is bad enough.[26] Apprehending the significance of something even more complicated, more plural, and more ephemeral – a political action, identity, or revolution – is even harder.

## The Singular Is Plural: We Are More Than One

For Hannah Arendt, art and action are distinct but are closely linked through the function of memory. Arendt held that art objects must "possess a certain permanence," as compared to the expendability of

[25] The diffuse 1990s origins for contemporary site-specific Iranian arts interventions also emerged in theater. Extraordinary performance work in (literally) underground theater was achieved in the 1990s by Hamed Taheri's experimental, intensely physical theater group Black Narcissus, including several different-length Tehran productions of Jean Genet's *The Blacks* using both male and female actors in gender-neutral costume (enabling them to work together in close physical contact without breaking the rules for mandatory *hejab*, since everyone was covered and no one was particularly gender-identified). See the entry for Black Narcissus on the source material website for Polish theater innovator Jerzy Grotowski, https://owendaly.com/jeff/grotowsc.htm. A video recording of the performance was made but is not publicly available.

[26] *Khaneh* means house; *khaneh-ha-ye* is the plural for the houses-to-be-destroyed.

"consumer goods ... whose duration in the world scarcely exceeds the time necessary to prepare them." But the object's qualities of either permanence or consumability are both at odds with "the products of action, such as events, deeds, and words, all of which are in themselves so transitory that they would hardly survive the hour or day they appeared in the world, if they were not preserved first by man's memory, which weaves them into stories, and then through his fabricating abilities."[27] Action becomes significant through memory, but memories are themselves fallible. Action is so plurally experienced and materially ephemeral that the individual memories of participant actors may be entirely accurate and a "trustworthy statement of intentions, aims, and motives," but the meaning of what has and has not been accomplished can be recognized only with time and perspective.[28]

Arendt describes action as a beginning with an unpredictable outcome, a temporal intervention that changes worldly possibilities even as it may seem to leave little trace. The implications of (an) action last well beyond its immediate, apparent end result because

[27] Arendt, "The Crisis in Culture: Its Social and Its Political Significance," (209) in Hannah Arendt, *Between Past and Future: Eight Exercises in Political Thought* (New York: Penguin Books, 1977), 197–226. Even if Arendt understood most works of art to be enduring (material) objects, she acknowledged a less solidified aesthetic:

> Poetry, whose material is language, is perhaps the most human and least worldly of the arts, the one in which the end product remains closest to the thought that inspired it. The durability of a poem is produced through condensation, so that it is as though language spoken in utmost density and concentration were poetic in itself. Here, remembrance, *Mnēmosynē*, the mother of the muses, is directly transformed into memory. (Hannah Arendt, *The Human Condition* (Chicago: University of Chicago Press, 1958), 169)

But Arendt treats poetry (and drama) as an art that is ultimately a text; she is not particularly interested in poetry as spoken word, or art as (dramatic) performance. See "Bertolt Brecht: 1898–1956," in Hannah Arendt, *Men in Dark Times* (New York: Harcourt Brace Jovanovich, 1968), 207–249; originally published in *The New Yorker*, 1966. Even when she states "the theater is the political art par excellence; only there is the political sphere of human life transposed into art," her conception of the essence of "theater" is of text rather than performance (which she considers an Aristotelian *mimēsis*, an imitation of "the living flux of acting and speaking"). See Arendt, *The Human Condition*, 187–188.

[28] For Arendt, action can only be solidified through the power of collective institution building and foundation. See Arendt, *The Human Condition*, 192.

action occurs in a world of human interactions, and all human individuals are themselves subject to the possibility of reacting to and initiating their own action(s) and stories.[29] Actions, both aesthetic and political, attain significance through the work of memory: whose work; whose action; whose meaning; whose significance. The legacy of the achievement is always malleable, depending as much on unexpected continuities and freshenings of future perspectives as the past intentions of those originally involved and the present culminations of their actions.

The *Khaneh Kolangi* projects set the stage for vibrant twenty-first-century work of a new generation of younger Iranian artists, many of whom may not even have been aware of the exact details of those early experimental initiatives.[30] The projects together function as origin points for the transformation that both Sohrab Mahdavi and Khosrow Hassanzadeh note of contemporary Iranian artists' relationships with themselves, with each other, and with the possible spaces for intervention around them.[31] But the *Khaneh-ha-ye Kolangi* – especially

[29] The basis for Arendtian action is human natality: the fact that we are born and that each new life is a possibility for a new beginning. The requirement for action is human plurality: the diversity of our common experience and the mutuality of our shared exchange. See Arendt, *The Human Condition*, 177–178, 190–192, 231–233.

[30] After this chapter had been written and early versions publicly presented, the online arts journal *Field* hosted an entire issue (guest curated by Saba Zavarei) dedicated to essays by Iranians on contemporary interventionist arts practices in Iran, mostly outside of conventional gallery and museum spaces. Helia Darabi's essay, "Alternative Spaces: Site Conscious Practice in Contemporary Art form Tehran (1990s–2010s)," is primarily focused on contemporary examples. But Darabi addresses the local origins and evolutions of Tehran's site-specific art interventions, from some early prerevolutionary initiatives to their postrevolutionary reemergence in (what she calls) *Project 71* and *Experience 98*: the *Khaneh Kolangi* projects of 1992 and 1998. Darabi's identification of the significance of the *Khaneh Kolangi* projects, as well as the correct identification (despite spelling issues) of the artists involved – as "Mostafa Dashti, Shahrokh Ghiassi (1952–1396), Sassan Nassiri, and Farid Jahangir" is most welcome (even though she identifies them all as "painters"). See *Field: A Journal of Socially Engaged Art Criticism*, (21) (Spring 2022), https://field-journal.com/category/issue-21.

[31] The particular self-reflective social making that was inherent to the *Khaneh Kolangi* projects is still relatively rare. For another collective example not mentioned by Darabi, see the collaborative, site-specific installations that were part of artist Negar Farajiani's project "Tehran Monoxide" (2011), in collaboration with artists Neda Razavipour and Rambod Vala's project "Hushhh!" All of the (interactive) work highlighted the issue and experience of

the first house in 1992 – also functions as a metaphor for the fuzziness of shared beginnings. I remembered the material objects and images from the physical installation, even though the artwork of the To-Be-Demolished House(s) was emphatically ephemeral, site-specific, and performative. But the reason I remembered them was because the project's reflexive emphasis on material fragility and worldly mortality also opened up the implicit question of plural alternatives and shared beginnings: of creative origin and authorship, of present choices and future possibilities.

The artist Bita Fayyazi, who is known for her crows on crates installations, credits the collective process of the 1998 To-Be-Demolished House with shaping her ensuing work and practice.

> My first experience of collaborative art projects was with the above [the 1998 To-Be-Demolished House], but over the years has evolved to involve many new facets. Working as a group has become an integral part of my practice and many of my projects would not have been realized were it not for the assistance and interaction of my co-workers, persons from different walks of life, social and aesthetic viewpoints plus even those with no artistic background as such. The process of developing the projects thus [is] becoming more interesting and challenging, since at any stage it is not clear exactly which direction it may take.
>
> I would begin with a rough concept of what I'm aiming to achieve and invite others to join and share their views and ideas.
>
> As a result during the development of the project (for want of a better expression) things happen! The process of realization of the artwork itself becomes part of the artwork. On the one hand there is the finished artwork on display to the public; coincident with it, a chronicle of the many happenings that led to it, documented on film and pictures.[32]

living with Tehran's high levels of air pollution (which has been exacerbated by international sanctions leading to the production and use of more polluting forms of gasoline). Note that Farajiani's website distinguishes between individual "works" and the more collaborative "projects," similar to the distinction maintained by several of the *Khaneh Kolangi* artists. See the Negar Farajiani's website at www.negarfarajiani.com. For analysis of Farajiani's initiatives, see Deanna Kashani, "Exhibiting the City: Site Specificity in the Photographs of Negar Farajani's Tehran Monoxide Project," in Abbas Daneshvari, ed., *Contemporary Iranian Photography: Five Perspectives* (Costa Mesa, CA: Mazda Publishers, 1980), 51–69.

[32] Author correspondence with Fayyazi.

Rather than a singular intention, collaborative work and collaborative action depend on the unexpectedness of plural contributions.[33] Rather than the autonomy presumed to be the sovereign attribute of the individual self, collaboration reveals and extends multiplicity: possibilities beyond the limits of the apparent one. Plural involvement can blur the boundaries and make it harder to figure out exactly what is going on. But plural involvement also implies multiple and alternative possibilities, beyond the limits of the obvious, single one.[34]

Writing about alternative possibilities for feminine identity (beyond the traditional focus on the lack of male physiognomy and masculine characteristics), the French philosopher Luce Irigaray theorized an alternative model of plural experience and relation. Instead of the singular, phallogocentric, authoritative claim to a (masculine) sovereign self, Irigaray posited a (feminine) plural self continually imbricated with themselves: a multiple experience of being-in-relation (with oneself and with others) that complicates singularity even as it deepens and expands the possibilities. Other philosophers have also theorized the internal dialog of thinking as a mind in relation to its (othered) self.[35] While most of these philosophical inquiries are based on the

[33] Documentation for groups engaged in ongoing collaborative arts production, especially of visual and performance arts, can be especially hard to find, as the organization of the group is often quite loose and intentionally informal. See the interviews in *Group Work*, ed. Temporary Services (New York: Printed Matter, 2007).

[34] In his essay, "Against Competition," the artist/publisher Marc Fischer makes a short, sharp intervention into the conventions of art world dynamics. Arguing for collaboration and against competition, Fischer celebrates a more collective approach to arts practice that provides for open-ended outcomes and plural possibilities. His contribution is part of an inclusive dialog among creative producers in the early twenty-first century, debating how to maintain the integrity and creativity of an arts practice that relies on community and is increasingly absorbed by the milieu of the market and the model of the sole (trademark) owner and the commodified object/subject. See Marc Fischer, *Against Competition* (Chicago: Temporary Services, 2015). The essay was originally published in the Chicago journal *B.A.T.*, April 2006.

[35] Hannah Arendt explores thinking as an internal plural dialog across a number of her writings. In *The Life of the Mind: Volume One/Thinking*, she focuses on the philosophical implications, particularly in chapter 3, "What Makes Us Think?," Sections 17 ("The answer of Socrates") and 18 ("The two-in-one"). But in *Thinking*, Arendt's focus is on the individual's ethical relation with the divided self. In other work, she explores the political possibilities and significance for an individual who can engage the possibility of political plurality even when on their own and under totalitarian conditions. This is particularly

example of dialogic but abstracted mental activity, Irigaray's prompting metaphor is the complex physical overlap and embodied intimacy of female genitalia. Rather than the conventional understanding of (the) female "sex" as a singular hole or lack (of a phallus, of an identity, of agency), Irigaray reconceived an alternative (feminine) mode of being by making a metaphor of what is there materially rather than what is apparently absent: a plural, connected complexity of internal and external; surfaces, overlaps, repetitions, and capacities. "This sex which is not one," and yet collectively, is.[36]

Irigaray's post-Lacanian, psychoanalytically informed theory is of an alternative, more productive version of female/feminine identity and desire that is not simply posed as a poor reflection of the male/masculine. The inherently reflexive and mutual aspects of this version of being are more open-ended and less easily recognized as complete. Irigaray's model of a plural self, constantly engaged with themselves to such an extent that the multiple positions of that relation seem both to cross-reference and cancel out any one localized identity, has other implications as well. Instead of the singular, autonomous phallus providing the model of a comprehensive, authoritative self who acts with clear self-sufficient agency, Irigaray offers a conception of (a) dynamic mutual self/ves extending beyond the limits of conventional ascription: a potential model for plural agency and collective action. Which part does what, and how do we know to give credit, while they all seem to be relationally involved in this together?

Arendt's understanding of the productive open-endedness of action, Fayyazi's discussion of the dynamic but amorphous process of collaboration, and Irigaray's theory of a plural, dispersed, but active self provide us with intersecting hints for political interpretation. What are we missing when we simply look for conventional order, form, and independent agency? What potential possibilities may we have

noteworthy in her discussion of minor, transcendent heroism of Anton Schmidt, the Austrian sergeant in the German army in Lithuania who helped Jews and "'did not do it for money'." See Hannah Arendt, *The Life of the Mind: Volume One/Thinking* (New York: Harcourt Brace Jovanovich, 1977), 166–193, and Hannah Arendt, *Eichmann in Jerusalem: A Report on the Banality of Evil* (New York: Penguin Books, 1977), 230.

36 See the various essays in Luce Irigaray, in *This Sex Which Is Not One* (Ithaca, NY: Cornell University Press, 1985; originally published in French as *Ce sexe qui n'en est pas un*, Editions de Minuit, 1977), especially "This Sex Which Is Not One" (23–33) and "When Our Lips Speak Together" (205–218).

overlooked or worse, misrecognized as a lack? We know the heroic, Homeric model of historical impact shaped by outsized men and petty gods is a myth. But how, and where, do we learn to see a different story and recognize a different version of political action, solidarity, and achievement?

## Revolutionary Possibilities: We Are More Than One

Is the *Khaneh Kolangi* a metaphor for the possibilities for alternative beginnings and unexpected results inherent in the 1979 Iranian Revolution, and beyond?

When does a revolution begin? When does it end? Who makes it? If it's hard to establish one specific origin to a revolution, there may not be one specific end point either. When, and where, do the implications and aftereffects of a revolution come to rest? Is a legacy of revolutionary possibility as significant as whatever a revolution achieves in institutions and codified state structures?

When do we judge a revolution? At the moment of liberation, when one regime is toppled? With the foundation of the first new government, so often a hopeful but unstable effort? During the period when the former opposition consolidates its new role as state authority with the tempting monopoly of state force? A generation later, when a new leadership and often a new regime have usurped the leadership role? During a period of reaction, or a period of renewal? After a week, a month, a year, one generation or several, or centuries? A revolution is not a coup or a simple change of government. Full revolutions are combined social and political movements that cohere a national population and challenge both the state and the naturalized order of society, don't happen often, and they are significant far beyond their national borders. Can we now judge the American or French Revolutions a success? Or the Russian a failure? At what point did they definitively succeed or fail? And at what point did we decide that we could adequately judge?

Michel Foucault, writing dispatches on the Iranian Revolution from Iran in 1978 for the Italian newspaper *Corriere della sera*, felt he was observing the concrete manifestation of the "political myth" of revolutionary "collective will," and he acknowledged that it was a shocking experience. "I thought that the collective will was like God, like the soul, something one would never encounter … Well, you have to salute it; it doesn't happen every day."[37] Foucault was overgeneralizing; even in 1978, there was factionalism and dissidence within the Iranian revolutionary movement. But he had a point. Like the French and Russian Revolutions, the Iranian Revolution made manifest the success of a new radical ideology – in the Iranian case political Islam – in forging national consensus to uproot an internal regime while challenging the existing social order. Like those other two great, tragic revolutions, the Iranian Revolution made widely relevant the hope and threat of its unexpected political promise. If revolutions are inevitably doomed to fail their utopian promise, they also provide for forms of revolutionary possibility. Foucault was right: the brief utopian incandescence of a new revolutionary movement doesn't happen every day.[38]

But revolutions are miserable to live through, particularly once the glorious moment of popular liberation has been achieved and the revolutionaries must set themselves the task of both consolidating and dividing state power. This is Hannah Arendt's theory of revolution: that the successful revolution must encompass both liberation and foundation, and that foundation is actually the more difficult project.[39] A social and political revolution must reconstitute effective governmental structures and social values, and the most dangerous temptation is always toward the limitless proof of pure revolutionary zeal. Thanks to Arendt's analysis, we can recognize Foucault's enthusiasm for the liberatory potential of the first stage of the Iranian Revolution during 1978 and also identify the extent to which the darkening tone of his writings during 1979 coincided with the failures of the second,

[37] Michel Foucault, "Iran: The Spirit of a World without Spirit," conversation with Claire Brière and Pierre Blanchet, in Janet Afary and Kevin Anderson, *Foucault and the Iranian Revolution: Gender and the Seductions of Islamism* (Chicago: The University of Chicago Press, 2005), 253.

[38] Foucault's writing on Iran has remained controversial (most commentators who mention it do so to deplore it) or untouchable (many commentators simply don't mention it at all, as though the whole subject remains too hot to handle). There have been several more nuanced analyses, attentive both to Foucault's intellectual trajectory and the Iranian historical political context. See especially Behrooz Ghamari-Tabrizi, *Foucault in Iran: Islamic Revolution after the Enlightenment* (Minneapolis, MN: University of Minnesota Press, 2016). See also Jessica Whyte, "Foucault's 'Distrust of Legalism': On Human Rights and the Revolution in Iran," in *Law and Philosophical Theory: Critical Intersections*, ed. Thanos Thartaloudis (New York: Rowman & Littlefield, 2018).

[39] Hannah Arendt, *On Revolution* (New York: Penguin Books, 1991).

state-founding stage, when the national coherence of the collective will began to give way to authoritarian internal repression sponsored by a faction of the clerical elite.

But what Foucault recognized was an intervention, an alternative, and a new configuration of the possibility for (revolutionary) utopia. The significance was not the apparent religiosity of the discursive form of the Iranian Revolution: not a fundamentalist structure of authority and rules. What Foucault witnessed was the possibility of a renewed (utopian) ethics of possibility, a break with the apparent inevitability of rationalized disciplinary power and/or autocratic domination. What Foucault thought he saw in the streets of Iran in 1978 was a plural alternative aimed at an open horizon of possibility. Shi'a Islam was its metaphor.[40] But it was just that: a metaphor. And like all enduring religions, Shi'ism has at its heart an ethics that transcends the application of rules. The enunciation of the fundamental ethics of the major monotheistic religions and their sectarian divisions are recognizable and surprisingly exchangeable: "Follow God"; "Love Your Neighbor"; "Strive for Justice." For Shi'ism, striving for justice begins and continues with a losing battle against the powers that be. Shi'a Islam as (revolutionary) metaphor rather than (religious or political) institution posited a horizon of justice grounded in a plural struggle. That is one interpretation.

But it is an important one. And it has had lasting effect. In 2009, during the massive protests against the apparently stolen Presidential election results, ordinary urban Iranians did a curious thing. Going up

[40] Foucault's celebration of the "political spirituality" of the Iranian Revolution has often been understood by critics to be a reification of (Shi'a) Islam. Along with Behrooz Ghamari-Tabrizi, I understand his enthusiasm as being a recognition of the significance of a renewal of popular (revolutionary) political power (in the Arendtian sense). Foucault's emphasis is on the transformative *political* spirit of the Iranian revolution; if Shi'a religiosity was a metaphor for a reinspired popular, political, plural, and successful fight for justice, Foucault seems to have felt, "so be it." A revolution (rather than a coup) that is going to bring down a highly militarized state needs belief. Foucault had recognized that after the disenchantment with the consolidation of elite authoritarianism that followed the anti-colonial national liberation struggles, Iran's awkward national struggle with its own internal(ized) authoritarianism could offer the promise of (re)new(ed) beginnings. But as the egalitarian *political* energy of the revolution was appropriated as a clerical *spiritual* orthodoxy to establish a (theocratic) state, Foucault withdrew his focus from Iran as a subject and turned his energies towards other things.

onto the flat roofs or residential buildings in the evening, supporters of Reformist candidate Mir-Hossein Mousavi appropriated the common evening rooftop chant of the 1979 Revolution: "*Allahu Akbar*" (God is Great). That phrase had been closely associated with the Islamist position in the Revolution; secular and leftist activists did not use it then. But thirty years later is meant something else: not a literal religious allegiance, but a statement of ethical critique. Many if not most of the chanters in 2009 were secular identified, protesting the claims of the conservative religious political factions that they had won the right to rule. If the chant had been understood as a literal religious call, it would not have made sense for it to have been used by these protesters. But the chant now meant something else: the call to a model of an ethics beyond the authority of institutions; a call (to strive) for justice.

Many if not most Iranians now regard the postrevolutionary Iranian state as irreparably compromised. The "Woman, Life, Freedom" popular uprisings of 2022 did not make use of "Allahu Akbar" as a political chant; people went onto their roofs to protest and make noise, but those seeking justice weren't calling to God. Nonetheless, the Revolution may still offer a distanced promise: a contested historical legacy and also a plural metaphor. Like the *Khaneh-ha-ye Kolangi*, it is both destroyed and an ongoing haunting, present memory within which lurk resurgent questions of possibility.

## Questions: Interventions

Can absence offer a choice? Can a lack be an opening? Who has the right to be the subject of our dreams, and the agent of our realities? The path to self-recognition is full of misdirections, but accepting complexity – the pluralities of one's identity and the contradictions of one's desires – can open up less restrictive possibilities. What does it mean to begin? To begin is to bridge the impossible gap of past and future. To begin is to take a chance, one step at a time. To begin is simultaneously to make a space for possibility and to keep on going. To begin is to see an opening, to step through it, and to leave the way open.

The horizon is always distant; utopia is always lost. They exist as a doubled mirage, a promise, and a direction. The Revolution itself was a bloody door, but the path from there is a winding road of shifting views, whether looking back or looking forward, whether traveled alone or together. The Iranian Revolution and the postrevolutionary society that lives its inheritance are an ongoing experiment in possibility, frustration, and change. The path the Revolution opened, despite the pitfalls, remains a prospect (to be) created by those who travel it. Like Shariati's intentionally vague, open invitation to Iranian women to make an active identity out of a model he would not quite completely specify (who is the Fatima who is, who she is?), the Iranian Revolution was a singular historical marker and is a plural possibility. It is a living inheritance of sorrow, hope, and promise, a collective memory of what must be, what may be, and what is to be done.

# 12 *Coda: Thinking in Practice – Arendt, Foucault, and the Challenge of Freedom*

## Thinking about Iran

These final considerations grow out of the theoretical inquiry behind the specific project of this book. For various reasons, some conceptual and some pragmatic (in terms of the volatility of the political situation on the ground in Iran), I have intentionally sidestepped a direct analysis of the state and the nearly intransigent political deadlock among Iran's institutional actors, along with the volatility of a system that is chronically both in crisis and under threat. For the most part, I have also not directly addressed the weight of the heavy hand of state repression and censorship. Instead, I have examined the deeper constituent social practices that have supported the ongoing societal process of democratization since the 1979 Revolution. This process has often not been reflected in the public statements of formal state actors but has continued at the societal level, often despite the stated goals of the state and its institutional allies. Thus, the book is focused on the "politics of daily life," with chapters that consider the fine-grained nuances of particular practices, identities, and contexts that continue to shift the experience and expectations of Iranians. Notwithstanding the authoritarian tendencies of those who monopolize institutional political power and are determined to resist power sharing or more participatory processes of accountability, Iran continues to be a postrevolutionary society in the process of fundamentally democratizing experience at the daily level of both individual expectations and community demands.[1]

[1] Asef Bayat has addressed the phenomenon of "quiet encroachment" in which social actors make individual decisions that collectively add up to societal change without social movements. His work is essential to understanding the pent-up frustrations and seething social changes that are affecting many population segments (youth, women, etc.) in some of the most dominated states of the Middle East and elsewhere. But Bayat's emphasis on fragmented actions that are repeated widely but individually and accumulate atomistically does not address

Perhaps especially in the US, Iran is a haunted field of inquiry, a subject trapped in a caricature of mutual historical entanglements and misrecognitions. How not to be stuck fighting off someone else's ghosts?[2] For this book, I pursued a different method, breaking with the borders and disciplinary formalities of academic knowledge production (the regimes of research and writing that define what is worthy of serious attention in the encounter with such a fearsome national "other") by exploring questions and narrating the complexity of experiences. I was not trained in Middle East or Iranian Studies; I caught up in these fields out of necessity, in order to be able to consider seriously the fundamental transformations I was able to observe and the daily quandaries I encountered over extended periods in Iran. Throughout the process, it became ever clearer to me that my training as a political theorist was informing the entire project.

For any study focused on the politics of daily lives and based on site-specific fieldwork, the obvious theoretical referents lie within feminist theory and social histories of gender as well as in the empirically grounded social theories of Pierre Bourdieu and Michel de Certeau. From feminism, we learn to notice the gendered constructions of social life and social power, and particularly to attend to their erasures. From Bourdieu, we learn to pay attention to the "logic of practice" embedded and revealed in the minutiae of ordinary details, patterns, and structural trends.[3] From de Certeau and his collaborators, we are charged to avoid the twin academic temptations of overarching social science generalizations (epitomized by positivism and the obsession with the scientific falsifiability of social data) or the encyclopedic

the shared social awareness, and the deep-seated sense of political entitlement that I have found in Iran. See Asef Bayat, *Life as Politics: How Ordinary People Change the Middle East*, 2nd ed. (Stanford, CA: Stanford University Press, 2013).

2 For a fuller explication of how the recognition of "haunting" can productively lead to an alternative methodology in itself, see Avery F. Gordon, *Ghostly Matters: Haunting and the Sociological Imagination* (Minneapolis, MN: University of Minnesota Press, 2008).

3 See Pierre Bourdieu, *The Logic of Practice*, trans. R. Nice (Stanford: Stanford University Press, 1990) as well as examples of theorizing through the interpretation of granular detail in *Distinction: A Social Critique of the Judgement of Taste*, trans. R. Nice (Cambridge, MA: Harvard University Press, 1984).

cataloging of historical arti/facts (social or material) without theoretical self-reflection.[4]

This focus on daily life as a subject of empirical and theoretical inquiry caught fire in the 1980s as a painstaking inquiry into ordinary and bodily practices, and a conception of identity as embedded in social relations, social power, and social space. Identity as practice is both deeply ingrained and utterly contingent and malleable. Thus it is both implacably structured and always open to modification and evolution, stubbornly resilient despite willed alterations.[5] But this method of intellectual critique became generally overwhelmed in the 1990s amid the exuberance of surplus commodity culture, and with it, the shift toward identity as a question in itself, more akin to a thing than a set of practices.

This project reconnects with that other approach to theoretical inquiry, which was itself eerily present in the Iran of the 1990s and early 2000s, with its odd combinations of dynamic political renewal and forcible repression, social liberation and constraint. The method matched the time and the place. Iran's internal contradictions took place in a context of unusual economic isolation. As opposed to the apparent flourishing of neoliberal policy in much of the world during much of that period, the Iranian economy and economic decision-making were hemmed in by international sanctions and internal rivalries that short-circuited efforts at full-scale structural adjustment. We were happy enough to be able to buy a shiny new blender! Yet Iran as an economic backwater, despite social integration (and increasing global cultural integration), allowed for a pause in the onslaught of global consumerism, and a retention of otherwise apparently outmoded possibilities for critical analysis of the past, present, and future.

4 See Luce Girard, "Times and Places," in *The Practice of Everyday Life, Volume 2: Living and Cooking*, ed. M. D. de Certeau, L. Giard, and P. Mayol, trans. T. J. Tomasik (Minneapolis, MN: University of Minnesota Press, 1998).

5 Bourdieu's concept of habitus provided a theoretical formulation for this understanding of identity as practices located in the full detail of material and intangible structures. Feminist Luce Irigaray theorized an alternative to the phallic conception of identity (whether applied to men or women) by metaphorically locating it in the material structures and physical experiences – the practices – of the female body. But while Bourdieu's work was recognized as a theoretical intervention, and not just a detailed analysis specific only to French society and culture, Irigaray's theoretical intervention has been mistakenly reduced to an essentialist prioritization of the female body. It is not.

This was a window of possibility in which development (economic, political, social) was being actively contested. Yet this project is not an exercise in nostalgia. The theme of inquiry running through the book is an examination of power.

## Learning from Others' Thinking: Foucault and Arendt

Power is not only domination, which is more akin to force. How do we think about power without being trapped in a haunted binary of either/or submission or domination? Michel Foucault's writings clearly could have some theoretical relevance for apprehending the evidence for the emergence of an empowered, although constrained, Iranian postrevolutionary self. Foucault is constantly preoccupied with power: its fluid workings, inequalities, and institutional constructions (especially when those institutions are not the formal suspects of oppression). Foucault's examinations of the situated self, its unexpected blockages and channeled agency, as well as his 1978–1979 writings from Iran on the Revolution, gave his work obvious relevance. Hannah Arendt, a political theorist known for her hostility to feminism and the social, would seem more of a stretch. Despite or because of my own earlier work on Arendt, I had assumed that her thinking would be only tenuously related to my own about Iran.

Yet even as I reconfigured my own research approach and method, I relied on Arendt's conceptual distinctions: between (repressive) force and (shared) power; between totalitarian and authoritarian regimes.[6] Arendt's political thinking kept returning as an interpretive fulcrum throughout this project. This is not only because Arendt's visceral hostility to the threat of the social to individual freedom, was what could suddenly illuminate the trap of obligation a younger generation of Iranian women felt when confronted by their mother's social imperative of "our culture." Or because during the Iranian reform period (1997–2005) students, journalists, and other activists became increasingly interested in Arendt's theories of revolution, civil disobedience, and political action as speech, all especially relevant in

[6] Arendt's conceptualization of totalitarianism as a state system that is defined by the implementation of genocidal state policies against its own population (not just as an especially brutal or encompassing version of violent authoritarianism) underpins my own insistence that Iran is not a totalitarian state, according to Arendt's definition.

a postrevolutionary national situation in which public institutions seem closed off to most citizens, the streets are sites of potential violence, and reform and resistance were initially concentrated in a burgeoning independent print press.

Arendt and Foucault, with a nod to Irigaray, provided the conceptualizations of power that run through all my interpretation. Their juxtaposition provides its own set of theoretical problems. Although both Arendt and Foucault are known as scholars of power, their theoretical approaches are not always considered in relation. Both were skeptical of the modern structures of social, political, and economic life and engaged contemporary questions of politics and power through detailed considerations of primarily historical examples. Their writings are densely detailed and require concentrated focus from their reading audiences. Both were committed to thinking through and with theoretical contradictions, loyal to the integrity of their questions even if the process of examining them led to controversial new arguments that challenged conventional interpretations. And both took an unusual risk (unusual for themselves, as well as for most of the scholarly profession) to get out of the theoretical armchair (of the office, the library, the archive) to go and try to observe, think, and write about an ongoing political event for the serious but popular public press. To use Arendt's words, they attempted to "think what we are doing," and at least in one instance, to do it in public.[7]

## Thinking in Public: A Political Commitment

Any critical intervention, even the most nuanced, finds itself structured by discursive preconditions. Arendt's writings on the Eichmann trial,[8]

[7] Hannah Arendt, *The Human Condition* (Chicago: University of Chicago Press, 1958), 5.

[8] Arendt's original essays on the 1961 Eichmann trial in Jerusalem were commissioned by *The New Yorker* magazine and first published as serial installments. The essays were then edited and published together as Hannah Arendt, *Eichmann in Jerusalem: A Report on the Banality of Evil* (New York: Viking Press, 1963). The revised and enlarged 1965 edition includes a general response by Arendt to some of the controversy raised by the publications; her written responses to individual criticisms have been published in Hannah Arendt and Ron H. Feldman, eds., *The Jew as Pariah: Jewish Identity and Politics in the Modern Age* (New York: Grove Press, 1978), and Hannah Arendt, Jerome Kohn, and Ron H. Feldman, eds., *The Jewish Writings* (New York: Schocken Books, 2007). The controversy as a whole has been exhaustively covered and commented upon.

and Foucault's writings on the Iranian Revolution,[9] are often reductively batted away as foolhardy mistakes because they escape the paradigm of what we think we know. These authors' challenges to conventional expectations – their willingness to think afresh about that which is already subject to preexisting judgment – have been used by some to condemn their entire theoretical oeuvre.[10] Ironically, the dynamics of orthodoxy have even been employed to appropriate their legacies of independent critical thinking, as the tribal considerations of identity and its proper *Herzenstakt* (literally "heart's tact," but used by Arendt to mean something closer to required sentimentality and group blood-loyalty) continue to demand conformist loyalty.[11] Reengaging the arguments over the specific historical details of the Islamist politics of the Iranian Revolution, or Arendt's determination to historicize antisemitism as a recognizably political problem rather than a unique ethno-religious curse, is beyond the scope of this project. Neither Arendt's writings on the Eichmann trial nor Foucault's on the Iranian Revolution are complete analyses of the phenomenon they are observing. They are insightful precisely for their determination to think about

[9] Foucault's publications on Iran first mostly appeared in the Italian newspaper *Corriera della Sera* during 1978 and 1979. The English language publication that includes most of Foucault's published writings on Iran (as a long appendix) is Janet Afary and Kevin B. Anderson, *Foucault and the Iranian Revolution: Gender and the Seductions of Islamism* (Chicago: University of Chicago Press, 2005). Foucault's related public statements on Iran, and his response to the controversy over his Iran writings, are included in the interview with Farès Sassine in Laura Cremonesi, Orazio Irrera, Daniele Lorenzini, and Martina Tazzioli, eds., *Foucault and the Making of Subjects* (New York: Rowman & Littlefield, 2016).

[10] I am taking as a given that they weren't simply "wrong" in their analyses and that their writings on these fraught twentieth-century events are not the signs of some fundamental flaw in their entire intellectual endeavor and approach to the world. The vilification of Arendt for her interpretation of Eichmann and his trial has been well documented. Regarding Foucault, see my book review of Afary and Anderson in *International Journal of Middle East Studies*, 38(3) (2006), 492–494.

[11] See Arendt's letter of July 24, 1963, in "'Eichmann in Jerusalem': Exchange of Letters between Gershom Scholem and Hannah Arendt (January 1964)," in *The Jew as Pariah*, 247. The renewed demand for (Jewish) *Herzenstakt* is exemplified by the brouhaha over Masha Gessen's receipt of the Heinrich Böll Foundation's Hannah Arendt Prize, elicited by a very personal essay Gessen had published in *The New Yorker* on the politics of (Holocaust) memory and its intersection with contemporary state violence. See Masha Gessen, "In the Shadow of the Holocaust: How the Politics of Memory in Europe Obscures What We See in Israel and Gaza Today," *New Yorker*, December 9, 2023.

what they are immediately observing and to try to consider its immediate details in context, but without freezing them within a preexisting narrative of reductive assumptions.

Arendt's coverage of the Eichmann trial in Jerusalem for *The New Yorker*, and her developing argument on the bureaucratic nature of genocidal evil that could be at once "profound" and "banal," challenged conventions of guilt, responsibility, and complicity. Foucault's dispatches from Iran during 1978 and 1979 for *Corriera della Sera* argued that what was happening on the ground was indeed a social and political revolution, even if it didn't fit the conventional theoretical and experiential paradigm that had come to dominate the established interpretive tradition of modern revolutions. Further, Foucault claimed that the politics of popular self-determination he was glimpsing around him in Iran had revived the possibility that the "collective will" could be a fleeting political reality rather than "a theoretical tool . . . like God, like the soul, something one would never encounter."[12] So how did both Arendt and Foucault manage to develop such unexpected and – I would insist – insightful analyses about these volatile subjects?

Strikingly, in both cases the authors volunteered to write for the public on immediately unfolding events. They were working as journalists – writing for general audience publications without benefit of the longer gestation period that theoretical scholarship usually demands. Is this significant? Does it matter that they physically went into the field and did so in order to observe rather than to advocate?[13] For both authors, this was an unusual choice. Both were recognized scholars, but in these cases both Arendt and Foucault seemed to try to sidestep their supposed expertise, and its accompanying discursive apparatus. They went to open themselves up to unfolding historical events, to observe, to learn, and to think; they had to pay attention to what was going on around them, in its multiplicity of detail, and try to make sense of what it means without simply relying on what they think

[12] Michel Foucault, "Iran: The Spirit of a World without Spirit," conversation with Claire Brière and Pierre Blanchet, in Afary and Anderson, *Foucault and the Iranian Revolution*, 253.

[13] On-the-ground (feminist) interventions during the Iranian Revolution by well-intentioned advocates (from Kate Millet to Simone de Beauvoir) were notoriously counterproductive. But they also insistently projected their own local experiences and understandings of feminism onto Iranian women's situation (and often conflated any wearing of *hejab* with absolute subjection to patriarchy).

they know – on the familiarity of their own experience. Crucially, they both treated what was happening in front of them as the instances of an unfolding event, not as precategorized evidence. Yet this neutrality of perspective, a willingness to think about what one is seeing combined with a scholar's attention to detail, led to remarkable theoretical insights. Both Arendt and Foucault had already published controversial, problematic public interventions (Arendt on racial segregation; Foucault on prison reform). But the *New Yorker* and *Corriera della Sera* essays are sustained examinations, not one-off commentaries that were thought better of with the passage of time.[14] They represent the unusual instance of philosophers leaving the armchair or the archive to go into the empirical field, not as a researcher or expert but as a reporter and interpreter: as someone willing to think in public.

What difference might it make to our theoretical understanding if we bring into relation these two efforts at political theory as thinking in public, by theorists who go into the field to get out of the box? Is there any discernible shared method to their thinking – their combinations of observational detail and theoretical analysis – that enables them to make original sense of what they see? Can an ethical commitment to thinking – about the ongoing relation between power and the self – provide a method for defamiliarizing us from what we think we know, and moving beyond the conventional wisdom of stereotypes, whether intellectual or ethno-religious? This is both a familiar and a fundamental question. Both Arendt and Foucault answer it by reconceptualizing thinking itself as critique, at least to the extent the thinking process is an engagement with plurality or alterity.

[14] Perhaps Arendt had learned (belatedly) of the dangers of projecting what you think you know (and want to assert) onto an event rather than attending to the actual reality of its contradictions and complexities. In a private letter to Ralph Ellison (July 29, 1965), she admitted that in writing "Reflections on Little Rock," controversial even before it was published in *Dissent* 6(1) (Winter 1959), she had been projecting her own German Jewish childhood experiences of social discrimination onto the experiences of Black children challenging legal discrimination in the US. She had not understood the profoundly different level of immediate violence that saturated their experience (and therefore had not known what she was talking about). Her Eichmann observations, in contrast, were based in historical awareness and personal experience of the social and political conditions of European antisemitism and its effects. See Elisabeth Young-Bruehl, *Hannah Arendt: For Love of the World* (New Haven, CT: Yale University Press, 1982), 308–318.

## Trying to Think with Arendt and Foucault (about Iran)

These considerations are prompted by my own similar perplexities about the challenges of thinking about Iran, from the background of a political theorist observing the immediate day-to-day unfolding of social change and political events during a period of profound transformations. Reading Arendt's *Eichmann* and Foucault's Iran essays and interviews provides us with the experience of thinking; itself the intention of the best political theory. But since these texts are about thinking through the details of what are assumed to be given judgments (Eichmann's genocidal guilt; the fanaticism of the Iranian Revolution), are they made more vulnerable to backlash over the ethics of questioning (given) judgment?

Arendt comes close to providing a synthesizing theoretical argument (or at least a theoretical catchphrase) through the notion of "the banality of evil." But this isn't really adequate to convey her concern with the possibility of evil being intrinsically related to the absence of thinking; the challenge that perfectly ordinary behavior (a careerist focus on "doing one's job") by respectable people can mean doing terrible things. Arendt's challenge is that she considers that Eichmann may be sincere in his commitment to professionalism before ideology; the difference between Eichmann and the defendants of the Nuremberg trials (for Arendt) seems to have been that she took seriously the possibility that the excuse was actually an explanation (although not an exculpation). Her elaborate inquiry into Eichmann's unimpressive personal and professional accomplishments until he found his niche as a Nazi bureaucrat is intended to establish his lack of exceptionalism, and therefore offer back a reflexive consideration of the possibility that devils don't always wear horns. But to a cursory reader, it risks seeming sympathetic, as though being a sad-sack loser is necessarily a form of innocence.

Similarly, Foucault finds his theoretical questioning drawn toward a notion of "political spirituality." A careful tracing of what exactly he is trying to get at with this phrase hints at a renewed version of the possibility of utopia: the ability to take seriously that we could make things other than they are.[15] But "political spirituality" has usually

[15] The best evaluation of Foucault's Iran writings, including awareness of the historical context of the Iranian events as well as their significance in relation to

been reduced to institutional religion or sectarian faith, framing Foucault's advocacy of the Iranian Revolution as a naïve endorsement of Islamic theology and/or Islamist ideology. For many Western intellectuals, for whom secular identity has become a stand-in for modernity, it is then easy to dismiss Foucault's Iran observations as bizarre slippage into gullible premodern superstition, or a revelation of his personal weakness for unreliable charismatic leadership. It doesn't particularly help that Foucault takes such sharp note of the Iranian revolutionaries' willingness to face death; the phenomenon of ordinary people (not ideologs, not the vanguard) in revolt in the face of violent repression.[16] Foucault is struck by the political possibility inherent in this inexplicable interruption in the status quo of society and politics, of life itself. He connects this to the social justice traditions woven into Shi'ia Islam (with its multiple, ritualized memorializations of those who struggle for justice against the state), and to the availability of religious symbolism to represent political critique (a subaltern politics of indigenous meaning). But conventionally orientalist and modernist presumptions of Muslim fanaticism easily conflated national political commitment (even unto death) with a religious cult of bloodthirsty martyrdom; Foucault gets accused of becoming an apologist for the enemies of (Western) modernity and civilization.

With the trick of available hindsight, Foucault's appreciation for the newness of collective (Iranian) revolutionary possibility gets read back against the violent repressions of the postrevolutionary state. In other words, his critics conflate the Arendtian moments of liberation and foundation and ignore the specific time frame Foucault insisted he was observing: the months leading up to and culminating in the liberatory period of the revolution, and not the ideological consolidation (and accompanying exclusionary violence) of postrevolutionary regime institutionalization. Similarly, Foucault's observations on the

his later work, is Behrooz Ghamari-Tabrizi, *Foucault in Iran: Islamic Revolution and the Enlightenment* (Minneapolis, MN: University of Minnesota Press, 2016). In attending closely to how a philosophical encounter with revolution is unexpectedly refracted in a philosopher's subsequent writing, Ghamari-Tabrizi's work is comparable to Susan Buck-Morss' *Hegel, Haiti, and Universal History* (Pittsburgh, PA: University of Pittsburgh, 2009). Both are repositioning the assumed relation between theory and history in order to reevaluate contemporary arguments over the Enlightenment.

16 Foucault, "Is It Useless to Revolt?" in Afary and Anderson, *Foucault and the Iranian Revolution*, 263–267.

political significance of the moment-facing-death get reduced to nihilism (itself understood as utter negation, rather than its original form as radical institutional critique in the service of utopian possibility).

The philosophical presumption that agency is predicated on a relation to mortality has a long and venerable genealogy. But an equation of revolutionary action only with the moment of revolt (the instant of the "man in revolt" facing death) short-circuits itself. A revolution that can sustain itself only by staying in the streets is a society in chaos; the institutionalization period of a revolution is all about closing off the open-ended potential of the new through a process of formalization. This is the internal contradiction of a postrevolutionary inheritance that young Iranian activists wrestle with and the entrenched governing faction recognizes and tries to suppress: "nothing threatens the very achievements of revolution more dangerously and more acutely than the spirit which has brought them about" (Arendt).[17] Revolution defined by martyrdom leads to an impossible choice: revolt and face mortality, or accept quietism and the stultifying status quo. This is the problem if mortality is assumed to be the only relevant revolutionary category of being: mortality in itself is inevitably a negation (we are all dead soon). Revolution must also be about the possibility of beginning; its relevant category of being, emerging from the ashes of mortality, is natality.

"I think we live at a moment of extreme darkness and extreme brightness. Extreme darkness, because we really do not know from which direction the light would come. Extreme brightness, because we ought to have the courage to begin anew" (Foucault).[18] Foucault himself understood that revolution must be about more than a willingness to face death to achieve a change of government; the goal of revolution must be creating a postrevolutionary subject who is freer than under the old regime.[19] He transfers his new-found attention to

[17] Hannah Arendt, *On Revolution* (New York: Penguin Books, 986), 232.
[18] Foucault in "Dialogue between Michel Foucault and Baqir Parham," in Afary and Anderson, *Foucault and the Iranian Revolution*, 185.
[19] Shirin Saeidi presents a sensitive analysis of how women adopted this possibility for creating a new and freer subjectivity during the early period of the revolution. Saeidi explores how women pursued self-conscious processes of "self construction" and "spiritual acts of citizenship" that positioned individuals as agents within a collective context of dynamic change that extended across both public and private. Strategies included (for pious women) relying on religious legitimacy to challenge conventional restrictions to women's independence, or

the possibility of revolutionizing freedom onto the genealogy of the (Western) self, as constructed through inter-relational practices and powers, a self whose private and public ethics merge in an essentially reflexive dynamic.[20] As always in the work published in his lifetime, Foucault attends to the minutiae of social relations and is skeptical of too close a fascination with the formal arrangements of state power.[21] But to appreciate the implications of his insights into the Iranian Revolution, and how they enable him to shift to a less teleologically stuck inquiry into relations of freedom, agency, and (social) power, we may need to keep shifting our own focus, back and forth dialectically between both Foucault and Arendt.

In posing natality as the fundamental aspect of the making of the new, Arendt offers a conceptual category that entails the possibility of growth and continuation. Like Irigaray's conception of an alternative possibility of the self modeled on the metaphor of the plural female (rather than the phallic male) body, Arendt's conception of natality is philosophically and politically metaphorical rather than literally and physically maternal. Natality is the continuing possibility of new life, not simply its momentary appearance. Revolution is not only a division of liberation and foundation. If revolution is to remake and make new possibilities for freedom, it must be an extended process of societal

(for secular women) relying on poetic models to craft an alternative subjectivity. See Shirin Saeidi, *Women and the Islamic Republic: How Gendered Citizenship Conditions the Iranian State* (Cambridge: Cambridge University Press, 2022), especially chapter 3, "Revolutionary Citizens: The Confrontation of Power and Spiritual Acts of Citizenship from 1980 to 1988," 67–105.

20 Ghamari-Tabrizi's *Foucault in Iran* provides a sustained exposition of how Foucault's subsequent writing on the self in relations, particularly in the later volumes of *The History of Sexuality*, is not a turn toward solipsism but rather a resolute investigation of the connection between our most intimate self-practices and collective political possibility. Foucault "views freedom as a ceaseless act of becoming, which is realizable only through the care of the self," but it is a self that is inherently relational, as is its care. See Ghamari-Tabrizi, *Foucault in Iran*, 176–177.

21 It can be argued that Foucault's Collège de France lectures, with their valuable conceptualizations of biopolitics and governmentality, were tracing the genealogy of the modern neoliberal self, but one stuck in the immediacy of familiarity. The estate has permitted editing and publishing of the lectures, but as Foucault left instructions that none of his unpublished work should be published after his death, it is hard to know exactly what form or emphasis he might have given more fully revised versions published under his supervision.

transformation, a back-and-forth dynamic of individual and collective self-definition through the myriad details of daily life.

## Thinking, Freedom, and Power

In general, we can say that a philosophy based on self-consciousness is necessarily related to the idea of freedom. And this is very good, but the philosophy or thinking whose subject matter is not self-consciousness, but real practice or social practice, relates to the theory of power. In other words, instead of self-consciousness and freedom, we reach practice and power. (Foucault)[22]

This book has developed theoretically out of a set of encounters, between (my training in) Arendt's political thinking with (the doubled encounter of) Foucault's social theory and his and my encounter with Iran itself. Arendt theorizes power (as opposed to strength or force) as a collective, plural capacity; Foucault's merging of private and public modes of self-creation is one of his most significant contributions. Both recognize that neither freedom nor power can be atomistically produced; they are essentially relational and interactive experiences. Arendt theorizes political action, with its remarkable power to constitute a reflexive self through mutual engagement with others, as an ephemeral (revolutionary?) moment. Foucault observed a revolution and then attempted to delineate some of the constitutive possibilities it revealed for the socially embedded self. Initially emerging as liberation, and despite its always problematic institutionalization, the experience of revolution has the possibility of becoming an ongoing (political) process of small, daily practices that add up to the social realities of an alternative collective possibility: a free political subjectivity.

Foucault witnesses the Iranian Revolution, writes about it, and then withdraws from the controversy and turns his attention to (related) other things. Not so Arendt. Her observations on the Eichmann trial prompted even more vehement accusations against her judgment than Foucault's on Iran, but she maintained her commitment to the integrity of the process of her work; she maintained her commitment to an ethics of thinking in public. Perhaps this difference is, in part, the difference between the philosopher and the political theorist; Arendt

22 Foucault in "Dialogue between Michel Foucault and Baqir Parham," in Afary and Anderson, *Foucault and the Iranian Revolution*, 188–189.

insisted on the accessibility of politics, and (political) thinking, while philosophy (and philosophers) have perhaps tended to privilege a certain distance. Arendt remained committed to the challenge of political (inter)action, even while she remained hostile to the possibility of social analysis. But what is her analysis of Eichmann as an individual but a social portrait – a merging of the private and the public – with political implications? It is in the details, of ordinary choices made or not, of policy reduced to procedure, and responsibility to acquiescence and ambition, that Eichmann's political guilt becomes an ethical lesson. It is in the spectacle of a collective becoming political – of a revolution – that Foucault begins to reconsider the possibility for freedom, for the possible interruption of the set structures of the already given present. In both observing and thinking about the open-ended continuations of a revolutionary process of beginning, and the political implications of its social practices – of the small but significant shifts in the (Iranians') care of the self and their relations to freedom – I have tried to follow their lead.

# Bibliography

Abbasi, A. (Director). (2022). *Holy Spider* [Film]. Iran.
Abbasi-Shavazi, M. J., McDonald, P., & Hosseini-Chavoshi, M. (2009). *The Fertility Transition in Iran: Revolution and Reproduction*. Springer.
Abu-Raddad, L. J., Ghanem, K. G., Feizzadeh, A., Setayesh, H., Calleja, J. M. G., & Riedner, G. (2013). HIV and Other Sexually Transmitted Infection Research in the Middle East and North Africa: Promising Progress? *Sexually Transmitted Infections*, *89*(Suppl. 3).
Adle, C., & Hourcade, B. (1992). *Téhéran, capitale bicentenaire*. Institut français de recherche en Iran.
Afary, J. (1996). *The Iranian Constitutional Revolution, 1906–1911: Grassroots Democracy, Social Democracy, and the Origins of Feminism*. Columbia University Press.
Afary, J., & Anderson, K. B. (2005). *Foucault and the Iranian Revolution: Gender and the Seductions of Islamism*. University of Chicago Press.
Afary, J. (2009). *Sexual Politics in Modern Iran*. Cambridge University Press.
Afkhami, A. A. (1999). Defending the Guarded Domain: Epidemics and the Emergence of an International Sanitary Policy in Iran. *Comparative Studies of South Asia, Africa and the Middle East*, *19*(1), 122–136.
Ahmed, L. (1992). *Women and Gender in Islam: Historical Roots of a Modern Debate*. Yale University Press.
Akkad, M. (Director). (1976). *Mohammad, Messenger of God* [Film]. Libya, Morocco, Lebanon, Syria, United Kingdom.
al-Dowleh, S. A. M. A. (2014). *Life at the Court of the Early Qajar Shahs* (M. M. Eskandari-Qajar, Trans.). Mage Publishers.
Alavi, N. (2009, June 2). Iran: A Blind Leap of Faith. *Open Democracy*.
Alinejad, M. (2014, June 4). Iranian State Television Faked My Rape. *Time*. http://time.com/2820082/iranian-state-television-faked-my-rape/.
Allaqoli, L., Saeedi, Z. A., Azin, A., Hajaan, S., Majd, H. A., & Molavi, N. (2014). Socially Damaged Women's Perceptions of Sexually Transmitted Infections: A Qualitative Study. *Life Science Journal*, *11*(4s), 244–250.
Amin, C. M. (2002). *The Making of the Modern Iranian Woman: Gender, State Policy, and Popular Culture, 1865–1946*. University Press of Florida.

(2004). Importing "Beauty Culture" into Iran in the 1920s and 1930s: Mass Marketing Individualism in an Age of Anti-Imperialist Sacrifice. *Comparative Studies of South Asia, Africa and the Middle East*, *24*(1), 79–95.

Amirani, A. (Director). (2005). *Trans-Sexuality in Iran* [Film]. Iran.

Anvari, H. (2006). Power of Cliché [Lecture and Slides]. Vimeo. https://vimeo.com/61602790.

Arendt, H. (1958). *The Human Condition*. University of Chicago Press.

(1964). *Eichmann in Jerusalem*. Penguin Books.

(1965). *On Revolution*. Penguin Books.

(1968). *Men in Dark Times*. Harcourt Brace Jovanovich.

(1969). *On Violence*. Harcourt Brace Jovanovich.

(1972). *Crises of the Republic: Lying in Politics, Civil Disobedience on Violence, Thoughts on Politics, and Revolution*. Harcourt Brace Jovanovich.

(1973). *The Origins of Totalitarianism*. Harcourt Brace Jovanovich.

(1974). *Rahel Varnhagen: The Life of a Jewish Woman*. Harcourt Brace Jovanovich.

(1977). *Between Past and Future: Eight Exercises in Political Thought*. Penguin Books.

(1977). *The Life of the Mind: Volume One/Thinking*. Harcourt Brace Jovanovich.

(1977). *Eichmann in Jerusalem: A Report on the Banality of Evil*. Penguin Books.

Arendt, H., & Feldman, R. H. (1978). *The Jew as Parish: Jewish Identity and Politics in the Modern Age*. Grove Press.

Arendt, H., Kohn, J., & Feldman, R. H. (2007). *The Jewish Writings*. Schocken Books.

Aristotle. (2017). *Aristotle, "Politics": A New Translation* (C. D. C. Reeve, Trans.). Hackett.

Attari, S. (Director). (2006). *It Happens Sometimes* [Film]. Iran.

Azarbayjanis, N. (Director). (2011). *Facing Mirrors* [Film]. Iran.

Babaie, S. (2008). *Isfahan and Its Palaces: Statecraft, Shi'ism and the Architecture of Conviviality in Early Modern Iran*. Edinburgh University Press.

Bagheri, N. (2017). Tehran's Subway: Gender, Mobility, and the Adaptation of the "Proper" Muslim Woman. *Social & Cultural Geography*, *18*(5), 304–322.

Bahari, M. (Director). (1998). *Art of Demolition: Ephemeral Art in Tehran* [Film]. Iran.

(2002). *And Along Came a Spider* [Film]. Iran.

Bahramitash, R., & Esfahani, H. S. (2011). From Postrevolution to the Reform: Gender Politics and Employment. In R. Bahramitash & H. S.

Esfahani (Eds.), *Veiled Employment: Islamism and the Political Economy of Women's Employment in Iran* (pp. 83–122). Syracuse University Press.

(2011). *Veiled Employment: Islamism and the Political Economy of Women's Employment in Iran*. Syracuse University Press.

Bahramitash, R. (2013). *Gender and Entrepreneurship in Iran: Micro-enterprise and the Informal Sector*. Palgrave MacMillan.

Bahramitash, R., & Olmsted, J. (2014). Choice and Constraint in Paid Work: Women from Low-Income Households in Tehran. *Feminist Economics*, *20*(4), 260–280.

Bahrampour, T. (1999). *To See and See Again: A Life in Iran and America*. University of California Press.

Bahreini, R. (2008). From Perversion to Pathology: Discourses and Practices of Gender Policing in the Islamic Republic of Iran. *Muslim World Journal of Human Rights*, *5*(1), Article 2, 1–49.

Banakar, R. (2015). *Driving Culture in Iran*. I. B. Tauris.

Bani-Etemad, R. (Director). (1998). *The May Lady* [Film] Iran.

(1995). *The Blue Veiled* [Film.] Iran.

Bardenstein, C. (2002). Transmissions Interrupted: Reconfiguring Food, Memory, and Gender in the Cookbook-Memoirs of Middle Eastern Exiles. *Signs: Journal of Women in Culture and Society*, *28*(1), 353–387.

Barthes, R. (1961). Vers une psycho-sociologie de l'alimentation moderne. *Annales: Économies, sociétés, civilisations*, *16*(5), 977–986.

Bateson, M. C. (1979). "This Figure of Tinsel": A Study of Themes of Hypocrisy and Pessimism in Iranian Culture. *Daedalus*, *108*(3), 125–134.

Bayat, A. (1997). *Street Politics: Poor People's Movements in Iran*. Columbia University Press.

(2007). A Women's Non-movement: What It Means to Be a Woman Activist in an Islamic State. *Comparative Studies of South Asia, Africa and the Middle East*, 27(1), 160–172.

(2010). *Life as Politics: How Ordinary People Change the Middle East*. Stanford University Press.

Beck, L., & Huang, J. (2006). Manipulating Private Lives and Public Spaces in Qashqa'i Society in Iran. *Comparative Studies in South Asia, Africa and the Middle East*, 26(2), 303–325.

Beeman, W. O. (1976). What Is (Iranian) National Character? A Sociolinguistic Approach. *Iranian Studies*, 9(1), 22–48.

Behnam, B., & Amizadeh, N. (2011). A Comparative Study of the Compliments and Compliment Responses between English and Persian TV Interviews. *3L: The Southeast Asian Journal of English Language Studies*, *17*(1), 65–78.

Behrooz, M. (1994). *Rebels with a Cause: The Failure of the Left in Iran.* I. B. Tauris.

Beyzaie, B. (Director). (1989). *Bashu, the Little Stranger* [Film]. Iran.

Blum, V. (1998). Ladies and Gentlemen: Train Rides and Other Oedipal Stories. In H. Nast & S. Pile (Eds.), *Places through the Body* (pp. 263–280). Routledge.

Bonnet, F., Vanek, J., & Chen, M. (2019). *Women and Men in the Informal Economy: A Statistical Brief.* WIEGO.

Bourdieu, P. (1984). *Distinction: A Social Critique of the Judgement of Taste* (R. Nice, Trans.). Harvard University Press.

(1990). *The Logic of Practice* (R. Nice, Trans.). Stanford University Press.

(2002). Pierre Bourdieu on Marriage Strategies (E. Forster, Trans.). *Population and Development Review*, *28*(3), 549–558.

Boydston, J. (1994). *Home and Work: Housework, Wages, and the Ideology of Labor in the Early Republic.* Oxford University Press.

Bromberger, C. (1994). Eating Habits and Cultural Boundaries in Northern Iran. In S. Zubaida & R. Tapper (Eds.), *A Taste of Thyme: Culinary Cultures of the Middle East* (pp. 185–201). Tauris Parke Paperbacks.

Brown, P., & Levinson, S. C. (1987). *Politeness: Some Universals in Language Usage.* Cambridge University Press.

Buck-Morss, S. (Autumn 1986). The Flaneur, the Sandwichman and the Whore: The Politics of Loitering. *New German Critique* (pp. 99–140). No. 39.

(1991). *The Dialectics of Seeing: Walter Benjamin and the Arcades Project.* MIT Press.

(2009). *Hegel, Haiti, and Universal History.* University of Pittsburgh.

Burgin, V., Donald, J., & Kaplan, C. (1986). *Formations of Fantasy.* Methuen.

Burnett, J. (1989). *Plenty and Want: A Social History of Food in England from 1815 to the Present Day*, 3rd ed. Routledge.

Burns, N. K., & Greenwood, J. T. (2017). *Rediscovering an American Community of Color: The Photographs of William Bullard, 1897, 1917.* Worcester Art Museum and Clark University.

Butler, J. (1990). *Gender Trouble: Feminism and the Subversion of Identity.* Routledge.

Carver, A. (2004). Dead Dogs: A Decade of Public Art Experiments in Tehran. *Bidoun*, (1).

Certeau, M. D., Giard, L., & Mayol, P. (1998). *The Practice of Everyday Life, Volume 2: Living and Cooking* (T. J. Tomasik, Trans.). University of Minnesota Press.

Chardin, S. J. (1988). *Travels in Persia, 1673–1677.* Dover Publications.

Chatterjee, P. (1993). *The Nation and Its Fragments: Colonial and Postcolonial Histories.* Princeton University Press.

Chehabi, H. E. (2003). The Westernization of Iranian Culinary Culture. *Iranian Studies*, *36*(1), 43–61.
Chernyshevsky, N. (1989). *What Is to Be Done?* (M. Katz, Trans.). Cornell University Press.
Cheshire, G. (1998). *Projection*. Faber & Faber.
Cohen, P. C. (1992). Safety and Danger: Women on American Public Transport, 1750–1850. In D. O. Helly & S. M. Reverby (Eds.), *Gendered Domains: Rethinking Public and Private in Women's History* (pp. 109–122). Cornell University Press.
Cornell, D., & Seeley, S. D. (2016). *The Spirit of Revolution: Beyond the Dead Ends of Man*. Polity Press.
Costa-Gavras. (Director). (1969). *Z* [Film]. Greece, France.
(1972). *State of Siege* [Film]. France.
Counihan, C., & Van Esterik, P. (Eds.). (2008). *Food and Culture: A Reader, Second Edition* (pp. 28–35). Routledge.
Cremonesi, L., Irrera, O., Lorenzini, D., & Tazziol, M. (2016). *Foucault and the Making of Subjects*. Rowman & Littlefield.
Dabashi, H. (1999). Mohsen Makhmalbaf's *A Moment of Innocence*. In R. Issa & S. Whitaker (Eds.), *Life and Art: The New Iranian Cinema* (pp. 26–43). National Film Theater, The British Film Institute.
Dalrymple, W. (2019, August 30). Lessons for Capitalism from the East India Company. *The Financial Times*. www.ft.com/content/0f1ec9da-c9a6-11e9-af46-b09e8bfe60c0
Damandan, P. (2010). *The Children of Isfahan: Polish Refugees in Iran, Portrait Photographs of Abolgasem Jala, 1942–1945*. Nazar.
Darabi, H. (2022). Alternative Spaces: Site Conscious Practice in Contemporary Art from Tehran (1990s–2010s). *Field: A Journal of Socially Engaged Art Criticism*, (21).
Davoodi, A. (Director). (1992). *Pickpockets Don't Go to Heaven* [Film]. Iran.
Day, C. M. (Director) (2017). *Saving Banksy* [Film]. USA.
De Beauvoir, S. (2011). *The Second Sex*. Vintage Books.
DeJong, J., Jawad, R., Mortagy, I., & Shepard, B. (2005). The Sexual and Reproductive Health of Young People in the Arab Countries and Iran. *Reproductive Health Matters*, *13*(25), 49–59.
Delafield, E. M. (1982). *Diary of a Provincial Lady*. Academy Chicago.
De Luce, D. (2023, August 18). The Beast of Mashhad. *The Guardian*. www.theguardian.com/film/2003/aug/18/edinburghfilmfestival2003.iran
Derambakhsh, K. (2016). Kambiz Derambakhsh, *Literary Series*. (Interview with Poupeh Missaghi.) *Asymptote*.
Derrida, J. (1994). *Specters of Marx: The State of the Debt, the Work of Mourning and the New International* (P. Kamuf, Trans.). Routledge.

Devictor, A. (2012). How Can Faith Be Filmed on the Battlefront and Experienced by TV Spectators? In F. Khosronejad (Ed.), *Iranian Sacred Defense Cinema: Religion, Martyrdom and National Identity* (pp. 161–173). Sean Kingston Publishing.

Doane, M. A. (1982). Film and the Masquerade: Theorizing the Female Spectator. *Screen*, *23*(3–4), 74–88.

Egan, E. (2005). *The Films of Makhmalbaf: Cinema, Politics & Culture in Iran*. Mage Publishers.

Ehsani, K. (1999). "The Conservatives Have Misjudged": A Conversation with Ahmad Bourghani. *Middle East Report*, *212*(3), 36–37.

(1999). Do-e Khordad and the Specter of Democracy. *Middle East Report*, *212*(3), 10–16.

(1999). Municipal Matters: The Urbanization of Consciousness and Political Change in Tehran. *Middle East Report*, *212*, 22–27.

(2003, July 15). "Our Letter to Khatami Was a Farewell": An Interview with Saeed Razavi-Faqih. *Middle East Report Online*. https://merip.org/2003/07/our-letter-to-khatami-was-a-farewell/

(2006). *The Politics of Public Space in Tehran's International Book Fair* [Unpublished Paper]. Middle East Studies Association.

Ehsani, K., Moruzzi, N. C., & Keshavarzian, A. (2009, June 28). Tehran, June 2009. *Middle East Report Online*. https://merip.org/2009/06/tehran-june-2009/

Ehsani, K. (2014). *The Social History of Labor in the Iranian Oil Industry: The Built Environment and the Making of the Industrial Working Class (1908–1941)*. PhD diss., Leiden University, the Netherlands.

Ehsani, K., & Keshavarzian, A. (2018, January 11). The Moral Economy of the Iranian Protests. *Jacobin*. https://jacobin.com/2018/01/iranian-protests-revolution-rouhani-ahmadinejad

Eisenberg, A. (2009, April 27). Tribeca Review: *About Elly* Brings the Iranian Middle Class Center Stage. www.flavorwire.com/18391/tribeca-review-about-elly

Elahi, B. (2012). Crossing Tehran Avenue. *Cultural Studies*, *26*(6), 956–981.

Emami, N. (2010, May 20). The Consolation of Philosophy: Hannah Arendt and the Green Movement. *Tehran Review*. http://tehranreview.net/articles/2780

Engelstein, L. (1987). Morality and the Wooden Spoon: Russian Doctors View Syphilis, Social Class, and Sexual Behavior, 1890–2005. In C. Gallagher & T. Laqueur (Eds.), *The Making of the Modern Body: Sexuality and Society in the Nineteenth Century* (pp. 169–208). University of California Press.

Erami, N., & Keshavarzian, A. (2015). When Ties Don't Bind: Smuggling Effects, Bazaars and Regulatory Regimes in Postrevolutionary Iran. *Economy and Society*, *44*(1), 110–139.

Esfandiari, H. (2009, October 21). Iranian Women Please Stand Up. *Foreign Policy*. https://foreignpolicy.com/2009/10/21/iranian-women-please-stand-up/

(2009). *My Prison, My Home: One Woman's Story of Captivity in Iran*. Harper Collins.

Eshaghian, T. (Director). (2008). *Transsexual in Iran/Be Like Others* [Film]. Iran.

Eshun, K., & Gray, R. (2011). The Militant Image: A Ciné-Geography. *Third Text*, *25*(1), 1–12.

Eslami-Rasekh, Z. (2004). Face-Keeping Strategies in Reaction to Complaints: English and Persian. *Journal of Asian Pacific Communication*, *14*(1), 181–197.

Esposito, J. (1986). Foreword. In A. Shari'ati & F. Rajaee (Eds.), *What Is to Be Done: The Enlightened Thinkers and an Islamic Renaissance* (pp. ix–xii). The Institute for Research and Islamic Studies.

Evans, S. M., & Boyte, H. C. (1992). *Free Spaces: The Sources of Democratic Change in America*. University of Chicago Press.

Fanon, F. (1965). *A Dying Colonialism*. Monthly Review Press.

Farhadi, A. (Director). (2011). *A Separation* [Film]. Iran.

Farman Farmaian, S., & Munker, D. (1992). *Daughter of Persia: A Woman's Journey from Her Father's Harem through the Islamic Revolution*. Crown.

Farshidfar, Z., Dastjerdi, R., & Shahabizadeh, F. (2013). Acceptance of Cosmetic Surgery: Body Image, Self Esteem and Conformity. *Procedia – Social and Behavioral Sciences*, *84*, 238–242.

Farzin, M., & Mahdavi, S. (2012). It Went Green and Then It Went Red. *ArteEast: The Global Platform for Middle East Arts*. Spring 2012/Artezinefile://localhost/, https://arteeast.org/quarterly/it-goes-green-and-then-it-goes-red/%3Fissues_season=spring&issues_year=2012.

Fatemi, M. J., Rajabi, F., Moosavi, S. J., & Soltani, M. (2012). Quality of Life among Iranian Adults before and after Plastic Surgery. *Aesthetic Plastic Surgery*, *36*, 448–452.

Fathi, N. (2004, August 25). Taarof. *Open Democracy*. www.opendemocracy.net/en/article_2117jsp/

(2014). *The Lonely War: One Woman's Account of the Struggle for Modern Iran*. Basic Books.

Federici, S. (1975). *Wages against Housework*. Falling Wall Press.

(2004). *Caliban and the Witch: Women, the Body and Primitive Accumulation*. Autonomedia.

Fenstermaker Berk, S. (1980). *Women and Household Labor*. Sage Publications.

Fernea, E. W. (1969). *Guests of the Sheik: An Ethnography of an Iraqi Village*. Anchor Books.

Fischer, Mark. (2004). Mute Dreams, Blind Owls, and Dispersed Knowledges: Persian Poets in the Transnational Circuitry. Duke University Press.

Flandrin, J. L., & Montanari, M. (Eds.). (1999). *Food: A Culinary History*. Columbia University Press.

Floor, W. M. (2006). Venereal Disease in Iran (1855–2005): A Public Affair. *Comparative Studies of South Asia, Africa and the Middle East*, *26*(2), 260–278.

Föllmer, K. (2011). Ardeshir Mohassess: Art and Satire in Iran. *Iranian Studies*, *44*(2), 302–306.

Forouzesh, E. (Director). (1987). *The Key* [Film]. Iran.

Foucault, M. (1978). *The History of Sexuality, Volume 1: An Introduction* (R. Hurley, Trans.). Random House.

(1985). *The Use of Pleasure, Volume 2 of The History of Sexuality* (R. Hurley, Trans.). Random House.

(1986). *The Care of the Self, Volume 3 of The History of Sexuality* (R. Hurley, Trans.). Random House.

(2007). *Security, Territory, Population: Lectures at the College de France, 1977–78*. Picador.

(2021). *Confessions of the Flesh, Volume 4 of The History of Sexuality* (R. Gros, ed., R. Hurley, Trans.). Pantheon.

Fraser, N. (2016). Contradictions of Capital and Care. *The New Left Review*, *100*, 99–117.

Freud, S. (1960). *Jokes and Their Relation to the Unconscious* (J. Strachey, Trans.). W. W. Norton.

Gazagnadou, D. (Spring 2006). Diffusion of Cultural Models, Body Transformations, and Technology in Iran: Iranian Women and Cosmetic Nose Surgery. *Anthropology of the Middle East*, *1*(1), 106–111.

Geiger, J., & Rutsky, R. L. (2005). *Film Analysis: A Norton Reader*. W. W. Norton.

Gessen, M. (2023). In the Shadow of the Holocaust: How the Politics of Memory in Europe Obscures What We See in Israel and Gaza Today. *New Yorker*.

Ghadarkhan, S. (2022, May 23). Iran's "Spider Killer" Is Re-Dramatised Two Decades after Original Documentary. *IranWire*. https://iranwire.com/en/society/104181-irans-infamous-spider-killer-is-re-dramatized-in-a-third-film/#:~:text=The%20story%20of%20the%20man,Cannes%20Film%20Festival%20on%20Sunday.

Ghamari-Tabrizi, B. (2016). *Foucault in Iran: Islamic Revolution after the Enlightenment*. University of Minnesota Press.

Ghazi Tabatabaei, M., Mehri, N., & Messkoub, M. (2013). *What Is Unpaid Female Labour Worth? Evidence from the Time Use Studies of Iran in*

*2008 and 2009* (Working Paper No. 562). Institute of Social Studies The Hague. https://repub.eur.nl/pub/41146/wp562.pdf

Gheissari, A. (2005). Despots of the World Unite! Satire in the Iranian Constitutional Press: The Majalleh-ye Estebdad, 1907–1908. *Comparative Studies of South Asia, Africa and the Middle East*, *25*(2), 360–376.

Gherovici, P. (2010). *Please Select Your Gender: From the Invention of Hysteria to the Democratization of Transgenderism*. Routledge.

(2017). *Transgender Psychoanalysis: A Lacanian Perspective on Sexual Difference*. Routledge.

Ghiabi, M. (2018). Under the Bridge in Tehran: Addiction, Poverty and Capital. *Ethnography*, *21*(2), 1–25.

Ghobadi, B. (Director). (2009). *No One Knows about Persian Cats* [Film]. Iran.

Girard, L. (1998). Time and Places. In M. D. de Certeau, et al. (Eds.), *The Practice of Everyday Life, Volume 2: Living and Cooking* (T. J. Tomasik, Trans.). University of Minnesota Press.

Golestan, Ebrahim (Director). (1965). *Brick and Mirror* [Film]. Iran

Gordon, A. F. (2008). *Ghostly Matters: Haunting and the Sociological Imagination*. University of Minnesota Press.

Graeber, D. (2011). *Debt: The First 5,000 Years*. Melville House.

Greenberg, C. (1965). Modernist Painting. *Art and Literature*, *4*, 193–201.

Guzman, Patricio. (Director). (1975). *Battle of Chile* [Film]. Chile, Cuba.

Haeri, S. (1989). *Law of Desire: Temporary Marriage in Shi'i Iran*. Syracuse University Press.

Hakakian, R. (2004). *Journey from the Land of No: A Girlhood in Revolutionary Iran*. Crown.

Hakimian, H. (2006). From Demographic Transition to Fertility Boom and Bust: Iran in the 1980s and 1990s. *Development and Change*, *37*(3), 571–597.

Hamedani, A. (Director). (2014). *Iran's "Sex Change" Solution* [Film]. Iran.

Harris, K. (2017). *A Social Revolution: Politics and the Welfare State in Iran*. University of California Press.

Hashemi, M. (2013). *Coming of Age in Iran: Poverty and the Struggle for Dignity*. Routledge.

(2015). Waithood and Face: Morality and Mobility among Lower-Class Youth in Iran. *Qualitative Sociology*, *38*, 261–283.

Heiman, R., Freeman, C., & Liechty, M. (2012). *The Global Middle Classes: Theorizing through Ethnography*. SAR Press.

Herzog, D. (1998). *Poisoning the Minds of the Lower Orders*. Princeton University Press.

Hosseini, F. (2009). *Whores or Wives: Discourses on Prostitution in Modern Iran, 1969–2006* [Unpublished Graduate Paper; MESA Graduate Student Paper 2009]. University of Maryland.

Hourcade, B. (2006). Iran: From Social to Political Change? *Woodrow Wilson International Center for Scholars*, *25*, 1–3.

Houshyar, S. (2013). Queer and Trans Subjects in Iranian Cinema; Between Representation, Agency, and Orientalist Fantasies. *Ajam Media Collective*.

(2015). LGBT Rights in Iran. *MERIP Blog in Middle East Research and Information Project*.

Human Rights Watch. (2010). *We Are a Buried Generation: Discrimination and Violence against Sexual Minorities in Iran* [Policy Report].

Huntington, S. (1993). The Clash of Civilizations. *Foreign Affairs 72*(3), 22–49.

Irigary, L. (1985). *This Sex Which Is Not One*. (C. Porter and C. Burke, Trans.). Cornell University Press.

Jafari, F. (2014). Transsexuality under Surveillance in Iran: Clerical Control of Khomeini's Fatwas. *Journal of Middle East Women's Studies*, *10*(2), 31–51.

Jafari, P. (2023). Revolt with a Revolutionary Perspective. *Iranian Studies*, *56*(3), *569–575*.

Javadi, H. (1988). *Satire in Persian Literature*. Fairleigh Dickinson University Press.

Javaheri, J., Shekarloo, M., & Keshavarz, N. (Spring–Summer 2008). News and Views [Interview with Jelve Javaheri, Iranian Feminist]. *Feminist Studies*, *34*(½), 329–342.

Javaheri, F. (2010). A Study of Transsexuality in Iran. *Iranian Studies*, *43*(3), 365–377.

Jefferson, C. (Director). (2023). *American Fiction* [Film]. USA.

Jeyrani, F. (Director). (1999). *Red* [Film]. Iran.

Johnston, S. (1999). Quietly Ruling the Roost. *Sight and Sound*, *9*(1), 18–20.

Jonze, S. (Director). (2002). *Adaptation* [Film]. USA.

Kadivar, M. A., Khani, S., Abedini, V., & Barzin, S. (2024). The Contingency of Structures: Triggers and the Social Geography of Revolutionary Episodes in Iran 2018–2022 [Working Paper].

Kalantar-Hormozi, A. (2013). A Brief History of Plastic Surgery in Iran. *Archives of Iranian Medicine*, *16*(3), 201–206.

Kandiyoti, D. (1988). Bargaining with Patriarchy. *Gender and Society*, *2*(3), 274–290.

Karamouzian, M., Nasirian, M., Sedaghat, A., & Haghdoost, A. A. (2014). HIV in Iran. *The Lancet*, *383*(9922), 1040.

Karim, P. M. (2013). In Praise of Big Noses (Personal Reflection). In A. Jafar & E. Masi de Casanova (Eds.), *Global Beauty, Local Bodies* (pp. 51–58). Palgrave MacMillan.

Karimi, P. (2013). *Domesticity and Consumer Culture in Iran: Interior Revolutions of the Modern Era*. Routledge.

(2017). Tourism, Voyeurism and the Media Ecologies of Tehran's Mural Arts. In J. Skinner & L. Jolliffe (Eds.), *Murals and Tourism: Heritage, Politics and Identity* (pp. 75–92). Routledge.

Karimi, Z. (2011). The Effects of International Trade on Gender Inequality in Iran: The Case of Women Carpet Weaver. In R. Bahramitash & H. S. Esfahani (Eds.), *Veiled Employment: Islamism and the Political Economy of Women's Employment in Iran* (pp. 166–190). Syracuse University Press.

Karimian, R., & Bahrampour, S. B. (1999). Iranian Press Update. *Middle East Report, 212*(3), 38–39.

Kashani, D. (2017). Exhibiting the City: Site Specificity in the Photographs of Negar Farajani's Tehran Monoxide Project. In A. Daneshvari (Ed.), *Contemporary Iranian Photography: Five Perspectives* (pp. 51–69). Mazda Publishers.

Katouzian, H. (2008). Private Parts and Public Discourses in Modern Iran. *Comparative Studies of South Asia, Africa and the Middle East, 28*(2), 283–290.

Keshavarzian, A. (2009). Regime Loyalty and *Bāzārī* Representation under the Islamic Republic of Iran: Dilemmas of the Society of Islamic Coalition. *International Journal of Middle East Studies, 41*, 225–246.

(2023). Protests, Participation and Representation in an Improvisational Polity. In M. Kamrava (Ed.), *The Sacred Republic: Power and Institutions in Iran* (pp. 47–65). Hurst.

Khatam, A. (2009). The Islamic Republic's Failed Quest for the Spotless City. *Middle East Report, 250*, 44–49.

Khomeini, A. S. R. M. (1984). *A Clarification of Questions: An Unabridged Translation of Resaleh Towzih al-Masael* (J. Borujerdi, Trans.). Westview Press.

Khosravi, H., Djalali, A., Riedijk, M., Marullo, F. (2017). *Tehran: Life within Walls: A City, Its Territory, and Forms of Dwelling*. Hatje Cantz Verlag.

Khosravi, S. (2008). *Young and Defiant in Tehran*. University of Pennsylvania Press.

Kia, M. (2016). Indian Friends, Iranian Selves, Persianate Modern. *Comparative Studies of South Asia, Africa and Middle East, 36*(3), 398–417.

Kianfar, N., & Mohr, D. (Directors). (2006). *The Birthday* [Film]. Iran.

Kian-Thiébaut, A., & Ladier-Fouladi, M. (2002). *Survey of the Social, Cultural, and Economic Situation of Families*. Monde Iranien (Paris) & Statistical Center of Iran (Tehran).

Kian-Thiébaut, A. (2005). From Motherhood to Equal Rights Advocates: The Weakening of Patriarchal Order. *Iranian Studies*, *38*(1), 45–66.

Kiarostami, A. (Director). (1987). *Where Is the Friend's House?* [Film]. Iran.

(1988). *Homework* [Film]. Iran.

(1990). *Close-Up* [Film]. Iran.

(1992). *And Life Goes On* [Film]. Iran.

(1994). *Through the Olive Trees* [Film]. Iran.

(1997). *Taste of Cherry* [Film]. Iran.

(1999). *The Wind Will Carry Us* [Film]. Iran.

Koolaee, E. (2009). Iranian Women from Private Sphere to Public Sphere, with Focus on Parliament. *Iran and the Caucasus*, *13*(2), 401–414.

Koutlaki, S. A. (2002). Offers and Expressions of Thanks as Face Enhancing Acts: *tae'arof* in Persian. *Journal of Pragmatics*, *34*(12), 1733–1756.

Kowsar, N. (2012). Being Funny Is Not that Funny: Contemporary Editorial Cartooning in Iran. *Social Research*, *79*(1), 117–144.

Kundera, M. (1973). *Life as Elsewhere* (Aaron Asher, Trans. (2000)). Harper Collins.

Lacan, J. (1966). The Insistence of the Letter in the Unconscious. *Yale French Studies*, *36/37*, 112–147.

(1977). *Écrits: A Selection*. Norton & Co.

Larrabeiti, M. D. (1998). Conspicuous before the World: The Political Rhetoric of the Chartist Women. In E. J. Yeo (Ed.), *Radical Femininity* (106–126). Manchester University Press.

Laudan, R. (2004). The Mexican Kitchen's Islamic Connection. *Saudi Aramco World*, *55*(3), 32–39.

Lee, M. Y. H., & Inuma, J. M. (2023, June 16). Japan (Finally) Changes a Century-Old Law: The Age of Consent Is Now 16. *The Washington Post*. www.washingtonpost.com/world/2023/06/16/japan-age-of-sexual-consent-16/

Lenehan, S. (Spring 2011). Nose Aesthetics: Rhinoplasty and Identity in Tehran. *Anthropology of the Middle East*, *6*(1), 47–62.

Levy, P. (2007, November 27). Reay Tannahill: Accidental Pioneer of Food History and Bestselling Romantic Novelist. *The Independent*, www.independent.co.uk/news/obituaries/reay-tannahill-accidental-pioneer-of-food-history-and-bestselling-romantic-novelist-760621.html

Longinotto, K., & Mir-Hosseini, Z. (Directors). (1998). *Divorce Iranian Style* [Film]. England.

Maclagan, I. (2000). Food and Gender in a Yemeni Community. In S. Zubaida & R. Tapper (Eds.), *A Taste of Thyme: Culinary*

*Cultures of the Middle East* (pp. 159–172). Tauris Parke Paperbacks.
MacLeod, A. E. (1991). *Accommodating Protest: Working Women, the New Veiling, and Change in Cairo*. Columbia University Press.
Mahdavi, P. (2009). *Passionate Uprisings: Iran's Sexual Revolution*. Stanford University Press.
Mahdavi, S. (2002). Women, Shi'ism, and Cuisine in Iran. In S. Ansari & V. Martin (Eds.), *Women, Religion, and Culture in Iran* (pp. 10–26). Curzon Press.
Mainardi, P. (2007). The Politics of Housework. In E. Freedman (Ed.), *The Essential Feminist Reader* (pp. 288–294). Modern Library.
Majidi, M. (Director). (1997). *Children of Heaven* [Film]. Iran.
Makhmalbaf, M. (Director). (1992). *Once Upon a Time, Cinema* [Film]. Iran.
(1995). *Salaam Cinema* [Film]. Iran.
(1996). *Gabbeh* [Film]. Iran.
(1996). *A Moment of Innocence* [Film]. Iran.
Makhmalbaf, S. (Director). (1998). *The Apple* [Film]. Iran.
Márai, S. (1993). *Les confessions d'un bourgeois* (G. Kassai and Z. Bianu, Trans.). Albin Michel.
Marefat, M. (1988). *Building to Power: Architecture in Tehran 1921–1941*. PhD diss., Massachusetts Institute of Technology.
Marx, K., & Engels, F. (1988). *The German Ideology*. International Publishers.
Marx, K. (1990). *Capital: Volume 1* (B. Fowkes, Trans.). Penguin Books.
(1902). *Wage-Labor and Capital* (Harriet E. Lothrop, Trans.). New York Labor News Company.
Massey, D. (1995). Thinking Radical Democracy Spatially. *Environment and Planning D: Society and Space*, *13*(3), 283–288.
Matthee, R. (1996). From Coffee to Tea: Shifting Patterns of Consumption in Qajar Iran. *Journal of World History*, *7*(2), 199–230.
(2005). *The Pursuit of Pleasure: Drugs and Stimulants in Iranian History, 1500–1900*. Princeton University Press.
Matthews, G. (1989). *"Just a Housewife": The Rise and Fall of Domesticity in America*. Oxford University Press.
Mauss, M. (2002). *The Gift: The Form and Reason for Exchange in Archaic Societies* (W. D. Halls, Trans.). Routledge.
MEE Correspondent (2019, July 8). Iran's 199 Student Protests: The Hot Summer that Shook Tehran. *Middle East Eye*. www.middleeasteye.net/big-story/irans-1999-student-protests-hot-summer-shook-tehran
Mehdizadeh, N. (2011). Gender and Reconciliation of Work and Family in Iran. *International Labour Review*, *150*(3–4), 405–417.

Mejdi, I. (2023). The Nexus Between Kinship and Politics During Times of Democratic Crisis in Tunisia [Working Paper].

Mehrjui, D. (Director). (1969). *The Cow* [Film]. Iran.

(1993). *Sara* [Film]. Iran.

(1996). *Leila* [Film]. Iran.

Mendelson, C. (2005). *Home Comforts: The Art and Science of Keeping House*. Scribner.

Mennell, S. (1996). *All Manners of Food: Eating and Taste in England and France from the Middle Ages to the Present*. University of Illinois Press.

Mernissi, F. (1994). *Dreams of Trespass: Tales of a Harem Girlhood*. Perseus Books.

Meshkini, M. (Director). (2000). *The Day I Became a Woman* [Film]. Iran.

Metz, C. (1975). Story/Discourse. A Note on Two Kinds of Voyeurisms. In *The Imaginary Signifier: Psychoanalysis and the Cinema*. Indiana University Press.

Milani, T. (Director). (1991). *Legend of a Sigh* [Film]. Iran.

(1999). *Two Women* [Film]. Iran.

(2001). *The Hidden Half* [Film]. Iran.

Minder, R. (2023, October 14). Lunch with Agnieszka Holland: "It's Possible to Commit the Worst Crimes and Never Pay." *The Financial Times*. www.ft.com/content/8586d37e-164d-4e42-b6e6-7abdff4199bb

Mirbakhtyar, S. (2006). *Iranian Cinema and the Islamic Revolution*. McFarland & Co.

Mir-Hosseini, Z. (Summer 2001). Iranian Cinema: Art, Society and the State. *Middle East Report* 219.

Mirgholami, M. (2012). From Traditional *Mahallehs* to Modern Neighborhoods: The Case of Narmak, Tehran. *Comparative Studies of South Asia, Africa and the Middle East*, *32*(1), 214–237.

Moaveni, A. (2005). *Lipstick Jihad: A Memoir of Growing Up Iranian in America and American in Iran*. Public Affairs.

Modarres, A. (2006). *Modernizing Yazd: Selective Historical Memory and the Fate of Vernacular Architecture*. Mazda Publishers.

Mofrad, G. H. (2015). (Sur)vivre et naviguer entre deux eaux: Histories de ruse, de résistance et de "par-être" chez les femmes téhéranaises. [Unpublished Dissertation]. Université catholique de Louvain, Belgium.

Moghadam, V. M. (2000). Hidden from History? Women Workers in Modern Iran. *Iranian Studies*, *33*(3–4), 377–401.

Mohammadi, S. A., Ramezankhani, A. A., & Majd, H. A. (2011). Poor Reproductive Health among a Group of Socially Damaged Middle Eastern Women: A Cross-sectional Study. *International Journal of Women's Health*, *3*, 399–403.

Mohammadshahi, M., Pourreza, A., Orojlo, P. H., Mahmoodi, M., & Akbari, F. (2014). Rhinoplasty as a Medicalized Phenomenon: A 25-Center Survey on Quality of Life before and after Rhinoplasty. *Aesthetic Plastic Surgery*, *38*, 615–619.

Mohassess, A. (2008). *Art and Satire in Iran* (S. Neshat & N. Nikzad, Eds.). Asia Society.

Molana, H., Ranjbar, A. M., & Razavi, S. (2023). Woman, Life, Freedom: Decoding the Feminist Uprising in Iran. *Political Geography*, *103*, 102834.

Montanari, M. (1994). *The Culture of Food*. Blackwell.

Moruzzi, N. C. (1994). A Problem with Headscarves: Contemporary Complexities of Political and Social Identity. *Political Theory*, *22*(4), 653–672.

(Autumn 1999). Women's Space/Cinema Space: Representations of Public and Private in Iranian Films. *Middle East Report*, *212*, 52–55.

(2000). *Speaking through the Mask: Hannah Arendt and the Politics of Social Identity*. Cornell University Press.

(2006). Janet Afary and Kevin B. Anderson, Foucault and the Iranian Revolution: Gender and the Seductions of Islamism (University of Chicago Press, 2005). *International Journal of Middle East Studies*, *38*(3), 492–494.

Moruzzi, N. C., & Sadeghi, F. (Winter 2006). Out of the Frying Pan, into the Fire: Young Iranian Women Today. *Middle East Report*, *241*, 22–28.

Moruzzi, N. C. (2007). Paradise Lost: Gone Shopping. *Middle East Report*, *245*(37), 42–43.

(2008). Trying to Look Different. *CSSAME*, *28*(2), 225–234.

Motahari, M. (1980). *The Rights of Women in Islam*. World Organization for Islamic Services.

(2013). *The Islamic Modest Dress*. CreateSpace.

(2016). *Sexual Ethics in Islam and in the Western World*. Sadra.

Motamedian, B. (Director). (2008). *Sex My Life/Tedium/Khastegi* [Film]. Iran.

Mottahedeh, N. (2008). *Displaced Allegories: Post-Revolutionary Iranian Cinema*. Duke University Press.

(2009). Iranian Cinema in the Twentieth Century: A Sensory History. *Iranian Studies*, *42*(4), 529–548.

Mulvey, L. (1975). Visual Pleasure and Narrative Cinema. *Screen*, *16*(3), 6–18.

Naficy, H. (2001). An Accented Cinema: Exilic and Diasporic Filmmaking. Princeton University Press.

(2004). Islamizing Film Culture in Iran: A Post-Khatami Update. In R. Tapper (Ed.), *The New Iranian Cinema: Politics, Representation and Identity*. I. B. Tauris.

Nafisi, A. (2003). *Reading Lolita in Tehran: A Memoir in Books*. Random House.

Naghibi, N. (2007). *Rethinking Global Sisterhood: Western Feminism and Iran*. University of Minnesota Press.

Naguib, N. (2006). The Fragile Tale of Egyptian Jewish Cuisine: Food Memoirs of Claudia Roden and Colette Rossant. *Food and Foodways*, *14*(1), 35–53.

(2013). Doing the Right Thing: Fathers, Husbands and Food in Contemporary Egypt. Paper presented at the 2013 Annual Meeting of the Middle East Studies Association, New Orleans.

Najafi, M. A. "*Yek Emarat-e Tarikhi-i Digar dar Khatar-e Virani*" ("Another Historic Building in Danger of Ruin: Urban Renewal Assessments as Blight on Beautiful Historic Buildings"). *Ettela-at, Mordad 27*, 1352 (August 18, 1973).

Najmabadi, A. (1991). Hazards of Modernity and Morality: Women, State and Ideology in Contemporary Iran. In D. Kandioti (Ed.), *Women, Islam and the State* (pp. 48–71). Temple University Press.

(1997). Feminisms in an Islamic Republic. In J. W. Scott, C. Kaplan, & D. Keates (Eds.), *Transitions, Environments, Translations: Feminism in International Politics* (pp. 390–399). Routledge.

(Summer 2005). Mapping Transformations of Sex, Gender, and Sexuality in Modern Iran. *Social Analysis*, *48*(2), 54–77.

(2005). Truth of Sex: While trans-sexuality in Iran is made legitimate, homosexuality is insistently reiterated as abnormal. *Iran.com*.

(2005). *Women with Mustaches and Men without Beards: Gender and Sexual Anxieties of Iranian Modernity*. University of California Press.

(Fall/Winter 2008). Transing and Transpassing across Gender Walls in Iran. *Women's Studies Quarterly*, *36*(3&4), 23–42.

(Summer 2011). Verdicts of Science, Rulings of Faith: Transgender/Sexuality in Contemporary Iran. *Social Research*, *78*(2), 533–556.

(2013). Genus of Sex or the Sexing of *Jins*. *International Journal of Middle East Studies*, *42*, 211–231.

(2014). *Professing Selves: Transsexuality and Same-Sex Desire in Contemporary Iran*. Duke University Press.

Nasirian, M., Karamouzian, M., & Haghdoost, A. A. (2013). Why Is the Number of HIV/AIDS-Related Publications Low in the MENA Region? *Sexually Transmitted Infections*, *89*(Suppl. 3), iii10.

Nguyen, M. T. (2010). The Biopower of Beauty: Humanitarian Imperialisms and Global Feminisms in an Age of Terror. *Signs* 36(2), 359–383.

Nomani, F., & Behdad, S. (2012). Labor Rights and the Democracy Movement in Iran: Building a Social Democracy. *Northwestern Journal of International Human Rights*, *10*(4), 212–230.

O'Leary, A. (2019). *The Battle of Algiers*. Mimesis International.

OECD/ILO (2019). *Tackling Vulnerability in the Informal Economy*, Development Centre Studies, OECD Publishing, Paris, 3. https://doi.org/10.1787/939b7bcd-en.

Ogle, M. (1996). *All the Modern Conveniences: American Household Plumbing, 1840–1890*. Johns Hopkins University Press.

Olmsted, J. C. (2011). Gender and Globalization: The Iranian Experience. In R. Bahramitash & H. S. Esfahani (Eds.), *Veiled Employment: Islamism and the Political Economy of Women's Employment in Iran* (pp. 25–52). Syracuse University Press.

Olszewska, Z. (November 2013). "Classy Kids and Down-at-Heel Intellectuals: Status Aspiration and Blind Spots in the Contemporary Ethnography of Iran." *Iranian Studies*, 46(6), 841–862.

Onsanloo, A. (2020). *Forgiveness Work: Mercy, Law, and Victims' Rights in Iran*. Princeton University Press.

OutRight Action International. (2016). *Human Rights Report: Being Transgender in Iran* [Policy Report].

Paidar, P. (1995). *Women and the Political Process in Twentieth Century Iran*. Cambridge University Press.

Panahi, J. (Director). (1995). *The White Balloon* [Film]. Iran.

(1997). *The Mirror* [Film]. Iran.

(2022). *No Bears* [Film]. Iran.

Peiss, K. (1986). *Cheap Amusements: Working Women and Leisure in Turn-of-the Century New York*. Temple University Press.

(1998). *Hope in a Jar: The Making of America's Beauty Culture*. Metropolitan Books.

Perkins Gilman, C. (1966). *Women and Economics*. Harper & Row.

Phadke, S., Khan, S., & Ranada, S. (2011). *Why Loiter: Women & Risk on Mumbai Streets*. Penguin Books.

Pilling, D. (2018 June 6). The Real Price of Vanilla. *The Financial Times*, 7.

Pitkin, H. F. (1998). *The Attack of the Blob: Hannah Arendt's Concept of the Social*. University of Chicago Press.

Pontecorvo, G. (Director). (1966). *Battle of Algiers* [Film]. Italy, Algeria.

Pourjavady, N., & Wilson, P. L. (1978). *Kings of Love: The Poetry and History of the Ni'matullahi Sufi Order*. Imperial Iranian Academy of Philosophy.

Rahimi, S. (2009, April 29). The Unconscious: Metaphor and Metonymy. *Somatosphere*. https://somatosphere.com/2009/unconscious-metaphor-and-metonymy.html/

(2009, May 3). The (Lacanian) unconscious: structure and negative ontology. *Somatosphere*. https://somatosphere.com/2009/lacanian-unconscious-structure-and.html/

(2012, December 16). Subjectivity at the Intersection of Metaphoric and Metonymic Functions. *Somatosphere*. https://somatosphere.com/2012/subjectivity-at-the-intersection-of-metaphoric-and-metonymic-functions.html/

(2017, April 27). Subjectivity After the Subject. *Somatosphere*. https://somatosphere.com/2017/subjectivity-after-the-subject.html/

Rahimieh, N. (2001). Capturing Cultural Transformation on Film: Makhmalbaf's *A Moment of Innocence. Edebiyat*, *12*, 195–214.

Remus, E. (2019). *A Shopper's Paradise: How the Ladies of Chicago Claimed Power and Pleasure in the New Downtown*. Harvard University Press.

Reza-Sadr, H. (1999). Contemporary Iranian Cinema and Its Major Themes. In R. Issa & S. Whitaker (Eds.), *Life and Art: The New Iranian Cinema* (pp. 26–43). National Film Theater, The British Film Institute.

(2006). *Iranian Cinema: A Political History*. I. B. Tauris & Co.

Richards, E. S. (1908). "Ten Years of the Lake Placid Conference on Home Economics; Its History and Aims." *Lake Placid Conference on Home Economics, Proceedings of the Tenth Annual Conference* (pp. 19–25). American Home Economics Association.

Rosenbaum, J. (1992, October 23). Iranian Sights [Life and Nothing More]. *Chicago Reader*. https://jonathanrosenbaum.net/2024/07/iranian-sights/

Rosenberg, J. (2014). The Molecularization of Sexuality: On Some Primitivisms of the Present. *Theory and Event*, *17*(2), https://muse.jhu.edu/article/546470.

Ross, K. (Winter 1994). Starting Afresh: Hygiene and Modernization in Postwar France. *October*, *67*, 22–57.

Ross, M. L. (2012). *The Oil Curse: How Petroleum Wealth Shapes the Development of Nations*. Princeton University Press.

Rostam-Kolayi, J., & Matin-Asgari, A. (2014). Unveiling Ambiguities: Revisiting 1930s Iran's *kashf-i hijab* Campaign. In S. Cronin (Ed.), *Anti-Veiling Campaigns in the Muslim World: Gender, Modernism and the Politics of Dress* (pp. 121–148). Routledge.

Rubin, M. (2000). Iran's "Dialogue of Civilizations" – A First-Hand Account. *Middle East Quarterly*, *7*(1), 31–38.

Russell, M. (Fall 2010). Marketing the Modern Egyptian Girl: Whitewashing Soap and Clothes from the Late Nineteenth Century to 1936. *Journal of Middle East Women's Studies*, *6*(3), 19–57.

Rutsky, R. L., & B. J. Macdonald. (2003). *Strategies for Theory: From Marx to Madonna*. State University of New York Press.

S*. (2023, January). Anger Piled Atop Anger: Iran Diary. *Bidoun*.

Sadeghi, F. (2008). Negotiating with Modernity: Young Women and Sexuality in Iran. *Comparative Studies of South Asia, Africa and the Middle East*, *28*(2), 250–259.

(2010, March 15). "Temporary Marriage" and the Economy of Pleasure (F. Afary, Trans.). *Tehran Bureau*. www.pbs.org/wgbh/pages/frontline/tehranbureau/2010/03/temporary-marriage-and-the-economy-of-pleasure.html

(2023). From Women's Revolution to *Jiyanist* Democracy (S. Shohadaei, Trans.). *Journal of Middle East Women's Studies*, *19*(3), 458–468.

Sadjadi, S. (2013). The Endocrinologist's Office – Puberty Suppression: Saving Children from a Natural Disaster? *Journal of Medical Humanities*, *34*, 255–260.

Sadjadpour, K. (2012). The Ayatollah under the Bed (Sheets). *Foreign Policy*, *193*, 74–80.

Sadr Ameli, R. (Director). (1999). *The Girl in Sneakers* [Film]. Iran.

(2002). *I Am Taraneh, Fifteen* [Film]. Iran.

Saeidi, S. (2022). *Women and the Islamic Republic: How Gendered Citizenship Conditions the Iranian State*. Cambridge University Press.

Saeidzadeh, Z. (2016). Transsexuality in Contemporary Iran: Legal and Social Misrecognition. *Feminist Legal Studies*, *24*, 249–272.

(2019). Understanding Socio-Legal Complexities of Sex Change in Postrevolutionary Iran. *TSQ: Transgender Studies Quarterly*, *6*(1), 80–102.

Saravi, F. K., Navidian, A., Rigi, S. N., & Montazeri, A. (2012). Comparing Health-Related Quality of Life of Employed Women and Housewives: A Cross Sectional Study from Southeast Iran. *BMC Women's Health*, *12*(1), 1–5.

Schwartz Cowan, R. (1983). *More Work for Mother: The Ironies of Household Technology from the Open Heart to the Microwave*. Basic Books.

Sciolino, E. (2000). *Persian Mirrors: The Elusive Face of Iran*. The Free Press.

Scott, J. C., Tehranian, J., & Mathias, J. (2002). The Production of Legal Entities Proper to States: The Case of the Permanent Family Surname. *Comparative Studies in Society and History*, *44*(1), 4–44.

Scott, J. W. (1988). *Gender and the Politics of History, Revised Edition*. Columbia University Press.

Sevom, A. (2014). Masha Shekarloo: Women's Rights Activist, Internet Pioneer. www.arsehsevom.net/2014/09/mahsa_shekarloo/.

Shahrokni, N. (2000). *Women in Place: The Politics of Gender Segregation in Iran*. University of California Press.

Shaida, M. (1998). The Poetry of Persian Food. In H. Walker (Ed.), *Food in the Arts: Proceedings of the Oxford Symposium on Food and Cookery* (pp. 182–189). Prospect Books.

(2002). *The Legendary Cuisine of Persia*. Interlink Books.

Shakerifar, E. (2011). Visual Representations of Iranian Transgenders. *Iranian Studies*, *44*(3), 327–339.

Shams, L. (2012, July 10). Presenting Our Video about "*Tarof*"! *Chai and Conversation*. www.chaiandconversation.com/2012/presenting-our-video-about-tarof

Shariati, A. (1982). *Fatima Is Fatima* (L. Bakhtiar, Trans.). The Shariati Foundation.

(1986). *What Is to Be Done? The Enlightened Thinkers and an Islamic Renaissance*. The Institute for Research and Islamic Studies.

Shariati, A., & Abedi, M. (1986). Nowruz. *Iranian Studies*, *19*(3–4), 235–241.

Shekarloo, M. (2005). Publicly Intimate Tehran: Desiring Subjects in Buses and Cabs. [Unpublished Paper]. Presented at the Conference "Private Lives and Public Spaces in Modern Iran," St. Anthony's College, University of Oxford.

Sherkat, S. (2009, June 2). Telling the Stories of Iranian Women's Lives. *Nieman Foundation*. https://nieman.harvard.edu/articles/telling-the-stories-of-iranian-womens-lives/

Shirani, Z., Partovi, P., & Behzadfar, M. (2017). Spatial Resilience in Traditional Bazaars; Case Study: Esfahan Qeisariye. *Bagh-e Nazar*, *14*(52), 57–68.

Shirazi, F. (2005). The Sofreh: Comfort and Community among Women in Iran. *Iranian Studies*, *38*(2), 293–309.

Shirazi, S. (2023, September 6). Iran: Campus Persecutions Ramp Up as Protest Anniversary Looms. *University World News*. www.universityworldnews.com/post.php?story=20230906121905590

Shrinivasan, R. (2013, March 10). No Country for Working Women: A Story in 5 Graphs. *The Times of India*. https://timesofindia.indiatimes.com/blogs/developmentdialogue/numbers/

(2013, May 19). Working Women Numbers Don't Add Up. *The Times of India*. https://timesofindia.indiatimes.com/home/sunday-times/deep-focus/working-women-numbers-dont-add-up/articleshow/20130046.cms

Siamdoust, N. (2011). Pardis Mahdavi, Passionate Uprisings: Iran's Sexual Revolution (Stanford University Press, 2009). *International Journal of Middle East Studies*, *43*(1), 155–158.

Sohrabi, N. (2022). Writing Revolution as If Women Mattered. *Comparative Studies of South Asia, Africa and the Middle East (CSSAAME)*, 42(2), 546–550.

Sprachman, P. (1995). *Suppressed Persian: An Anthology of Forbidden Literature*. Mazda Publishers.

Statistical Center of Iran. (2012, 2013, 2023). *A Selection of Labor Force Survey Results*.

Steedman, C. (2009). *Labours Lost: Domestic Service and the Making of Modern England*. Cambridge University Press.

Strasser, S. (2000). *Never Done: A History of American Housework*. Henry Holt & Co.
Subramanya, R. (2013, October 8). Why Female Labour Force Participation in India Is Low. *Business Standard*. www.business-standard.com/article/economy-policy/why-female-labour-force-participation-in-india-is-low-113100800029_1.html
Sullivan, Z. T. (1998). Eluding the Feminist, Overthrowing the Modern? Transformations in Twentieth-Century Iran. In L. Abu-Lughod (Ed.), *Remaking Women: Feminism and Modernity in the Middle East* (pp. 215–242). Princeton University Press.
(2001). *Exiled Memories: Stories of Iranian Diaspora*. Temple University Press.
Sundriyal, D. (2023, April 8). Is Holy Spider's Arezoo Rahimi a Real Life Journalist? Where Is She Now? *The Cinemaholic*. https://thecinemaholic.com/is-holy-spiders-arezoo-rahimi-based-on-a-real-journalist-where-is-she-now/
Tahami, R. (Summer 1994). Iranian Women Make Films. *Film International*, *2*(3), 4–13.
Tannahill, R. (1973). *Food in History*. Stein and Day.
Tavakoli-Targhi, M. (2001). *Refashioning Iran: Orientalism, Occidentalism and Historiography*. Palgrave Macmillan.
Terman, R. (2014). Trans[ition] in Iran. *World Policy Journal*, 28–38.
Thompson, N. (2012). *Living as Form: Socially Engaged Art from 1991–2011*. The MIT Press.
(Curator). (2019). *Living as Form (The Nomadic Version)*. Independent Curators International. https://curatorsintl.org/exhibitions/living_as_form_the_nomadic_version.
Torab, A. (2007). *Performing Islam: Gender and Ritual in Iran*. Brill.
(2017). Conditional Gifts for the Saints: "Gift" and "Commodity" as Gender Metaphors in Shi'a Ritual Practices in Iran. In M. Joy (Ed.), *Women, Religion, and the Gift* (Sophia Studies in Cross-Cultural Philosophies of Traditions and Cultures), vol. 17 (pp. 139–157). Springer.
Trollope, F. (1927). *Domestic Manners of the Americans*. Routledge.
Varzi, R. (2004). A Ghost in the Machine: The Cinema of the Iranian Sacred Defense. In R. Tapper (Ed.), *The New Iranian Cinema: Politics, Representation and Identity* (pp. 154–166). I. B. Tauris.
Walkowitz, J. (1980). *Prostitution and Victorian Society: Women, Class and the State*. Cambridge University Press.
(1992). *City of Dreadful Delight: Narratives of Sexual Danger in Late-Victorian London*. University of Chicago Press.
Watson, K. (2015, September 2). Sharwarma: Taco al pastor's Culinary Ancestor. BBC. www.bbc.com/news/magazine-33993719

Weinbaum, A. E., Thomas, L. M., Ramamurthy, P., Poiger, U. G., Dong, M. Y., & Barlow, T. E. (2008). *The Modern Girl around the World: Consumption, Modernity, and Globalization*. Duke University Press.

Werner, L. (2010). Mexico's Colors of Three Cultures. *Saudi Aramco World*, *61*(1), 34–43.

Whyte, J. (2018). Foucault's "Distrust of Legalism": On Human Rights and the Revolution in Iran. In Z. Thartaloudis (Ed.), *Law and Philosophical Theory: Critical Investigations*. Rowman & Littlefield.

Wilber, D. N. (1967). Language and Society: The Case of Iran. *Cross-Cultural Research*, *2*(1), 22–30.

Willard, F. E. (2014 [1895]). *A Wheel within a Wheel: How I Learned to Ride the Bicycle, with Some Reflections By the Way*. Frances Willard Historical Association.

Williams, P. (2013). "Happy" (Official Music Video). www.youtube.com/watch?v=y6Sxv-sUYtM

Williamson, C. (1999). Art Matters: The Films of Abbas Kiarostami. In R. Issa & Sheila Whitaker (Eds.), *Life and Art: The New Iranian Cinema* (pp. 90–104). National Film Theatre, The British Film Institute.

(2001). The Making of an Iranian Filmmaker Abbas Kiarostami. In H. Dabashi (Ed.), *Close Up: Iranian Cinema, Past, Present and Future* (pp. 33–75). Verso.

Women's Group on Public Welfare (1943). *Our Towns: A Close-Up*. Oxford University Press.

*Women & Struggle in Iran: A Publication of the Women's Commission of the Iranian Student Association (ISA-US, Supporters of O.I.P.F.G.)*. (Summer 1984). No. 3.

World Bank, Gender Data Portal (2023). *France*. https://genderdata.worldbank.org/countries/france/

World Bank, Gender Data Portal (2023). *India*. https://genderdata.worldbank.org/countries/india/

Wright, L. (1960). *Clean & Decent: The Fascinating History of the Bathroom and the Water-Closet*. Penguin Books.

Yeo, E. J. (1998). *Radical Femininity: Women's Self-Representation in the Public Sphere*. Manchester University Press.

Young-Bruehl, E. (1982). *Hannah Arendt: For Love of the World*. Yale University Press.

Yousefzadeh Faal Daghati, S. (2013). *Childhoods Embargoed: Constructing and Reconstructing Multidimensional Child Poverty in Iran, 1984–2009*. Boekenplan.

Zojaji, R., Arshadi, H. R., Keshavarz, M., Farsibaf, M. M., Golzari, F., & Khorashadizadeh, M. (2014). Personality Characteristics of Patients Seeking Cosmetic Rhinoplasty. *Aesthetic Plastic Surgery*, *38*, 1090–1093.

# Index